How to Travel in the Deep Way to Understand the Truth

كيف الطريقة إلى معرفة الحقيقة

kayfa-l-ṭarīqa ilā maʿrifati-l-ḥaqīqa

2010 teachings of
Sidi Shaykh Muḥammad Saʿīd al-Jamal ar-Rifāʿī ash-Shādhulī

How to Travel in the Deep Way to Understand the Truth

كيف الطريقة إلى معرفة الحقيقة

kayfa-l-ṭarīqa ilā maʿrifati-l-ḥaqīqa

2010 teachings of
Sidi Shaykh Muḥammad Saʿīd al-Jamal ar-Rifāʿī ash-Shādhulī

يَا أَيُّهَا النَّاسُ إِنَّا خَلَقْنَاكُم مِّن ذَكَرٍ وَأُنثَىٰ وَجَعَلْنَاكُمْ شُعُوبًا وَقَبَائِلَ لِتَعَارَفُوا إِنَّ
أَكْرَمَكُمْ عِندَ اللَّهِ أَتْقَاكُمْ إِنَّ اللَّهَ عَلِيمٌ خَبِيرٌ

*"Oh humankind! We have created you from a male and a female,
and made you into nations and tribes so that you may know one another.
Truly, the most honorable of you with Allāh is that who has taqwā (piety).
Truly, Allāh is all-knowing, all-aware."* (49:13)

بسم الله الرحمن الرحيم

الحمد لله رب العالمين

الرحمن الرحيم

مالك يوم الدين

إياك نعبد وإياك نستعين

اهدنا الصراط المستقيم

صراط الذين أنعمت عليهم غير المغضوب عليهم ولا الضالين

Cover art: Rahima Wear
Cover design: Amina Stader-Chan

ISBN 978-0-9762150-5-9

For information, address the Shadhiliyya Sufi Center
P.O. Box 100 Pope Valley, CA 94567
(707) 965-0700

Table of Contents
Chronological

Introduction i

Acknowledgments iii

Welcome Weekend

The Queen of Divine Love 5

Everything Depends Upon Tawba 17

The Grave's Two Paths 31

The Day of Judgment's Two Paths 37

Sufi School West

Say Yes to Divine Love 51

Repent Like the Man Saʿīd Ibrāhīm Helped 66

The Messenger's Intercession for Us 75

The Real Baqāʾ in the World of Allāh 89

Midwest Sufi Gathering

The Prophet's Night Journey and Ascension 108

Portland

Everything is from the Love 133

USHS July

The Divine Science of Pregnancy, Birth and Parenting 121

Allāh Opens His Door to the Sincere Ones 153

A Drop of the Wine of the Deep Essence of Knowing 170

Tawba is the Door to Goodness 192

The Straight Path to Love 209

Sufi School East

The Best of Allāh's Creation Are Those Who Make Tawba 229

The Emigration to Allāh 247

How to Travel in the Deep Way Like the Prophet Ibrāhīm 263

Austin

The Table of Divine Love..............289

The Light of ʿĪsā and Maryam..............308

Florida Mystical Sufi Weekend

The Story of ʿĪsā..............340

The True Meaning of Ḥajj..............363

USHS October

How to Care for Your Body..............325

The Healing for Many Diseases..............376

Ibrāhīm's Sacrifice for the Face of Allāh..............386

Remedies for Healing in the Way of Allāh..............406

San Diego

Allāh's Orders Are a Gift..............416

Final Teaching

The Family's Beautiful Fragrance..............430

Appendices & Indices

Appendix I: Prophets, Angels, ʿAwliya..............445

Appendix II: Glossary of Arabic Terms..............449

General Index..............456

Qurʾān Index..............466

Ḥadīth Index..............470

Ḥadīth Qudsī Index..............472

Table of Contents
By Topic

TAWBA

Everything Depends Upon Tawba 17
Allāh Opens His Door to the Sincere Ones 153
Tawba is the Door to Goodness 192
The Best of Creation Make Tawba 229

THE GRAVE, THE DAY OF JUDGEMENT, INTERCESSION

The Grave's Two Paths 31
The Day of Judgment's Two Paths 37
The Messenger's Intercession for Us 75

PROPHETS & ʿAWLIYĀ

The Prophet's Night Journey and Ascension 108
How to Travel Like the Prophet Ibrāhīm 263
The True Meaning of Ḥajj 363
Ibrāhīm's Sacrifice for Allāh 386
The Light of ʿĪsā and Maryam 308
The Story of ʿĪsā 340
The Queen of Divine Love 5
Repent Like the Man Saʿīd Ibrāhīm Helped 66

TEACHINGS WITH DIVINE MUSIC

Everything is from the Love "A Drop of the Love" 133
A Drop of the Wine "A Drop of the Love " 170
Allāh's Orders Are a Gift "A Drop of the Love " 416
The Real Baqāʾ in the World of Allāh "My Heart Tells Me" 89
The Straight Path to Love "My Heart Tells Me " 209
The Table of Divine Love "Everything is From Love-Portland " 289
Allāh Opens His Door "The One Who Knows All the Secrets " 153

Tawba is the Door "The One Who Knows All the Secrets " 192
The Emigration to Allāh "Oh Lord, Guide Us " 247

DIVINE LOVE

The Queen of Divine Love *Children of the Truth* 5
Say Yes to Divine Love *The Traveler's Journey of Healing* 51
The Table of Divine Love "Everything is From Love-Portland " 289
The Family's Beautiful Fragrance *Conversations in the Zawiya* 430

HEALING

The Divine Science of Pregnancy, Birth and Parenting 121
How to Care for Your Body *The Migration of the Truthful Traveler* 325
The Healing for Many Diseases 376
Remedies for Healing in the Way of Allāh 406
The True Meaning of Ḥajj *Secret of the Spirit* 363
The Family's Beautiful Fragrance *Conversations in the Zawiya* 430

2010 PUBLICATIONS

Spiritual Discourses at the Blessed Al-Aqṣā Mosque

The Grave's Two Paths 31
The Day of Judgment's Two Paths 37
The Messenger's Intercession for Us 75
Repent Like the Man Saʿīd Ibrāhīm Helped 66
The Prophet's Night Journey and Ascension 108

The Migration of the Truthful Traveler

The Rituals of Worship 325

The Traveler's Journey of Healing

Say Yes to Divine Love 51
Everything Depends Upon Tawba 17
Allāh Opens His Door 108
Tawba is the Door to Goodness 192
The Best of Allāh's Creation 229

Introduction

بسم الله الرحمٰن الرحيم

We witness that Allāh (ﷻ) is the One, the Eternal, the Sustainer and the Generous. We send our prayers and blessings to all of the prophets (عليهم السلام), their companions and families (رضي الله عنهم) and all of the beloveds who know and love Allāh, beginning with the Prophet Muḥammad (ﷺ), the Prophet Ibrāhīm (عليه السلام), the Prophet Mūsā (عليه السلام) and the Prophet ʿĪsā (عليه السلام). We ask Allāh (ﷻ) to bless our beloved guide and to give him strength, and we thank Allāh (ﷻ) for sending him to us and for providing this rich, nutritious table of divine knowledge. Yā Allāh, yā Rabb, yā Mujīb!

As we can attest, all of Sidi's teachings are based in the divine message; and yet, each year his teachings evolve. In 2010, Sidi continued to have his poetic, inspired teachings read aloud while accompanied by music performed by Shaykh Yasīn Tuhamī. Because Sidi used a greater diversity of readings, we chose to group the teachings chronologically as we have in years past.

Divine knowledge is an underlying theme in this year's teachings, as is evidenced in this year's book title, which Sidi selected himself (as he always does). Highlights of 2010 include:

- Sidi recounts and adds detail to several khutbas included in *Spiritual Discourses at the Blessed Al-Aqṣā Mosque* that focus on death, the grave, the Day of Judgment, the Prophet's intercession (ﷺ) and the Prophet's night journey and ascension (ﷺ). Based in the Qurʾān and ḥadīth, these teachings are incredibly beautiful and they create a feeling of containment, light and truth.

- Sidi gave many beautiful teachings on divine love this year in a variety of contexts, including: how to live in al-baqāʾu-l-bi-llāh (subsistence in Allāh ﷻ), remembering Allāh (ﷻ) through Sidi's lyrical teachings set to music, and the example of Rabiʿa al-ʿAdawiyya (رضي الله عنها).

- Focusing on family, Sidi gave an extremely detailed teaching on pregnancy, childbirth and parenting, along with a most beautiful teaching on marriage and the family.

- Prophetically, Sidi focused on the lives of the Prophet Ibrāhīm (ؑ) and the Prophet ʿĪsā (ؑ) as examples of how to truly emigrate to Allāh (ﷻ) and how to receive deeply from Allāh's table of divine nourishment.

- For the first time, Sidi gave us specific remedies for different physical conditions *that were not read from one of his healing books*, addressing concerns such as hair loss, high blood pressure, weight gain and more.

- As usual, Sidi encourages us to make tawba in every moment, including the need for every single part of our physical bodies to make tawba, as well as our minds, hearts and spirits.

Each year we find that there are more teachings than can fit in one 500-page volume. Inshāʾa-llāh, in May 2010, we plan to release a supplement containing a selection of the missing teachings that will be free of charge to those who have purchased this book. If you wish to receive your free copy of the supplement, please complete the form on the last page and submit it to the SSC Gift Shop.

We realize that we have undoubtedly made errors of fact or judgment for which we alone are responsible and for which we seek Allāh's forgiveness (ﷻ). Our prayer is that this book will provide spiritual support and healing for all people seeking to travel deeply to find the truth of Allāh (ﷻ). May Allāh will it (ﷻ).

Wadude Laird and Shams Wesley

Acknowledgments

بسم الله الرحمٰن الرحيم

The editors would like to gratefully acknowledge the generous assistance given by many beloveds who stepped forward in every instance to contribute exactly what was needed. We begin by thanking Dr. Hadeel Barak and Ibrahim Ali who translated the teachings Sidi Muḥammad gave originally in Arabic into English. Their dedication to transmit not only the literal but also the transcendent meanings of the teachings will, we believe, offer the reader greater access to the full richness of what Sidi has offered.

We want to acknowledge all those who made this year's events with Sidi possible: the directors, staffs, hosts and many beloveds around the country who contributed in various ways, large and small. We especially thank each community for allowing us access to their audio recordings, ensuring the successful completion of this project.

Our transcription team continuously and selflessly gave deeply of themselves throughout this year's project. Their dedication, love, commitment and patience have made this book possible, and we thank Allāh (ﷻ) for providing us with such excellent assistance. We humbly thank: Abdullah Ray Rivers, Sumayya Beth Allen, Bilqis Loeliger, Aisha McGuffey, Munsif Montgomery, Aʾamina Sandy Thomason, Salima Christina Tate, Hamda Leslie Rodgers, Ahmed Tarrell Rodgers, Safiyyah Naomi Miller, Mariam Upshaw, Iman Kim Corrick, Saberra K. Morrow, Shamsa Houck, Rabiʿah Houle, Rahima Witt, Hadia Tirben, Mahabba Fran Bell, Salima Peggy Abedoi, Laila Wallace and Sara Baber.

Once again, Rahima Wear has blessed us by allowing us to use her radiant original artwork for our cover and Amīna Stader has, as usual, designed an elegant cover that beautifully reflects her love of Allāh and His way. We are sincerely grateful for the generosity and trust extended to this project by all donors, past and present. As always, we extend our gratitude to Salih Kent and Ihsan Rose, our brother and sister in the way, for their love, kind-heartedness and enthusiastic commitment. May Allāh (ﷻ) accept our walking, our work and our giving. Āmīn.

The Queen of Divine Love

Wednesday, June 16, 2010 AM, Welcome Weekend
"Rābiʿa Al-ʿAdawiyya" from The Children of the Truth

لا إله إلا الله – لا إله إلا الله – لا إله إلا الله – محمد رسول الله عليه صلاة الله
لا إله إلا الله – لا إله إلا الله – لا إله إلا الله – ابراهيم رسول الله عليه صلاة الله
لا إله إلا الله – لا إله إلا الله – لا إله إلا الله – موسى رسول الله عليه صلاة الله
لا إله إلا الله – لا إله إلا الله – لا إله إلا الله – عيسى رسول الله عليه صلاة الله
اللهم انت السلام ومنك السلام و إليك يعود السلام
تباركت ربنا وتعاليت يا ذوالجلال والإكرام

Āllahumma (Oh Allāh), help us to mention You all the time and do not let us forget You. May peace be upon you, my beloveds, my daughters, those who Allāh loved, those who came here to worship Allāh and to know the truth and to know everything. The human being needs knowledge. Our Prophet said:

> If you pass close to the Garden, drink.

And he said:

> Know that any group of people who sit and mention Allāh, angels will surround them and mercy will be with them. Love will be with them.

That means they are in a high garden, a very beautiful garden. I am asking Allāh to let you be able to carry the message of the truth and it will be enough for everything.

I would like to enter this lesson and I want to explain to you how those who fall in love with Allāh live their lives in the circle of the divine love as, for example, Rābiʿa al-ʿAdawiyya. She is one of the lovers. She is the queen of divine love. How did she reach this position? She struggled with many things and she passed through very hard times, but she never looked back. She never looked back, because she was part of the divine beauty, the patience—the divine patience. Allāh selected her because she was honest and He gave to her as He gave to His holy daughter Maryam (Mary) when He sent her the spirit. He gave to her as He gave to the mother of the Prophet Mūsā (Moses),

Asiya (☼). This holy woman took Sayyidinā (Our Master) Mūsā[1] (☼) in her arms from the sea and she raised him.

The women who worship Allāh (☼), who are honest with Allāh (☼), and who know what love is...love is a very patient thing and anyone who loses love loses everything. Now we will be under the recitation of Lady Rābi'a (☼), may Allāh (☼) protect her with His care.

We need to drink from the cup that Sayyida (Lady) Rābi'a (☼) carries—the cup of love, the glass of love. In Islām, the woman, she is a jewel. We should take care of her. We should love her and she should contain all the love she received from Allāh (☼). I would like to tell all of you, my sons, my daughters; I want to tell you how Sayyida Rābi'a (☼) walked to Allāh (☼)—how she reached this position.

...how the sun of the deep secret love carries the message of God (☼). I want everybody to walk like she walked. This is what Allāh (☼) says, because she gave the promise to Allāh (☼) after what happened in her life. She said, "God, take me. I keep the love and send the love through my heart to walk through what You want from me." God accepted her through her walking. Bismi-llāh.

"Rābi'a Al-'Adawiyya" from *The Children of the Truth*[2] is read from the beginning and continues until, "And while he (Rābi'a's father) was sleeping he dreamed that the Prophet Muḥammad (☼) came to him and said, "Do not be sad. The girl child which has just been born is a queen amongst women who will be the mediator for seventy-thousand from my community.""

---

[1] Hadeel gives us this word in Arabic throughout the summer before certain names. It means master or lord and is a term of address for people in a high class. It usually refers to people, not Allāh (☼). Variations include: Sayyidinā (our Master), Sayyida (Lady), Sayyidī (my Lord), Sayyidatī (my Lady, feminine), Sayyidatunā (our Lady)

[2] Sidi Muhammad, *The Children of the Truth*. Petaluma: Sidi Muhammad Press, 1998. 65-84.

She is the queen of the love, the sun of the deep secret love from Allāh (ﷻ) from when she was born.

The reading continues until, "'To set right your forgetfulness, give this man four hundred dinar, which he has lawfully earned.' And when he awoke and remembered his dream..."

Allāh (ﷻ) cared about Rābiʿa (ؓ) and He sent for her...because He cared for her. She is the queen of the love and she taught all the people how to go to the deep secret love, to drink, to be in the real life. Yes, Allāh cares and protects.

The reading continues until, "Their father, Ishmael (ؓ), worked as he could to make a living for his family in the desert, but when the eldest daughter was about twenty years old and Rābiʿa (ؓ) was about eleven, their father died, leaving behind him his wife and four daughters, all of whom were very poor."

Trust Allāh (ﷻ). He cares about everything.

The reading continues, "Rābiʿa's master took her to Baghdad where he immediately set about using her in a way that was most profitable for himself. She was very beautiful. She also had a very lovely voice and so her master taught her how to sing and play the oud."

She started in this job. Allāh (ﷻ) let her be perfect for this job to reach Him through this music. This is not strange. Allāh (ﷻ) directed this holy woman and He cared about her and helped her to reach what Allāh wanted for her. She wanted to teach people how to reach Allāh (ﷻ) through music. Music is food for the spirit and Allāh (ﷻ) helped her.

The reading continues, "This continued until she was about thirty-six years old, when one day as she was singing at a wedding she found herself singing in a different way. Songs were coming from her heart for her Beloved."

Come to My way. Sing for Me to show you the meaning about what I asked you to be—the queen of the love.

The reading continues, "Songs were coming from her heart for her Beloved who was her true love, because, Allāh, the Almighty (ﷻ) had awakened Rābi'a (ؓ). From that moment she left everything that she had done before and she refused either to sing or dance or to play any music for anyone except her beloved God (ﷻ)."

...for her Beloved Allāh (ﷻ). She sung for Allāh (ﷻ), not for the people. Allāhu akbar!

The reading continues, "This made her master very angry, because he could no longer use her to make money for himself, so he began to ill treat her and to beat her. He even put burns on her body, hoping this would frighten her into returning to her former ways."

She did not care about what he said. She was strong...

The reading continues, "But she refused anything that her master tried to do to her. She had begun to pray all through the night crying to her beloved God (ﷻ) to help her in her desperate state. After a time, her master, seeing that he could not influence her in any way and because she was no longer of any use to him, decided to sell her. He put a cord around her neck and took her to the slave market in Baghdad."

This is her life. It was a strong life, yes, but in this was a deep teaching about how to give, how to not care (about anything except Allāh ﷻ) and how to be with Allāh (ﷻ). She did not care about any other master.

The reading continues, "And there a holy man took Rābi'a (ؓ) to his home and gave her food and simple clothes and told her that he didn't want anything from her except that she could pray and be free in his house. Rābi'a (ؓ) thanked him with all her heart..."

...the person who knows because he feels the presence. He recognized this was not a common lady. There was a deep relationship between her and Allāh (ﷻ), so Allāh (ﷻ) sent this guide for her.

The reading continues until, "Rābi'a (ؓ) thanked him for his kindness and consideration, and she said that she did not want to marry anyone but was grateful for the way that he cared for her in her deep need."

She had only one Beloved. She was waiting for Him. She was not for a human being; she was for Allāh (ﷻ).

The reading continues until, "For Rābiʿa's case was that she heard the voice of her Beloved who was Allāh (ﷻ), and none other than He. She had no need for any earthly husband, because the only true marriage for her was with Allāh, Himself, alone (ﷻ).

This is the human being, the complete woman. She (﵂) opened her heart and Allāh (ﷻ) gave her the complete love in order to test this love and to keep her walking toward Him. He gives all people the knowledge of how to reach Him with this love.

The previous paragraph of the reading is repeated.

He is the Only One (al-Wāḥid). We can say, "He is the Rich, Yā Allāh al-Ghanī." He is the Great (al-Aḍhīm) and the Rich, and God (ﷻ) let her be satisfied. He gave her love and she started to give this light to all the people, especially the poor people and those who were suffering. She (﵂) gave them love and she let the divine paradise of love appear to all people, because He is the complete food.

Within Allāh the Living (al-Ḥayy), nothing can be in the right way, just with Allāh (ﷻ). You can find true love, pure love, if Allāh (ﷻ) will give it to you. You should give it to others to know Him and to drink from His love.

Who can live without love? Tell me, who can live without love? There is one condition: it must be divine love, because you are a tree. You are a human being which is like a tree. You are like a tree. Your source...and her head in the sky and this tree will perpetually give divine fruits to all people. Let others carry these fruits, this love, to let the eternal life continue.

What is the reason for all the disasters and suffering you see now in the world? What, what is the reason for all of these things and for wars? They happen because those people lost the divine love and they went to their human wars, and so they became beasts—animals! They eat the meat of each others, the flesh of others. This is exactly what happened between Hawwāʾ (Eve) (ﷷ) and Ādam (ﷷ) when they disobeyed Allāh (ﷻ). They ate from the holy tree. Allāh (ﷻ) told them, "Leave the Garden. I put you here to let you plant a good plant."

Allāh (ﷻ) wants us to carry the divine message. This divine message is the source of life—pure, clean love. If a person tries to cheat or to be dishonest with this love, he will lose everything. You should keep this love holy. You should just go to Allāh (ﷻ). He is the light of the skies and the air. Allāh (ﷻ)—His light is like a light in a glass.

All this light comes from the tree of love. It is in the earth and her branches reach high into the sky. Everything in this earth has a good fragrance. Everything will have this good fragrance and everything will be happy. Everyone will be happy and satisfied if they have divine love. With this divine love, all people will be alive and other trees will be planted: trees of peace, trees of freedom, trees of justice. This is what you need.

This holy lady wanted to be a divine example, to transform her life and travel to Allāh (ﷻ). Allāh (ﷻ) tested her. She passed through very hard times, but she told Allāh (ﷻ), "I'm traveling to Allāh (ﷻ)." She started to emigrate to Allāh (ﷻ) by love and she started to teach others how to reach the divine love.

The first way for us is love. After love, love can produce peace; love can produce mercy, if there is real love. If there isn't love, how can you come here and how can I talk to you? This is the will of Allāh (ﷻ) within you. Allāh (ﷻ) says:

> Through love I created the human being from clay,
> so I created him from clay by love! This is a divine matter. (Sidi)

The beginning is not Rābiʿa (ﷷ). Its beginning is "Be," "Kun." He created us in a perfect picture. Allāh (ﷻ) created you; after He created you, He told you; and after He told you, He gave you the secret. He gave you something that no one else can give you. He blew from His spirit within you. This is love. Have you ever received a greater secret than this? The child of Ādam (ﷷ) carried the message when He said:

> Truly, We did offer the trust to the heavens and the earth,

> and the mountains
> but they declined to bear it and were afraid of it.
> But the human being (both male and female) bore it. (33:72)

The first thing Allāh (ﷻ) did was to blow His spirit within this clay, and He ordered the angels (ﷺ) to pray for this Ādam (ﷺ): not for Ādam's body but for Allāh (ﷻ) who manifested within this clay, within this body, and who carried the divine love. Thus, He said:

> He loves them, so they love Him. (5:54)

He also said:

> But those who obey Allāh's orders
> and keep away from what He has forbidden,
> will be above them on the Day of Resurrection.
> (We will let you see there is no cover between Me and you.)
> (2:212 and Tafsir)

When someone obeys Allāh (ﷻ), Allāh (ﷻ) calls, "I love this one!" Through this, all people will love him. This lover will plant the tree of love, the tree that gives the light. Allāh (ﷻ) is the divine light that covers all worlds by the order of Allāh (ﷻ), and that light appeared in order to carry the message.

What is the message? Again, it is the message of love. This message will give you a peaceful mind. It will give you happiness and if you stopped giving anyone this water, he would die—he would start screaming. The people are thirsty; they need the water. When you ask, "Why are you screaming?" They will say, "I lost my mother and I lost what my mother gives me. I lost the love, because my mother fed me love when I was a child. However, when I rose up and I was powerful and strong, I started to disobey her."

You should be polite. You should go to her and give her pure love. If the human being loses love, I'm telling you, He will lose everything and his life will stop. Because of this Allāh (ﷻ) says:

> You are between Our eyes. (Sidi)

Who will you love? You will love dunyā—the lower world. You will love the human being. Love al-Bāqī. Al-Bāqī is one of Allāh's names, the Eternal One.

Everything is from Him. Everything is from His provision. Allāh (ﷻ) will be pleased with this love. He will be attached to this love; all of the prophets (عليهم السلام) give and all the prophets (عليهم السلام) taught us about such love. All people around the world need love, and if you see a lot in the news about wars, criminals and killers, they have lost the love and so they don't care about the happiness of others.

People have lost their houses. They have lost their money. Why? Because the kings and the presidents run away from Allāh (ﷻ) and they disobey Him. Thus, Allāh (ﷻ) told them, "Wait. I will let you see. I will not let you last forever." Those who took the love from the hearts of mothers and children took away love from the human being, and so people are like animals—not just like animals, but worse than animals.

Sayyida Rābiʿa (رضي الله عنها) taught divine love. She (رضي الله عنها) helped many poor people and many women and many men and she taught them what the divine love is. She gave them life because, as I mentioned, without love there is nothing. There is no life and she was talking with Allāh (ﷻ). Sayyida Rābiʿa (رضي الله عنها) was talking to Allāh (ﷻ) when she said:

> I love You with two kinds of love:
> one because I love the love,
> and the second kind is because You deserve it.
>
> I don't love You because I need money or the lower world.
> I love You because You send the love to me to be alive
> and to give it to others—to let others know love.
> The real servant will know what I mean by this love.

No one can ruin love; it will be saved. May peace be upon all people. People can, at that time, hear the song of the angels (عليهم السلام). Did you hear about this verse? Allāh (ﷻ) said:

> Indeed, We have sent it (the Qurʾān) down in the night of Qadr,
> during which descend the angels (عليهم السلام) and the rūḥ
> by Allāh's permission with all decrees,
> There is peace until the appearance of dawn. (97:1, 4, 5)

The reading continues until, "She (ﷺ) never married, but she had many children. And Allāh (ﷻ), pleased with her, said..."

This is the truth. He speaks the truth. I hope to see all beloveds be the children of Rābiʿa (ﷺ), the tree of the love, and to be the love for everyone, the tree of life.

I am asking Allāh (ﷻ) to make you all become the divine mirror, and I'm sure of what I'm telling you. Allāh (ﷻ) says:

> They want to extinguish Allāh's light with their mouths,
> but Allāh (ﷻ) will not allow anything
> except that His light will be perfected. (9:32)

They want to stop the light of Allāh (ﷻ). They want to, but Allāh (ﷻ) will complete His light. You will see this light in all countries and you will hear the divine song in every house, whether they accept it or not. Allāh (ﷻ) will complete His light.

Allāh (ﷻ) gave us lessons through the Prophet Nūḥ (Noah) (عليه السلام). When Nūḥ (عليه السلام) came to the people and told them, "Come to worship Allāh (ﷻ) and carry the message," they hurt him. He stayed with them for 950 years while they threw stones at him, ruined and destroyed the earth. He was patient and he was always saying, "Maybe they will come," so he kept giving them the message. "Maybe the next generation...maybe the third generation." He reached the tenth generation and even they hurt him. Then Sayyidinā Nūḥ (عليه السلام) invoked Allāh (ﷻ) against those people and he asked Allāh (ﷻ), "Oh Allāh (ﷻ), let them disappear. Let them die, all of them, because they will give to those who will disobey You."

Then what happened? Allāh (ﷻ) told Nūḥ (عليه السلام) to make a ship and said, "Don't invoke against the disobedient ones or ask Me to forgive them." The disobedient ones didn't deserve the love, the tree of this love. They destroyed people's hearts.

Then Nūḥ (عليه السلام) invoked, he asked Allāh (ﷻ), "Allāh (ﷻ)! Take them away! Let no one be left alive on this earth." Then Allāh (ﷻ) sent His angels (عليهم السلام), because Sayyidinā Nūḥ (عليه السلام) asked Allāh (ﷻ) to destroy the disobedient people, to finish them. Allāh (ﷻ) let water cover the entire earth so that all of the people at that time died.

Then Nūḥ's son came after he built the ship. When the water reached his son, Nūḥ (ﷺ) said, "Come my son. Come to be safe, because Allāh (ﷻ) will destroy everything." Allāh (ﷻ) told him, "Nūḥ, this son is not from your family, not from you, because he was disobedient." His son destroyed the earth and had never believed in divine love, so Allāh (ﷻ) destroyed him. I'm telling you now, Allāh (ﷻ) will not let all those people who do horrible things to humanity—to the orphans and to the poor—remain unpunished. Allāh (ﷻ) will let them live like this for a while, but He will catch them; and when He catches them, He will not let them be safe again.

Allāh (ﷻ) is the Merciful. He does not want to punish us, but people transgress limits against themselves. Allāh (ﷻ) is the Most Merciful. I'm asking Allāh (ﷻ) to spread peace and love to all of your families, to your children and to all people.

The reading continues until, "Not only did Rābiʿa (ﷺ) never marry, but she also never had a shaykh to guide and instruct her, for she received everything that she knew directly from Allāh (ﷻ), the Most High..."

She is the holy mother.

The reading continues until, "The same writer also said that Rābiʿa (ﷺ) was 'that one set apart in the seclusion of holiness, that woman veiled with the veil of sincerity, that one inflamed by love and longing, lost in union with God (ﷻ)...'"

She was different than any other saint. Allāh (ﷻ) never disappeared in her eyes for even a moment. She was always in existence with Allāh (ﷻ) and He never was absent from her. She was with Him all the time.

The reading continues until, "Rābiʿa remained behind, alone in the vast desert all around her. And she prayed to her Lord saying, "Oh my God (ﷻ), do kings deal thus with a woman, a stranger who is weak? You are calling me to Your house, but in the middle of my way You have suffered my donkey to die and You have left me alone in the desert."

Hardly had she finished praying when her donkey began to move. Finally, it stood up, Rābiʿa put her baggage onto it and continued on her way."

The first thing that the donkey said, he began to sing his song. Yes, so for the love of Rābiʿa (ﷺ), He gave life for her.

The reading continues until, "Then, they rest face to face with their Mighty King, and the tongue of their asking is as Rābiʿa who said, 'Everyone who prays to You from fear of the Fire and if You do not put them in the Fire this is their reward, or they pray to You for the Garden, full of fruits and flowers and that is their prize...'"

The people ask...he says, "Why do you pray?" Maybe I can take my chance to be in the Garden. Be in the Garden now! Be one when you pray to know how to carry the message.

The reading continues until, "She said, 'I have fled from the world and all that is in it and my prayer is for union with You, Allāh (ﷻ)! That is the goal of my desires.' Then, since she was always attributing her illnesses and misfortunes to the will of her beloved God (ﷻ)..."

This is the story of lovers. She came to teach us how to maintain love, why to keep this love—to keep this love to help those who are suffering and in pain. She never put anything in her mind. She just wanted to help others. The only thing she cared about was being with Allāh (ﷻ) and saving, keeping and taking care of the divine tree, the divine love, and giving this love to all people.

She left us many things, including how to keep this love within us, and she said, "Renew your promise with Allāh (ﷻ)!" This is a prayer. This is a real prayer from Sayyida Rābiʿa to all human beings without discrimination, regardless of color or gender.

If you want to receive divine love, you should come and promise Allāh (ﷻ) that you love Him and it will return back to you. You can take the love from Allāh (ﷻ) to ease the heaviness of this tree. Our backs carry this tree. All of you will be on the ride back to Allāh (ﷻ) and you will be happy, so you should put the flag of love in your houses. Allāh (ﷻ) will save your children, your families and your beloveds.

Lā ʾilāha ʾilla-llāh. Lā ʾilāha ʾilla-llāh. Give us love—that love You gave to all the prophets and gnostics (عليهم السلام), because the tree of love is eternal. Let us test this love. Keep our bodies, our hearts and our spirits to reach You safely, with mercy for all our families, for our beloveds, for our sons, for our daughters and for our homes.

Oh Allāh (ﷻ), I ask You to give the shadow of love
as You did for Your lover Sayyida Rābiʿa (رضي الله عنها),
as You did for all the prophets (عليهم السلام).
You accept their supplications
and You gave them the message to give their love to all people.
We promise You that we will walk like gnostics, like lovers,
Your lovers.
Āmīn. Āmīn.

Everything Depends Upon Tawba

Compilation of Tawba Teachings from *The Traveler's Journey*

Friday, June 18, 2010 PM, Welcome Weekend

لا إله إلا الله - لا إله إلا الله - لا إله إلا الله - محمد رسول الله عليه صلاة الله
لا إله إلا الله - لا إله إلا الله - لا إله إلا الله - ابراهيم رسول الله عليه صلاة الله
لا إله إلا الله - لا إله إلا الله - لا إله إلا الله - موسى رسول الله عليه صلاة الله
لا إله إلا الله - لا إله إلا الله - لا إله إلا الله - عيسى رسول الله عليه صلاة الله
اللهم انت السلام ومنك السلام و إليك يعود السلام
تباركت ربنا وتعاليت يا ذوالجلال والإكرام

Peace be upon you. Thanks to God (ﷻ), thanks to Allāh (ﷻ). I praise God (ﷻ) for letting me be His servant, carrying His message. I praise Him, I thank Him, because He makes it easy for me. He carries me on His wings, by His grace. He came in this time with people suffering in every country, in this country and everywhere. They are suffering from pain and starvation. They are being destroyed because of bad people.

I am asking my God (ﷻ), my Lord (ﷻ), in these days for peace, love, mercy, freedom and justice for all those who are suffering from sickness, hunger and all horrible things. I love to come here because I was busy in my ṣalāh in al-Aqṣā in the Holy Land. I was there near the Holy Rock, the rock of Muḥammad (ﷺ), Ibrāhīm (Abraham) (ؑ) and ʿĪsā (Jesus) (ؑ). I spent the whole night asking God (ﷻ) to help people. God (ﷻ) gave me permission and I came here within 24 hours. Allāh (ﷻ) guides me. Allāh (ﷻ) let me come.

I am telling you from my deep heart, that I love you and I love all those who love Allāh (ﷻ) and I love all those who carry the love of God (ﷻ), the message of peace and mercy. I ask God (ﷻ) to carry all of you kindly. I ask Him to protect your bodies and your hearts and your spirits. Allāh (ﷻ) cares about you!

Allāh (ﷻ) is with us. We are full of sins. Allāh (ﷻ) directed us to His angels (ؑ) in the sky. He says:

> They used to sleep but little in the night. (51:17)

There are those who will ask forgiveness at midnight because they didn't obey God (ﷻ) as they should.

He created us. He is the Holy One. He asks us to pray for Him and to obey Him. He is the Beloved; no one is a beloved, just Him. He is the Love. He says on the tongue of His Prophet (ﷺ):

> The heavens and the earth cannot contain Me,
> but the heart of My faithful believer and lover contains Me.

God (ﷻ) will settle in the hearts of those who know the truth and know why God (ﷻ) created them. Those who have fallen in love with God (ﷻ) know in every moment that He created them to obey Him. He does not need anything from them. He does not want them to provide for Him. We are poor—He is rich.

You should be with God (ﷻ) and follow His orders, so that you will not be far from Him. If you believe in God (ﷻ), if you love God (ﷻ), you will keep your prayers (ṣalāh). You should know why you are praying. What is the meaning of ṣalāh, what is the meaning of rakʿāh and sujūd?[3] You should know the meaning of ṣalāh. There are many deep meanings within it. This is the food for your spirit. This is the manifestation of God (ﷻ). Through it you can feel and love God (ﷻ). Our Prophet (ﷺ) says:

> The closest we can be with God (ﷻ)
> is when we pray and are on our knees.

He will ask you how loyal you are. You should renew your promise. Ask Allāh (ﷻ) for forgiveness, If you want Allāh (ﷻ) to accept you and to provide for you, you should obey Him and you should pray for Him. If you are like that, you will be the air and the tongue and the hand and the leg of God (ﷻ). You will be a divine slave and if you will say to anything, "Be," that thing will be, by the will of God (ﷻ).

This is the real truth. We carry the Beloved in our hearts and we will be slaves to you, my children, my lovers of God (ﷻ), to help you be good slaves to God (ﷻ) and obey God (ﷻ). You will be with God (ﷻ) all the time. You will be with Allāh (ﷻ) alone, and you will be in the divine presence.

---

[3] A rakʿāh is a cycle of ṣalāh. Sujūd means prostration.

If you are like this, you will be the child of unity, the child of the existence of Allāh (ﷻ).

This reading is comprised of excerpts from *The Traveler's Journey of Healing through Divine Love, Knowledge and Truth.*[4]

"I ask Allāh (ﷻ) to make us steadfast in His way.
Make us firm in Your Way and forgive our faults.
Conceal our mistakes and bestow Your Mercy upon us.

Oh Allāh (ﷻ), I ask You by the reality of Your lofty essence
and by the reality of Your praiseworthy Prophet (ﷺ).
Please do not let any one of us be miserable or sad, or suffer.
And please do not forsake us
and put us in shame on the Day of Judgment,
but forgive us and bestow Your mercy upon us.
Grant us happiness, all of us.
Āmīn.

Know that everything depends upon tawba. Tawba is your first step and it is a continuous step. It is like changing the oil in your car. Can you actually drive a car when it doesn't have oil or when it has a different problem? No, you have to fix it in order to drive it. You are like this vehicle and you are full of things that need to be fixed, rectified, washed and cleaned in order to drive and arrive at the divine presence."

If Allāh (ﷻ) took away our electricity, could our cars continue to work? Can anyone make cars work without electricity? Do you know the secret of electricity? No one knows the secret, and the evil ones ask for this secret. They want to destroy the earth. Allāh (ﷻ) says:

> We will soon show them Our signs in the universe and in their own souls, (41:53)

Allāh (ﷻ) will let you see many things, divine things from Him. In one year you will see things that are smaller than an ant or a similar insect.

---

[4] Sidi Muhammad, *The Traveler's Journey of Healing Through Divine Love, Knowledge and Truth*. Pope Valley: Shadhiliyya Sufi Center, 2010.

You have not heard about many things that have happened, like how Allāh (ﷻ) stops everything: airplanes in the sky, volcanoes...If Allāh (ﷻ) sent something like a fire, what would happen? No one could stop it. And other signs...something should happen.

We ask God (ﷻ) for eternal love, divine love. We ask Him to be merciful to all people without discrimination. We ask Him to let them know the right way, and to turn back to Him and to build a divine place for all people.

The reading continues, "The path to Allāh (ﷻ) is full of obstacles and danger and you must continue to purify yourself by walking this path until you become fully conscious of the divine presence. You must purify the body and your soul through tawba. You need to repent because our bodies and hearts and souls accumulate dirt that causes illness. We must purify ourselves and truly follow the divine way by following His commands and prohibitions.

Do not fear anyone except Allāh (ﷻ). Revere Allāh (ﷻ) and walk to Him through the essential gate, which is the gate of tawba.

Tawba of the Body

The purification of the body is known. What does it mean? It means that you do not use your limbs, your hands or your eyes in a way that is not pleasing to Allāh (ﷻ). Your limbs should not be killing or violating someone's rights or doing something wrongful and displeasing to Allāh (ﷻ).

You should not spy on people, for example, or feel envious of others. Your tongue should be purified, too. It should fast from backbiting and speaking ill of others. It should fast from offending others. Your hearing, your ears, should also fast. All of your limbs, all of your senses, have to be purified and returned to their original state through tawba. Tawba is important."

From here, you should know: tawba should not be made only with your tongue. Your tongue is a jewel and this jewel is pure and very sensitive. We should take care of it and we should use it just to obey Allāh (ﷻ). We shouldn't use it to hurt other people. Keep your tongue clean; this tongue can be a snake, something that could hurt you. Because of that, Allāh (ﷻ) says:

> The recording angels (عليهم السلام) record all of your actions,
> one sitting on the right and one on the left. (50:17)

These angels (عليهم السلام) write every detail of what you say and do, everything. They will record your good deeds and bad deeds. The one on the right will write your good deeds and the one on the left will write your bad deeds.

He who comes to Allāh (ﷻ) on the Day of Standing with his book in his right hand will go to his family happy. From this point, you are a human being.

He created you in a complete picture. Do not think you are a simple thing. Within you there is a large world. You carry the message of the truth. The mountains could not carry the message, but you can carry it. The sky does not carry it; no one can carry it except for the human being. The human being carries it and the human being does not know the worthiness of the message. Because of that, you should be humble. Do not forget who you are. The human being is created weak and he cannot do anything for himself if God (ﷻ) does not give him permission.

Everything knows God (ﷻ) and praises God (ﷻ). Everything, even the insects, the ants praise God (ﷻ). Insects keep the promise of God (ﷻ) and they thank God (ﷻ) all the time. The human being is the only creature who does not know what he carries. He does not know how to praise God (ﷻ) or how to accept the truth that he is weak and he should obey God (ﷻ) all the time.

You are a jewel and you should protect your existence. You are the pride of the divine presence. Because of that, God (ﷻ) asks the angels (عليهم السلام) to pray for you. Allāh (ﷻ) tells the angels (عليهم السلام):

> (I) breathed into him out of My spirit (My own light)
> (so pray for them). (35:71 and Tafsir)

At that time, Allāh (ﷻ) manifested in Ādam (ؑ); Ādam (ؑ) is the manifestation of Allāh (ﷻ). Allāh (ﷻ) said on the tongue of His Prophet (ﷺ):

> I created Ādam (ؑ), the human being, in My image.

Allāh (ﷻ) said, "human being," He didn't say man or woman; He didn't say male or female. Why do you deceive yourself? Why do you cause harm to yourself?

God (ﷻ) lets you know that you carry the message. Allāh (ﷻ) is the Most Merciful, the Most Compassionate. Allāh (ﷻ) knows you carry the message, and He helps you to carry the message. Allāh (ﷻ) knows what you do all the time and that you make mistakes all the time, but He opens the door of tawba.

Allāh (ﷻ) opens the door of tawba for those who believe in Allāh (ﷻ) and who promise Allāh (ﷻ) that they will not return to their mistakes again. He will accept their tawba, but it will not work if you give your promise and tawba in the morning and at night you return back to the same bad actions. Allāh (ﷻ) knows everything and He sees everything. He sees the ants inside of a rock, so who are you trying to cheat?

A man comes to a master, one who knows Allāh (ﷻ), and he has many sins. The man asks the master, "My Master, how can I get rid of my mistakes and return back to Allāh (ﷻ)?" The master told him, "If you can make true tawba, God (ﷻ) will accept you. If you want to eat, earn pure, clean money from people. Do not steal it. Even if you steal from people who cannot see you, know that Allāh (ﷻ) can see you."

How can a person steal from God (ﷻ)? The master told him, "No, you should make a true and honest tawba, because Allāh (ﷻ) is the Hearing and the Seeing." Allāh (ﷻ) said to Harūn (Aaron) and Mūsā (Moses) (ؑ) that anywhere they went He could see and watch them. Because of that, we should announce our tawba.

The reading continues, "*Tawba of the Soul.* After tawba of the body, there is tawba of the soul. What is tawba of the soul? I will give you an example. Sometimes you see someone in a good state or receiving a blessing and you say, 'That is not fair. Why does he have this and I do

not? He does not deserve it.' You start to think these thoughts and to feel badly. This is not right. This is envy. This is jealousy and envy and it is not a blessed feeling. It is not encouraged by the prophets and messengers of Allāh (ﷻ). You must discipline your commanding ego. Your soul desires to fast, too. This ego listens only to Iblīs, the evil one, the devil.

Sometimes you may hear ideas or have thoughts that are coming from teachers who are not knowledgeable, and so they impart incorrect information. They make you think you can see and hear things that are not real. You cannot listen to these teachers because they live in illusions and pictures. You should not be listening to them or to the devil, the evil one, the shayṭān."

Many of the stupid people, those who say, "I see Allāh (ﷻ) and I hear what Allāh (ﷻ) is saying," still live in clay, in mud. Everyone should be polite and should understand the words of God (ﷻ) though His Qur'ān. No one should live in illusions, in pictures. No one can guide you to good deeds; Allāh (ﷻ) is the only one who can lead you to good things through His prophets (ﷺ).

No one can help you, because no one can see inside you. No one can tell you how many hairs there are on your head. How could anyone know these hidden things? A person can only know these things if Allāh (ﷻ) teaches him.

If you obey Allāh (ﷻ), Allāh (ﷻ) will teach you many things that you never knew before. If you obey Him, He will teach you. He will let you understand everything. He will send you a messenger; He will teach you how to walk and how to sit and everything. This is the mercy of Allāh (ﷻ).

The reading continues, "You must know the stations of the soul and go through them, one by one. You must understand the language of each station, of each level, and go through it. Your ego can whisper to you in many ways in accordance with your station or spiritual level, so you must understand the language of these stations.

I have clarified this for you and explained the stations in many of my books, such as *Music of the Soul*[5] and *He Who Knows Himself Knows His Lord.*[6] I have explained how to discipline the ego and how to check it. You should make use of these books. Read them, write them and comprehend them, understand them and follow them—this is how you will purify your soul."

You are of this world, but you are the master of all the worlds. Don't think you are a small star; this is the science of Allāh (ﷻ).

The reading continues, "*Tawba of the Heart*

Afterwards, there is a level of purifying the heart. What is the heart? The heart is something magnificent. It is a house. It is the house of your Lord (ﷻ), the house of God (ﷻ). The heart is the house of Allāh (ﷻ). Allāh (ﷻ) says on the tongue of His Prophet (ﷺ):

> My heavens and My earth could not contain Me,
> but the heart of My faithful believer contains Me.

This means that the heart should be empty of hate, jealousy and anger and should be tranquil and peaceful. It should be full of love and care for others and full of mercy and free of evil. It should be purified of every blemish. It goes through seven levels.

When you are making tawba, you must feel regret for what you have done. The meaning of seeking forgiveness is feeling sorrow for everything you have done that was wrong and that deviated from Allāh's way (ﷻ). If you have stolen something or violated someone's rights with your tongue or your hand, if you backbit someone, if you discriminated against someone, if you were racist or if you betrayed your wife or husband, you must seek forgiveness for it. This includes whatever your hand, eyes, ears or tongue did to violate another human being. You should make tawba for whatever you did that Allāh (ﷻ) prohibits and was not merciful.

---

[5] Sidi Muhammad, *The Music of the Soul*. Petaluma: Sidi Muhammad Press, 2002.
[6] Sidi Muhammad. *He Who Knows Himself Knows His Lord*. Petaluma: Sidi Muhammad Press, 2007.

Also, you must understand that you must return any rights that you took from others unjustly. You must return those rights to where they belong, if you know how to and if you can. For example, if you took money that was not yours to take, you must return it to the person you took it from and ask for his forgiveness. You must return the money to that person if you still have it. Even a sheep will come before Allāh (ﷻ) if it was kicked or violated to ask for justice. Also, animals will be held accountable for their actions; so what about the human being who violates the rights of many creatures?

If you took money from someone, you will stand before Allāh (ﷻ) on the Day of Judgment and Allāh (ﷻ) will command, "Return the money."

You will answer, "I do not have any money."

Then Allāh (ﷻ) will say to the abused, "Take the blessings and rewards he received for doing good deeds."

What if all of your blessings and rewards are taken to right wrongs you committed, but you still owe others?

Allāh (ﷻ) will say to the abused, "Place your sins upon him."

Then your balance will be full of sin and if you still owe you will be thrown into the Hellfire.

This is how it will be, but a person in this world can still repent, return rights he took from others, ask for their forgiveness and apologize to them; then Allāh (ﷻ) will intervene on his behalf.

Allāh (ﷻ) will say, "He apologized, he asked for your forgiveness, he returned your rights to you. It is all right, forgive him," because Allāh (ﷻ) is fair.

Allāh (ﷻ) will say to the abused, "Look at the heavens."

The abused will turn and he will see his house in the Garden.

Allāh (ﷻ) will say, "This is what I will give you if you will forgive your abuser."

Because Allāh (ﷻ) is the Most Merciful, Most Compassionate, He will give the abused compensation for forgiving the abuser. He will forgive the abuser if he seeks tawba.

What can help an abuser or a person who has wronged others or committed sins? Offer a sacrifice. This is a testimony of his faithfulness and sincerity in regretting what he did and in seeking forgiveness. He must show his sincerity in this world before Allāh (ﷻ) will take him on that Day and say, "Let him stand and be accountable."

If a person cannot return money he has stolen, he must still ask forgiveness from the one he stole from. In this way, he continues to be in his repentant state until he earns the money and can return it. What if he dies before he has finished returning it? If he has apologized and asked for forgiveness and repented, then Allāh (ﷻ) will compensate that person through the money that is paid for the sacrifice (upon his passing).

No one should despair about anything he has done, because Allāh (ﷻ) is the Most Compassionate, Most Merciful. If, in your heart, you have the intention to return the money and you cannot do so now, and you die with that intention, that is good. If you offer even a little sacrifice and say, "This sacrifice is to show my tawba," it will go to help the poor, the needy and the ill. In this way you will be forgiven, it will be accepted from you, because this sacrifice goes to build a road, a school or a hospital, etc. It goes to help people. This is why you can be forgiven through giving a sacrifice. Through that sacrifice, Allāh (ﷻ) returns the right you took wrongfully to the victim after you die, and He accepts your tawba.

Let go of the past. Allāh (ﷻ) gives the abusers, the oppressors, the chance to repent. But if they do not, He captures them by force and they will taste the consequences of what they have done and they will suffer. Allāh (ﷻ) says:

> Allāh (ﷻ) gives respite to the oppressor,
> but when He takes him over, He never releases him.

> Such is the seizure of your Lord
> when He seizes towns in the midst of their wrong:
> His seizure is indeed painful and severe. (11:102)

For this reason, do not dwell in pain from the past. Trust Allāh (ﷻ) with it and move forward; if you hold on it will make you sick. If you make others dwell in it, then you are sick and you will make them sick.

You people, you are in poverty. You are in need of Allāh (ﷻ), your Creator who is self-sufficient. You are in need of Him; you are all in need of Him. We need to make tawba, to ask Him to accept us and to give us the strength to keep walking in the right way. No, Allāh (ﷻ) will punish you first and then choose you like He did with the Prophet Mūsā (ﷺ)."

This is Allāh's order; this is a divine order expressed in the Qur'ān and through the prophets (ﷺ). Allāh (ﷻ) says that the prophets (ﷺ), all of them, talk about the divine order. Allāh (ﷻ) taught them. He brought them to help us understand and to teach us.

Do not be with illusions; do not be with those who carry black minds. You should know how to open your white, illuminated mind. This is easy for you to know if you are honest. If you want to be a true follower, be like Ibrāhīm (ﷺ) who says:

> I am emigrating to my Lord. He will guide me! (37:99)

Be like the Prophet Ibrāhīm (ﷺ), just go to Allāh (ﷻ) and do not stop.

The reading continues, "An attribute of the true lover is true fasting in order to please Allāh (ﷻ) by living up to His truth and His reality. This is the true translation of the word "fasting." Are you ready to do this type of fasting? If you are truthful and you say, "Yes," then you must ask Allāh (ﷻ) to give you the strength, because alone you cannot do it. You must repent to Him for this reason.

Look at what we recite in the Fātiḥa when we pray. We say, "'ihdina-ṣ-ṣirāṭal-mustaqīm" which means, "Guide us to the straight way." We ask for His help because this is the true way. You are now on the path, so you must translate the true tawba and the true meaning of fasting. You must follow it truly and be like Mūsā (ﷺ)."

This world has been in existence for many millions of years. No one can create a human being. No one can create an insect. No one can make it rain. No one can do that. But evil people can create chemicals to kill others and to kill other beings. These are people who create bad things on the earth. But those who love Allāh (ﷻ) try to spread love. Those who don't know Allāh (ﷻ) are dirty in their time and in their deeds. They say many things, but they do not do anything. They work against the human being, and Allāh (ﷻ) tried to let all human beings be happy.

The reading continues, "When Mūsā (ﷺ) once asked his Lord (ﷻ):

> "Oh my Lord! Show me (Yourself) that I may look upon You."
>
> Allāh (ﷻ) said, "You cannot see Me." (7:143)

Allāh (ﷻ) said this to Mūsā (ﷺ) even though he was a prophet and a messenger and a gnostic. He was in the station of existence and so He said:

> Take off your shoes,
> for you are standing in the Valley of Ṭuwa. (20:12)
>
> (If you want to see Me) look upon the mountain. (7:143)

Which mountain did Allāh (ﷻ) mean? Where is this mountain? The mountain is that which can contain Allāh (ﷻ) and it is a metaphor of the human heart.

Allāh (ﷻ) says in a ḥadīth qudsī:

> My heavens and My earth cannot contain Me.
> Only the heart of My faithful servant contains Me.

The heart of the one who is purified from all sins and has truly repented to Allāh (ﷻ) can contain Him. You must purify yourself. Leave this world and the pursuit of the pleasures of this world and the next and animate yourself; become consumed in your worship for Allāh (ﷻ) and your desire for Allāh (ﷻ) until you become nothing, like water.

When you lose yourself like that in Allāh (ﷻ), then Allāh (ﷻ) will revive you.

When Allāh (ﷻ) revived Mūsā (ﷺ) back to this life, what did he say? Mūsā (ﷺ) said, "I am always in poverty; I am always in need of you, despite all of Your bounty." Mūsā (ﷺ) looked at the mountain, which means the mountain of his life, after everything had been purified and he was trained and disciplined.

This is why we must declare our tawba from every bad deed we have committed. We must purify ourselves from the actions that Allāh (ﷻ) does not like. If you do so, you will experience true peace; the whole world will experience true peace, divine peace, until when even a chicken can walk among people or wolves and it will not be eaten. You will see the world full of love, full of mercy. All people will love each other and help each other.

This is why I invoke Allāh (ﷻ) by His greatest name and by His encompassing mercy—to save all of humankind, to guide them to return to Him and to repent from their sins. May they all return to adopt divine love as their creed! May peace and mercy become their creed so that no one faces the death that is experienced by tyrants and oppressors who are not conscious of Allāh (ﷻ) and do not guard themselves against evil, and all people can rejoice in a happy, eternal life without death. Āmīn."

This is a precise picture. This is how you will be in a good relationship with Allāh (ﷻ). This is the real tawba. Sign a contract with God (ﷻ) saying that you will purify your body, your spirit, your heart and your senses. You should ask Allāh (ﷻ) for forgiveness and you should renew your promise with Allāh (ﷻ) to let Allāh (ﷻ) look at you. Allāh (ﷻ) says in a ḥadīth qudsī:

> Oh My worshipful slave,
> if you did not make mistakes
> I would create another creation that would make mistakes
> and that would repent to Me,
> and I would give them tawba and forgive their mistakes.

He knows that you are weak and you will sin. When you do sin, you should remember Allāh (ﷻ) and ask forgiveness.

Now I am asking you to renew the oath between you and Allāh (ﷻ). I am asking you to renew your tawba. I am asking Allāh (ﷻ) to forgive you all. You are most welcome if you want to come and Allāh (ﷻ) will help us. This is a divine opportunity, and by the order of Allāh (ﷻ), I am asking you, I am calling you. You should announce from the bottom of your heart, the bottom of your spirit, that you are and want to be with His divine presence. He says:

> Say: "Oh My slaves who have transgressed against themselves!
> Do not despair of Allāh's mercy. Truly, Allāh (ﷻ) forgives all sins.
> Truly, He is the one who is Often Forgiving, Most Merciful."
> (39:53)

You should promise Allāh (ﷻ) that you will not return back to you sins/ Be like a child. The child is clean and his spirit is pure. If you want to be like that, you should renew your oath with Allāh (ﷻ) to protect your body and to be just for Allāh (ﷻ) in your self, your heart and your spirit. If you want that, you should ask Him for forgiveness. The door is open and it has never been closed. Allāh (ﷻ) says:

> Oh My angels (عليهم السلام), this is My slave.
> He came to me asking My forgiveness.
> I will let you be My witness that I accept his forgiveness
> and I forgive all his sins.

This is Allāh (ﷻ), the Most Merciful and Compassionate. Are you ready to keep the promise? Āmīn.

The Grave's Two Paths

"The First Discourse: On the Torment of the Grave and Its Severity"[7] from *Spiritual Discourses in the Blessed Al-Aqṣā Mosque* Saturday, June 19, 2010 AM, Welcome Weekend

لا إله إلا الله - لا إله إلا الله - لا إله إلا الله - محمد رسول الله عليه صلاة الله
لا إله إلا الله - لا إله إلا الله - لا إله إلا الله - ابراهيم رسول الله عليه صلاة الله
لا إله إلا الله - لا إله إلا الله - لا إله إلا الله - موسى رسول الله عليه صلاة الله
لا إله إلا الله - لا إله إلا الله - لا إله إلا الله - عيسى رسول الله عليه صلاة الله
اللهم انت السلام ومنك السلام و إليك يعود السلام
تباركت ربنا وتعاليت يا ذوالجلال والإكرام

As-salāmu ʿalaykum wa raḥmatu-llāhi wa bārakatuhu and may peace be upon our prophets (عليهم السلام) who ask us to do righteous deeds and to stop doing bad deeds. I praise God (ﷻ) for this day, that He provides me the strength and understanding to apply His message, to give His message as He wishes, in detail and with brevity. I am a poor servant of Allāh (ﷻ). Allāh (ﷻ) gave me this command, this order, through the teachings of all our prophets (عليهم السلام) and through my beloved Prophet Muḥammad (ﷺ). My grandfather Ibrāhīm (Abraham) (عليه السلام) and all other prophets (عليهم السلام) said, "I am poor; I am poor; I am poor."

I am asking Allāh (ﷻ) to give you what He gave me. I am asking Allāh (ﷻ) to let you understand His orders and to help you to follow them. I am asking Him to help you carry His message so that you can establish happiness for you and your family, your sons and your beloveds.

I ask Allāh (ﷻ) for all of you to live under Allāh's tent. You will live in peace, justice, freedom and love. I am asking Allāh (ﷻ) to allow me to give this peace, freedom and love so that you can give it to others and earn a way to be under the tent of Allāh (ﷻ) and under the tent of the poor people. Our Prophet (ﷺ) says:

> Give the poor their rights, take care of them,
> and give them peace and love.

---

[7] Sidi Muhammad, *Spiritual Discourses in the Blessed Al-Aqṣā Mosque*. Petaluma: Sidi Muhammad Press, 2010, pp. 16-18.

Allāh (ﷻ) says that there is a nation that He loves. The poor people, who you should help and love, are honest. I don't mean just the poor people who don't have money; no, I don't mean that. I mean those who are really loyal to Allāh (ﷻ) and carry the message of Allāh (ﷻ). Their hearts are full of justice, freedom and love. Those who devote their lives to being a big deal, their lives are not a big deal. Those who want to live in this life on ḥalāl (lawful) money should just ask for the love of God (ﷻ). They want to love the One who created them (ﷻ), the One who gave them health and happiness in this world and the next. This is the first emigration to God (ﷻ); this is the dunyā, this life.

If you obey His orders, I am sure Allāh (ﷻ) will accept you and give you what you want, the desires of your heart. You will see what no eyes have seen before and you will hear what no ears have heard before. Allāh (ﷻ) gives those who follow Him this gift. Our Prophet (ﷺ) says:

> Those who believe in Him are in the Garden now.

Take your chance in this life and know it is a temporary life; it is just an illusion. It is a short life. Other lives will come and this one will disappear like an illusion or a dream. You will live for twenty or seventy or one hundred years and then you will leave this life. You will begin other journeys. You will travel from this world of Mulk (lower world) to the world of Malakūt (dominion, the unseen).

We call this journey a journey of al-barzakh. There is a critical line you will travel to another life through the barzakh. You will be carried on His name. When you die it is not a real death, because you will travel to other worlds. For example, imagine taking a trip on a plane and sitting in the airplane for 10-20 hours, then finally the airplane stops and you get out at a new destination and start your real life.

This is a holy journey, a blessed journey, for those who are blessed by God (ﷻ). You can find everything on this journey. This journey is supplied with many things. This is the journey that takes you to divine truth. This is the journey of the examination, the true test. You are preparing yourself for questions.

Others will take from you; after death did you leave anything behind for all those people? Yes, you left a home, you left money, you left everything. Did you take anything with you? When you die they will even take your clothes. They will leave you with just yourself and they will put strange clothes on you. Then they will put you in a ditch, in a grave. What is a grave? It is a great thing. Our beloved Prophet (ﷺ) says:

> The grave can be the Garden or it could be Hell.

Which one will you choose?

This is the journey of the spirit, of the heart and of the self. It is not an easy thing. I will explain the grave to you. All the prophets (عليهم السلام) went to the grave; they left this physical life and traveled to the divine presence.

I will explain what the followers of our beloved Prophet (ﷺ) said after he passed away. They went out with our Prophet (ﷺ) after he was cleaned. They carried him to his grave with the intention to put him inside it. All the people were around him and they were very sad. They started to feel pain in their hearts and they were thinking, "Will we all be like this? What kind of life is this? What did I do?" Inshā'a-llāh.

Our Prophet (ﷺ) said:

> Ask Allāh (ﷻ) for forgiveness three times.

Ask Allāh (ﷻ) to open the door for you and say, "You are in charge of all the doors, You are the Benefactor and You are the Most Merciful, the Most Compassionate. You created me. You are the Provider. Please, my Lord, don't punish me. I am poor between Your hands." This is what the honest believer, who follows the commands and orders from God (ﷻ), says.

All the prophets (عليهم السلام) went sad and silent. They were scared like birds who were on their heads. It was not easy for all the (truly) poor people who strayed from God (ﷻ) and those who did not accept His message. All those who had their bodies cremated and their ashes spread are feeling as if they will not be found and that they have been taken from Allāh (ﷻ). They are afraid that they might be put in a prison filled with fire. Has any prophet ever been cremated? No prophet has died and burned; it is the devil, the shayṭān, that is to be burned.

People wonder whether they are the only ones put in front of God (ﷻ) if they are put in a grave. The answer is no, everyone will be in front of God (ﷻ), because I am saying all human beings who work politely on this earth, from this earth, will go to God (ﷻ). You do not know what is inside this earth; you will return to this earth. It is not proper to destroy human beings at the time of death through cremation. Our prophets (عليهم السلام) tell us to ask God (ﷻ) for forgiveness if we have done this.

Believe in the truth and believe in Allāh (ﷻ). Follow our prophets (عليهم السلام) and leave everything behind. Just as our grandfathers left everything behind we, too, will not have anything. When my grandfather died he told me to take my hand like this (open and empty) and I asked why. He said, "Because I want all the people to know I passed away empty. My hands are empty."

After death, the angels (عليهم السلام) come down and the spirits show how Allāh (ﷻ) created Ādam (عليه السلام) from His spirit. Those angels (عليهم السلام) who come down, come to the honest believers and followers who keep their promises with Allāh (ﷻ). The angels (عليهم السلام) come down and bring the light, the brightness of the sun. They take true believers to the Garden and they bring special things to the person who has died.

They tell you to get up and the angels (عليهم السلام) will sit upon them. The angels (عليهم السلام) are by your side before you die to take you to the Angel of Death, Izrāʾīl (Azrael) (عليه السلام). If you are honest and ask for forgiveness and acceptance of God (ﷻ), all the angels (عليهم السلام) are governed and take your spirit to a celebration. It will be like a wedding. They are waiting,

If you are dishonest, you will have the devil waiting for you. Only the honest people go to a celebration. Those who do not give love to others will have no celebration; only those who showed love will have a celebration.

When the spirit is carried by the angels (عليهم السلام), its beautiful fragrance and the essence of who the person was will be shared with all the world and the heavens. All the angels (عليهم السلام) will smell this beautiful fragrance. The Angel of Death (عليه السلام) will tell all the other angels (عليهم السلام) this good spirit's name. Because he was good and carried the orders of God (ﷻ), all the angels (عليهم السلام) will celebrate him. This is the greatest celebration a person can ever have. It is greater than any wedding. Your spirit will hear and your heart will hear, also. Allāh (ﷻ) will write a book in the highest sky and you will be returned back to the earth. This is why Allāh (ﷻ) says:

> From her (the earth) We create you
> and into her We will return you. (20:55)

Then the spirit who died will come back to himself along with the two angels Munkar and Nakīr (ﷺ). When you return, these two angels will ask you who your Lord is, who your prophet is, and what religion you practice. You are to answer, "My religion is the same as all the prophets (ﷺ) and my God is Allāh (ﷻ). I have followed the prophets (ﷺ) who are the messengers of God (ﷻ). I have followed these messengers."

Then, other angels (ﷺ) from the sky will also answer and say, "Yes, he is being honest." They will say, "Now, prepare a place in the Garden for him. Open the door to the Garden and you will see a big road that opens and leads you inside."

A beautiful angel full of a beautiful fragrance will greet you. This is your day in the Garden. The angel (ﷺ) will ask, "Who are you?" You will answer, "I am your righteous deed and I want to return back to my family." This is what the good believer will find.

When those who disobey Allāh (ﷻ) die, they will see angels of darkness (ﷺ). The disobedient ones will not be able to see the angels and the angels of darkness will take him. The Angel of Death, Izrā'īl (ﷺ), will come and ask the dying one in his last living moment to give him a chance to change this. The angel will tell him to go to Allāh (ﷻ) so that his spirit and his death will not have an ugly fragrance. No one can put up with this smell.

He will go to each sky with the angels (ﷺ) and they will ask, "What is this smelly spirit?" They will call him bad and dirty names, and then he will be returned back to the grave and the angels (ﷺ) will come to him. They will test him and ask him to go to the angel of Allāh (ﷻ).
If he refuses, they will take his spirit to the Fire which has been prepared for him for a thousand years. This fire burns over 100 yards. His grave will be narrow and he will feel pain in his body. Many snakes

will come to eat the body and he will stay in pain until the Last Day of Judgment.

Judge yourself before Allāh (ﷻ) judges you and ask yourself about every deed you have done every day. Every day we should ask ourselves if we have caused any harm to another. Check every day, because the Fire will come to you every day if you are not good. The believers will be in the eternal garden.

Each person chooses whether he wants the Garden or the Fire; you have complete freedom to choose. Sidi asks, "Which do you want, my beloved? Help others and help those who have passed away, especially those who disobeyed Allāh (ﷻ). Without your prayers they will be kept in the eternal Fire.

This is from all the prophets (عليهم السلام) and they have all mentioned this same message in all of the holy books. The prophets (عليهم السلام) will lead you away from this physical, material, temporary life. I was given the order 4 years back in the Holy Land and I continue to give to them in order to let you and others know the truth. People think that when you die there is nothing further, but I wanted to explain that this is part of faith,[8] so do what is right and obey Allāh (ﷻ) and protect yourself and your family from the Fire.

---

[8] In Islām there are certain beliefs you must hold as true to be within the boundaries of the religion. These beliefs are called the articles of faith (imān). The six articles of faith are: 1. to believe in One God (ﷻ), 2. to believe in the angels, 3. to believe in the holy books, 4. to believe in the prophets (عليهم السلام), 5. to believe in the Day of Judgment/afterlife, and 6. to believe in the supremacy of God's will.

The Day of Judgment's Two Paths

"The Second Discourse: On the Horror of the Day of Judgment and the Terror of Events" from *Spiritual Discourses in the Blessed al-Aqṣā Mosque*

Sunday, June 20, 2010 AM, Welcome Weekend

لا إله إلا الله – لا إله إلا الله – لا إله إلا الله – محمد رسول الله عليه صلاة الله
لا إله إلا الله – لا إله إلا الله – لا إله إلا الله – ابراهيم رسول الله عليه صلاة الله
لا إله إلا الله – لا إله إلا الله – لا إله إلا الله – موسى رسول الله عليه صلاة الله
لا إله إلا الله – لا إله إلا الله – لا إله إلا الله – عيسى رسول الله عليه صلاة الله
اللهم انت السلام ومنك السلام و إليك يعود السلام
تباركت ربنا وتعاليت يا ذوالجلال والإكرام

This day is a holy day because it is from a holy month. This month is the month of Allāh (ﷻ) and its name is Rajab. During this month Allāh (ﷻ) created the whole world. When He said, "Be," "Kun," everything appeared. He created seven heavens and seven earths. In this month, also, He said to the angels (عليهم السلام):

> I am going to create a man from dried clay of altered mud.
> So, when I have fashioned him completely
> and breathed into him (from My spirit)
> the soul which I created for him... (15:28-29)

This means, "I will create this human being as My manifestation, a worthy thing, and I want you to know Me through Ādam (عليه السلام), the human being."

He created the whole world and then He created Ādam (عليه السلام). When He sent His spirit to Ādam (عليه السلام) He said, "Be," and just like that everything happened. This happened during this month of Rajab. It is the month of Allāh (ﷻ) and it is very special.

Everything created in the sky or on the earth should pray to Allāh (ﷻ), because He created you. Do you think you are small? You contain the whole world within you. Do not think you are a small thing: you are everything. You are the father of all of creation. When He created Ādam (عليه السلام) He told the angels (عليهم السلام):

> I am going to create a man from dried clay of altered mud. .
> So, when I have fashioned him completely and breathed into him (from My spirit) the soul which I created for him,
> then fall down prostrating yourselves to him. (15:28-29)

This means that the angels will pray for Allāh (ﷻ) who manifested Himself in Ādam (ﷺ).

Everything created is a manifestation of Allāh (ﷻ). Because of this, if someone kills any part of creation, it is as if he has killed all the world. To kill others is to be against Allāh (ﷻ) and His manifestation.

The human being is very dear to Allāh (ﷻ), so why do you disobey Him? If the human being knew the truth of his existence, he would go to Allāh (ﷻ) and thank Him.

Why does Allāh (ﷻ) ask us to pray to Him and prostrate only to Him (ﷻ)? We ask Allāh (ﷻ) to let us be in His divine existence and witness His station. We ask Him to witness His station. You should reach this station. You hold all the secrets of the world. He told us, "You think you are small, but the whole world is within you." Why do you disobey Him?

Don't say "I am," because there is no lā ʾilāha ʾilla-llāh in those words. Our beloved Prophet (ﷺ) said:

> You will be very close to God (ﷻ) when you pray to Allāh (ﷻ).
>
> Those who ask Allāh (ﷻ) for forgiveness and pray at midnight
> and those who thank Allāh (ﷻ), those who fear Allāh (ﷻ),
> those who worship Allāh (ﷻ), male and female...

Allāh (ﷻ) gathered you and Allāh (ﷻ) told you, "I am your Lord." Allāh (ﷻ) gives you your sons and your daughters from your vice-regency and He talks to the spirits. It was in the pre-eternal world that He asked:

> "Am I not your Lord?"
> They said, "Yes! We testify,"
> in case you should say on the Day of Resurrection,
> "Truly, we have been unaware of this." (7:172)

What is the meaning of ṣalāh? It is the connection and the relationship between you and Allāh (ﷻ). You are a divine light. That divine light is inside your heart and sprit.

What is the meaning of the rūḥ, the spirit? If you study and try to figure out what the spirit is, you will understand that it is the first word that came down to our Prophet Muḥammad (ﷺ) and all of our other prophets and messengers, like Ibrāhīm (Abraham) (عليه السلام) and Mūsā (Moses) (عليه السلام). The Ḥadīth tells us:

> Allāh (ﷻ) told the Prophet (ﷺ), "Read" and the Prophet told Him, "I don't know how to read or write."
>
> Allāh (ﷻ) said it again and the Prophet (ﷺ) responded with the same answer.
>
> Then, for the third time He told him to, "Read" and the Prophet (ﷺ) said, "I don't know how to read."

Then, Allāh (ﷻ) supported him by sending him the spirit and secret of Allāh (the Archangel Jībrīl (Gabriel)) who told him:

> Read, in the name of your Lord who has created (everything). (96:1)

After that, He taught you everything. You should thank Him all of your life.

Do not say "I am." Allāh (ﷻ) taught you. He gave you a spirit, a divine spirit. We call it the white mind. It is a divine machine; it is Allāh's machine. You are talking by the tongue of Allāh (ﷻ). Do not think that it is just a piece of meat and you are just talking. Allāh (ﷻ) manifested on your tongue and so you started to talk. He lends you ears with which to hear so that you can hear by Allāh (ﷻ) and see by Allāh (ﷻ) and walk by Allāh (ﷻ).

This is the right path, If you want to know Allāh (ﷻ), follow His orders through His prophets and messengers. Allāh (ﷻ) prepared something for those to return back to the divine presence, to the divine word.

How did He create us? How did He create different colors? Allāh (ﷻ) promised that He would return everything to His first being. I have permission to tell you, so that maybe it will enter your heart. This is just for those who have a heart or who have a divine ear and a divine heart. They will understand what I am saying. Allāh (ﷻ) says in a ḥadīth qudsī:

> My heavens and My earth cannot contain Me.
> Only the heart of My faithful, honest servant contains Me.

Allāh (ﷻ) appeared to all the worlds: the seven heavens and the seven earths, a total of 14 worlds. Allāh (ﷻ) appeared to everything in those 14 worlds: to the human beings and to the jinn. Allāh (ﷻ) created everything. Some creatures you know and some you do not know. Because He is the Most Merciful, He will not let you see everything, because if you were to see something Allāh (ﷻ) did not want you to see, you would not be able to live for another moment.

Allāh (ﷻ) asks you to extend your knowledge. You should follow what the prophets and messengers (عليهم السلام) gave you. They gave you knowledge you would have never known without them. He lets you know how to use seeds to plant trees and to eat vegetables. He taught you: this is oil, this is water and this is God (ﷻ). He taught you everything. Do not say, "I am" or "I am from my grandmother or grandfather or ancient people."

> And He taught Ādam the names of all things (2:31)

He asked him (عليه السلام), "Are you ready to carry and keep My message, or are you like Iblīs who disobeyed Me and would not follow My orders?" Allāh (ﷻ) says:

> Truly, We did offer the trust to the heavens and the earth,
> and the mountains.
> but they declined to bear it and were afraid of it.
> But the human being bore it. (33:72)

Allāh (ﷻ) created many other worlds. We know some of them but not all of them. Allāh (ﷻ) asked the created ones in the skies and the created ones on the earth's and all of them said, "We cannot carry the message." Even the jinn said, "No, we cannot carry the message." Even the mountains said no. All of them said, "We cannot carry the message; it is very heavy." However, human beings can carry the message.

So what is this secret? The human beings do not know (exactly what they are agreeing to), so they accept Allāh's request and take the promise with Ādam (ؑ). Ādam (ؑ) asks them, "Is Allāh (ﷻ) your Lord?" They say, "Yes," and Allāh (ﷻ) sends His understanding to them regarding how to follow His message.

By nature, the human being is polite. He behaves well and carries the qualities of Allāh (ﷻ). This is from love. If you love Allāh (ﷻ), He loves you. Even if you believe that you are not here by yourself, Allāh (ﷻ) is here. He gives you many signs inside you, just to know Allāh (ﷻ).

The Prophet (ﷺ) takes care of you. He wants you to be an honest servant and he is kind and compassionate. He is the lover for all of you, of all human beings. Our beloved Prophet (ﷺ) said:

> If any of you are haunted by a small darkness,
> I will feel your pain.

This is our Prophet (ﷺ). This is the will of the Prophet (ﷺ). He never discriminates between any of the other prophets (ؑ). He is from the same clay as Ibrāhīm (ؑ), ʿĪsā (Jesus) (ؑ) and Mūsā (ؑ).

God (ﷻ) gave them special land. He says, "This is Allāh's land and it is no place for criminals and horrible people who play games and hurt others. This is no place for them. If you return, I will return back and I will let the Fire be your fate."

He will order a plan. It will be quick in action. He will destroy everything. Everything will disappear. This is the order of Allāh (ﷻ). I am sure that everything will appear suddenly while you are sleeping, driving your car, or at the airport. Everything will stop. Allāh (ﷻ) will make something very small happen in the air, for example. What could an airplane do if this happened? An airplane could do nothing. Who can protect us from this? No one but Allāh (ﷻ).

You must hear His words and obey His orders to carry His message, the message of unity: lā ʾilāha ʾilla-llāh. We should carry the message of peace and truth in His name. He is the Peace. He is the Merciful, the Compassionate. We should carry the message of peace, mercy, justice, freedom and love for all people.

Our beloved Prophet (ﷺ) told us the story of the woman who refused to feed or give water to her cat. Allāh (ﷻ) puts this woman in the Fire. What do you think of the people who hurt others and let others die of hunger or sickness or those who kill innocent people? Allāh (ﷻ) says:

> Oh people, We have created you from a male and a female,
> and made you into nations and tribes
> so that you may know (and love) one another. (49:13)

I will continue to the other world with you now. Excuse me for giving a long talk and a long introduction. It is not from me. It is from Allāh (ﷻ). I am His servant.

Now, I want to let you know one of the secrets you do not yet know. You do not know what is in the other world after the grave. I told you that the grave could be a Garden or Hell. We want to continue the journey.

Allāh (ﷻ) says that He is calling to all jinn and human beings. I advise you to take heed of your deeds and your actions. If those things that are recorded in your book are good, thank God (ﷻ) for that. If something bad is written in your book, you cannot blame anyone other than yourself.

If your book is full of bad deeds, Allāh (ﷻ) will order Jahannam, the Fire, Hell. A creation named Anak will appear from the Fire. Allāh (ﷻ) will punish those who disobey Him through this creation, Anak. This is the punishment for those who steal, kill or spread poisons into the sea and throughout the world. This creature's name is Anak; it is huge and has a long neck. This creature can contain the whole earth and the whole sky. Anak has a bright light and following it is darkness. He speaks by the will of Allāh (ﷻ). He will say, "Allāh (ﷻ) says."

Allāh (ﷻ) says, "I tell you all the time, do not worship the devil. I told you, oh son of Ādam (ﷺ), not to listen to the devil, to illusions or pictures. I told you not to listen to the self that tells you to do bad things." This is the black mind that follows Iblīs. Those who do these things follow Iblīs.

Allāh (ﷻ) says, "I told you not to follow him or worship him; he is your enemy, always and forever." Allāh (ﷻ) said, "Just worship Me, this is the straight path." Allāh (ﷻ) told us, "This is your nation—one nation; this is My path, the straight path. It is not winding. Come to My path, worship Me, follow Me."

We say in al-Fātiḥa, "Give us the straight path." God (ﷻ) will guide those who love Him to the path. Those who want happiness in this life and the last life, know that this is an examination. This dunyā, this life, is the home of the examination. In the end, some people will be happy and some will be sad and in Hell.

Allāh (ﷻ) says you should look to other people, other nations, who let Iblīs mislead them. Do you have minds to think about this? Iblīs came in the shape of human beings and he started to make everything beautiful. He is the strong and he can do everything. He will give to you. He is the provider. He will tell you, "I will help you, I will make you happy." This is Iblīs. He promises the human being, saying that he will let you be happy if you follow him.

Iblīs has many sons on this earth. Those who follow Iblīs are also Iblīs. Allāh (ﷻ) says that many people have been mislead by Iblīs. Don't people have minds to think about the truth, to figure out the straight path? Allāh (ﷻ) will say, "This is the Hell I promised you, come and enter the Fire because you disobeyed Allāh (ﷻ). You are covered with your deeds and you will enter the Fire."

At this point, this event is the same as the Day of Judgment. Allāh (ﷻ) will gather all the people, the ancient and everyone. How will the people be? All nations will be gathered. You will see every nation and they will be called by their books. The judgment will be strong and Allāh (ﷻ) will be the Judge. This will be the punishment. What is this the name of this day? This is Yawm al-Jabarūt. All the jinn and all the human beings will be present on this day, the Day of Judgment. This is the strongest day; this is not easy.

Do you think that one day you will pass away and die very soon? Do you think about which place you would want to be in? This is the day. Allāh (ﷻ) says, "We promised you this day and this is the day. We will punish you. Come, you who have disobeyed Me, who have disobeyed their fathers and mothers. Come, you who never helped anyone, who never helped the poor or the sick."

Do you think you will live forever? Have you ever seen anyone live forever? Everyone will die. Every moment of your life was planned in detail by Allāh (ﷻ) before you were ever born, including how you will live and how you will die; whether you are female or male; if you are to live a happy life or a sad life.

A doctor can tell you the sex of your baby with a sonogram. This doctor cannot tell you whether you will be happy or sad or how long you will live. Who knows that when he is still just a drop of sperm? The doctor received the knowledge of the sonogram and the ability to determine the sex of a child through a drop of Allāh's knowledge, through Allāh's mercy. So, he should pray for Allāh (ﷻ) and worship Allāh (ﷻ) because Allāh (ﷻ) gives him this knowledge. He should fear Allāh (ﷻ). He should know that Allāh (ﷻ) is the Creator. He should not say, "I know." He should say, "Allāh (ﷻ) gives His knowledge to me."

Allāh (ﷻ) will put the honest scientists, those who hold knowledge, in high places. He will not accept any scientist or doctor who uses his knowledge to harm others. This is a message from God (ﷻ). The knowledge is a message from God (ﷻ) to be kind to all people, to be humble and to help people with this knowledge. If he does this, Allāh (ﷻ) will put him in a good place.

If a scientist or doctor does not do this, Allāh (ﷻ) will put him with those nations who say, "I am and I know." He will put him with those who disobey Allāh (ﷻ), who kill or steal. He will say, "The ants are better than you, because the ants do not disobey Me or kill or steal." Those who kill destroy peace, so to them Allāh (ﷻ) says, "I am your Lord, the Highest One." Who created you? You are poor. Allāh (ﷻ) created you.

After Mūsā (ﷺ) escaped Egypt, Allāh (ﷻ) let Firʿawn (Pharaoh) die in the sea with his followers and his friends. To this moment, Allāh (ﷻ) has allowed Pharaoh's body to be preserved in the sea. It is a miracle: if you visit a museum in Egypt, you can see the preserved body of Pharaoh. It is mentioned in the Qurʾān that Allāh (ﷻ) would save his body and He saved his body.[9] You can go to the museum and see his body. This is what Allāh (ﷻ) promised him; this is an act of Allāh (ﷻ).

I am so sorry that those in prison all over the world did not receive the message Allāh (ﷻ) sent through him. Allāh (ﷻ) will not give criminals anything. Allāh (ﷻ) says:

> And you will see each nation humbled to their knees;
> each nation will be called to its record (of deeds).
> This Day you will be recompensed
> for what you used to do. (45:28)

You will see every nation come and meet Allāh (ﷻ) on their knees. All the nations will be on their knees, from Ādam (ﷺ) to the Last Day. They will ask to bring their books of their deeds and Allāh (ﷻ) will tell them, "This is your fault."

Those who bring their books in their right hands are the servants of Allāh (ﷻ). They are the honest slaves and good people who have clean, pure hearts and hands. They are beautiful. Their eyes are beautiful and they are happy. Those who bring their books in their left hands will face a severe punishment

Then Allāh (ﷻ) will gather all the people. He will have them sit down. Allāh (ﷻ) will punish all of them. You may ask, "How will Allāh (ﷻ) punish all of those millions of people?"

Allāh (ﷻ) will not just judge the human being, He will punish the jinn and animals, too. If an animal does something to another animal that is unlawful, it will be punished. Animals have their own nations. Allāh (ﷻ) says in the Qurʾān:

---

[9] "So this day We will deliver your (Pharaoh's) body so that you may be a sign to those who come after you!" (10:92)

> They (animals) are but nations like yours. (6:38)

Story of Sidi and the Birds Who Danced and Sang with Him

I will tell you a story now. I was in a place 30 meters away from the rock. I used to feed the dogs and birds. I fed those birds 30 years ago. They came to me when they saw me, because they knew I would feed them.

After five weeks I saw two black birds, crows. Those two birds would stand in front of me while I was saying lā ʾilāha ʾilla-llāh. Then those two birds began to make dhikr in front of my face, and when I saw that, they started to dance and sing with me.

Allāh (ﷻ), Allāh (ﷻ), Allāh (ﷻ) (said in a singing voice). I stopped and they stopped, I started again, they started again. There was a group of tourists who saw that when I began to sing, the birds began to sing.

There was one person, a minister. The minister said, "Sidi, how do they sing lā ʾilāha ʾilla-llāh?" I said, "Who created them?" He said, "Allāh (ﷻ), Allāh (ﷻ)."

Allāh (ﷻ) says, "Every creation, every nation—your nation and other nations—I taught them how to pray and how to mention My name. I taught everyone."

The man asked me if I could make them sing again. I said, "Yes, but for what reason?" He said that he would like to take a picture. I do not believe in any picture. I destroyed the picture. I knew what he wanted, (Sidi laughs here).

When he went left the group, most of them were crying, sure. When I saw them, I began to sob. It was very strong. The group saw another animal and then I began to sing and dance again with them. (laughing) and I told them: Go! Enough!

That is what happened. That is what I saw. Others saw all of it. I ask Allāh (ﷻ). This is from Him. Allāh (ﷻ) says when He called Dāwūd (David):

> And indeed We bestowed grace upon Dāwūd from Us (saying):
> "Oh you mountains, glorify (Allāh ﷻ) with him! And you birds!

> And We made the iron soft for him." (34:10)

Allāh (ﷻ) asks the mountains and the birds to pray, so pray with Dāwūd (عليه السلام).

Pray for this area and this land. This land is very holy. What Allāh (ﷻ) created is holy. America is holy. Everywhere is holy. Africa is holy. Allāh (ﷻ) created it all. Allāh (ﷻ) created it all holy and He gives all people what they need.

You should use this land for good things. You should not destroy this land because it is your mother. Allāh (ﷻ) says:

> From her (the earth) We create you
> and into her We will return you. (20:55)

She will protect you. Do not disobey His orders. You should respect the earth. Use this earth in the right way. Do not leave it without use. Plant beautiful flowers, trees, fruits and vegetables. Allāh (ﷻ) does not want you to be lazy.

Allāh (ﷻ) will punish everyone who does bad things to others. At that time on the Day of Judgment, people will judge each other in front of Allāh (ﷻ). They will say, "This person took my money; this person killed me; this person destroyed my things."

Allāh (ﷻ) will bring them together in front of all the nations and He (ﷻ) will ask them, "Did you take his money? Did you kill him? Did you betray him? Did you cause him any harm?" The person will tell Him, "Yes." He cannot lie to Allāh (ﷻ).

Allāh (ﷻ) will ask the wrongdoer to give his rights to the one he wronged. He will say, "How do I give him anything? I have nothing to give." Allāh (ﷻ) will take from the wrongdoer's good deeds until his good deeds are used up. What will he do then? Allāh (ﷻ) will tell him that He will take the bad deeds of the person he stole from and add them to his own.

No one will help you on this day, not your son or your daughter. No one will help you. Everyone will take their rights on this day.

One of the friends of the Messenger (ﷺ) asked him how they will be governed at the Day of Judgment. He told him that everyone will come. Everyone will be gathered naked, as they were when they came into this world.

The wife of our Prophet (ﷺ), ʿĀʾisha (ﷺ) asked him:

> "How can this be, this nakedness? This is shameful—everyone will see and watch each other."
>
> The Prophet (ﷺ) said. "The people will be busy and will not have time to look to each other. Their eyes will be looking to something else. They will be busy with their deeds and unable to watch anything else around them.
>
> Everyone will see only Allāh (ﷻ). No one will be able to look to the left or the right. They will ask Allāh (ﷻ) for mercy. No one will be able to talk to other people because they will be so busy. They will look to the sky. They will stand and wait for 40 years with no food.

No one will be saved from punishment. Everyone will be punished. Then the divine order will be finished. On this day, the father will go to his son asking for help. He will say, "Oh my son, I was your father; I helped you. I raised you. Please help me and give me some of your good deeds. I need them to save me from the punishment."

The son will tell the father, "I can't do that, because what you fear, I also fear. No one will help me, either." Neither your money nor your sons can help you. The man will go to his wife and say, "Please, give me some of your good deeds." She will also say no and that she afraid of punishment. She will say, "I fear Allāh (ﷻ)." He will tell her that he loves her, and she will say that she loves him, too, but that she is in the same situation.

Everyone will be busy with themselves. This is the divine order. This is the truth. All the prophets (ﷺ) say this. All the prophets (ﷺ) told us this. This is a promise from Allāh (ﷻ) and Allāh (ﷻ) swears by the Day of Judgment. No one will be safe—no king, no prophet, no one will be free of punishment. Everyone will receive punishment and everyone will be scared. At this point, we should return to Allāh (ﷻ). We should not go beyond the boundaries. This is the divine order.

"The Second Discourse: On the Horror of the Day of Judgment and the Terror of Events" from *Spiritual Discourses in the Blessed al-Aqṣā Mosque*[10] is read from the beginning.

This is a good question (referring to where did you earn your money and where did you spend it). Where is the money for the poor people? What did you give to the people? Do you give medicine to them? This is not an easy thing. Allāh (ﷻ) is the Judge.

Allāh (ﷻ) says, "I created your body. How did you use your body to help people? Do you make something bad? Did you destroy people or their land?" He asks, "From where did you get this money?" Allāh (ﷻ) knows, but He wants the person to say, "I steal." This was not his money. He will ask, "How did you use your body? Did you use it to help others? Did you use it to pray in the right way? Did you follow the right way?"

The reading continues.

Allāh (ﷻ) asks you about every cent. He makes you bigger and bigger and then He asks you where you spent it. If you say that you used it in the wrong way to make bad machines in order to destroy people, then Allāh (ﷻ) says, "For you there is no help." When you use money to help those who are crying, you help yourself.

This is the answer. Allāh (ﷻ) knows everything. If Allāh (ﷻ) does not like how the money is used, He will put you in the Fire.

The reading continues.

This is enough. Now my love, I want to describe the other worlds, the Malakūt. I will continue to explain. You should know this world. Do not deceive yourself. I will give you the secrets and the truths that Allāh (ﷻ) sent to the other prophets (ﷺ). I will let you know the secret to being happy in this life and the next.

---

[10] Sidi Muhammad. *Spiritual Discourses in the Blessed al-Aqṣā Mosque*, pp. 17-20.

This is not from me. This is from Allāh (ﷻ) and from our prophets (عليهم السلام). I want to explain this in detail to you. I will continue. This lecture I published 14 years ago and I gathered all those lectures into a book. It will be published and given as a gift to all my sons and daughters. I want you to be on the straight path so that you can know Allāh (ﷻ) and know the truth. I want to encourage you and motivate you to walk on this straight path. Āmīn.

Say Yes to Divine Love

Compilation of Teachings on Divine Love from *The Traveler's Journey*

Friday, June 25, 2010 AM, Sufi School West

لا إله إلا الله - لا إله إلا الله - لا إله إلا الله - محمد رسول الله عليه صلاة الله
لا إله إلا الله - لا إله إلا الله - لا إله إلا الله - ابراهيم رسول الله عليه صلاة الله
لا إله إلا الله - لا إله إلا الله - لا إله إلا الله - موسى رسول الله عليه صلاة الله
لا إله إلا الله - لا إله إلا الله - لا إله إلا الله - عيسى رسول الله عليه صلاة الله
اللهم انت السلام ومنك السلام و إليك يعود السلام
تباركت ربنا وتعاليت يا ذوالجلال والإكرام

Allāhumma (Oh Allāh ﷻ), You are the Peace, to You return the peace. You are the Great, oh Allāh (ﷻ), yā dhul jalāli wal ikrām (oh Lord of Majesty and Bounty).

May peace be upon you, my beloveds. It is my honor to be with you. I am grateful that you supported me so that I could come here again. I ask Allāh (ﷻ) to be able to come next year and to give the peace, love, mercy, justice and freedom to all those who are suffering without discrimination—there should be no discrimination.

All of you should love each other. In the name of Allāh (ﷻ), I ask Allāh (ﷻ) to protect you from harm, poverty, hunger, disasters, volcanoes, in this world. I ask Him to protect you from all the criminals and those who try to destroy and ruin the earth.

I ask Allāh (ﷻ) to save this earth for all people—black and white and yellow. All people are from their father Ādam (عليه السلام) and their mother Hawwā' (Eve) (عليها السلام). They should not fight each other because He said in His Qur'ān:

> Oh people, We have created you from a male and a female,
> and made you into nations and tribes
> so that you may know (and love) one another.
> Truly, the most honorable of you with Allāh (ﷻ)
> is that who has taqwā (piety).
> Truly, Allāh (ﷻ) is all-knowing, all-aware. (49:13)

Our Prophet (صلى الله عليه وسلم) said:

> All creatures are the children of Allāh (ﷻ),
> and the most beloved to Him
> are the ones who are most beneficial to His children.

He also said:

> The one who will be loved by Allāh (ﷻ) should be close to his
> people, to the friends.
> Without love there is no right life.

Because of that, Allāh (ﷻ) says:

> He loves them, so they love Him. (5:54)

He started with Himself by saying, "I love you." He did not order the human being to love, He started with His love and He gave it to everyone: the human beings, the animals and the birds. Allāh (ﷻ) said to Sayyidinā Dāwūd (Our Master David) (عليه السلام):

> And indeed We bestowed grace upon Dāwūd from Us (saying):
> "Oh you mountains, glorify (Allāh ﷻ) with him! And you birds!
> And We made the iron soft for him." (34:10)

He ordered the mountains and the birds—different nations all of them—to praise Him, but not the human being. He ordered this because all of them want to start a wedding with Dāwūd (عليه السلام), singing about love and sending the message of truth.

All the prophets (عليهم السلام) gave the same message. Because of that, the letter "alif" is the first letter of the name of Allāh (ﷻ). Alif. He started love, al-ḥubb. He loved them and they loved Him. Because of that, Allāh (ﷻ) says, "Obey My orders. I see what has been covered over.[11] Through My love you will see everything."

---

[11] The idea of being "covered over" is expressed in the understanding of kufr, which means non-belief. A kafīr is a person who disbelieves in Allāh (ﷻ), His angels, His prophets, His holy books, the Day of Judgment/the afterlife, or the supremacy of Allāh's will). The literal translation of kafīr is: one who covers over the truth.

If Allāh (ﷻ) loves you and you love Him, you will listen to Him because if you love someone you, listen to him. You should listen to what has been sent down to all the prophets and messengers (ﷺ). This is one of His conditions. If you want to be loved, you should love. Allāh (ﷻ) asks you to love Him. He says, "I love you. If I did not love you, I would not have created you."

He says in a ḥadīth qudsī:

> I was a hidden treasure and loved to be known.
> Therefore, I created the creation so that I might be known.

"I let you know Me and everything around you, all the heavens, all the animals and everything around you and the waters the seas, the mountains, the jinn; all of those manifestations. I have been manifested within those things because My name, adh-Dhāhir, manifested."

You are carrying the mirror of the divine, the mirror of Allāh (ﷻ). If you are honest and obey His orders, you will be a mirror walking between the people. You will see everything with Allāh's eyes. He told you, "Look what you are seeing. Are you seeing yourself? Are you seeing evil?"

Yes, if he will be leading by shayṭān, he will see shayṭān. Do not use money to disobey Allāh (ﷻ). Would you use money to kill others, to kill human beings, women, kids? Do you want to steal people's money and their lives? How do you hold His manifestation? How can you ruin His manifestation? All of them are manifestations of Allāh (ﷻ). Because of that, Allāh (ﷻ) says:

> If anyone kills a person or spreads mischief in the land—
> it is as if he has killed all humankind. (5:32)

In the sharīʿa, the laws of Allāh (ﷻ), it is forbidden to kill others. All of the other prophets (ﷺ) asked people to obey this order.

Allāh (ﷻ) said the first words, "I love you," so love Him. This love is the first element, the most important element that exists in all creatures. He wrote the words that they should love Him. Do not kill, do not steal, and do not do bad deeds.

He created everything in this earth. He created the earth and the skies for all of you. Without love, there is nothing. This love is like a light, it is like a candle in a glass. His light (ﷻ) is like this light. It is like this globe. This glass contains the light. It is from Allāh's love, from the olive oil. (24:35)

This olive gives the love, the truth that Allāh (ﷻ) is a manifestation like a big globe, a big light. Allāh (ﷻ) will light all the people. He will send life, because of that.

Allāh (ﷻ) let this holy olive oil, not from the olive trees. No. This is different. This other meaning of olive is alternative. You are the olive if you are filled with love, peace, mercy, justice and freedom. You will be the olive, the holy olive.

Allāh (ﷻ) manifested in it and made two eyes and two ears for you. He made everything to you, so you should prostate to Allāh (ﷻ) for the manifestation of Allāh (ﷻ) who sent it within you. When He said:

> And (remember) when your Lord said to the angels (عليهم السلام):
> "Indeed, I am going to place (humankind)
> generations after generations on earth."
>
> They said: "Will You place upon the earth
> those who will make mischief and shed blood,
> while we glorify You with praises and thanks and sanctify You?"
> He (Allāh ﷻ) said: "I know that which you do not know." (2:30)

Allāh (ﷻ) manifested by Himself, within Himself! He took from His light and He said, "Be," so everything exists. Thus, Allāh (ﷻ) revealed Himself by His name upon everything because He said on the tongue of the Prophet (ﷺ):

> I was a hidden treasure and loved to be known.
> Therefore, I created the creation so that I might be known.

The first important issue: He let love be existence. When He revealed and manifested to Ādam (عليه السلام), He put love within the heart of Ādam (عليه السلام). This is the truth of the divine existence.

The angels (﵈) had been ordered to pray to Ādam (﵇) because he was the manifestation of Allāh (ﷻ), not because he was Ādam (﵇). The word "Ādam (﵇)," means dust. In Hebrew and Arabic, "adim" means dust.

Because of that, we should prostrate just to Allāh (ﷻ), not to dust. We should obey Allāh (ﷻ) and prostrate to Allāh (ﷻ), to His manifestation. This is why the human being is holy and he is the most worthy thing in this universe. The human being who obeys Allāh's orders and says, "I hear You, my Lord. I listen to You."

Everything needs the water of the love because Allāh (ﷻ) says:

> And We have made from water every living thing. (21:30)

This is holy water. This is holy water. You should not do bad things to this water or ruin this water. If you break the love, you will be against Allāh (ﷻ), you will start a war against Allāh (ﷻ).

Our way, our path, is from the path of Allāh (ﷻ). First of all, with everything within us we obey Allāh (ﷻ) by His holy names, the Peaceful, the Merciful. We believe that the human being should obey Allāh's orders because this is the truth and why he has been created.

I would like to let you listen to what I have said in your language.

The reading is comprised of excerpts from *The Traveler's Journey of Healing through Divine Love, Knowledge and Truth.*

"As-salāmu ʿalaykum, my beloveds. May Allāh (ﷻ) bless you and open your hearts, souls, bodies and senses in order to know the true love that Allāh (ﷻ) revealed to His prophets and messengers (﵈).

Allāh (ﷻ) says in a ḥadīth qudsī:

> **My servant continues to draw near to Me**
> **with voluntary works**
> **until I love him.**
> **When I love him, I am**
> **his hearing with which he hears,**
> **his seeing with which he sees,**
> **his hand with which he strikes and**

> **his foot with which he walks.**
> **(If he says, 'Be,' then it is.)"**

Who is this human being who carries the face of Allāh (ﷻ), who carries the heart of Allāh (ﷻ)? I am not talking to this body that can see, this body from dust. I am talking with Allāh (ﷻ) by His name which manifests upon you. Because of that, He said:

> Truly, We did offer the trust to the heavens and the earth,
> and the mountains
> but they declined to bear it and were afraid of it.
> But the human being bore it. (33:72)

The human being carried this message. Allāh (ﷻ) used the word "insān" which means "human being," man or woman. It refers to all of humankind, not only the men or women. Allāh (ﷻ) manifested in the human being, each one is the offspring of the other. Each one is from the other and the world of divine truth.

In this material world, Allāh (ﷻ) said, "This is man, this is woman," but because He is the One, you are from each other. This is the truth until Allāh (ﷻ) will establish His orders and you are the sign of Allāh (ﷻ), the miracle.

We should bow to Allāh (ﷻ) and behave well with everything He has created. If you are well-behaved with others, you will be well-behaved with Allāh (ﷻ).

If you love, love Allāh (ﷻ) in His manifestations. It is not acceptable for the human being to be impolite or to misbehave. You should be full of love, you should be full of mercy, and you will carry all of these things, the mercy, justice and love, and they will carry you because you are their mirror. You will see yourself in this mirror. If you love someone you will see yourself.

Just obey Him. You have only one mirror. Take care of it. Be careful. You have just one mirror. If you want to look left and right, Allāh (ﷻ) will destroy you.

This is a holy thing. You are holy and the mirror is holy. Everyone is holy because he looks at himself in this mirror established by love.

The reading continues, "In the realm of divine reality there is only the Real (ﷻ), the truth that comes from one spirit. A woman can be a leader of guidance as Rābiʿa al-ʿAdawiyya (ﷺ) was. Rābiʿa carried the message of divine truth: real mercy, real peace and real love for everyone. She said:

> **I love You, Allāh (ﷻ), with two types of love:**
> **a love that is passionate and a love because You should be loved.**
>
> **I do not care if the whole world is ruined for me**
> **as long as my relationship with You is not ruined,**
> **because everything made from dust will return to dust**
> **and only the Real will continue to exist for certain.**

Rābiʿa (ﷺ) said her heart was empty of everything except Allāh (ﷻ) and she offered everything as a sacrifice for Allāh's sake."

It is important to give a sacrifice for your heart. You carry the love; keep the love inside, do not try to look left or right but look for Allāh (ﷻ) inside of you. And know that He exists within you, He is not absent. He is with you. Hear and see.

The reading continues, "Many of the saints, men and women, in the past and now, offer themselves to serve people. How sweet are the tears of love? How sweet are the tears of a lover..."

These are the tears of love. When the lover cries it will illuminate the dark and all of the existence. Why? Why do you forbid yourself from shedding these wonderful tears? Here I'm saying that love is the principle of life. The Prophet (ﷺ) said:

> The one who believes in Allāh (ﷻ) now, this minute,
> is in the Garden.

This is what our Prophet (ﷺ) said. If you believe in Allāh (ﷻ), you are now, this moment, in the Garden. You should live now, in this moment, in the Garden. Which garden? It is the garden of love and peace. This is the truth. It will be moved from this material world to the witnessing world. Witnessed.

The reading continues, "How sweet are the tears of the lover who weeps yearning for his beloved. For I become absent in my beloved."

This is the first degree because he found what he is searching for and, from this state, his life will start. I am not talking about finding the love of a wife or husband. I am talking about the truth of the human being, the man who knows what love is, the man who knows how to protect love, how to protect life and how to be happy and full of mercy. The human being, man or woman, should only live in love and happiness. Through the water of the love—you cannot live without water. Love is the water of life. Allāh (ﷻ) says:

> And We have made from water every living thing. (21:30)

What is your opinion? If Allāh (ﷻ) stopped sending water for two months and there was no water anymore, not a drop, what would airplanes, or weapons, or anything do? What would they do with them? They would be finished. For this reason, you should know for certain that this water is the secret of life. It is not easy to speak about the secret of this love. Continue.

The reading continues, "I become absent in my Beloved and my Beloved becomes absent in me. This is the meeting in which we drink the wine of love.

If a person does not have manners, he does not have love. The secret of Allāh's knowledge is through love. Love is the way to know Allāh (ﷻ). If you do not love something, you will never know what love is.

There are signs of love: politeness, mercy and beauty in your creation and in your manners. If you speak, you speak with politeness and when you speak, you smile. You would not dare take anything without permission.

If a person does not have manners, then he does not have love. The beloved is obedient for the Beloved. If you love Allāh (ﷻ), then you must

obey His commands. You must truly know and taste through the divine commands, manners and mercy.

A person comes to my guide (☀) one day. He had wanted to be student of my guide (☀) for maybe forty-six years. I was there in Damascus with my guide (☀). He told my guide (☀) that he wanted to be a follower of the teaching, a murīd.

> My shaykh (☀) says to him, 'Have you tasted the love?'
> The man replied, 'How can I taste the love?'
> 'Oh,' he (☀) told him, 'You are a very poor one.'
> 'How I can taste the love?'
> My shaykh (☀) answered, 'Go and love whatever you wish, even if it is a donkey, so that you can understand the meaning of love.'"

This has a deep meaning. It is not an outside one. He wanted to teach him how to be polite.

The birds know love. The animals, even sheep, know love. The bird keeps singing because he is in love. His singing is a prayer. Allāh (☀) says:

> Each one (of His creatures) knows his ṣalāh
> and his glorification (of Allāh ☀). (24:41)

Everyone has his own prayer. Everyone knows how to pray to Allāh (☀). I think that you know the story of the nightingale with Sulaymān (Solomon) (☀). When he went, Sayyidinā Sulaymān (☀) was searching for his birds and there was this bird.

> The bird said, "He (Sulaymān) left me, and I love him.
> He left me without telling me.
> I love his voice. He disappeared.
> Why did that happen?"

Then the bird came and he asked Sulaymān, "Where were you?"

He said, "I was in Yemen and I saw a lady. They did not worship Allāh (☀). They worshipped the sun instead of Allāh (☀).

> Sayyidinā Sulayman (ﷺ) wanted to test him, to examine him, because he was one of his lovers.
>
> He told this bird, "Take this letter and give it to Bilqīs."
>
> This is a bird. One the birds said, "How did he know the language of the birds?"

Allāh (ﷻ) said:

> And Sulayman inherited (the knowledge of) Dāwūd.
> He said: "Oh humankind!
> We have been taught the language of birds..." (27:16)

Sayyidinā Sulayman (ﷺ) is not just Sulayman. We know many things we did not know. He is al-ʿAlīm (the Knower). He manifested within you by his name al-ʿAlīm, so He let you know many things you do not know.

You think your eyes see. The water in your eye is the part of your eye that would not see unless Allāh (ﷻ) put life into it. Allāh (ﷻ) revealed His secrets within your eye. You hear by the name of Allāh (ﷻ). Allāh (ﷻ) revealed His secrets to your ears, to your eyes and you started to see. You started to hear.

> Sulayman went and he asked,
> "Who will bring me the throne of Bilqīs?"

Sulayman (ﷺ) had jinn under his command. They are believers, faithful, committed to Allāh (ﷻ), Muslims.

> One of those jinn told him, "I will go and bring her kingdom."

Just like that. It was very quick. It was very fast. It faster than the rocks. It is the slave of Allāh (ﷻ).

This bird, the nightingale, was praising Allāh (ﷻ) or mentioning Allāh (ﷻ) all the time. Pray. This is Allāh's order. If there is no love, no one can sing. Everyone is singing his prayer to Allāh (ﷻ), praising Allāh (ﷻ).

The reading continues, "This has a deep meaning. It is not an outside one. He wanted to teach him how to be polite, for if you do not go to

the door of politeness in the special way that Allāh (ﷻ) wants, the door will not open for you. So beloveds, be polite.

When you look at the bee, do you see how she is flying? When she is flying, she remembers Allāh (ﷻ). She chooses beautiful flowers for herself. She smells and when she feels free like it is right, she is very useful."

I want to you to be like the bee. Our Prophet (ﷺ) wants us to be like a bee, clean, pure, loyal, kind and generous. She gives honey to others. We can get medicine and recovery from her stomach. Medicine is not just in the honey, even the sting of the bee there is medicine, cure. Everything has love. Do you want to live in love life?

The reading continues, "The bee goes gently so as to be polite. She is not trying to break any window. If you break it, you lose everything. If you love a person, it is important to know how to love in the right way, not in the rubbish way. This is what I mean."

You should be well-mannered, you should be polite. Everyone should know he is talking to a station of Allāh (ﷻ). He should not break the wall of al-adab, good manners.

The reading continues, "If you love Allāh (ﷻ), you will obey what Allāh (ﷻ) says and you will become polite. You become polite with the one you love. When you love someone, you are polite with him. Who are you, oh human being?

Divine love covers the heart and it comes out of the senses, and in this way Allāh (ﷻ) guides us to the straight and right path. Without good manners and following a straight path and the divine commands, humanity will never see peace and love.

The Prophets (ﷺ) Teach Us How to Live in Love

In order to walk to Allāh (ﷻ) you need a vehicle. What is the vehicle, or the way, to Allāh (ﷻ)? The way is through the beloveds of Allāh (ﷻ), the prophets (ﷺ) and the holy ones (ﷺ). The way is through those who taste the love of Allāh (ﷻ). All of the messengers and prophets (ﷺ) are the image of the Real (ﷻ). They love with a deep love that has no beginning and no end. They die in obedience to the divine commands and in being in service to Allāh (﷾). These people have mercy on animals, birds and everything that Allāh (﷾) has created.

The Prophet (ﷺ) said:

> All creatures are the children of Allāh (﷾),
> and the most beloved to Him are the ones who are most beneficial to His children.

All of the prophets (ؑ) of Allāh (﷾) knew the taste of the love. They lived obediently and followed Allāh's commands. The lovers are the witnesses and the beloveds of Allāh (﷾).

Love is not just living with my tongue and my body. I love with my heart and my soul. The food of the soul is to be only with the love. The soul wants the music of love. Without this music, the soul is not near divine love. With divine music the soul comes closer to divine love.

Allāh (﷾) is a great lover who created you with no price. He created you from His love for you in order to see His light through you so that He could enjoin you with the true image of love. Become soft and subtle so that you can give this love to everyone. This is what He wants."

This is the depth of love. I will pray two cycles to Allāh (﷾) and I will ask Allāh (﷾) to be close to Him.

The reading continues, "With divine music, the soul comes closer to divine love. Allāh (﷾) is a great lover who created you with no price. He created you from His love for you in order to see His light through you..."

To live in His circle.

The reading continues, "...so that He could enjoin you with the true image of love.

Beloveds, become soft and subtle so that you can give this love to everyone. This is what Allāh (﷾) wants. He did not show you this directly but He sent his messengers with the message and He sent His command to do ṣalāh, the daily prayer. Ṣalāh is your connection to Allāh (ﷻ) because He speaks to you every time you pray."

I pray my ṣalāh to my Love. I hope He will let me be with Him in His presence and I feel so happy to be with Him every minute, every minute in my life; in the night and in the day. That is what Allāh (ﷻ) wants from you. He will give you everything you want, happy in His Paradise, in His Garden.

The reading continues, "Follow this divine teaching through His prophets (ﷺ) who tell you how to live in peace and love. Allāh (ﷻ) does not love those who destroy the houses of Allāh (ﷻ), and for this reason Allāh (ﷻ) said:

> If anyone kills a person or spreads mischief in the land—
> it is as if he has killed all humankind. (5:32)

This is like one house. If you destroy one house, you destroy all houses. You have destroyed the love. The world will never be at peace unless it comes to a place where it can recognize love, be in love and live in love. Live this love through the divine teaching of Allāh (ﷻ). Allāh (ﷻ) said:

> I was a hidden treasure and loved to be known."

This is the end, but I want to say how to taste love and how to be absent in this love. One word from a poem:

If you love someone you will obey him. He will not say, "No," to his love. He will say, "Yes." You will be absent in love and you will be in this station of eternity by mentioning Allāh (ﷻ). Obey Him in all His orders, in everything. Try and you will see, inshāʾa-llāh.

The reading continues, "We uncover, unveil, and give our love to whoever loves us. Allāh (ﷻ) said to His angels (ﷺ), 'This is one whom We love. All of creation will hear that this is Our beloved. There is no fear or grief among Our worshippers.'

When those who carry the sharīʿa, the divine law, and the ḥaqīqa, the divine reality, prostrate, they always prostrate to the Real (ﷻ)."

Do not say, "I do not want the law of Allāh (ﷻ), I am a Sufi. I will tell you that you are liars. This is the sharīʿa, the law of Allāh (ﷻ). This is the door, this is a gate. How will you be able to enter the, ḥaqīqa, divine truth? You should open the door. You should learn how to open the door; then the Owner of the home will open it for you. You should obey the divine truth. You should obey the sharīʿa, the law of Allāh (ﷻ), or you will never be able to reach. I will give you example.

If you want to go to the home of your lover, or if you want to take something to visit him, will you enter his home through the window or the front door? The law of Allāh (ﷻ), the sharīʿa, is the front door of the divine truth because everything in the sharīʿa words holds the divine truth.

Allāh (ﷻ) ordered all His prophets (عليهم السلام) from Ādam (عليه السلام), Ibrāhīm (Abraham) (عليه السلام), Nūḥ (Noah) (عليه السلام), Mūsā (Moses) (عليه السلام) and ʿĪsā (Jesus) (عليه السلام). He told them, "I am Allāh (ﷻ), the divine unity, and I created all of you. Pray, and pray for Me, give zakāh and fast."

These are doors. These are doors. What is the meaning of "pray?" It means, "Be with Me, to let you know what love is. I do not want you to be in this world, in this existence. I love you and want you to be in My witnessing station."

From here I say, "He who knows himself, knows His Lord (ﷻ)." I wrote a book about this and I put secrets within it. I told you how to know your selves—then you will see and know your Lover (ﷻ), the Great Lover (ﷻ), Allāh (ﷻ).

I give you this and this is like a lake. I let you swim in this lake to know Allāh (ﷻ), the divine love. You should search, and I taught you how to reach this station. Do not stand by illusions and pictures. We are the sons of divine truth. We want to touch divine truth. We know the divine truth. I know and listen. He told Hārūn (Aaron) and Mūsā (عليهما السلام). He told them:

> Do not be afraid: for I am with you,
> I hear and see (everything). (20:46)

He is hearing and seeing and taking care of us. He provides us with food. He is the generous. I say that and ask Allāh (ﷻ) for forgiveness.

Repent Like the Man Sa'id Ibrahim Helped (رضي الله عنه)

"The Commands of the Saint...Who Knows Allāh to the One Who Is Seeking Guidance" from *Spiritual Discourses in the Blessed Al-Aqṣā Mosque*
Friday, June 25, 2010 PM, Sufi School West

لا إله إلا الله – لا إله إلا الله – لا إله إلا الله – محمد رسول الله عليه صلاة الله
لا إله إلا الله – لا إله إلا الله – لا إله إلا الله – ابراهيم رسول الله عليه صلاة الله
لا إله إلا الله – لا إله إلا الله – لا إله إلا الله – موسى رسول الله عليه صلاة الله
لا إله إلا الله – لا إله إلا الله – لا إله إلا الله – عيسى رسول الله عليه صلاة الله
اللهم انت السلام ومنك السلام و إليك يعود السلام
تباركت ربنا وتعاليت يا ذوالجلال والإكرام

Peace upon our Prophet Muḥammad (ﷺ) and upon all the messengers and prophets (عليهم السلام). We praise Allāh (ﷻ). He supported me and with His support I carry the message of divine truth, the message of justice, love and freedom for all people. I invoke Allāh (ﷻ) from the bottom of my heart to keep you in this path, in this faith, the faith of unity. And I ask God (ﷻ) to give all of you happiness, to give you all that you wish for, and to carry the message of divine truth. Āmīn.

This is a holy day. This is from the month of Rajab, the month of Allāh (ﷻ). This is a very important day. Soon Sha'ban will come, the month of our Prophet (ﷺ). Then Ramaḍān will come.

I ask Allāh (ﷻ) for all of you to have happiness and health and to be full of love and mercy. I ask Allāh (ﷻ) to support all those who need help, all those who suffer and pass through hard times everywhere, and those who need medicine or food all over the world, without discrimination.

I would like to tell you how the gnostics were at that time: how they depended totally upon Allāh (ﷻ) and how they trusted Allāh (ﷻ). They left the earthly life and just asked Allāh (ﷻ) for His truth. There are many complete men and women. One of the women was Rābi'a al 'Adawiyya one was al-Junayd. Also, Muḥyi-d-dīn ibn al-'Arabī was a philosopher.

My shaykh (ق) entered us in a retreat for forty days with those gnostics of Allāh (ﷻ). It is like the Garden to be on this straight way, to know how to act and how to let Iblīs, shayṭān out of his life. It is a blessing to be honest and to be on a straight path. I will tell you this story about the gnostic of our beloved gnostics who knows Allāh (ﷻ).

Story of the Gnostic and the Sinner

One man went to one of the gnostics of Allāh (ﷻ) and asked, "I made every mistake you can imagine. I killed, I did many hurtful things, I stole. I want your advice: how can I go to Allāh (ﷻ)?"

The door is open. Tawba to Allāh (ﷻ) is available all the time because Allāh (ﷻ) says:

> The one who comes with tawba and a full heart,
> I will transform his bad deeds into good deeds. (5:39)

Allāh (ﷻ) will accept your tawba. Allāh (ﷻ) wants you to give your promise that you will make real, honest tawba. Do not say, "If I were to repent would I maintain it?" You should be honest in your tawba and your tawba and you should not return back to your mistakes.

Do not be scared. Allāh (ﷻ) will not reject you. Allāh (ﷻ) will tell you, "Do not be scared. I am the one who will forgive you. I am al-Ghafūr (the All-Forgiving). I will open the doors. Come close and do not be scared."

Allāh (ﷻ) says:

> All my servants, I created you, I gave you life.
> I provided for you, and I created you by My hands.
> I gave you sight, I gave you hearing, I gave you a heart.
> I provided you with everything.
>
> I ordered you to obey Me, but you disobey Me all the time.
> I am the Merciful One.
> If you come to Me in tawba,
> I will be your lover and I will forgive you.
> If you disobey Me and you come to Me, I will accept you.
> I will never close the door in front of you.
>
> Anyone who makes mistakes and wants My forgiveness,
> I will give it to him.
> If he comes to Me walking, I will run to him.
> You are crying because you have turned your heart,

> but I am telling you I am the Merciful, the Most Compassionate.
> If you are honest, if you really want Me,
> if you really want to get rid of the horrible things in your life,
> I will accept you. I will accept you.
>
> I will accept all tawba up until the moment of your death.
> If you come to Me, I will open all the doors of mercy.
> My servant, I give you everything,
> I am He who gave you everything.

I told you there are two paths. There is the path of happiness, the Garden, and there is the path of the Fire. Choose which one you want. This is your choice. If you are still alive, you should choose one of them. Do not let your mistakes stop you from returning to Allāh (ﷻ); do not let anything stop you from coming to Allāh (ﷻ).

Allāh (ﷻ) will take care of you; Allāh (ﷻ) will purify you. The Prophet (ﷺ) said:

> Allāh is kind and He loves kindness,
> and confers upon kindness
> that which He does not confer upon severity,
> and does not confer upon anything besides it (kindness).

If you will be kind to others, He will be kind to you. Do not be one of the followers of Iblīs. Allāh (ﷻ) says on the tongue of His Prophet (ﷺ):

> Oh My worshipful slave,
> if you did not make mistakes
> I would create another creation that would make mistakes
> and that would repent to Me,
> and I would give them tawba and forgive their mistakes.

You will not be in need for anyone for anything—you just need Allāh (ﷻ). If anyone asks you who Allāh (ﷻ) is, Allāh (ﷻ) is very close to you. Allāh (ﷻ) is able to hear your supplications, to hear your needs, and Allāh (ﷻ) can provide everything. You do not need to go to a judge, to the courts; you should go directly to Allāh (ﷻ). Allāh (ﷻ) will forgive you. You do not need someone else to ask for tawba for you, just talk to Him.

Many people make mistakes and they think Allāh (ﷻ) will not be able to see them. One went to one of the gnostics, one of the physicians of the heart and the soul. He went to Sidi Ibrāhīm Adham[12] (☒) who was a gnostic; he was a complete man.

Story of Sidi Ibrāhīm ibn Adham (☒): Five Pieces of Advice

Sometimes a gnostic is in other worlds, not this world, so if you go to a gnostic, he will be in a witnessing station and absent and he will not hear you. Thanks be to Allāh (☒), at that time of this story the gnostic Sidi Ibrāhīm ibn Adham (☒) was not in absence.

> The man said to Sidi Ibrāhīm (☒), "As-salāmu ʿalaykum, Ibrāhīm (☒)."

> Sidi Ibrāhīm (☒) did not hear him because he was absent, so the man said, "As-salāmu ʿalaykum. Yā Ibrāhīm (☒), which Ibrāhīm are you? Which Ibrāhīm are you, this one or the Prophet (☒)? I want you."

> Ibrāhīm (☒) answered, "Do you want me or do you want my master? You knocked on my door and I am a faqīr. I cannot do anything. I cannot provide you with anything. Go and search for your master. Your master will take care of you. What you want from me? I am a servant. I am poor."

> The man said he had a question and Ibrāhīm (☒) told him to hold on and wait. He said, "Let me pray two rakʿah and ask permission from Allāh (☒) to listen to your question and to answer you. Are you able to be patient and hear from me?"

> After praying Ibrāhīm (☒) said that he could ask his question.

> So the man told him, "I am full of sins. Can you advise me? Can you offer me any advice on how to get rid of these sins and to return back to Allāh (☒)?"

He could have asked his shaykh but he was ashamed and he was afraid of what his shaykh would do to him.

> Sidi Ibrāhīm (☒) answered him, "Yes. If you are able to achieve five qualities, Allāh (☒) will accept your tawba."

---

[12] Sidi Ibrāhīm's name is pronounced Ad-ham (أدهم).

This man answered, "I am ready, please go ahead."

Sidi Ibrāhīm (ﷺ) told him, "If you want to disobey Allāh (ﷻ), do not eat from His provision."

The man thought about this. Everything in the earth and the sky is provision from Allāh (ﷻ).

He started to cry and asked, "How can I do that?"

Allāh (ﷻ) says, "If you want to disobey Me, go and eat from anyone, but not from Me." Do not eat ḥarām food, do not take aid from others, and do not take anything. You should be on the right path.

This disobedient man said, "How you say that, Ibrāhīm (ﷺ)? This is unbelievable. Everything is for Allāh (ﷻ) and from Allāh (ﷻ). Allāh (ﷻ) provides us with everything: food, clothes, a place to live, everything, so I cannot do that. I cannot go to somewhere to disobey Allāh (ﷻ) and not to eat His provision. Everything is from Allāh (ﷻ)."

The gnostic Sidi Ibrāhīm (ﷺ) told him, "If you know everything is from Allāh (ﷻ), shame on you for disobeying Allāh (ﷻ) and eating from His provision. He supports you and He feeds you and after that you disobey Him? That is not acceptable."

The man said, "Please tell me the second piece of advice."

Ibrāhīm (ﷺ) said, "If you want to disobey Allāh (ﷻ), search for a place to live that does not belong to Allāh (ﷻ). Go and disobey Him. Search. There is just one place. Go to the shayṭān, Iblīs, to guide you to the Fire."

"No I cannot do that," the man told him, "I cannot do that."

"Allāh (ﷻ) sees and hears everything and everything is for Allāh (ﷻ). Everything is for Allāh (ﷻ) and from Allāh (ﷻ): all of the air, all of the skies.

Ibrāhīm (ﷺ) told him, "If you know that everything in the earth and in the skies is for Allāh (ﷻ), then how can you disobey Him? Do you have a mind to use in order to think about this?

"Here is your third piece of advice: if you want to disobey Allāh (ﷻ), then go to a place that Allāh (ﷻ) will not be able to see you."

The disobedient man answered, "How can I do that?"

"Allāh (ﷻ) hears the footprints of the black ant on a rock in the night. He sees everything. He sees and knows all things."

This is not easy issue. Anyone who says, "Allāh (ﷻ) will not see me," I will tell him go to his brother the shayṭān.

The disobedient man asked for his fourth piece of advice.

Ibrāhīm (ﷺ) told him if the Angel of Death, Izrā'īl (ﷺ), comes to capture your soul, tell him, "Not now, come back some other time."

The man told him, "How that could be? It is impossible." Allāh (ﷻ) says in His Qur'ān, 'And Allāh (ﷻ) grants respite to none when his appointed time (death) comes. (63:11)' How can I say to the Angel of Death, 'Go away and come back later?' You are crazy. You know that the Angel of Death will come to capture your soul no matter who you are or where you are. It is the day. It is the time. No one can postpone it; no one can advance it. So, you cannot do that."

Then Sidi Ibrāhīm (ﷺ) said, "At the Day of Judgment the angels (ﷺ) of punishment will come because you are a criminal. Tell them, 'Do not take me. I do not want to come with you.' They will not hear from you because you are full of dirt and they will take you to the Fire."

Then the disobedient man said, "Please, please you have given me enough. I will repent to Allāh (ﷻ) and I will be honest. I will pray to Allāh (ﷻ) and I will ask Him for forgiveness. Allāh (ﷻ) who helps me, who provides for me, who gives me help, I will be honest with Him."

My daughters and my sons, you should remember this story. Allāh (ﷻ) sees you, hears you, and your provision is from Allāh (ﷻ). No one can protect you, just Allāh (ﷻ). There is no choice, no choice, just Allāh (ﷻ), no choice but Allāh (ﷻ).

This gnostic Ibrāhīm (ق) told his students be like Ibrāhīm the Prophet (ﷺ). You should prepare yourselves for emigration. You will not live forever. No one can live forever. This life is temporary. Prepare yourself.

I am telling you my beloved daughters and sons, there is no escape from Allāh (ﷻ); there is just Allāh (ﷻ). From here if you want to be sure that you are on the safe path, the right path, do not turn, do not try to look behind you, do not try to return back. Keep these five qualities I have just told you about with you. Sell this world and buy the real one. This world is nothing. It is internment; it is a game. Collect anything and everything and millions of dollars, but you will leave them.

You cannot take any of your fortune with you, not even your clothes. They will put you in a coffin and you will be with empty hands. Your family, your brothers, and all those who say, "You are my beloved," will search everything you have in order to take it, to put it in their pockets. Then they will put you in the grave. In the grave there is punishment.

The man started to cry about his sins and how he harmed himself, his spirit and his soul. So Sidi Ibrāhīm (ق) told him, "Come, you directed your face honestly to Allāh (ﷻ) and you promised to Allāh (ﷻ) and repented. Even if you have sins as big as the ocean you came to Allāh (ﷻ) honestly. Do not be scared."

You should return back. You should rectify the rights of others and give them back their due. If you are honest, Allāh (ﷻ) will take care of all those problems in your life and if you do not break the promise between you and Allāh (ﷻ), He will be the Most Merciful and Compassionate. If you do not keep the promise, nothing, nothing will help you. No sons, no daughters, no families, no money will help you, just your healthy, pure heart.

The reading, "The Commands of the Saint, the Gnostic who Knows Allāh to the One Who Is Seeking Guidance" from *Spiritual Discourses in the Blessed Al-Aqṣā Mosque* is read from briefly.[13]

---

[13] *Spiritual Discourses in the Blessed al-Aqṣā Mosque*, p. 76.

Sidi Ibrāhīm (ﷺ) said when he started his journey that there was a man who went to ask him: who will guide me to Allāh (ﷻ)? He was searching for someone to help him and he held the lights and tried to find someone who could help him. When he reached someone he asked him, "Please let someone guide me, take my hand," and he was crying.

A young child, twelve years old, took him and told him, "Come sinner. I will let you know who will help you recover, who will give you the cure. You are hurt, you are injured, and your smell is not good, it is nasty."

This bad smell came from sins. The man disobeyed the child and then this child took up his stick and told him, "Go, this door can lead you. Knock on this door." The gnostic heard the voice of the person who knocked and said, "No one knocks on our door, just the friend of the shayṭān from his smell." The gnostic can smell a person's sins even if it the person is 1,000 miles away.

When the gnostic recognized that he was really crying and he was honest, he was asking for forgiveness, he told him, "Come, come what do you want?" The gnostics of Allāh (ﷻ) will never be angry. They are water. They are full of a beautiful fragrance. They are the physicians of hearts and spirits.

The gnostic told him, "Do not feel scared. Because you have real intention to emigrate to Allāh (ﷻ), I am your servant. I will guide you. I will guide you on the way, on the path. This way will take you to the place of security and peace, it will save you."

The gnostic never told him to go away or that he did not want to help him or answer him. He helped his heart. He gave him illumination, he lit his heart by the grace of Allāh (ﷻ) and he did not say, "Enough." He told him to come and take this secure, clean cloth and to go take a bath.

He did not mean to take bath for his body. He meant that this gnostic sent his soul to him, his spirit to him, and he was asking him to go to get back to your soul. So he took a bath and he repented to Allāh (ﷻ) and after two years he was very fat because he was eating ḥarām foods.

So, after two years, one day he was walking in the street Sidi Ibrāhīm (ؓ). Sidi Ibrāhīm (ؓ) asked him, "Where is the man who came to me?" He told him, "That man has died, he has passed away. Nothing from that man is left. He told him, "You saw my death. You gave me something that killed all of my sins and turned back my soul and you sent me to Allāh (ﷻ) again. I am between your hands."

Have you ever tasted the meaning of the divine love? This man did. He said to Sidi Ibrāhīm (ؓ), "Allāh (ﷻ) took me from the bad situation with the nasty smell gave me a wonderful situation. Allāh (ﷻ) sent you to me."

Sidi Ibrāhīm (ؓ) told him, "You have been changed because you had an honest intention. You wanted to give your tawba to Allāh (ﷻ) and so because of that, Allāh (ﷻ) let you find me. I supported you because Allāh (ﷻ) knows that you were honest."

This is a great opportunity to come to Allāh (ﷻ) with your pure honest heart.

Sidi gives the promise.

The Messenger's Intercession for Us (ﷺ)

"The Messenger's Intercession to Hasten the Day of Judgment"

from *Spiritual Discourses in the Blessed Al-Aqṣā Mosque*

Saturday, June 26, 2010 AM, Sufi School West

لا إله إلا الله - لا إله إلا الله - لا إله إلا الله - محمد رسول الله عليه صلاة الله
لا إله إلا الله - لا إله إلا الله - لا إله إلا الله - ابراهيم رسول الله عليه صلاة الله
لا إله إلا الله - لا إله إلا الله - لا إله إلا الله - موسى رسول الله عليه صلاة الله
لا إله إلا الله - لا إله إلا الله - لا إله إلا الله - عيسى رسول الله عليه صلاة الله
اللهم انت السلام ومنك السلام و إليك يعود السلام
تباركت ربنا وتعاليت يا ذوالجلال والإكرام

May peace be upon you, my beloveds. May the mercy of Allāh (ﷻ) be upon you. This is a holy day. It is the beginning of another holy journey. This journey is to the worlds of al-Malakūt and al-Jabarūt, and you will travel during this journey to al-Laḥūt. This is part of the journey to Allāh (ﷻ). You will be all together, from Ādam (عليه السلام) to Sayyidinā (Master) Muḥammad (ﷺ).

This journey is for those who walk to Allāh (ﷻ) and want to know Allāh (ﷻ). This is the journey of walking to Allāh (ﷻ). You will find how your bodies and your selves and your souls and your spirits will be purified, from Ādam (عليه السلام) to the others who came after him. Prepare yourselves, for Allāh (ﷻ) will purify you.

Allāh (ﷻ) wants you to be purified and He wants you to remove all of the dirt from you so that you have pure souls. Come to Allāh (ﷻ) with your heart and your spirit. Be humble. Pray to Allāh (ﷻ). Make prostration to Allāh (ﷻ), like the prophets (عليهم السلام) did. You can find the spirits of the messengers and the prophets (عليهم السلام) and the gnostics, the complete people who know Allāh (ﷻ). The spirits of the masters will be on this journey.

Are you ready for this journey? Prepare yourselves to receive a purification by the water of knowledge that He gives to His beloveds. You should be prepared to take the divine promise if you wish to be purified by the grace of Allāh (ﷻ). Give this beloved the holy water, the clean water so that Allāh (ﷻ) will purify you. Now listen to what Allāh (ﷻ) says in His Qurʾān:

> When Allāh (ﷻ) will let all of the people arise from their graves
> and they will come between His hands to receive His mercy.

This is an opportunity for anyone who has a heart. If he listens it is like he has been murdered—his self dies. From here all of the people will be gathered in front of Him. I meant by al-Khalq the Creator of human beings, jinn, angels, prophets, messengers and gnostics of Allāh (ﷻ).

There will be a place for those who transgressed the limits against themselves. They will come to Allāh (ﷻ) asking for purification. Allāh (ﷻ) says in His Qur᾿ān to us:

> And they have not honored Allah with the honor that is due to Him; and the whole earth will be in His grip on the Day of Resurrection and the heavens rolled up in His right hand; glory be to Him, and may He be exalted above what they associate (with Him). (39:67)

This is a revelation of the beginning of the end, and Allāh (ﷻ) will give His order. He will order Isrāfīl (Raphael) (ﷺ) to start and Isrāfīl (ﷺ) will blow his trumpet. Everyone will hear the voice of the trumpet. He will gather the jinn and angels (ﷺ) and all will be shocked when they hear the voice of the trumpet.

> And the trumpet will be blown, and all who are in the heavens
> and all who are on the earth will swoon away,
> except he whom Allāh (ﷻ) wills.
> Then it will be blown a second time,
> and behold they will be standing, looking on (waiting). (39:68)

All who are on the earth and in the skies will be shocked and they will arise from their graves. Again, Isrāfīl (ﷺ) will blow the trumpet. All of the people will be shocked. The angels (ﷺ) and prophets (ﷺ) and gnostics (ﷺ), the complete human beings, will be in their places, surrounding all of the human beings and jinn, those who Allāh (ﷻ) protects. After that, Allāh (ﷻ) will order the trumpet to be blown again.

> And the earth will shine with the light of its Lord
> and the book will be placed (open);
> and the prophets (ﷺ) and the witnesses will be brought forward;
> and it will be judged between them with truth,
> and they will not be wronged.

> And each person will be paid in full for what he did;
> and He is the Best Aware of what they do. (39:69-70)

The will all be standing, looking to Allāh (ﷻ). The oppressors and those who disobeyed Allāh (ﷻ) and those who selected the wrong path to Allāh (ﷻ) will all look to Allāh (ﷻ). They will see His throne, which contains all of the heavens and the earth. Then, Allāh (ﷻ) will begin meting out punishment.

The lights will appear in the earth because Allāh (ﷻ) will reveal Himself. This is the light, this is al-jalāl (the majesty). So all of those people—the criminals, the murderers, those who disobeyed Allāh (ﷻ), those who did not hear the order of Allāh (ﷻ) through the prophets and messengers (ﷺ)...those who carried the message of justice and love and freedom will stand between Allāh's hands.

All of the criminals will come to Allāh (ﷻ) standing, and they will all be before Allāh (ﷻ). They will be awaiting their punishments, naked, with nothing. They will tell Him, "Oh Allāh (ﷻ), we are poor before You."

Allāh (ﷻ) will say, "Are you lying to Me? You are criminals, you are oppressors. This is the day I will punish you. You never repented during your lower dunyā. I will gather all of you and transfer you to al-Malakūt or al-Jabarūt." Al-Jabarūt is the world of fear and punishment. All of the people who had been treated badly by others will take their rights. Allāh (ﷻ) is the Merciful.

The earth will have been lit by the light of Allāh (ﷻ). Everything will be lit by Allāh (ﷻ) and the book (containing all deeds) will be open. Allāh (ﷻ) will ask the first row of prophets, the martyrs, the gnostics and those who know Allāh (ﷻ) to come to the first row with His mercy. Allāh (ﷻ) will cover them with shadows of happiness and give light to all of those who heard the voice of Allāh (ﷻ), the order of Allāh (ﷻ).

They will say, "Oh, my Lord (ﷻ), we heard someone who was calling us to the truth. We heard him and we obeyed. We obeyed. We obeyed." They will fall down crying to Allāh (ﷻ), happy because Allāh (ﷻ) gives them His mercy. All of the obedient ones who carried His message in this life and obeyed Him are in this situation. This is the grace of Allāh (ﷻ) on them.

After this Allāh (ﷻ) will say, "They will not be judged. They will be happy by Allāh's grace. Thank Allāh (ﷻ)." These are the beloveds of Allāh (ﷻ) who followed Allāh's orders through His prophets and messengers (عليهم السلام). They sacrificed themselves to Allāh (ﷻ) and they obeyed Him in every issue, large and small.

Then everybody will take what he did and they will not be wronged. He knows everything. He knows everything in the skies and in the earth. This is the truth, it is divine truth. It is not imagination or pictures or images. It is the truth and He sent it to all of the prophets (عليهم السلام), from Ādam (عليه السلام) to our beloved Prophet Muḥammad (ﷺ). He sent it to ʿĪsā (Jesus) (عليه السلام) and Mūsā (Moses) (عليه السلام), the prophets and beloveds of Allāh (ﷻ).

What happens next? Now comes the punishment. Allāh (ﷻ) will refer to the book (containing all deeds). Don't try to lie. Don't think you can lie. There are witnesses. Why did you do this? Why have you killed that? Why did you ruin this? Why did you destroy the earth? Why did you ruin the ocean? Why did you use things We sent to people for their benefit to destroy them?

First of all, He will punish those who are criminals and oppressors. There are many angels (عليهم السلام) who will take them to Jahannam, Hell. Allāh (ﷻ) says:

> Those who disbelieved will be driven to Hell in groups. (39:71)

I ask Allāh (ﷻ) not to be among the people in those groups.

I am asking Allāh (ﷻ) to reveal Himself to you with all His beauty. I swear by the name of Allāh (ﷻ), this is the truth. As I am talking, I swear as you hear my voice, it is the truth. This is the emigration. This is the emigration to al-Jabarūt. Allāh (ﷻ) will be able to know every detail in the sky and in the earth.

When they are taken to Jahannam, they will reach Hell. Allāh (ﷻ). The angels (عليهم السلام) will open the doors of Hell to let those punished groups enter.

The doors will be opened by the angels (عليهم السلام) and those who gave up doing good deeds will enter. These are the angels (عليهم السلام) who guard the Fire. First they will question them, asking, "Didn't you ever hear about the Real (ﷻ) and the message of Allāh (ﷻ) from a prophet or messenger (ﷺ)? Didn't you meet any of the gnostics or prophets like Sayyidinā Ibrāhīm (Abraham) (ﷺ) or Sayyidinā ʿĪsā (ﷺ)?"

Allāh (ﷻ) says, "I sent you 124,000 prophets (ﷺ) I sent them to you, but you treated them badly and you disobeyed them. You killed some of them and you did not hear the message." Some of those in the punished groups will say, "We did not kill them; we did not cause any harm to them. We just heard the message and we didn't follow it."

Allāh (ﷻ) says, "I am the One who knows everything. I know everything. I hear everything. Are you saying that you did not hear and meet prophets (ﷺ) or gnostics? That you did not meet a complete human being sent to teach you and lead you to Me?"

There are witnesses among you, within you, from your body. Allāh (ﷻ) will ask your skin, your hands, your feet. They will be witnesses. Allāh (ﷻ) will order all of your body parts to be your witnesses. They will tell the truth. They will tell the truth if you killed with your hand. If your tongue said bad things about people, ruined the reputation of people, and was not merciful, it will tell Allāh (ﷻ). They are criminals. Allāh (ﷻ).

Those parts of your body will tell the truth on the Day of Judgment. Do you need other witnesses? You cannot lie because Allāh (ﷻ) knows everything. Allāh (ﷻ).

The prophets and messengers (ﷺ) were reciting this to you. They warned you about this day. They will say, "Yes, we did." No one can say no. Don't lie. Don't kill. Every part of your body will testify against you. Allāh (ﷻ) will say, "I am Allāh (ﷻ) and there is no other Lord, no other God (ﷻ), just Me. Pray to Me and obey Me. This is your day."

Justice will come to all of the people who did bad things, who killed. Allāh (ﷻ) will tell those groups, "Go! And remain in Hell for eternity. This is your home, this is your place. This is for the people who were disobedient."

To the other groups containing the people Allāh (ﷻ) blesses, who obeyed Allāh (ﷻ), who loved Allāh (ﷻ), who carried the message of unity and peace and love and justice and freedom, Allāh (ﷻ) says, "The angels (ﷺ) will come to them kindly and they will make a divine wedding for them."

I am asking Allāh (ﷻ) to be among those people, those wonderful people, those who obey Allāh (ﷻ), those who wanted to be under the tent of justice and mercy, the tent of Allāh (ﷻ).

The angels (ﷺ) will come to the obedient ones and take them to the wedding, with the prophets and messengers (ﷺ), to the high Garden. They will find everything they desire. No one can imagine the beauty of this Garden. No one can even think about this beauty.

Then, when they reach Paradise, the doors will open by themselves. No one will open the Garden, by the order of Allāh (ﷻ). The doors will be open. The guards of this Garden will tell them, "As-salāmu ʿalaykum." They will welcome them. You will inhale a wonderful smell, a beautiful fragrance, a nice smell. It is a million times better than the good smells experienced in this life.

> And those who kept their duty to their Lord
> will be led to Paradise in groups until they reach it,
> and its gates will be opened
> and its keepers will say:
> "As-salāmu ʿalaykum!
> You have done well, so enter here to abide within." (39:73)

The angels (ﷺ) will tell them, "Enter the Garden and remain here forever. This is your home forever." They will start to sing the song of, "Al-ḥamdu li-llāh," meaning, "Thank God (ﷻ), this is what Allāh (ﷻ) has promised us. This is what Allāh (ﷻ) promised those who obey Him. Allāh (ﷻ) gave us what He promised us, a wonderful, marvelous garden."

For everyone who obeyed Allāh (ﷻ) there is a chair, a place. They will say, "We thank Allāh (ﷻ)! You sent us to this other place, more beautiful than the one where we lived before." No one can imagine the beauty of these gardens. By the grace of Allāh (ﷻ), we are happy in the Garden of al-Jabarūt." This garden is full of happiness and completeness.

This is because they had polite manners and helped people. They were humble and they never hurt anyone. Without any discrimination, they were kind to all people. They will say, "Allāh (ﷻ), we obeyed You in everything You asked of us or ordered us to do." Then they will say, "Al-ḥamdu li-llāh. All praise and thanks to Allāh (ﷻ). He let us be free!"

You will receive all of this because you obeyed Allāh (ﷻ). This is your payment. Another wedding will be prepared for them by the angels (ﷺ). You will see the angels (ﷺ) surrounding the chair of Allāh (ﷻ), praising Allāh (ﷻ) and their songs are, "Allāhu Akbar!" and "Al-ḥamdu li-llāh!" This is the divine wedding. Allāh (ﷻ) and His angels (ﷺ) will celebrate you, all of the honest believers. Allāh (ﷻ) will judge them and they will say "Al-ḥamdu li-llāh." This is the beginning.

The companions of Sayyidinā Muḥammad (ﷺ) said that he woke up in the morning one day. He prayed the morning ṣalāh (fajr) and he kept sitting until the dhuhr prayer. Then Sayyidinā Muḥammad (ﷺ) was laughing and sat down in his place. He prayed the afternoon prayer, and then he was silent. Then he (ﷺ) prayed the evening prayer. Then he (ﷺ) went to his family.

The people went to Sayyidinā Abu Bakr (ؓ), the khalīfa. They asked him, "Could you ask Sayyidinā Muḥammad (ﷺ) why he did acted in this way today? He has never done that before." Sayyidinā Muḥammad (ﷺ) told Sayyidinā Abu Bakr (ؓ) what had happened. Then, Sayyidinā Abu Bakr (ؓ) told the people that Sayyidinā Muḥammad (ﷺ) had learned what will happen on the Day of Judgment, and it is what Sidi just told you. Sayyidinā Muḥammad (ﷺ) described all of the details I just told you.

Allāh (ﷻ) will gather the believers and the disbelievers and they will sweat until they are about to drown in their own sweat. On some people the sweat will reach their knees, on some people it will reach to their cheeks, to their necks, and they will be waiting. What are they are waiting for? The order of Allāh (ﷻ). This is a hard issue. This is a great thing. They will stand like this for 40 years.

Then, the people will go to Ādam (ﷺ), the father of us all, the father of humanity. They will ask him, "Please, Ādam (ﷺ), you are our father and

Allāh (ﷻ) has selected you. Please, we need your intercession." They will ask him to help them. He will tell them, "I can't do it." They will ask him, "Please help us, please forgive us." He will tell them, "It makes no difference, for I am in the same situation." Allāh (ﷻ) said in the Qur'ān:

> Allāh chose Ādam (عليه السلام),
> Nūḥ (Noah) (عليه السلام),
> the family of Ibrāhīm (عليه السلام)
> and the family of ʿImrān (عليه السلام)
> above (the rest of) humankind and the jinn. (3:33)

People will go to these four and ask them for intercession.

They will go to Nūḥ (عليه السلام) and they will ask him, "Please, we need your intercession. Allāh (ﷻ) selected you and He answered your supplication." Nūḥ (عليه السلام) will say, "I can't. I am in the same situation as you."

They will go to Ibrāhīm (عليه السلام), for he is beloved of Allāh (ﷻ) and he has been selected by Allāh (ﷻ). Ibrāhīm (عليه السلام) will tell them, "I emigrated from this world to His world." They will ask him for intercession and he will respond, "I can't help you." They will ask him again, "Please, please, intercede for us." He will tell them. "I can't do it. Go to Mūsā (عليه السلام). Allāh (ﷻ) spoke with him; maybe he will be able to help you."

Then they will go to Mūsā (عليه السلام). Sayyidinā Mūsā (عليه السلام) will tell them, "I can't do it, for it is not within my ability. Go to ʿĪsā (عليه السلام), son of Maryam (Mary) (عليها السلام). ʿĪsā (عليه السلام) was given miracles of healing; he brought dead back to life and he helped heal people." Sayyidinā ʿĪsā (عليه السلام) will say, "I can't do it. Go to the master of the children of Ādam (عليه السلام). Go to Sayyidinā Muḥammad (ﷺ) and ask him to intercede for us, to ask for Allāh's forgiveness."

They will hurry to Sayyidinā Muḥammad (ﷺ). When they go to Sayyidinā Muḥammad (ﷺ), the Angel Jībrīl (Gabriel) (عليه السلام) will also go. When they see the face of Allāh (ﷻ) they will fall down into prostration and they will stay in that prostration for a week, just to ask Allāh's forgiveness (ﷻ). Allāh (ﷻ) will talk to Sayyidinā Muḥammad (ﷺ) and Jībrīl (عليه السلام). After they are in absence, praying to Allāh (ﷻ) and in prostration to Allāh (ﷻ) for one week, Allāh (ﷻ) will say, "Tell me Muḥammad (ﷺ), tell me Jībrīl (عليه السلام), I will hear you and I will accept your intercession."

The Prophet Muḥammad (ﷺ) will look to his Lord (ﷻ), to the face of Allāh (ﷻ) and again, he will fall down into prostration for one week. Allāh (ﷻ) will say, "Go ahead and ask Me to forgive your people." When the Prophet (ﷺ) looks at Allāh (ﷻ) again he will start to fall into prostration again, and then Jībrīl (ؑ) will come and hold Sayyidinā Muḥammad (ﷺ) under his arms to support him.

Sayyidinā Muḥammad (ﷺ) will start to invoke Allāh (ﷻ) and make du'ā', asking, "Yā Allāh (ﷻ), forgive these people." He will start to ask Allāh (ﷻ) for forgiveness for the people who followed him. When Allāh (ﷻ) accepts his supplication and forgives him, every prophet (ؑ) will come with his followers. He will tell them, "Ask the martyrs and gnostics and those who know Allāh (ﷻ)." Then Allāh (ﷻ) will reveal Himself by His name the Beauty, al-Jamāl. To those who never created partners with Allāh (ﷻ), He will say, "By My name al-Jamāl, enter My Garden."

After this Allāh (ﷻ) will say to those who He has forgiven, "Go to the Fire and look to see if anyone is in there who did any good." Maybe because He is the Merciful He will ask those in the Fire, "What good things did you do in life?" One of those people will say, "I never associated a partner with my Lord (ﷻ)."

Allāh (ﷻ) will ask another one, "What did you do during your life?" This man was a merchant and he was easy when he sold and when he bought, and in this way he helped poor people. He loved people and he was easy with them. He supported them and he tried to be kind to those who were suffering. He helped orphans and poor people. This man said, "I did all those good things, but I ordered my son to cremate me and spread my ashes in the ocean." Allāh (ﷻ) will say, "Why did you do that?" He will respond, "Because I disobeyed You and I was scared of You. I knew I would be punished and I did this so that You would not be able to gather me for the Day of Judgment."

This man asked to be cremated because he felt afraid of Allāh (ﷻ). He burned his body because he was scared of Allāh (ﷻ). "Maybe Allāh (ﷻ) will forgive me because I am repenting to Allāh (ﷻ)." I am not telling you to do this because it is forbidden. It is forbidden to all people, even to the prophets (ؑ), the messengers and all human beings, because they are trying to escape from their disobedience. You should know that this is forbidden. We should follow Allāh (ﷻ) so that we can be the children of Allāh (ﷻ).

I am telling you to ask for Allāh's forgiveness (ﷻ) and I ask for forgiveness for myself and for all of you. He is the Most Merciful and Compassionate.

This is how Allāh (ﷻ) created us. He created us, humankind and the jinn, just to worship Him. He says:

> I do not seek any provision from them,
> nor do I ask them to feed Me. (51:56-57)

"I don't want them to feed Me. I am al-Ghanī, the Rich. I am the Most Merciful and Compassionate. I open the door of tawba. I never close this door, even to those who transgress against themselves. I am the Most Merciful. Come to My doors. Come to My words." Allāh (ﷻ) hears you and sees you. Lā ʾilāha ʾilla-llāh.

This knowledge I have just given you is from Allāh (ﷻ) through His prophets (ﷺ). I do not intend to frighten you, I just want you to know the truth and I want to save you, to protect you. Do not go and turn away from peace, justice, freedom and love. I am telling you this because I want to explain in detail what people will find on the Day of Judgment if they kill or if they steal and they think no one saw them. Allāh (ﷻ) sees and He hears. Allāh (ﷻ) is the Just. He gives Paradise to the believers and the Fire to the disobedient.

Our beloved Prophet (ﷺ) said:

> Oh Allāh (ﷻ), in the time before the Day of Judgment,
> You will find some people pretending they are religious.
> They will pretend to know Allāh (ﷻ).
> They will say, "Allāh says," and, "The prophets say."
> They will smell like dirty animals. They will have a very nasty,
> bad smell because they are lying to people.
> They talk sweetly, like honey, but they are liars.

Allāh (ﷻ) says, "They cannot lie to Me." They will try to cheat Allāh (ﷻ) and the prophets (ﷺ).

They can't do that. They will cheat just themselves. Why aren't they truly religious people? Why won't they teach people that Allāh (ﷻ) is the One and the knowledge that will help them in this life and next life? Those people will receive severe punishment from Allāh (ﷻ).

Allāh (ﷻ) says, "I swear by Myself, I will send them conflict in order to let them suffer during their entire lives. I will give them a punishment I have never given to any other human beings, because they cheated people, they took their money without right, and they never did any good deeds. Why won't they be honest? Why won't they tell them about the other worlds? Why won't they tell them the truth?

Because of this I want to explain how to emigrate from the world of al-Mulk, this lower world, to the world of al-Jabarūt. Some human beings will pass the exam of this life. Who is asking the questions in this exam? Allāh (ﷻ) is asking the questions. If you want to pass this exam, obey Allāh (ﷻ). You will pass. I do not want you to be scared.

Some people among you think that I want to scare you. No. This is in the Holy Qurʾān. This is what He tells us. This is not from me. It is an order from Allāh (ﷻ) to me to let you know what will happen, and I am trying to tell you the truth. If you give up doing good deeds, you will find Hell. You should follow the orders of Allāh (ﷻ). You should know that Allāh (ﷻ) has prepared a wonderful, gorgeous garden for you. But those who followed shaykh Iblīs, the shayṭān, are prepared for the Fire. We should be clear. We should ask ourselves, "Why did He give us minds? Why do we carry this message?"

Recognize the difference between these two paths. If you let even a young child see fire, he will pull himself away from it with fear. If you give him dates, sweet things, he will take them and eat them. You should recognize which path you want. You should choose. This is why Allāh (ﷻ) gave you a mind. Lā ʾilāha ʾilla-llāh.

It is an order from Allāh (ﷻ) for me to inform you of all these details. Inshāʾa-llāh, I will be honest about Allāh (ﷻ), about His holy books and all of His prophets (عليهم السلام). We should be honest about the Tawrā (Torah), the Injīl (Gospel), the Qurʾān and all of the holy books. I should tell you everything as Allāh (ﷻ) has asked of me.

I am telling Allāh (ﷻ). Allāh (ﷻ), be my witness. I told Your people the truth. There is much grace from Allāh (ﷻ) for this emigration. You are in a holy position now. I am sure that if you take the promise and give your honest tawba, Allāh (ﷻ) will accept you.

I have explained everything. I accept the Qur'ān. I am a servant of Allāh (ﷻ), I am a slave. If Allāh (ﷻ) did not order me to speak, I would never speak. I cannot say anything unless it is an order from Allāh (ﷻ). Did you hear me?

People: Yes

Did you hear the words of Allāh (ﷻ)?

People: Yes

Did you promise Allāh (ﷻ)?

People: Yes

To follow Allāh (ﷻ)?

People: Yes

This is it. Now I invoke Allāh (ﷻ) to purify you and to accept your tawba. I am asking you by His saying:

> Who is he that will lend Allāh (ﷻ) a goodly loan
> so that He may multiply it for him many times?
> (2:245 and see 57:11, 5:2, 57:18, 64:17, 73:20)

Allāh (ﷻ) will grace this money for you. Allāh (ﷻ) will give you more and more and more. Allāh (ﷻ) is asking you to give anything you can to help the orphans, poor people and hungry people. If you give this, you are giving it to Allāh (ﷻ). If you help the poor people and those who are suffering everywhere, you are giving to Allāh (ﷻ).

Lend the money to Allāh (ﷻ). Don't think about groups of people. Be without discrimination. There are no Christians, no Jews, no Muslims. He did not say, "I am the Lord of the Muslims" or, "I am the Lord of the

Christians." He said, "I am the Lord of all human beings." For that reason you should help everyone.

If you help orphans, poor people, widows...if you give to sick people, if you give to those people through a sacrifice, you will keep your health and you will keep your money. Allāh (ﷻ) will praise you. Be generous. Allāh (ﷻ) is the Generous. Be generous in order to save the people who are suffering everywhere.

This dunyā is a temporary life, a temporary world. It will disappear very soon and you will leave everything behind. You will travel very soon. Do not be cheap with your money. Give to people. Who will lend a loan to Allāh (ﷻ)? Allāh (ﷻ) will praise him. Allāh (ﷻ) will give him back seven hundred times more than what he gave. This is the last word I am telling you. Thank Allāh (ﷻ).

Anyone who wants to give, may Allāh (ﷻ) bless you. I am very sorry about what I see now. Many people are crying from the deep suffering everywhere. I want to give my heart, my body, my life, what I have, as a sacrifice for everyone crying from the deep suffering. Āmīn. Beloveds, I invite you. Bismi-llāh, Al-ḥamdu li-llāh. Take your chance.

Ṣalīḥ Kent: Sidi says now is the time. If you would like to see some of the videos that would not show yesterday, he is going to show them now. They are videos of the Jerusalem Kindergarten's graduation where Sidi speaks, then kisses each child in blessing as their names are called.

Sidi: I am very happy to see those children receive help. They came to learn how life will be in the future. These children carry the message of Allāh (ﷻ) in the right way. They are learning how to be polite and well-mannered, to carry the love and peace and to carry the message of Allāh (ﷻ).

I want to gather the orphans because people have given up helping these poor children. I have made myself a servant to them. I consider myself to be like their father and I am trying to provide a good life for them, with food and clothing.

This is a divine issue. This divine issue makes me work day and night to help these children. Some of them have disabilities. They are orphans, 250 children from different religions. I am trying to love them and to teach them how to love others.

There is no difference between a girl and a boy. This school is a school for love. I am trying to plant the love within their hearts and within their spirits to let them carry the message of Allāh (ﷻ). I do not want them to be astray in the streets. Maybe they will learn bad manners from the streets. I do not want that and Allāh (ﷻ) does not want that.

With the support you and others gave, we opened this school. With your support and the support of others, we will help many other people, not just in this school. We support other people who are in prison. They do not have anything: no food, medicine or clothing. I am not a physician of the spirit, I am a physician of hearts and bodies and Allāh (ﷻ) ordered me about that. Because of that:

> Who is he that will lend to Allāh (ﷻ) a goodly loan
> so that He may multiply it for him many times?
> (2:245 and see 57:11, 5:2, 57:18, 64:17, 73:20)

Every good deed is something you give to Allāh (ﷻ).

The Real Baqa in the World of Allah (ﷻ)

"My Heart Tells Me" and Music
Sunday, June 27, 2010 AM, Sufi School West

لا إله إلا الله – لا إله إلا الله – لا إله إلا الله – محمد رسول الله عليه صلاة الله
لا إله إلا الله – لا إله إلا الله – لا إله إلا الله – ابراهيم رسول الله عليه صلاة الله
لا إله إلا الله – لا إله إلا الله – لا إله إلا الله – موسى رسول الله عليه صلاة الله
لا إله إلا الله – لا إله إلا الله – لا إله إلا الله – عيسى رسول الله عليه صلاة الله
اللهم انت السلام ومنك السلام و إليك يعود السلام
تباركت ربنا وتعاليت يا ذوالجلال والإكرام

I beg You, Allāh (ﷻ). I direct my faith in walking to You. Please protect all of my beloveds who came to hear how the human being can walk and purify himself with holy water in order to travel from al-Jabarūt to al-Laḥūt, the world of Allāh (ﷻ), the eternal world.

I hope all of you will be able to open your hearts and spirits to be in the ocean of the eternal love that Allāh (ﷻ) wants for you. Purify your hearts and sprits and bodies and obey Allāh (ﷻ) to be in the eternal life with happiness.

Allāh (ﷻ) says;

> My slave is trying to be close to Me
> and he keeps doing good things so that he can be close,
> so that he will be in a divine state.
> If wants something, I will give it to him, for sure.
> He paid his toll and his sacrifice to Allāh (ﷻ) who created him
> in a beautiful picture.

At this point I am asking you to give a promise to Allāh (ﷻ) to be in a divine state so that you can live your life in the divine world. I hope you have prepared yourselves to live in the eternal world, walking toward Allāh (ﷻ). You can invoke Allāh (ﷻ) and ask Him for anything and He will answer your supplication. You can ask Allāh (ﷻ) to help your beloved and to help those who have passed away. You can ask Allāh (ﷻ) to have mercy for them.

This is a divine petition; no one can stop this. Ask Allāh (ﷻ) to help your beloveds and to give them the knowledge to know His divine love. Open your heart and spirit and promise Allāh (ﷻ) with a complete promise.

I want to take your hand so that Allāh (ﷻ) can purify you with the eternal, holy water of love. Life is to be saved, to be protected by Allāh (ﷻ). Allāh (ﷻ) says in His holy books that He will protect you from everything—and Allāh (ﷻ) is not half of the protector!

This is my daughter. A few years back I was telling her to come while she was a doctor at Baghdad University. She replied to me and came after what happened in Iran. I was waiting for her to teach Arabic and Qur᾿ān in our spiritual Sufi order. Her place is here; she will teach Qur᾿ān and Arabic inshā᾿a-llāh.

What I want to give you through her is not from me, it is from Allāh (ﷻ). It is a special gift from Allāh (ﷻ) to learn how to read the Holy Qur᾿ān in the right way. She has the full understanding from me on how to teach Qur᾿ān. If you don't know how to read Arabic, how will you know how to read and understand this book? The Qur᾿ān continues the teachings of all of the holy books and all the teachings of our beloved Allāh (ﷻ).

Anyone who likes can contact her. I am sure Ṣalīḥ can help her on the internet, I don't know this machine. I have something more than the internet, and it is a gift from Allāh (ﷻ) for Him to use my tongue as He pleases.

Now I would like to start to give something from deep within my soul. I and one of my brothers from a long time ago made pilgrimage, and on the holy mount on ʿArafat we made dhikr and sang. I'd like to explain what Allāh (ﷻ) says to the enamored of Allāh (ﷻ) and what He says of the deep, secret love. I want you to know how to walk with Allāh (ﷻ) always.

This is my case: I am always with Allāh (ﷻ). I ask Allāh (ﷻ) to give this light to everyone and to grant them understanding. Always be with Allāh (ﷻ). May Allāh (ﷻ) protect all my children.

For this teaching Sidi used an unpublished reading, "My Heart Tells Me," which is based upon the music of Shaykh Yasīn at-Tuhamī with Sidi's lyrics.

The lyrics of the music are bold, italicized and indented. The reading is in bold text. Sidi's live commentary is in plain text.

Music plays.

"Beloved Yasīn says:

> ***My Beloved's heart tells me:***
> ***You will make me disappear.***
> ***I will annihilate.***
> ***I sacrifice my spirit to You, whether You know it or not.***

I knock on the door of love, asking for a drop of love. I ask Him to accept me. This is divine love, for He manifested Himself through the world of love.

Many praises to You, Allāh (ﷻ), You are the only One. You are the One who revealed Himself in a beautiful picture.

Beloveds, before you come to the land of Allāh (ﷻ), you should swim in the sea of love to know my story, to know my secret through my singing and my understanding. If this is the secret of life, then I will become absent in this secret. If this is the matter, then it deserves a sacrifice. I will give a sacrifice. I will give a sacrifice to receive just one drop. I will give a sacrifice to cease my existence. In order to deserve this love, I will die, I will pass away. I will die to live an eternal life.

This eternal life is from you, Allāh (ﷻ). You let me into Your divine world, Your holy world, in order to free me from imagination and illusion. I am just an atom of love and this love gives me life. Prevent me from dying for any reason except for the sake of the One I love (ﷻ).

Oh Allāh (ﷻ), you say, 'My follower, come, for My door is open to those who are honest and come directly to Me, without turning left or right.'

My beloved, you revealed yourself with the light from the Eternal (ﷻ), so spread your perfume and fragrance in the world. This fragrance is the secret of life given to all people who fall in love with You. Give them a taste if they will sacrifice their hearts to You."

This is the path of divine love.

Beloved, you should get rid of everything if you want to swim in the divine ocean and receive purification. You should get rid of everything and avoid everything impure; stay only with Allāh (ﷻ). Be between Allāh's arms. Divorce everything. Make Allāh (ﷻ) your private lover—He will give you the love, and the love will give you eternal life. This love will give you the secret to live in the eternal world of lovers, and this is the life of subsistence, eternal existence (baqā').

There is no death in this world. You will move from a material death to an eternal life. When you are in this life, Allāh (ﷻ) will purify you and give you clean clothing, full of happiness. Allāh (ﷻ) will give you eternal existence and you will be dressed in His beautiful clothing. You will be a singer, like a bird singing on the branch of a tree. This is a holy tree.

This is a different life than the life of this lower world, which is full of suffering. There is no suffering anymore in this life. No tree will withhold food from you. The divine tree will give you fruit and flowers because you became a divine slave, because you obeyed Allāh (ﷻ). Be like this. Over there you can sing a song full of the secret.

This emigration is unlike the emigration of any of the prophets, gnostics or knowers of Allāh. He will take care of you. He will change this material world into an eternal one. He will give you an examination—maybe you will pass it and maybe you won't. You should try to pass. I am asking Allāh (ﷻ) to help you with this.

So, my beloved, I ask you: are you willing to sacrifice your heart for Allāh (ﷻ)?

The reading continues, “Your heart is the heart of Allāh (ﷻ); no one else can make a place in it. No one can know where or when. There is nothing like Him. Do you see?

My heart is absent because my heart is the manifestation of divine truth. When I was a child, I drank a drop of Allāh’s praiseworthy love. I will be drunk with Your love and I will sacrifice myself to give it to others who want to be with this love. This love is Your love, Allāh (ﷻ).”

I would like to be a child or one of the children of Allāh (ﷻ). Allāh (ﷻ) gifted me with a pure milk, even before I came into this world. I ask Allāh (ﷻ) to give it to the whole world. I ask Allāh (ﷻ) to give mercy and freedom to their hearts and to help them deal with each other in divine love, not material love. l would like your heart to be pulled by real love, real love by the divine presence.

The human being is always hungry and thirsty. I don’t want people to drink only material water, I want them to drink holy water.

Don’t think that you will die and that other people will die (and that life ends there). I would like to tell you that I want you to die into Allāh (ﷻ) by obeying His orders and emigrating to him like the Prophet Ibrāhīm (Abraham) (عليه السلام) did. This is what I want to explain to you, and I would like to explain this love to you in order to guide you.

The reading continues, “I will be drunk with Your love and I will sacrifice myself for Allāh (ﷻ) in order to give to other people who want to be with this love, who want to be with You. For this love is Your love, Allāh (ﷻ), and I cannot receive anything beyond what You give me. So please let me have love without beginning or end, for You are my eyes. You are always in my heart. Let me forever be in the spring of prostration.

Allāh (ﷻ) says, ‘Oh my friends, you are singing the song of the lovers. How can you reach if you will not give Me the things I gave you from the eternal life? Your life hasn’t any beginning. This contains the secret of eternity.’

Oh Allāh (ﷻ), You are the pleasure, You are the Giver, You give the whole world the melodies of prostration. You give them eyes that see everything and lights revealed upon them, and You give to them through Your existence.

Allāh (ﷻ) is the Generous. He is the Love. Only love Allāh (ﷻ), nothing else.

Oh Allāh (ﷻ), through Your existence You give them everything in this world. They become drunk from the wine of this knowledge and then they become absent. They witness You."

Beloveds, I would like you all to become absent from everything, to be only with Allāh (ﷻ). Drop from your mind, I am sure He will make you absent.

The reading continues, "The lovers are absent from everything but the truth. There is no prostration if you don't know love."

This love is forbidden, it is just for those who obey Allāh (ﷻ). For those who disobey Allāh (ﷻ) there is Hell. Those in Hell have killed people, they have destroyed others, they have lost the love they tasted. They chose that path.

Allāh (ﷻ) says:

> And (I have) shown him the two ways (good and evil). (90:10)

He says, "I gave you two paths; this is the good one and this is the bad one, so choose."

And Allāh (ﷻ) says:

> This, your (human) nation, is one nation,
> and I am your Lord so worship Me (alone). (21:92)

He says, "I am the only one that gives life to all of you."

He is the Giver. He created everything in a perfect picture. He wants you to always pray and to let Him give you divine love all the time.

The reading continues, "Those who become absent from their selves into His self, let them know they shouldn't go beyond My borders. Don't stop following My commands and My prohibitions.

Beloveds, I send my voice to all those who search for the deep, secret love. I call all my children to come and knock on the door, to hear the song of the Holy Qur'ān, and I am sure that anyone who comes will come with a deep sincerity. He will be completely absent from the dense world to be inside the world of the truth. This is the world of the love.

Don't wait, my beloveds, time is very short. Really, the truth is that there is no time for anybody. Only this moment exists; this is the time of your beloved God (ﷻ). So listen for His flute; if you listen, you can remember, you can understand. If you like to be absent from everything, if you like to only be with your Beloved, then now is the time for you. This is the real time between you and Allāh (ﷻ). This is the time to be only with Allāh (ﷻ), to be in the arms of Allāh (ﷻ).

Don't lose your time, don't give it to anyone who doesn't understand, who doesn't follow Allāh (ﷻ) in everything. This is the real drink of the source of love. He will give you the real life, not a false life. I am a child from His children, and I like to sing what He wants from me."

Music plays.

> *My heart tells me all the time,*
> *"Oh my love, You will always be my love.*
> *Let me be absent, let me disappear...I will sacrifice my soul..."*

Beloved, either you know my intention or you don't. Oh Allāh (ﷻ), I swim in Your ocean to drink Your deep, secret love.

Allāh (ﷻ) loves you. Allāh (ﷻ) told me and taught me. He will teach you what you never knew before through the Qur'ān. He taught me English and He has given me other languages. Don't wonder how I am speaking English, because Allāh (ﷻ) can do that.

The reading continues, "Give me the time to swim all my life in the ocean of the essence of truth and to know You, Allāh (ﷻ), and to be with You and to carry what You want from me and to be a real, real slave for You.

Oh Allāh (ﷻ), teach me how to walk, show me where there is a holy door to cross to You, for without You there is nothing. Take me from this material world to the world of Your essence, because You are my beloved. Destroy all of my humanity and return me to Your spirit, for my spirit comes from Your spirit.

You gave to the father of all human beings (ﷺ), and if I don't understand the meaning of this then I will lose everything, and I will be without Your help.

You told me, 'Read My Qur'ān and you will find and know the essence of the deep secret love, and you can drink. You will help yourself to remain always with Me and to listen to everything I say. For that reason, you can't take anything if you do not give Me the essence of your heart. This is the price. This is the sacrifice.'

This is like what the Prophet (ﷺ) said:

> Die before you die."

This is the real life.

The reading continues, "Oh Allāh (ﷻ), How can I reach You if you do not accept me? If You do not help me? If You do not give me a new life and a new creation? For that reason, I keep my heart behind Your door until I see Your door is open.

I searched for a long time to drink from the source of Your love, Allāh (ﷻ). Then You gave me the real life to be with You. For that reason I call to You, 'Oh my heart, my poor heart. Without Your love, Allāh (ﷻ), I am nothing.'

For this reason, I give myself completely, not only in my heart but in my spirit. I like to clean myself in the way that Allāh (ﷻ) wants. I like to purify myself, to be a poor slave for You. I don't want to travel unless You show me how I can travel within the holy song of lā ʾilāha ʾilla-llāh.

Music plays.

> *Oh Allāh (ﷻ), oh my Love,*
> *I sacrifice my spirit for You,*
> *whether You know it or not.*

Sure, He knows everything, but it is important for everyone to be as Allāh (ﷻ) wants. Surrender completely and do not say 'I.' Only say, 'Allāh (ﷻ),' for He is the love,

He is the one of the truth, and for that reason He created everything. He gives and He puts the essence of all His knowing in everything. Then He puts us in the Garden through His way (ﷻ), not the way of those who do not how to walk to Him.

It is not easy for anyone to say 'I am.' It is forbidden for anyone to say 'I.' Instead, look inside this mirror and see this essence; then Allāh (ﷻ) will teach you.

I do not need even one moment to see the face, to see the light, of my beloved Laylā. Then I throw myself into prostration between His arms (ﷻ) and drink from His water (ﷻ), for He gives me eternal life without death. This is al-baqāʾu-l-bi-llāh (subsistence in Allāh ﷻ).

For anyone that has heard my voice, there is permission to listen to the song of God (ﷻ) through my spirit, but it is important to be gentle and to be polite when you are around the Beloved. Āmīn.

> *Oh Allāh (ﷻ), I didn't pay you the rights of Your love.*

I spent all my time and You gave it to me without taking anything.
And for that reason I cry to You, "Give me just a drop from You" to give me the real life.

I have been waiting a long time to see with my real eyes, not my earthly eyes, the beauty You give to all that You have created, Allāh (ﷻ).

This is the real life.

> *I didn't give You the rights of Your love.*
> *There are no rights for love, and I didn't give anything.*

Allāh (ﷻ) says, 'My beloved, carry My love to help those who have been crying for a long time.' I answer, 'Yes, I will,' in my heart. There is no way to say, 'No, Allāh (ﷻ).' I listen for Your notes, for Your flute, and I follow Your words from when You said: 'Kun.'

This is the real life. I don't like to die in a way that people don't understand."

I like to die between the arms of Allāh (ﷻ).

The reading continues, "I don't like not giving people a chance to see Your face, because of all of Your beauty. Everyone is so thirsty for Your love, Allāh (ﷻ). You are the Merciful. Give a drop of this mercy to those who open their hearts in order to explain the real idea of love and how to love in the right way. I want my beloveds to love Your face, my Lord (ﷻ), as I love only Your face."

Beloveds, I want you to be in the presence of Allāh (ﷻ), not in the presence of human beings. From here you should get rid of everything. Then Allāh (ﷻ) will give you a beautiful life full of love and happiness and peace and you will live forever. This is the answer to the question of how He created you.

For this reason, Allāh (ﷻ) says His Qur'ān, "I created Ādam (ﷺ). I revealed Myself within My holy name of al-Āḥad to let you exist here." He says, "I am the Most Merciful and Compassionate." He sent the prophets (ﷺ) to be His mercy for all people. He sent them (ﷺ) to be full of mercy, to be generous.

You should be humble; you should not be like the mountains. You cannot reach the mountains, so do not put hatefulness inside your heart. Help the people who are suffering everywhere. Give them peace and love so that you can see His light in your life.

We were created for this life, the real life, not for the material life. Allāh (ﷻ) says, "For this reason I created jinn and human beings and animals and all of creation."

Beloveds, we should be in the world of knowledge, because the one who revealed Himself is Allāh (ﷻ). Through His name, through His qualities, He revealed Himself and gave mercy to all of creation. For this reason you should be polite with yourself, with your children, and with other people, even with animals and birds. Learn love from the birds. Isn't this the truth? Birds are always praising Allāh (ﷻ). Every creature praises Allāh (ﷻ) in its own language.

Why are birds happier than human beings? Because they hear and obey Allāh (ﷻ) when He calls them. You should be like this. They follow His order. Everything in this world follows the order of Allāh (ﷻ) except human beings; only the human being disobeys Him. I ask Allāh (ﷻ) to bring the disobedient people to the way and to open their hearts.

Birds are happy; they are free and they don't even have to pay taxes to this rubbish government. Those who live in the garden of Allāh (ﷻ) listen to the voice of Allāh (ﷻ), and they don't have to pay for the rubbish government. They are very happy. People would be happy to dance with the birds.

Music plays.

The reading continues, "Oh Allāh (ﷻ), how can I leave Your love? How can I live without Your love? This is the love. This is the real life for everyone who wants to travel to reach Your real Garden. Oh my Beloved, keep me under Your foot to know how to make the real prostration to Your face. Please teach me, Allāh (ﷻ), how to thank You. Teach me how to serve You, and how to be the poor slave, the real slave, like what You want from me. Give me a chance to travel only for Your face, and for me to see the face of my Beloved who created me, and to be only for His face.

Oh my beloved children, follow me in this way to drink from the cup of Allāh (ﷻ). This is my voice submitting to the voice of the Greatest One who carries everything (ﷻ).

Oh Allāh (ﷻ), give everyone a drop of Your love so that they can reach the real baqā' in the world of God (ﷻ).

My children, if you'd like to walk in a deep, deep way then be polite, open your heart, and leave everything to clean yourself. Be only spirit, for without Allāh's spirit you could not walk, because God (ﷻ) changes the heart to be His spirit.

Life without the essence of His love, beloveds, is nothing. This singer likes to explain this in the song, but he does not have the real words to explain it.

I am a very poor slave and I will try to explain it. I will make a real prostration for Allāh (ﷻ) in order to drink from His source, and I will not leave because He gave me this chance to explain this song of His love, to explain the real love of Allāh (ﷻ) to my children. Whoever takes the real love has the real life and he carries what Allāh (ﷻ) says.

Listen to His voice (ﷻ). Listen to His tone (ﷻ). He will teach you what you have never known before. This is just from obeying Him and following His orders and commands in this life. Without His help you can't do anything, not even walk.

If a person drinks from His love like He asks us to, then I'm sure he will sing His song. He will always dance and will not stop. He will not stop through his ṣalāh and he will say, 'Bismi-llāhi-r-raḥmāni-r-raḥīm.'

This is the key to the home of Allāh (ﷻ). For this reason, anyone who likes to come, to be and to follow—to see what He likes to give and to follow what He likes to say—I am sure Allāh (ﷻ) will give him a chance to know himself, to clean himself and to clean his heart. Then he will see that the Kaʿba is love and he will circumambulate it and kiss the stone that the Prophet Ibrāhīm (ؑ) brought.

On Ḥajj

This stone is the center of divine love. A few people understand the meaning of what Allāh (ﷻ) says to Ibrāhīm (ؑ), 'Build My home, the home of love. Make ṭawāf (circumambulation) around My home, the home of love. Here is the first home for everyone that likes to drink from the source of his beloved God's love.'

So why does He say, 'Throw the stones?'[14] It means to leave everything and to not listen to Iblīs. Throw the stone that Allāh (ﷻ) gave to Ibrāhīm (ﷺ) to discharge everything that is not from and for Allāh (ﷻ). Then, my children, you will have made the real Ḥajj, because you will say, 'labayk-allāhumma labayk.' Now, not tomorrow, my children.

You will say, 'Here I come, Allāh (ﷻ).' Then you will see that in the home of love, love walks around you. This is the real bride. It is the real wedding for you to dance around the Kaʿba.

When you have the deep knowing of what Allāh (ﷻ) says in the Qur'ān, and when you know everything that He sends through His beloved prophets (ﷺ), you will know real love.

Don't search for false love, my children. You will lose your chance if you don't wake up. Excuse me if I give something of this secret, but I am nothing without Him. I am just a drop from His essence (ﷻ). He sent me to explain this song, the song of His deep praying. I will. Let us continue to see what He says.

Music plays.

> *I don't have anyone, Allāh (ﷻ), just You.*
> *I don't have anything except my spirit,*
> *and even this I sacrifice.*

If Laylā asks me to give everything for her, then I give everything without asking why or what.

Why? Because I like to drink from His milk. I like to live a real life and return everything that He gives, and to live in the way He wants. I want to always be in the tajjalī al-jamāl (beautiful ongoing revelation) when He reveals Himself in beauty. Through His love I reach to be complete.

---

[14] Sidi is referring to the part of Ḥajj where pilgrims throw stones at three walls called, "jamarāt" in the city of Mina just east of Mecca.

Then I begin to use the flute to sing, 'Oh Allāh (ﷻ). Oh Allāh (ﷻ).'

He gave me the flute of Dāwūd (David) (عليه السلام) to send His voice to everyone, for every bird, for everything in creation to hear His voice. This is the flute of the prophets who love Allāh (ﷻ). My Master Muḥammad (ﷺ) who sent his voice to all people, said:

> Say: 'If you love Allāh then follow me.' (3:31)

He says, 'Follow me, for I am of the child of God (ﷻ). I have this flute through saying, "Allāhu Akbar" to carry His message.'

This is some of the deep meaning of what Allāh (ﷻ) has said.

> *The one who sacrifices himself for the sake of his Lover*
> *is not wasteful.*
> *The one that loves and spends his life sacrificing himself for*
> *his Lover did the right thing.*
>
> *Oh my Love, oh yes, my Love*
> *I did not suffer much in Your love.*
> *You are right, I should suffer, and I didn't suffer much.*
> *If you are the One then I will give my soul for You.*

This is my life. My Lover gave me this life, the life He wants me to have. It will not be as I want it to be, because I want His wish. There is nothing before or after His wish.

There is no place or time that is eternal. It is one. He created everything with beauty, as He wished. He gave me His love in every way. He let me be His lover, as He wished. He used me to be a lover. He gave me an atom of His love.

This atom contains the entire existence of humanity, the jinn, the plants and everything. This chair contains all of the skies. This is the earth in a small atom of what He created. So excuse me if I sing the song of the Eternal (ﷻ). Who initiated that? Who lit this song with His light and His love?

Oh my beloved, I am calling to all human beings, everywhere that you are, everywhere that you will be, in every time and place. My Beloved loves you, so love Him.

He gave you everything. You shouldn't prostrate just for His beauty, my beloved. Follow me everywhere I go, because I have no choice. I just want the beauty of His face and the wine that will give me eternal life. Recognize your life, my beloveds, my sons and my daughters, those who are thirsty and want to be full.

He gives you and your spirit life and then, through this spirit, you will speak with Allāh's tongue, with His words. You will be like a bird singing in al-Malakūt, al-Jabarūt and al-Lahūt. You will live the eternal life. There is no death, my beloveds, in this life.

If you understand what I am saying, then pray and prostrate to Allāh (ﷻ). I am nothing. I am nothing, but within Him I became everything. Can you understand what I am saying? Yes, you can. You can do it. You should forbid yourself to eat or drink from any other plate or cup; only drink from the cup of Allāh (ﷻ). Then, my children, you will be saved. If you are follow these instructions then you will hold a new creation. Allāh (ﷻ) said on the tongue of our Master Muḥammad (ﷺ):

> My servant continues to draw near to Me with voluntary actions
> (extra ṣalāh and worship)
> until I become the hearing with which he hears,
> the seeing with which he sees,
> the hand with which he strikes (and heals) and
> the foot with which he walks.
> I will be his life full of love.

This is the real life, the giving life.

My beloveds, you have a cure within you. You should give this cure to all who need it. How? Give it through sharing this divine medicine. When you give, you give to yourself, not to anyone else. You give to your life, to serve yourself, and for your Master (ﷻ). For this reason, always open your ears and your spirit. You should give this cure to all those who need it through what Allāh (ﷻ) has given you through Sayyidinā (our Master) Muḥammad (ﷺ).

This is just some of the meaning from the deep, secret garden that you all carry from your beloved God (ﷻ), so follow what He says.

I don't have anything, just my spirit.
One who will give himself is not spending much,
and he is not wasteful.

What would you like to give? You do not have anything because You have not created yourself. For this reason it is important to make the real fanā' through the beloved rūḥ (spirit). He says, 'I give you this spirit' because He is generous. He gave you life, but He wants you to live a real life.

You are more holy than the angels (عليهم السلام). Why don't you sing like the angels (عليهم السلام) sing? He gave you the flag of love, so why do you hide it? Follow the flag and then you will see yourself in the complete walking. This is the real baqā', the real existence.

If a person has nothing and wants to visit his Lover (ﷻ), bringing a gift from himself, he will go to Allāh (ﷻ) who created him. What gift will he bring Him? The person doesn't have anything to give but himself. What can he make? The only gift Allāh (ﷻ) asks of you is to be pure, to clean your heart, to clean your spirit and to say, 'My gift is all that I can give You, which is everything I have, for without You, I am nothing. I would only like You to give me some light so that I can see Your robe in order to drink from the source of Your love, my Lord.'

This is the water and it gives real life, for without real life from God (ﷻ), full of love, then you can't be anything.

If You do not accept me I will be so miserable.
I will live in deep suffering, deep sadness,
because I will lose the sense of the deep, secret life.
I only have a creation through You, Allāh (ﷻ),
and without that I will lose everything.

How can I live without Your love? I will suffer.
If You accept my gift, I will give myself as a gift to you.
If you accept it I will be the ransom, I will be the gift.

The tongue of my Beloved says, 'When you give to those who are crying, for those who love Me, then you give My love to everyone and then I accept your giving.' This is what He wants from you, my children."

This is the exact meaning of what Allāh (ﷻ) wants from us. Don't think you are the giver. He is the Giver. He wants you to constantly give, to constantly help those who are suffering around the world: the sick people, the poor people and the angry people. They are a manifestation of Allāh (ﷻ). Allāh (ﷻ) revealed Himself within them with His name.

Allāh (ﷻ) is the Provider and He gave you provision because He is the Giver. He gave you life, so give this life to those who are suffering everywhere, and praise Him for using you to help His manifestation.

You are poor, He is rich and He is the Provider of His provision. You came into this world crying and suffering and you didn't have anything. When you see anyone anywhere crying or suffering, help him without discrimination. Allāh (ﷻ) and His Prophet (ﷺ) say:

> All creatures are the children of Allāh (ﷻ),
> and the most beloved to Him
> are the ones who are most beneficial to His children.

The reading continues, "So when you give to those who are crying, who love Me, you give My love to everyone. This, I accept, and when you give you are only sharing a tiny portion of what I have given you.

My children, for this reason He wants you to be the tree of the love. He wants you to give the fruits from your tree to everyone, to help all voices sing the song of Allāh (ﷻ). Allāhu Akbar. This is the essence of the religion of God (ﷻ). for He is the Merciful, ar-raḥmāni-r-raḥīm. He contains everything.

> *How can I sleep deeply when I am suffering from Your love?*
> *If you refuse to give Your love to me, then how can I sleep?*
> *If you refuse to give me Your spirit,*
> *the essence of Your love, how can I sleep?*
> *How can I be in the real life?*

I will miss everything;
I will lose everything without help from You.
I will not be able to sleep.

You will let me put on the clothes of suffering
if You don't give me what I ask for—Your love.

Without Your love there is no life!

My lusting for You will kill me,
You will let me be nothing very soon.
Please be kind to me, my Love.
I am thirsty, so please give me a drop.

I am very thirsty. If You don't give me the water of Your love, then I will cry forever. I will cry all the time until I lose everything.

I am very weak.
My body is very weak.
Without the essence of the deep secret from You, Allāh (ﷻ),
I could not walk,
I could not stop,
I could not give anything, and my heart would be sick.
Please give me the real medicine from the sweet bees,
from the source of Your life, because you are al-Ḥayy.

I like to be patient, to give myself a chance to wait for the holy gift that You like to give.

This is all I hope for and my heart is open. All the doors that I have are open; they are only for my Beloved and nothing less. I am patient, I can wait. I am sure Allāh (ﷻ) is generous, for He lets me sleep between His arms like a child who drinks his mother's milk. This is enough for me because He gives me the real life. He gives me more than a new creation, but in the gentle way, the way of my Lord, and I like to spend all of my time in this way.

This is not a dream, this is the truth. This is my voice speaking to all who love God (ﷻ), and I hope everybody understands the meaning of this knowledge. I explain in the song how everyone who loves God (ﷻ)

should be in order to reach and how to be with his beloved Allāh (ﷻ). Āmīn."

This is a call to everyone who wants to be in love, to everyone who wants to open his heart to every single order and promise Allāh (ﷻ) to be obedient. This is for the one who wants to pay his heart and spirit as a sacrifice to Allāh (ﷻ) and who promises Allāh (ﷻ) a strong promise.

The one who does this will be under the divine love, under those wonderful shadows. If you promise Allāh (ﷻ), you will be happy and you will live an eternal life, because you will obey all of the orders He sent to the prophets (عليهم السلام). Are you ready to promise now? If you are ready, come. Come and give your promise.

The Prophet's Night Journey and Ascension (ﷺ)

"The Seventh Discourse: Concerning the Ḥadīth on Making the Five Prayers Obligatory on the Night Journey" from *Spiritual Discourses in the Blessed Al-Aqṣā Mosque* Saturday, July 10, 2010 AM, Midwest Sufi Gathering

لا إله إلا الله – لا إله إلا الله – لا إله إلا الله – محمد رسول الله عليه صلاة الله
لا إله إلا الله – لا إله إلا الله – لا إله إلا الله – ابراهيم رسول الله عليه صلاة الله
لا إله إلا الله – لا إله إلا الله – لا إله إلا الله – موسى رسول الله عليه صلاة الله
لا إله إلا الله – لا إله إلا الله – لا إله إلا الله – عيسى رسول الله عليه صلاة الله
اللهم انت السلام ومنك السلام و إليك يعود السلام
تباركت ربنا وتعاليت يا ذوالجلال والإكرام

Yā Allāh (ﷻ), I am asking You to prevent all disasters all over the world.
We ask You to give peace, love, justice, and freedom
to all people in this world without separation or discrimination.
May You prevent the pain of those who are suffering,
those who are imprisoned, and those who are treated in a bad way.
Give them freedom and correct their situations.
You (ﷻ) are able to do everything.

I am invoking Allāh (ﷻ), asking Him
to let all of the presidents come back to the truth
and prevent them from being offensive.
Allāh (ﷻ), please be merciful with our nations in this world.
Help these leaders to help people,
help them to guide people to happiness,
and prevent them from stealing people's money or fortunes.
Help them deal with each other with justice
and help them to obey Allāh's commands and orders (ﷻ).
Help them to live in deep justice,
full of mercy for themselves and for all others.
Help them to work to achieve peace, freedom, love, and mercy.
Allāh (ﷻ) is able to do everything.

I am pleased to see all of you this year, this second time. I invoke Allāh (ﷻ) to give to me from His divine knowledge. I am His servant between His arms (ﷻ). He can direct me as He wishes (ﷻ). It is my honor to be servant for the human being, following the example of all the prophets (ﷺ) and following the message of all the prophets (ﷺ), the message of unity.

As all of you can see, I am weak. I came here with this weak body, but it is full of His strength. I am an old man; I am 77 years old. Allāh (ﷻ) put within me the strength of youth and I praise Him because He gives me health. I am asking Him to give me the strength to be honest and to give His message, the sharīʿa (divine law), and unlimited love through this path, which is the truth.

From here I am talking to all of you and all of those who are suffering, with all of my love. Every night, every hour, my heart is with those who are suffering. I cry, asking Allāh (ﷻ) to help those who are suffering. I cry to Allāh (ﷻ) and invoke Allāh (ﷻ) with my tears to stop the pain, the anger, the pain. I ask Allāh (ﷻ) to help those who are suffering so much because of presidents who disobey the orders of Allāh (ﷻ) and disobey the message of all the prophets (ﷺ). It doesn't matter whether they are Jewish, Muslim, Christian, or Buddhist, I don't believe just in one message, it is all the message of Allāh (ﷻ). I am on this path because Allāh (ﷻ) ordered me to be this way.

I invoke Allāh (ﷻ) not to let me die while I am just standing. I hope I will be strong to the end and I hope Allāh (ﷻ) will answer my supplication, and I ask the same for all my beloveds who carry the same message.

Today is a wedding day for all the prophets and the angels (ﷺ). It is the wedding day for all believers, who believe in unity and are loved by Allāh (ﷻ). This is a holy day because it is the divine wedding.

Allāh (ﷻ) has ordered His prophets and messengers (ﷺ) to gather and pray for all those who are suffering. Through this wedding, Allāh (ﷻ) wants to let you know that this is a day of provision, divine provision. This divine provision...when Allāh (ﷻ) ordered Sayyidinā (our Master) Muḥammad (ﷺ) on the Night Journey of the ascent.

On that night Allāh (ﷻ) brought the Prophet (ﷺ) very close to Him in order to give him the orders that people should follow, including the prayer and how we should worship Him. All the prophets and the angels, all the gnostic people gathered on that day. Sayyidinā Muḥammad (ﷺ) narrated this ḥadīth from Allāh (ﷻ).

Bismi-llāhi-r-raḥmāni-r-raḥīm. The Prophet Muḥammad was reclining between al-Haṭim and Zamzam in Mecca, and he was praising Allāh (ﷻ), he was absent from this world and he was praying for all the people who are suffering, sick and poor. He was crying and his tears fell. His tears, his heart was crying for those people because he was the messenger of mercy. Allāh (ﷻ) says:

> We have not sent you but as a mercy for all the worlds. (21:107)

He sent our Prophet (ﷺ) not just to Muslims, Jews, or Christians, but to everyone, to all people. Allāh (ﷻ) sent him to all people and he was the first light. One of his friends, followers asked him, "Who was the first one Allāh (ﷻ) created?" The Prophet (ﷺ) told him:

> The first thing Allāh (ﷻ) created was the light of your Prophet, oh Jabbār.

He told him:

> I was a prophet before Adam (ﷺ) was made from clay.

So he asked him to let him know about the journey. He was absent and his spirit and his heart was crying and sad for what was happening in that world. At that time when a mother gave birth to a daughter those people would put her in a grave while she was still alive when she was 16 years old. They never suffered or felt sad about her. He was crying about that.

They used people badly then; they bought and sold the human being. This was a horrible thing. The strong man ate the weak man and used him. And people at that time never worshipped Allāh (ﷻ). They worshipped idols like Nimrūd and others. Some of them worshipped kings, like Firʿown (Pharaoh), who said, "I am your greatest and highest Lord and you should worship me."

Story of Mūsā and Firʿown (Pharaoh)

In Firʿown's nation, there was no choice; the one who did not worship Firʿown would be killed, like what almost happened to Mūsā (ﷺ) after his mother gave birth to him. Firʿown said, "There will be a prophet in this land and he will claim that he is a prophet." So he gave the order to kill any boys born because one of them could be his enemy. How can he be an enemy? He is a human being.

After Mūsā's mother gave birth to him, she put him in a box and put him in the Nile River. Allāh (ﷻ) ordered an angel to carry this box and this box reached Towendo. The wife of Firʿown (Asiya ؓ) saw this box and didn't know what was in it. She sent her servants to carry the box and they when they opened it they found a baby crying, saying, "Yā Allāh (ﷻ)," in a language that the Egyptians understood at the time.

The wife of Firʿown believed in Mūsā (ؑ) and she said, "This child is different from any other human being; he is holy." When Firʿown came she told him that Mūsā (ؑ) was a beautiful son, a beautiful child. She wanted to take him as a son, so she carried him and raised him up to look to the wisdom of Allāh (ﷻ).

This child needed milk. They tried to wet nurse him with all the ladies but he refused all of them. Then, his sister came (her name Maryam) and she told them, "Do you want me to guide you to someone who will feed this baby?" They said yes.

So she brought Mūsā's mother and they didn't know who she was. She fed him and the baby knew her immediately. Every day she fed him three times.

Mūsā (ؑ) grew up and was raised up in Firʿown's house, and He became a prophet. Allāh (ﷻ) sent him as a prophet and a messenger. He was strong. He said the first word to Firʿown, asking him:

> "Firʿown, who is your Lord? Who is your God?"
> Firʿown answered, "Who? I am your highest Lord."
> Mūsā (ؑ) told him, "My lord is Allāh (ﷻ) who created everything and He who provides us with everything."
> Firʿown replied, "I am our Lord."
> Mūsā said, "You will die one day, so worship the Lord who created you."
> So Firʿown told him, "You don't have any position here."
> Mūsā responded, "Allāh (ﷻ) is rich, I don't need your provision."

This was a divine situation. I like to let you know about such stories. I want to let you know how people were suffering all the time and how presidents and kings treated people. At that time they gave two or three or four servants, but now the bad presidents who corrupt the earth order all the nations to be servants to them. They steal money, they kill here and there, and they start wars all over the world. They give excuses for the wars they start. They say, "Those people don't deserve life." Is that right?

We are now in the days when the divine wedding has been completed for the prophets and all human beings. All people made a contract, a divine contract, between them and the prophets (ﷺ). There are 124,000 prophets and messengers besides the angels and the honest people and the gnostics and the perfect people.

In China there is a law that forbids people to have more than child. If they have more than one they are put in prison. If the women gets pregnant with another child she will sell her. This is now. You have heard about this. We have heard about this.

Listen, we hear about this every day. If you don't have a baby you can go to China to buy a baby. This is the truth; this is not right. They sell their hearts, their children are their hearts. The law has asked them to do that. If they do not do it they will go to jail. What can those people do? What can those people who try to cut the message of the Prophet (ﷺ) do?

That why Muḥammad (ﷺ), the Prophet, appeared. He was orphaned. He didn't have a father. His father passed away when he was in his mother's womb. Then his mother passed away when he was four years old. He was orphaned: he had no father and no mother. This child suffered a lot until he became prophet.

Story of the Prophet's First Revelation

Allāh (ﷻ) sent down to the desert a large amount of rain and this was a sign for our prophet's (ﷺ) appearance. He sent him as a prophet and he was worshiping Allāh (ﷻ) in the cave of Hirāʾ.

Allāh (ﷻ) told Jībrīl (Gabriel) to say, "Read" to the Prophet (ﷺ).

> The Prophet (ﷺ) told him, "I don't know how to read or write."
> So Jibrīl (﷐) told him, "Read in the name of Allāh (ﷻ) who created
> everything and who created you from a small sperm."
> Jibrīl (﷐) told him, "And Allāh (ﷻ) taught you everything you
> have ever known.

Sayyidinā Muḥammad (ﷺ) was scared. He didn't know what was going
on, so he went to his wife, Sayyidatunā (our Lady) Khadīja (﷠) and he
told her:

> "Something happened to me; my body cannot put up with this."
> Sayyidatunā Khadīja told him, "Don't be scared. You are honest
> and you are kind and this is a message from Allāh (ﷻ) to you."
> "Be careful," she told him, "There have been hints that you
> would appear, You will be sent to the people."

This holy prophet, this noble prophet had his miracles like the other
prophets (﷐), every one of them, had theirs.

Ibrāhīm Was Saved from the Fire

Sayyidinā Ibrāhīm (﷐), was put him in the fire, but because he was a
prophet, Allāh (ﷻ) saved him. Allāh (ﷻ) sent to him Jibrīl (﷐) while he was
in the fire and he asked Ibrāhīm (﷐), "Do you need anything?" Ibrāhīm
(﷐) answered, "No, I don't need anything from you. The One Who Knows
what I need, knows what I need and He will give me what I need." Then
Allāh (ﷻ) ordered the fire to be peaceful and cool. So everything was
changed into a beautiful garden for Ibrāhīm (﷐). This was the miracle of
Ibrāhīm (﷐).

Mūsā's Miracles (﷐)

Allāh (ﷻ) gave Mūsā miracles, too. At that time, there was lot of people
who dealt with magic, so Allāh (ﷻ) gave him something to deal with
those people who deal with magic. Allāh (ﷻ) told him, "Throw your stick
and it will become a snake." It did, it became a huge snake. She ate all
the other snakes of the other people who did magic.

Mūsā (﷐) parted the sea for his people and the sea became eleven
streams, each one representing one of his sons. Where Firʿown entered
the streets, the streets returned back into the sea. Allāh (ﷻ) destroyed
Firʿown and his soldiers in the sea.

We ask Allāh (ﷻ) to help those who are suffering. Allāh (ﷻ) always watches everything and protects people's rights. Allāh (ﷻ)will let the offending people treat others badly, but Allāh (ﷻ) will take him step by step and his punishment will be very severe. Allāh (ﷻ) said:

> My servants, I have made oppression unlawful for Me and unlawful for you, so do not commit oppression against one another.

I don't want talk about so much about that. This is a short introduction. I would like to let you know about those people at that time. The people now are like the people of that time, so there is one thing we can do to solve our problems: let people follow the message of all the prophets (ﷺ).

Story of the Prophet Muḥammad's (ﷺ) Night Journey and Ascension (al-isrā wal miʿrāj)

The Prophet (ﷺ) said that he was between al-Haṭim and Zamzam, in the Kaʿba, the house of Ibrāhīm (ﷺ). This was the first house for people, for holy rest.

The Black Spot is Removed

The Prophet Muḥammad (ﷺ) was reclining and a mysterious stranger came to him. And he heard him say, "Take the black spot from his heart." This was to prevent the devil from entering his heart. So there was an operation, a surgery. They took the spot of black blood from our prophet's heart, and in this way Allāh (ﷻ) purified him. They took out this spot of black blood from his heart.

The Prophet (ﷺ) said, "Then a gold tray of belief was brought to me and my heart was washed and filled with belief."

Then they came. A white animal (named Burāq) appeared to the Prophet (ﷺ). In our sharīʿa it was an animal, but in the truth it was an angel. It was smaller than a mule and larger than a donkey. Sayyidinā Muḥammad (ﷺ) rode this animal, and its step was very long, until they reached al-Quds. They arrived very quickly, like in the blink of an eye. It was faster than an airplane and or rockets and it was 1,400 years ago. The rockets of Allāh (ﷻ) are faster than the rockets now.

The Prophet (ﷺ) reached the al-Aqṣā Mosque, the Holy Rock, the rock of Ibrāhīm (ؑ) and the rock of all the messenger and prophets (ؑ) who were born near there. He was there. Jībrīl (ؑ) took him tied the animal to the west door of the mosque. To this moment you can see this door at the al-Aqṣā Mosque.

The First Heaven: Adam (ؑ)

After that, Jībrīl (ؑ) took him and they rode in the sky until they reached the first heaven. Its guard is an angel and he asked Jībrīl (ؑ), "Who is with you?" He said, "Muḥammad (ﷺ)." The angel asked, "Has Muḥammad (ﷺ) been called?" He told him, "Yes." So the angel welcomed him and the gate opened. Sayyidinā Muḥammad (ﷺ) said, "The gate was opened and I saw Adam (ؑ)." When he first saw him the Prophet (ﷺ) asked, "Who is this?" and Jībrīl (ؑ) told him, "This is Adam (ؑ), your father. Say, 'as-salām' to him." So Muḥammad (ﷺ) said, "as-salām," to him and Adam (ؑ) answered his salām and told him, "Welcome Muḥammad (ﷺ), oh pious son and pious prophet."

The Second Heaven: ʿĪsā and Yaḥyā (ؑ)

Then the Prophet (ﷺ) and Jībrīl (ؑ) traveled to the second heaven and Jībrīl (ؑ) knocked on the door. Sayyidinā Jībrīl said, "Muḥammad (ﷺ) is with me and Muḥammad (ﷺ) has been called." And the angels guarding the door said, "Welcome. Welcome. The gate has been opened." Sayyidinā Muḥammad (ﷺ) saw Yaḥyā (ؑ) and ʿĪsā (ؑ) (John the Baptist and Jesus Christ). They were waiting for him. They are the sons of his aunt. They said, "Greetings, as-salām. Welcome oh pious son, pious prophet."

The Third Heaven: Yūsuf (ؑ)

Sayyidinā Jībrīl (ؑ) took him to the third heaven. He knocked and they asked him, "Who is with you?" and he told them, "Muḥammad (ﷺ)." They answered, "He is most welcome." The Prophet (ﷺ) recognized Sayyidinā Yūsuf (Joseph) (ؑ) who paid his greetings to the Prophet (ﷺ) and said, "Welcome oh pious son, pious prophet."

The Fourth Heaven: Idrīs (ؑ)

They ascended to the fourth heaven and Jībrīl (ؑ) said, "Muḥammad is with me." Then they greeted him and when he reached he saw Idrīs

(Enoch) (عليه السلام). He greeted him and he welcomed him and he said, "Welcome, welcome pious son, pious prophet."

The Fifth Heaven: Hārūn (عليه السلام)

Then they ascended to the fifth heaven and he knocked on the door and the door was opened. The angels guarding the door asked, "Who is with Jībrīl (عليه السلام)?" Jībrīl answered, "Muḥammad (ﷺ) and Muḥammad (ﷺ) has been called." They said, "Welcome, welcome." Muḥammad (ﷺ) saw Hārūn (Aaron) (عليه السلام), prophet of Allāh (ﷻ), and he told him, "Welcome, my brother and my pious prophet."

The Sixth Heaven: Mūsā (عليه السلام)

And they ascended to the sixth heaven and Jībrīl knocked on the door and the door was opened. The angels guarding the door asked, "Who is with you, Jībrīl (عليه السلام)?" and Jībrīl responded, "Muḥammad (ﷺ) is with me." They welcomed him and Sayyidinā Mūsā (عليه السلام) was in this heaven and the Prophet (ﷺ) paid his greetings, saying, "As-salāmu ʿalaykum. You are the one who talked with Allah (ﷻ)."

Then Mūsā (عليه السلام) was crying and Muḥammad (ﷺ) asked, "Why are you crying?" Mūsā (عليه السلام) answered, "I am crying because there is a young man who was sent after me and more people from his nation will enter the Garden than from my nation." He is the nation of our prophets (عليهم السلام). Mūsā said, "You are a pious prophet and you are most welcome."

The Seventh Heaven: Ibrāhīm (عليه السلام)

In the seventh heaven they saw Sayyidinā Ibrāhīm (عليه السلام) and Jībrīl told him, "This is your father, Sayyidinā Muḥammad (ﷺ)." And Muḥammad (ﷺ) received his greeting and was told, "You are most welcome, pious son and pious prophet."

The Lote Tree

Then, he ascended to the holy Lote tree, to the gardens of the lights, the divine lights Allāh (ﷻ) placed there. There he saw what he had never seen. Then the house, one of His manifestations, lifted for him and they gave him a jug wine and a cup of milk and a jar of honey and was told to choose. He took the milk and he didn't take the wine, as all the other prophets (عليهم السلام) did not. Jībrīl (عليه السلام) told him, "You chose the natural one, how come?"

Don't you know that any creature in this world, the first thing it takes is milk. The first thing the baby and the animals will take is milk. If you give them wine they will not drink it, but those who are stupid drink wine to be crazy. They will cut themselves and have lots of accidents and kill people and kill themselves. This is the message of the prophets (ﷺ). This is the order of Allāh (ﷻ). He inspires him not to take this wine and the prophets (ﷺ) pass the exam every time.

Muḥammad (ﷺ) Receives the Ṣalāh

Here Allāh (ﷻ) obligates our Prophet (ﷺ) with the ṣalāh. Allāh (ﷻ) ordered him to do 50 prayers a day. The Prophet (ﷺ) returned and passed by Mūsā (ﷺ) and he told him, "My nation should worship Allāh (ﷻ) with 50 prayers a day." Mūsā (ﷺ) said, "Your nation cannot do that." He advised him and said, "I carried your message before you to the nation of Israel and it is very hard, I am telling you, they can't do that. Go back to Allāh (ﷻ) and asked him to reduce the number of prayers."

I am honest with you; people don't know how our Prophet (ﷺ) was graced with wisdom and mercy. He was a generous prophet. So he turned back to Allāh (ﷻ). Allāh (ﷻ) knows everything. So Allāh (ﷻ) reduced it by 10 to 40. Muḥammad returned back to Mūsā (ﷺ) and told him that Allāh (ﷻ) had reduced it to 40. Mūsā said that this was still too much.

So, the Prophet (ﷺ) returned back to Allāh (ﷻ) and He reduced it to 10. When Muḥammad returned to Mūsā (ﷺ), Mūsā said, "Even 10 your nation cannot do." So Sayyidinā Muḥammad (ﷺ) said, "I am ashamed to turn back to Allāh (ﷻ) to ask him again." Mūsā (ﷺ) told him to ask Allāh (ﷻ) to make it easy for his nation. I am honest with you, so Allāh (ﷻ) finally reduced the ṣalāh to 5 times a day, and Allāh (ﷻ) said those 5 prayers equal 50 prayers. So when you pray the 5 prayers a day and you keep those 5 prayers a day, Allāh (ﷻ) said those 5 prayers will equal 50 prayers. He said, "This is for my nation and this is the divine journey."

Allāh (ﷻ) took him on this night journey to see all the prophets (ﷺ). They were walking around the throne and they were surrounding the throne and he saw what he saw. He saw the Fire, the Garden and the people who are suffering, the murderers and the other people, the gnostics and the prophets (ﷺ). This is true and is in the Qur'ān. Praise Allāh (ﷻ)

who takes His servants from Mecca to al-Quds (Jerusalem), and we praise this area, this land, and the plants that surround this area.

Al-Quds has its borders. It, and of its all bordering lands, are very holy. In this land it is forbidden to do anything bad or to kill or to be away from the mercy. They should obey Allāh (ﷻ) with justice and freedom. Allāh (ﷻ) ordered them not to do anything against Allāh's order. Whether they are Jewish, Christian or Muslim, this is the order of Allāh (ﷻ).

This is a holy land to all the people who follow any of the prophets. When they attack this land, this holy land, and lots of children and old people are killed, Allāh (ﷻ) will not let this pass easily. Allāh (ﷻ) will avenge that; Allāh (ﷻ) will punish those people. Allāh (ﷻ) will reach them no matter where they are.

Allāh (ﷻ) said in Ḥadīth Qudsī that there are many snakes and beasts around holy land. Allāh (ﷻ) will send them to people who attack others, who kill others, who deal with others without justice and who are not be kind to others. Their needs will be poisoned. Those who will kill a child or tree or anything, will die. Allāh (ﷻ) will send him a severe punishment.

We ask Allāh (ﷻ) for peace, love, mercy and justice and to save all of the people who are suffering. We ask Him to help all people achieve love and mercy and to let them come back to their white minds and to the straight path. We ask Him to spread peace all over of the world.

Return to Al-Aqṣā

After this divine journey, Sayyidinā Muḥammad (ﷺ) returned back to the al-Aqṣā Mosque; he had ascended to the sky from the holy rock. His footprints are still on the on the Holy Rock. Allāh (ﷻ) ordered all the prophets (عليهم السلام) to come down with their real bodies and Sayyidinā Muḥammad (ﷺ) was their Imām and they prayed behind him.

From here, Allāh (ﷻ) took the promise from him, and he promised to take the promise from those who believe in the prophets and who believe in our prophet (ﷺ). This promise was between one hand and 124,000 prophets (عليهم السلام). All of those prophets (عليهم السلام) gave the promise to

Sayyidinā Muḥammad (ﷺ) to protect the message of unity and to follow this message. All the prophets (ﷺ) gave their promise to follow this message.

We carry this message and we took this message from them and we carry this message. Allāh (ﷻ) said he took the promise from Adam and all of his children.

> "Am I not your Lord?"
> They said, "Yes! We testify," (7:172)

They said yes. Allāh (ﷻ). They said, "We will deliver this message; we will give this message and ask the people to follow the message. You are the Lord of all people, and no one should be worshipped but You. We will follow all of Your orders in every single detail."

He orders them not to talk from their minds and their imaginations; we are just to teach them from the holy books. Allāh (ﷻ) said, "Muḥammad (ﷺ) was your father." He was the last prophet and messenger. All of them believed and they brought the good news of his appearance from here.

The promise the prophets (ﷺ) gave to Allāh (ﷻ), all of them, was to not worship anything but Allāh (ﷻ) and to not follow any other signs, just the signs of Allāh (ﷻ). The one who disobeys Allāh (ﷻ) will see a severe punishment, sickness and a bad life.

We should follow Him and we should hurry to Allāh (ﷻ). We should start to understand what all the prophets (ﷺ) taught us. He said that all of the prophets (ﷺ) believed the message and all of the people and there is no separation between the prophets (ﷺ). There is no separation between the messengers because they all testified to the message and they all followed it.

I would like to give this promise, the promise of the prophets (ﷺ). We should save and protect this promise. We should be honest and know the reality in what I said. It is important to deeply know the meaning of the journey.

"The Seventh Discourse: Concerning the Ḥadīth on Making the Five Prayers Obligatory on the Night Journey from the Ḥadīth Narrated by Ibn Malik" from *Spiritual Discourses in the Blessed Al-Aqṣā Mosque*[15] is read from the beginning.

Sidi gives the promise.

[15] *Spiritual Discourses in the Blessed al-Aqṣā Mosque*, p. 38.

The Divine Science of Pregnancy, Birth and Parenting

Tuesday, July 20, 2010 AM, USHS Year 1 Fall

لا إله إلا الله - لا إله إلا الله - لا إله إلا الله - محمد رسول الله عليه صلاة الله
لا إله إلا الله - لا إله إلا الله - لا إله إلا الله - ابراهيم رسول الله عليه صلاة الله
لا إله إلا الله - لا إله إلا الله - لا إله إلا الله - موسى رسول الله عليه صلاة الله
لا إله إلا الله - لا إله إلا الله - لا إله إلا الله - عيسى رسول الله عليه صلاة الله
اللهم انت السلام ومنك السلام و إليك يعود السلام
تباركت ربنا وتعاليت يا ذوالجلال والإكرام

Peace and mercy be upon you. Praise Allāh (ﷻ). Peace be upon our Prophet Muḥammad (ﷺ) and all of the prophets, messengers, the followers, gnostics (عليهم السلام) and all who know Allāh (ﷻ). We are knocking on Allāh's door (ﷻ) and we are His poor servants. We gave our promise to be His beloved. I ask Allāh (ﷻ) to bestow to you His mercy and His knowledge. Allāh (ﷻ) says:

> (I will teach) you that which you did not know before. (2:151)

His mercy upon you is great. This is a holy day. It is my honor to be among you. I can see that you are all the same. There is no discrimination between my sons and daughters. I wish for all people to be beloved brothers and sisters under the tent of Allāh (ﷻ), the tent that will protect you. Allāh (ﷻ) says:

> I will protect you. (see 5:67)
>
> I am the All-Hearer, All-Seer (see 4:58, 4:134, 17:1, 19:65, 20:56, 22:61, 22:75, 31:28, 40:20, 40:56, 42:11, 58:1)
>
> I am the Most Merciful, Most Compassionate.
> (see 1:1, 1:3, 2:163, 27:30, 41:2, 59:22)

I directed my heart and my spirit to all of you, asking Allāh (ﷻ) to look at you with His eyes full of mercy to protect you and to send down the angels (عليهم السلام) who Allāh (ﷻ) ordered us to invoke and to ask Allāh (ﷻ) for every good thing for you.

This lecture is about how Allāh (ﷻ) created the human being in the perfect shape. He created him in the picture that He wished. I would like to speak about how Allāh (ﷻ) created the human being through the Ḥadīth Qudsī directly from Allāh (ﷻ) to our Prophet (ﷺ).

Allāh (ﷻ) sent this ḥadīth down to the Prophet's heart (ﷺ) and this is a divine inspiration to the heart of the Prophet (ﷺ). My beloved Allāh (ﷻ) said to the Messenger of Allāh (ﷺ) that Allāh (ﷻ) will gather the human in the womb of the mother. The woman and the man will be together in a loud way. Each one of them will achieve the order of Allāh (ﷻ) when they are together and will be in a relationship that Allāh (ﷻ) allows. They will give the love to each other.

Allāh (ﷻ) created the gametes, the sperm and the eggs. The gametes and eggs of the woman contain millions of atoms that will create the human being. Allāh (ﷻ) will order the man to get the sperm and Allāh (ﷻ) will decree the creation of that time. No one knows about this moment, only Allāh (ﷻ). No one can understand or imagine the secret within the one sperm and one egg. Only Allāh (ﷻ) knows if the baby will be a male or a female.

As I told you, that there are millions of eggs and sperm; however, just one of each will come together and after that they will be in the womb of the mother for 40 days. All of us pass through this station. This station will continue and the sperm and the egg will meet each other during the forty-eight hours. When they are alive they will meet and know each other. Allāh (ﷻ) will order them to go and after forty days there will be a blood clot in the womb of the mother.

At this moment the building of Allāh (ﷻ) will start and Allāh (ﷻ) will send down many angels (ﷷ). Each angel (ﷷ) will be responsible for certain things within the man and the women. During the forty-eight hours that station will be for forty days and then after that the establishment of the baby will start. They will move to other stations. Therefore, after the blood clot it will then be a piece of meat. It is very small, only two centimeters. This station is also forty days. You now are at eighty days.

The first station is the blood clot then the second station is a piece of meat and the third station is after eighty days when He (ﷻ) will send out angels and the rūḥ, the spirit.

He (ﷻ) will send the spirit to this human being. The angels (عليهم السلام) will take this piece of meat with his hands and he will ask Allāh (ﷻ) if He wants this baby to be in this existence. If Allāh (ﷻ) wants this baby to be alive the angel will tell the other angel to write if he is a male or a female on fixed paper. He will ask Him how long he will be alive and when he will die. He will register if it is male or female and if this baby will be happy or sad.

This is a divine knowledge. Happiness or sadness has been written for this baby but Allāh (ﷻ) can erase it and give alternate orders to let him be happy here in a divine blink of Allāh (ﷻ). If you count eighty days and the other eighty days, the human being will be completed. He will have ears and hearing. He will have eyes and by the order of Allāh (ﷻ), he will have the parts that will be for his hands and his legs and everything will be within him. This divine view is the story of the creation of the baby in his mother's womb. It is the same thing with animals.

In the creation of a human being, it is not acceptable to kill a baby after it has been in the womb for four months. It is unacceptable to kill this baby because Allāh (ﷻ) sent His spirit to this baby and it would also be dangerous. There are some cases (in which it can be acceptable), for example, if the baby is not normal and there is a problem with this creation or if his mother will be in danger and may die. This is a different situation and it is acceptable to get rid of the baby. However, the decision should be made between both the man and the woman together.

If a woman gets rid of a baby without the permission of her husband, she will be considered to be making a mistake, because she does not know the meaning of this law. Many girls do this without getting permission from their husbands. She will be obligated to get rid of the baby, maybe because she will create a hardship with her family or with her community. This is an offensive thing, because this baby came in the right way. What is the mistake of this baby? If that happens, she should give a sacrifice to Allāh (ﷻ) asking for forgiveness, because she killed this spirit.

From where will this baby be fed? Allāh (ﷻ) created two veins for him. Those veins are attached to the stomach of the mother and they will be joined with other arteries. They will change when the baby breathes, and its food will not be blood after birth. It will change to be milk from the mother. This artery will be joined to other huge arteries. One artery will go to the right breast and the other will go to the left, because Allāh (ﷻ) decreed the baby's food. When the mother gives birth the milk will be ready for him.

The baby inside of the womb of his mother cannot talk; however, his spirit can speak. No one can understand him except Allāh (ﷻ) and the angels (ﷺ). The angels (ﷺ) let the baby make different movements.

After four months the baby will be completed. In the middle of the fifth month Allāh (ﷻ) will allow him to have concentration. When he is seven months old he will be completely perfect, his mind and feelings will be perfect. Everything will be perfect for him. He will have concentration. If the mother is sad, the baby will be sad. If the mother is happy, then the baby will be happy. If he listens to music, he will start to move and dance. He can understand because his spirit can understand and the music is food for the spirit and the body. This is a divine issue. Allāh (ﷻ) created you and perfected you in a perfect way.

After six months, he can recognize and feel. The first of the senses which the baby will gain is hearing. He will begin to hear. The next sense is from the eyes. He will not open his eyes until three to five days after birth. At birth he can see, but he cannot figure out pictures and shapes; he can only see shadows.

This is the divine science that Allāh (ﷻ) said to all of his prophets. The reason I am telling you this information is that you will be healers and if a pregnant lady comes asking for healing, you will have the knowledge about it so that you can try to heal this lady. Then the healer can put his hand in the correct and gentle way because she is pregnant and he will not offend the baby when he does healing with the mother.

You should ask the pregnant lady how many months she is and ask about the baby's movement. Be gentle when you touch the womb of the mother, because there is just two centimeters between the skin and the stomach and maybe he will be in a different direction. The womb of the mother will be his place and he is free to move in any direction. The movement of the baby is not from himself, but it is from the order of Allāh (ﷻ) to the angels (عليهم السلام) to let him move in this way or that way. The movement to the right and to the left and to the center is like exercise.

It is not like he is in a prison. Allāh (ﷻ) created him and the angels support him to move (عليهم السلام). He will move by the breath of the angels (عليهم السلام). This baby lives among the world of peace.

Allāh (ﷻ) says:

> (I) created you, fashioned you perfectly. (82:7)

He created everything in the perfect way.

We will describe what the breast of men and women hold. Allāh (ﷻ) created the liver. When Allāh (ﷻ) created the baby he placed him in the perfect situation. He covered his face with a very thin veil. He let the baby be comfortable in the womb, not be offended by the smell of the stomach.

After Allāh (ﷻ) put the cover on the baby to let him be comfortable, He created the liver as a recliner on the right side and the spleen like pillows on the other side to let the baby be comfortable. He let him breathe in the perfect way because the baby needs air, as he needs food.

After Allāh (ﷻ) created everything and all the parts, He ordered the heart to pump the blood and the lungs and all the parts in the exact quantities. Allāh (ﷻ) recovered all those parts and allowed the lungs to take air. Tell me who can create things such as this? Can anyone create things like this? No one can. Maybe someone would say they can, but no one can create things such as this. Those people who say, "I can create it," it is rubbish; they cannot create it. Ask them. Yes or no? This is the answer from the heart. Allāhu Akbar.

Then Allāh (ﷻ) will send his order to the angels (ﷺ). The physician thinks that he can take the baby from the mother, but it is a special moment. Who moves her? It is Allāh (ﷻ) who will order the angels (ﷺ) to let this baby to come out to this world, and He will carry the baby by the divine light from the angels (ﷺ).

Some women will have their babies standing in different positions. All women give birth only by the permission of Allāh (ﷻ).

Yes, Allāh (ﷻ) gave His knowledge to the physicians regarding the baby and how the baby moves his hands. There are a lot of physicians, both male and female, who are studying about the creation. It is important for the woman who wants to give birth to find a good doctor, either male or female, to help her give birth. The doctor should worship Allāh (ﷻ) and he should doctor this mother as if she were his daughter or sister. The physician should give love and care to the mother. If the nurse is good at her work, honest, loyal and having good knowledge, she can help this woman.

Some women want to give birth at home. She should select someone with knowledge who is perfect with her manners, medicine and are full of love. This mother is between Allāh's hands; if she were to make a mistake, she may cause a danger to the baby and to the mother. This is not a simple thing.

A man came to the Prophet and asked, "To whom should we be kind?" He told him, "Your mother." He asked this question three times and each time the Prophet answered, "Your mother." You should be kind to your mother. The next time he answered, "Your father."

The man asked why. The Prophet said, "Because your mother carried you in her body and you were fed through her blood. You were a part of her and without her food, which Allāh (ﷻ) provided for you, you would not be alive. She was between death and life with the pain that she had giving birth to you."

During the birth, He will cover her with His protection and He will support her. No one can imagine this pain and this woman never has never had this pain before. After she gives birth, she will take you between her arms and forget the pain. She will forget everything and look happily at you. She will not remember any of the pain, because Allāh (ﷻ) sends down the recovery through an angel (عليه السلام) who will clean everything and support her for no longer than two days.

The baby will be guided by the angels (عليهم السلام), by the divine knowledge. He will wash his face and will guide him to the breast of the mother. He will look to the baby for him to take the breast by his lips, and Allāh (ﷻ) taught him how to suck the milk. No one else taught him, only Allāh (ﷻ). Allāh (ﷻ) will open his eyes and the baby will see and know where his food is. Who can do that? This is the glory of Allāh (ﷻ).

He created you and then He gave you strength in your legs and hands. After one month, the baby will recognize who this is and that is and he will recognize his mother and his father. This is the divine tool through which Allāh (ﷻ) will send to his eyes and ears a precise, divine magnetic attraction to his mother and his father.

I would like to tell you that I am giving you this lecture because of its relation to your job. It is holy to have babies and to raise children from birth. The mother should protect her heart and body in order to be a pure heart and body. She should protect herself by following the orders of Allāh (ﷻ). It is not acceptable for her to sleep with other men because she will break the promise of the divine. She will walk on the path that Allāh (ﷻ) will never accept. She should be patient and follow Allāh's orders. Allāh (ﷻ) says to keep your sexual parts pure. He asks us to be pure.

In the divine law Allāh (ﷻ) says to all the prophets that He ordered us to protect our bodies and our selves. He wants us to be pure in order to help ourselves in this life. If you are not married, you should protect yourself. You should not be in this relationship in the wrong way because Allāh (ﷻ) created you and He will protect you. This is also true for the man. The man should keep his heart and his body pure. This is a great responsibility

Allāh (ﷻ) said:

> I am the Best of Protectors
> and I am the Most Merciful of the Merciful. (see 12:64)

He will cover her with His protection and He will support her. You should know that and I see that it is my responsibility to express how Allāh (ﷻ) created you and how He praises you on how to be a mother or a father. It is a great responsibility on our hands.

The law of this lower world destroys families. One hundred years ago the families in America lived together in the same house. They sat together at the same table. The father and mother took care of the family. Is that right? Your sons and daughters need your support and care. Even if they are eighteen they still need your help. It is not like the people living nowadays. Even the Prophet ʿĪsā (Jesus) (ﷺ) ordered us to be pure and ordered us to take care of our children. How did it come to be that our daughters are again between the hands of the lower, disobedient people? Allāh (ﷻ) sent down the law to protect you and to protect what Allāh (ﷻ) gave you.

What is happening now in the world? There are a many hardships and disasters now. Why? The human being, both male and female, will bring other human beings as their sons and daughters. The mother and father have the responsibility to love their children and to do what is best. Their sons and daughters should listen and obey their parents.

Do not believe that there is anyone else who will love you more than your mother and father. Your parents hope that you will be happy in your life. They brought you into this life and it is their responsibility to protect you, because Allāh (ﷻ) will ask them why they did not give you love and protection.

You should not say no to your father or mother. If you see your mother or father do something wrong you should advise them, but you should listen to the guidance of your mother or father. When the daughter is eighteen then she will be mature enough. If she wants to do something she should go to the mother or father and ask them what they think. She should go to her parents first and then ask other people. There is no one who will give you more loyal guidance then your parents. It is for this reason that many offenses occur, and it is the children's fault. It is a situation of the separation between the parents and the children. Your mother and father have a deep experience of this life.

You are a young man or daughter and you do not have that experience. You need your mother and father all the time, even if you are eighteen years old. You will be responsible in front of Allāh (ﷻ) with regard to your deeds. Young man and young woman, you will be responsible to Allāh (ﷻ) if you do not listen to your father and mother. You will be responsible for your faults.

You can see millions of divorces now with young girls in every country. However, in the Middle East I was a judge for thirty-six years and I only granted a divorce one time. In most of the marriages the children listened to their parents. What has happened? The parents know if he or she is good or not. It is not only through talking, but they make sure to know everything in order to be certain that he or she is acceptable, honest and sincere for the other. Are they going to be a real beloved for each other?

One beloved came to me and said, "Sidi, I have a beloved and he likes me and he is all right." I asked her if he follows Allāh (ﷻ). Is he honest, sincere and serving to you? Does he walk straight? Does he contain you? Does he love you or does he like to make pain? These are the questions I ask and I bring them both in front of each other with two people witnessing. If they say yes, then I tell them to write down what they say. I like to be a protector.

I then ask if he is acceptable, sincere and honest. Can he contain you and feed you? I ask him what his work is. Does he work or not? If he does not work I tell him to go and find work first. Then come and see me. How can you feed and serve her? You like to use her for what you want. No! This is important. However, when you go to a judge now, he does not care about that. The sharī'a, the divine law, asks every single thing. She is a human being and he wants her to be a wife for him. I ask him to tell me why he wants her for his wife. I care about what he says.

He says, "Sidi, I love her." I tell him, "That is not enough. Maybe you will change that love, break it up and make her sad. If you love her and you are sincere, honest and you serve her, then sign here." Then the two witnesses come. People cannot play with this state. She can bring him to court. This is the law of Allāh (ﷻ). It is not from us. Allāh (ﷻ) says to be free and choose what you want. However, it is not easy to choose what you want.

First, I like to ask him these questions. If he is acceptable then bismillāh. This is the life. However, if they go and he is with her maybe five years then what happens? Five years but for what reason, I do not know. Maybe he will cheat and love another lady. Then she will cry and ask what has happened with me and this boy? This is a very delicate thing. The love is very delicate. It is very important. This is the life. How can he break her heart? Also, there are many ladies who break the heart of the husband. What is the reason?

When anyone says that her beloved is bad then I put it on paper and get her beloved. I tell him what she said and if he says, "No," then I send them away for one week. Then I call for the neighbors and the friends to come and I ask them to tell me everything that they have heard about their neighbors. I tell them to put their hand on the Qurʾān in order to speak the truth and I ask them to tell me everything that they know. Allāh (ﷻ) judges them. I bring one person and when it is enough for that one person then I bring another person for the man. For the woman I need two ladies and I ask, "What have they heard about this person?"

Then, I bring the man to me and if he begins to lie then I tell him that he is not right and I bring in witnesses. He begins to move and he asks me, "What happened?" I tell him that this is what he is. I tell him that this is the chance for him to make peace now because they both would like to. They both must say astaghfiru-llāh al-ʿaḍhīm and make repentance and promise to love each other and serve each other as Allāh (ﷻ) wants.

When a person puts his hand on the Qurʾān and swears to tell the truth and he lies, then maybe Allāh (ﷻ) will send something when he is driving his car. Maybe someone will hit him and then he dies. It is important to care about Allāh (ﷻ). If you care about your beloved and she also cares about you, Allāh (ﷻ) will make you safe and happy. I only had one case in thirty-six years where I gave a divorce.

After that time, I was the judge of judges. I did not let any judge play games. It was very strong. If he did not come at the right time then I judged him. Allāh (ﷻ) wanted him to serve the people. When I came and I saw a long line in his court, I asked why the judge was not there. Then, I sat in this chair and when he came I looked at my watch and I saw that it had been one hour. I asked him why he had not come. "Why do you keep the people waiting for you?" Then he said, "Astag͟hfiru-llāh al-ʿaḍẖīm." I said, "I will accept it this time but after this I will not accept it." He was here to serve the people and care about the people.

This is not only true for this case but for everyone. Allāh (ﷻ) gives you work. Do not take money without work. Be honest, sincere and serve the people without separation.

This is the human being and Allāh (ﷻ) said:

> Truly, I am going to create a human being from clay. (38:71)

He does not need to look for you. Allāh (ﷻ) likes you to follow Him; then He loves you and then what you give He gives. This is what Allāh (ﷻ) says. I hope you understand what I say and what Allāh (ﷻ) teaches us from the prophets (ﷺ) to serve Allāh (ﷻ) with what He sent us. It is a message from Him (ﷻ) to His prophets (ﷺ). Āmīn

This is now the time for the students of healing in the university to give a promise to Allāh (ﷻ) to follow the teachings that come from Allāh (ﷻ) though the prophets (ﷺ) and to not use anything, only His teachings. You promise to be gentle, honest, sincere, real and to carry the love. This is a promise for Allāh (ﷻ). It is not from me, for I am a very poor slave, but I care and would like to see all of my beloveds sincere and honest and for them to trust Allāh (ﷻ). Do not stop with the pictures. Do not say, "I see Allāh (ﷻ)." No.

Allāh (ﷻ) sees when you make istikhāra.[16] As I explained, when you see that you would like to ask for something you should do wuḍuʾ and then

[16] The istikhāra is a practice we use in order to receive guidance from Allāh (ﷻ). As Sidi says here, start by making 2 voluntary rakʿāh (in addition to the obligatory ṣalāh) and recite a special prayer. For the exact instructions according to Sidi, contact the Shadhiliyya Sufi Center.

perform two rakʿāh. When you are praying, standing or in prostration, open your heart and ask Allāh (ﷻ) what is inside your heart. When someone asks Allāh (ﷻ) about his needs, Allāh (ﷻ) will answer him. There is a special duʿāʾ that I gave to ask what is inside your heart. When you are in wuḍuʾ, pray two rakʿāh and then ask what is in your heart.

Every prophet made the istikhāra. What are the signs you see in your dreams? What is the right time for making the duʿāʾ for the istikhāra? The right time is one hour before fajr. This is the right time.

The dream you have after making the istikhāra is not a regular dream. It is direct and everything you see means that Allāh (ﷻ) accepts your duʿāʾ. Some of the signs may be that you see a garden, trees or something. You may see a river and birds. You may see a person you love, and sometimes at that time the Prophet (ﷺ) may come if you are very holy and straight and if you walk straight like Allāh (ﷻ) wants. You see the Prophet (ﷺ) and he speaks direct to you or you may see one of the Prophets like Mūsā (Moses) (عليه السلام), ʿĪsā (عليه السلام) or Nūḥ (Noah) (عليه السلام). They are very holy. You may see one who loves Allāh (ﷻ) and who loves you. He will talk to you. This is right.

Maybe you will see something very dark. Maybe you will see huge animals or a big ocean coming to take you. This is what you like to make. Stop. However, if you see light, know that this is really the light of the Prophet (ﷺ) and that he is talking to you. Any prophet can visit and give you the true love of Allāh (ﷻ) and can help you.

For you to say, "I see Allāh (ﷻ)," no. Allāh (ﷻ) sent the prophets (عليهم السلام) and He spoke directly to Mūsā (عليه السلام) when he went to the mountain and He also gave him signs. This is a prophet and an ʿawliya, a perfect one who we would like to be like. Maybe he comes and he goes. This means that He accepts what you ask. This is the sign.

Sidi gives the promise.

Everything is from the Love

"A Drop of the Love" and Music
July 24, 2010, Portland

لا إله إلا الله – لا إله إلا الله – لا إله إلا الله – محمد رسول الله عليه صلاة الله
لا إله إلا الله – لا إله إلا الله – لا إله إلا الله – ابراهيم رسول الله عليه صلاة الله
لا إله إلا الله – لا إله إلا الله – لا إله إلا الله – موسى رسول الله عليه صلاة الله
لا إله إلا الله – لا إله إلا الله – لا إله إلا الله – عيسى رسول الله عليه صلاة الله
اللهم انت السلام ومنك السلام و إليك يعود السلام
تباركت ربنا وتعاليت يا ذوالجلال والإكرام

On this holy day, I am among you. I am here in my form, in my body. But when I leave and return to the Holy City, al-Quds, Jerusalem, I want you to know that I will keep my heart and my spirit praying for you and for everyone who is crying from the deep suffering in this world. I cry from my deepest spirit. I ask Allāh (ﷻ) to send His peace and His mercy and His love and His freedom and His justice to all people everywhere.

I ask that He help those who are crying from deep sickness everywhere. I ask that He send angel healers (ؑ) for everyone who is crying from deep sickness, that He clean this heart, clean this land, clean all the earth everywhere from the bad sicknesses, from the bad diseases and from chemicals.

I pray for Allāh (ﷻ) to stop war everywhere and to send the wind of peace. I want to see His flag of unity go directly to every heart. I ask Him to stop those who play games and those who are not right, and I ask Him to help those who do walk though this order that helps people become pure and learn to help each other. I am sure of what He says:

> And when My slaves ask you concerning Me,
> then (answer them), I am indeed near.
> I respond to prayers when they call upon Me. (2:186)
>
> I am inside his heart.
> I hear everything he asks and I hear his crying.
> I accept him if he has a deep heart
> and if he makes the real prostration.
> I am inside everything, and everywhere he looks, he finds Me.

Raise your hands and ask Allāh (ﷻ), and then let Him answer your supplications. Āmīn. Be honest and ask with deep sincerity for Allāh (ﷻ), for He hears you, He sees you and He is listening to you, yā Allāh (ﷻ).

In this place, in this time, in this room, there are angels (ﷺ) listening to the teaching, praising Allāh (ﷻ) and remembering Allāh (ﷻ), helping to clean everyone who is honest and sincere. This is a very holy time. Say:

Allāhu, Allāhu, Allāhu, Allāhu, Allāhu, Allāhu, Allāhu, Allāh.

Lā ʾilāha ʾilla-llāh, Lā ʾilāha ʾilla-llāh, Lā ʾilāha ʾilla-llāh, Lā ʾilāha ʾilla-llāh,
Lā ʾilāha ʾilla-llāh, Lā ʾilāha ʾilla-llāh, Lā ʾilāha ʾilla-llāh.

Oh, Allāh (ﷻ),
You answer our supplications,
You Answer our questions and our needs.
We are knocking on Your doors,
so please, Allāh, answer us.
You are the Forgiver, so please, Allāh (ﷻ),
accept us and answer our supplications.
Allāh!

My Master,
You are the essence of our existence.
We are Your mirrors and we are knocking on Your door.
You know what is going on inside us.
You know everything.
We ask You and You are the Only One.
Please, please, Allāh (ﷻ), answer our supplications.
We are between Your hands.
We are Your poor servants.
We are praying for those poor, poor people.
They are praying for You, for Your essence.
for You created us and You provide for us.
We direct our faces toward You,
asking You to heal us, to heal our daughters
and our beloveds all around the world.
We complain of our weakness to You and our poverty, Allāh (ﷻ).
We take refuge in You.

You are the Only One.
Please, Allāh (ﷻ), answer our questions and our supplications.
Yā Allāh (ﷻ).
Āmīn.

Excuse me, my beloveds, my heart is crying for those who cry from the deep suffering in the whole world. Āmīn, Āmīn, Āmīn.

I start in this holy place at this holy time for everybody to cry to Allāh (ﷻ). So who will answer our supplications? You are the only One Who Answers Supplications. The honest worshippers should not have any fear in their hearts and they will never be sad. Āmīn.

Al-ḥamdu li-llāh, praise Allāh (ﷻ). Allāh (ﷻ) accepts our prayers and our supplications and He accepts us among His worshippers. Āmīn. So please excuse me. I did that obeying His order.

On this day, we will enter through a huge door, a big door: the door of love. Love is the first thing to enter to Allāh (ﷻ) and to knock on Allāh's doors. Allāh's doors are open to you. Allāh (ﷻ) told Hārūn (Aaron) (ﷺ) and Mūsā (ﷺ):

> I hear and see (everything). (20:46)

He hears our supplications and He sees us. Now we are in the ocean of the love of Allāh (ﷻ). Prepare your hearts. Be honest. Don't lose this chance in this time of mercy. The angels (ﷺ) and the spirits of the prophets (ﷺ) are around us.

Be with me and my heart and my spirit because I am with you. I will give everything as a sacrifice, just for you to solve your problem. Ask Allāh (ﷻ) to help you, to let you be stable in your religion, standing, praying, fasting and prostrating. Purify everything that Allāh (ﷻ) has provided to you.

I will start with love, al-maḥabba. What is maḥabba, love? It is the first degree. It is the degree to enter the presence of the Truth (al-Ḥaqq). First of all, you should clean your tongue, your hearts, your minds and your selves, because Allāh (ﷻ) says:

> ...except the one who brings Allāh a whole heart.
> And Paradise will be brought near to the pious. (26:89-90)

One of the gnostics (ﷺ) said:

> You can find Allāh's existence everywhere,
> even if you escape somewhere deep within the earth.
> He will hear you and He will see you.
> He sees you and He knows what you are doing.
> He can see your hand and you can see.

I swear by His name that He loves you. Why do you turn away from His love? Why don't you listen to what He says? Why haven't you obeyed Him?

Come to the mercy of Allāh (ﷻ). Clean your hearts. Clean your spirits to be near Him in His place, to be in the ocean of love, the entire love.

He is the Manifester in everything and you are His mirror. So how can you be unable to see Him? You are the follower, the traveler to Allāh (ﷻ). He said on the tongue of His Prophet (ﷺ):

> I was a hidden treasure and I loved to be known.

By you, this manifestation, Allāh (ﷻ) revealed Himself in the human being. They know Him. Each person who doesn't live a true life full of love, love for the human being and for Allāh (ﷻ), giving everything for others if they need help...

When a person gives everything for the poor and sick people this is provision from Allāh (ﷻ) to him. Allāh (ﷻ) has allowed you to help others. This is a gift from Allāh (ﷻ) to you and to others, and this is a holy thing.

Do you want to live in the ocean and swim in the ocean of love? Come to the mercy of Allāh (ﷻ). The door is open. The door is open. There is no separation. In the world of Allāh (ﷻ) there is no separation or discrimination. He says, "Al-ḥamdu li-llāh rabbīl ʿalamīn," He is the Lord of all people. Those fragrances are full of peace and love. This is what we want: to say and to teach and to translate on this earth.

Allāh (ﷻ) says that this earth will be made into a Garden for all of His good people, good worshippers. Allāh (ﷻ) created the earth as a place for people to live in peace. If we want to stop disasters, wars, earthquakes, volcanoes from happening, we should return back to Allāh (ﷻ). There is no refuge other than Allāh (ﷻ). There's nowhere to go, just Allāh (ﷻ). By praying, worshipping and following the orders of Allāh (ﷻ).

We are the son of Sufism. Allāh (ﷻ) selected us to be His beloved because we follow the orders of Allāh (ﷻ). I am poor. I don't have anything in my hands. There's no separation between me and you. We are one body, one heart, one spirit, all of these manifestations of Allāh (ﷻ). This is a divine manifestation.

Even though we are different in our colors and languages, there is one language of Allāh (ﷻ). You can recognize it with your heart—it is one language. You can understand. We can understand each other with the language of the spirit and the heart. This is the highest station. It is not illusion. It is not pictures and imagination. It is not the words of Iblīs or his followers. The entire religion is the religion of unity.

Yes, people say and do anything they want. We don't want to put people in prison. We want them to obtain freedom, let them say and do anything. But, they didn't understand that Allāh (ﷻ) says:

> Not a word does he (or she) utter
> but there is a watcher by him ready (to record it). (50:18)

Allāh (ﷻ) says:

> Judge yourself before you are judged.

The lyrics of the music
are bold, italicized and indented.
The unpublished reading
"A Drop of the Love" is in bold text.
Sidi's live commentary is in plain text.
A video containing a few minutes of this teaching
is on YouTube under "Drop of the Love"

The reading begins, "I like to send the essence of the secret love through the essence of my holy spirit to explain to my beloveds the meaning of love. It's important to walk when you are ready. If you're hungry, to taste the drop from Him. I want to help you understand how to change everything in the life, to know the real meaning and how to be a real beloved for Allāh (ﷻ). Then, we can sing His song like Dāwūd (David) did, to explain to all those who haven't tasted..."

To hear the song of Dāwūd (ﷷ) and I sing his song, which is no more than the song of Allāh (ﷻ).

The reading continues, "(I want) to explain for all those who haven't tasted, how to be a real beloved for Allāh (ﷻ), how to become very pure and carry the message of His love, this love of Allāh (ﷻ). Then you will become clean and you will know how to walk like Allāh (ﷻ) wants you to walk. If you follow the real message you can reach the real knowing, how to give what Allāh (ﷻ) wants you to give for all those who are crying everywhere. Then, in that moment, he knows how to make the real prostration in the mosque of the love.

When I say, 'mosque' I mean He changes his heart because he is the throne of God. For that, he makes prostration for Allāh (ﷻ) through his pure heart, because Allāh (ﷻ) rubs and erases everything from before in that life, and he walks very deeply with the real medicine, the holy medicine, when he has the deep sincerity. For this reason, I like to give these words for all of you who love Allāh (ﷻ).

If you're ready to make the real wedding with your beloved God...are you ready, my beloveds, to make the real wedding with Allāh (ﷻ)? Then this song is like a yearning to move you from this material world to a more subtle world to clean yourself. You will become purified. Your prostration will be accepted.

The Great Beloved One will be very close to His beloved when he is in prostration, because when prostrating, in his heart there is no space for anything else. There is no space for humanity or anything in the world, because God has cleaned him to be one of the real beloveds for Him through what he gives. For that reason, I send my voice for all my beloveds, for all people, to come and make the real, real sajda. The food for the heart comes only through His spirit and His heart.

If you give everything that Allāh (ﷻ) gives you for the face of Allāh (ﷻ), God will change you from the material body to the pure body, more than that, the secret, to make you nothing but complete light. Then, you will begin to see what your real food is. If you love Allāh (ﷻ), then Allāh (ﷻ) is the real food for you. Then, you will begin to sing the song of the love, peace and mercy for everyone, without separation. In that moment it is important to care, to not open your door to anyone except Allāh (ﷻ).

My beloveds, it's important to follow all of His practices. Then you will see what Allāh (ﷻ) makes, for this is the real Garden. For that reason, the Prophet (ﷺ) says:

> Those who believe in Him are in the Garden now.

So pray, pray my beloveds. Keep your remembrance until you see yourself in His Paradise.

This is some of the deep meaning of the love. This is like a drop from the ocean, so excuse me, I keep many things inside, but everything comes in its time. Now we will begin the song, now you can hear some of what I explained from this song."

Music plays.

> *Let me hear about my Love.*
> *The conversation of my Love is my drink.*
> *I enjoy this drink, the wine of the love.*
> *Yes, come, mention the One I love, even if I hear His name in a dream.*
> *Because the conversation between me and my Beloved is my drink.*

The reading continues, "To begin, I say, if you want to be with Allāh (ﷻ), then I would like to give you a special gift through this song. In the beginning, I give you a drop of this love. I give this in a special cup to make you absent, to change you from everything that you have, to leave the past and discharge it and to go deep, my children. Then I give you to drink from a drop of His love. Please do not go far away. Be ready.

After you have all the sincerity..."

You are ready?

Audience: Yes!

Allāh!

The reading continues, "After you have all the sincerity, all the surrender, when you do not try to surrender to anything else or to your nafs, but surrender completely to the One you love, who created you to be pure, this is what I mean by 'be ready.' I would like to give you my holy cup, full of my essence of the deep secret love.

Then Allāh (ﷻ) will change your eyes and your ears. Everything in you, He will change. He will change you and bring you from this world to another world, to the world of the love.

This means the world of the real life and this means to be with Him. So if you love Him, then it is important to follow everything He says. Because every beloved listens and obeys every order when He sends it. So are you ready for that?"

Yes!

The reading continues, "If you are ready, then the water of His love is ready now. If you love me, follow me and listen. You have asked me many times, 'I would like to see Allāh (ﷻ).' Well, Allāh (ﷻ) is not absent, He is everywhere. He is in everything.

Do not keep your ears from hearing and your eyes blind. He wants you to be with Him and to follow Him and then you can understand everything. Always, Allāh sends love. He is always sending love. He never stops. He opens His arms for you. His arms are open for eternity. He says:

> Come, my beloveds.
> I am ready for everything that you give.
> So why do you go far away?
> You have been far away from your beloved God (ﷻ) long enough.

My beloved (Shaykh Tuhamī) is saying, 'Give me a drop of my Beloved.' This is not like a drop of the wine that people know. A drop of this wine is different. It makes you absent from this material world."

Allāh!

The reading continues, "Be ready, for this drop gives you the deep essence of knowing. It makes your eyes open so that you can see what Allāh (ﷻ) wants to show you.

> *At the same time, you will be drunk with His love.*

This means that Allāh (ﷻ) changes this drop of wine to be water, to be life, to be the real life. This is what I mean.

> *Yes, answer me, answer me.*
> *Allāh (ﷻ), please give to me, answer me.*
> *Please give me the words of my Beloved*
> *and what He orders me.*

I am ready, with Allāh's help."

Music plays.

The reading continues, "When He talks with me He gives me to be with Him completely and to understand what He says, and I am always ready to drink. I don't speak another word after that, for His word is enough for me, because it comes from the one who loves me and has cared about me all my life. Because I am in that case, I am absent from everything that people see, because I am with Him. Through my body, through my heart, through my self, through my spirit, there is no choice for me."

This is my situation. I am absent from everything that people see, because I am with Him in my body, heart, self and spirit. I have no choice. It is not easy to be in this situation if you do not surrender completely to your Beloved. He wants you to give a special sacrifice to your Beloved who created you. Listen to understand what He means. Allāhu Akbar.

The reading continues, "I just want to be alone with my beloved God (ﷻ) in the real life. This is the life I am waiting for—to not look left or right but to be only between His arms. Yā Allāh (ﷻ). Yā Allāh (ﷻ).

That is what I wait for. I wait to drink from His source and to swim in His ocean through my following of what He says. Yes, yes."

Music plays.

> *My Lover, my Beloved, my Spirit, my Love.*
> *Mention the name of the One I Fall In Love With even in my dreams.*
> *Let me hear His name.*

The reading continues, "My hearing witnesses that I love You. The dream that comes to my eyes, to my ears, to my heart, all of them witness that I love You. My ears, my eyes, everything that God (ﷻ) gave me are my witness that I do not return back. Always, I keep my deep spirit with my Beloved who loves me, Allāh (ﷻ). Even if I am far away and I do not see Him, He does not go far away. He never leaves me, not for one moment. This is a chance for me to be with Him. This is the real wedding.

It is my pleasure to hear remembrance within my witnessing and within my love. I am very lucky that Allāh (ﷻ) took me into His arms and that He supports me in obeying His orders to be always be in His eternal world. This is my pleasure and this is my hope and this is my end and this is my goal, that He puts me in front of His eyes and takes care of me. It is my deep wish to see all of you who love Allāh (ﷻ), everyone, in this holy station."

I like to see aaaaallll the world dance with each other. Real beloveds, real wedding for Allāh (ﷻ), for all the beloveds who love Allāh (ﷻ) and live in the ocean of His love.

The reading continues, "I want them all to reach and to hear the divine station, for Allāh (ﷻ) wants to position all of His creatures in this station. If they obey His orders (ﷻ) and the orders carried out by all the prophets (ﷺ), and if they carry the message of unity through the love that Allāh (ﷻ) gifted us..."

To be clean gives life to you and to everyone who is in this state, in this place and everywhere.

The reading continues, "He loved us, so He gave us this gift and so we love Him and obey Him."

He loves you and you love Him and you will be in His presence of love all the time. The real life is within Him and to follow Him, to obey Him, to be between His hands as He wishes. Because He says:

> I will be with you everywhere and anywhere. (20:46 and Tafsir)

This is the truth. How do you walk to Allāh (ﷻ)? This is the walking. I have explained this in all my books. This is what you need to know. If you speak from an ugly mind, you will not be able to reach Allāh (ﷻ). You will forget Him and you will turn away from Him. You will leave His Garden and you will go into the material world, the rubbish world, the recycle bin.

Allāh (ﷻ) wants to give you sweets, but you do not want them. What are you trying to say? You claim that you are a slave, but you do not follow His orders. You do not follow the commands that He sent down to His prophets and messengers (ﷺ).

You say you are a lover but you kill? You say you are a lover but you are a thief? What is that? Return back to Allāh (ﷻ)! The cure, the healing, is in Allāh (ﷻ). He provides you with everything. After that, how can you disobey Allāh (ﷻ) and follow the shayṭān, Iblīs? Allāh (ﷻ) says:

> (Escape to) Allāh, the true Guardian-Protector. (Tafsir of 2:257)

Allāh (ﷻ) is the supporter of those who are honest. Allāh (ﷻ) will forbid those who disobey Him from tasting the love. They will not be able to taste the love. Those who love Allāh (ﷻ), those who follow His divine law, will be under the tent of Allāh (ﷻ). They will be in the Garden with close branches where you can always find His provision.

> Say: 'If you love Allāh (ﷻ) then follow me.' (3:31)

The reading continues, "Allāh (ﷻ) gives me this special gift, Allāh (ﷻ), the only truth, al-Ḥaqq, He gave me a message for those who have already heard the divine call, but disobeyed. I hope and I ask Allāh (ﷻ) to open their hearts, their spirits and their minds to be among those who receive His mercy and are purified, because His message is the message of the Most Compassionate, the Most Merciful."

Music plays.

> *My love, my Spirit.*
> *By mentioning the name of the One I love, I will have eternal life.*

The reading continues, "When you mention the name of Allāh (ﷻ) with sincerity in your heart, it is not just your tongue that says the name—every part of you is saying the name, your twenty-seven trillion cells are saying the name."

Music plays.

The one who blames me because I want to close to Allāh (ﷻ),
I don't care about him,
Because I want to be close to Allāh.

The reading continues, "Please, Allāh (ﷻ), give me Your eternal love and let all Your other beloveds continue their lives as You wish, not as they wish. Most of the time they ask You for Your care because they're children at Your table and they're thirsty and hungry. They need food, but not the food of the material world.

People eat when they're hungry, but what they need is the real knowledge, the knowledge that will help them obey You through Your love. For Allāh (ﷻ), You are the Most Generous.

My beloveds, keep repeating, keep mentioning and keep remembering. Keep giving the water of life to your hearts and your spirits so that you can continue to be in Allāh's order, the divine order He commands us to follow.

It is the holy order to carry Your message and to save all the people from suffering around the world, and not only this world, but in all of Your worlds that You have created and given the real life. You asked and ordered them to carry the flags of happiness, pleasure and spirit, which will send Your love to their hearts, for You are our love. You are our Lord (ﷻ). Oh, my Lord (ﷻ).

I will not listen to people who say many different things, who try to distort the orders of Allāh (ﷻ) or make the orders of Allāh (ﷻ)..."

They live in illusion, in pictures that they talk about with false tongues. This is not what Allāh (ﷻ) wants. He wants you to throw your self and your heart and your spirit between the arms of Allāh (ﷻ) under His religion of unity. He wants you to follow everything that He says and then you will be a pure one.

Do not choose another way, my children. Do not choose dark and false ways. Be in the ocean of your Beloved, under His command, under what He says for you, because He cares about you. He wants you to live in the way that He wants for you. Then you will always be in His ocean, full of love. This is the life for you, my children.

The reading continues, "I will open my heart and my spirit to everyone who wants life. This life has already been given by You and the provision comes from You.

Many, many thanks Allāh (ﷻ), for You gave me the water of mercy. I ask You to accept my supplication and to give this holy water of mercy to others to allow them to live good lives.

Oh my beloveds, let us hear beautiful melodies. Let all of the people hear this beautiful music, Allāh (ﷻ). These are the prayers that You command us to pray and we obey You, as You wish."

The music, the essence of the music through the love is the real food for your spirits. It helps you to travel very quickly. In one moment you are in His Garden. If you do this, you know what I mean. I open the door for you. This is what Allāh (ﷻ) says. He says, "Come. Come to My Paradise!" He opens the door. He says, "Be in my Garden now, don't wait." Your beloved is waiting to make a real wedding for you.

This is the real life. There is no death, just life, if you follow what He says. But if you drink the dirty water, then how can you be in the real life? No one can. This is the real death. There is no life if you are not sincere.

It is the water of Allāh, at-tawḥīd, to say: Lā ʾilāha ʾilla-llāh. Do not just say it with your tongue but say it with your spirit. Use what He gave you like what He wants. Use your hands, your legs, your mind and your hearts only for what Allāh (ﷻ) has ordered. I want you to follow what He sent through His beloved prophets (عليهم السلام). Then, my children, you are happy.

Do not think you will die. If you die within Allāh by following His orders and the prophets, it is life. This I the real life of love. When you are under the tents of all the prophets and messengers (عليهم السلام), you will be with Allāh (ﷻ). His Prophet (ﷺ) says:

> Those who believe in Him are in the Garden now.

It's as quick as the blink of an eye. If you are sincere, honest, if you are with Allāh (ﷻ), in just one blink of an eye you will be with Him. Allāh (ﷻ) will accept you. Yes.

The reading continues, "When I follow what Allāh (ﷻ) asks of me and I avoid what Allāh (ﷻ) prohibits, my hearing will remain divine, and my seeing will always be divine, and I will hear everything that Allāh (ﷻ) says and I will be a giver. I will be giving all the time, but this giving is not from me."

Allāh says:

> Remember Me, I will remember you,
> and be grateful to Me and never be ungrateful to Me. (2:152)

> If you give thanks, I will give you more, but if you are thankless, truly My punishment is severe, indeed. (14:7)

The reading continues, "I will be giving all the time, but this giving is not from me; it is from my Lord who ordered me to obey Him. I say, 'Yes, I hear and I obey, my Lord. Please forgive us and we all return back to You.'

Oh Allāh (ﷻ), please keep this vision and witnessing in truth, for I continually hear everything You send to Your prophets and messengers (ﷺ). This is my life—this is the prayer, the ṣalāh, that You commanded me to follow. This prayer is the connection.

So I direct My face to You, Allāh (ﷻ). Please don't keep me distant, Don't cut off this prayer and please inspire me with all the knowledge. Send it to my heart to let me live an eternal life in Your holy world, for I want to see all of the worlds, everyone in this world and in other worlds that I've never seen. I want to see them singing the melody of love, the melody of peace, the melody of mercy, the melody of freedom, for all those melodies will obey You. I want to hear the melody of justice because You are the Most Just. You tell us, as Sayyidinā Muḥammad (ﷺ) said:

> All creatures are the children of Allāh (ﷻ),
> and the most beloved to Him
> are the ones who are most beneficial to His children.

I obey these words and I prostrate toward You. These words come through the mouth of our beloved Prophet (ﷺ). There is no discrimination between all the people. Āmīn."

Music plays.

The reading continues, "Please, Allāh (ﷻ), let my ears and my heart and my eyes be ready to accept You. Let me always hear these divine orders, these eternal orders, because this is the secret of my life. Even if these orders come in my dreams, I need them, and I don't want to be away from the love that You send me.

Even though this may bother others, those who mistreat people and deal with them badly, those who inflict suffering, I'm asking Allāh (ﷻ) to return them back to You, to give them mercy and understanding. This is my religion, this is the religion that You gave to me.

All these beautiful melodies, all these gifts that you gave to me...my spirit is overflowing and all the worlds are listening. I'm overjoyed with the beauty of this song, so I ask You to give all the people the beauty of this melody and to let them see You in everything that they look upon through Your name 'the Manifest (aḍh-Ḍhāhir).'

I ask You, Allāh (ﷻ), to let them hear the song of love through Your name, for my heart and my spirit don't know any quarreling with others. You send the light to all creatures by sending down the water. I mean by water when You said in the holy Quran:

> And We have made from water every living thing. (21:30)

Water here means life, the life that is full of everything.

I'm just a poor servant, for without You I am nothing. I was nothing and by You I'm everything. This, my beloveds, is the secret of my existence. Because of that I repeat: You sent all of these songs to all of Your messengers and prophets (ﷺ), and so I praise and glorify You with these melodies. I love those who brought these songs to us to help people life happily in this life. I hope that they will follow these melodies we received from all of the messengers and prophets (ﷺ) and that they will obey them.

Maybe, one day, I will finish this commentary, but I'm still with Allāh (ﷻ) and right now nothing is coming from me. Continue. Bismi-llāh. Continue, this is for you."

Music plays.

> *I love with two kinds of love.*
> *One of them is because I love You and one is because You deserve this love.*

Allāh (ﷻ) is the Only One who exists.

The reading continues, "I don't care. All the people advise me, the evil ones and the shayṭān, and I promise I will never, ever listen to those

voices. Those who try to take us away from our Beloved are making noise all the time. They want to be in their horrible situation."

No one can change me from the heart of my Beloved Allāh (ﷻ)! Without doubt He is my Beloved, al-ḥamdu li-llāh.

The reading continues, "They choose this and we let them know and we try to transmit the message of the prophets to them, but they refuse to accept it."

If I am with Allāh (ﷻ) completely, sacrificing everything for what He wants from me, He will not discharge me for one moment from the real world that He created. This is the case for every beloved. Choose for yourself. You have complete freedom, not the freedom of those who use false freedom. In the real freedom life is always for you when you remember His name and you are with Him.

You are not an easy one. You have a deep connection with your beloved God, but you need more. This is the real food. Eat and do not say, "Enough," but continue. Then you will take everything. Allāh (ﷻ) is the Generous. He does not forbid anyone to take from His holy water. This is very deep.

Allāh (ﷻ) created everything perfect and He is the Healer. I ask Him to keep His message for us and for the people. Āmīn.

The reading continues, "My beloveds, this message, this music, is the divine food like the food of Dāwūd (ﷺ) when he sang with his flute so that others could hear his melodies."

Sayyidinā Dāwūd (ﷺ) is singing. This is a very deep song. Open your ears. You can take the music of the spirit of the Prophet Dāwūd (ﷺ). Then Allāh (ﷻ) ordered the mountains and all the birds to sing with Dāwūd (ﷺ). They began the song of peace, love, mercy, justice and freedom.

This is what He wants: for us to be one body, one heart, to not make any separation. There is no separation. You cannot say, "I am a lady," or, "I am a man." There is nothing like that, only Allāh (ﷻ). For that reason He said: Lā ʾilāha ʾilla-llāh. This is the real purity. For that reason He says:

> Remember Me, I will remember you, (2:152)

He gives everyone the real life through the water of the unseen through His way. This doesn't die. Allāh (ﷻ) is always alive.

The reading continues, "He sang with his flute so that others could hear his melodies and come with love to Allāh (ﷻ). I don't care about those who refuse to obey. They choose to be disobedient, because Allāh (ﷻ) ordered them to hear Him and to treat others with love. Allāh (ﷻ) wants us to give the mercy and love to others.

What should I say? It makes me very sad and I hope they will open their ears and their hearts again, because Allāh (ﷻ) gave us a great gate, a big door, this door of repentance. He called His creatures and said to them:

> **Oh My worshipful slave,**
> **if you did not make mistakes**
> **I would create another creation that would make mistakes**
> **and that would repent to Me,**
> **and I would give them tawba and forgive their mistakes.**

They will see that all My doors are open, but only for the ones who are honest, sincere and give their real repentance and are willing to be guided. All of those, Allāh (ﷻ) will change and He will change their bad, offensive deeds to good deeds, because Allāh (ﷻ) is the Forgiver. This is the end of this talk because for each article, for every talk, there is a station."

Music plays.

I like to live with the real love to continue in the real life. Everything, even the birds, even the water in the river, sings the song of the love and they thank Allāh (ﷻ) because He created them to give life to everything. The water of the love is in every place.

Swim in His ocean. This is the love of Allāh (ﷻ), when you follow what He says. Follow the beloveds of Allāh (ﷻ), the prophets (ﷺ). Thank Allāh

(ﷻ) for what He sent us. They are carrying the peace, love and mercy for all of the people for Allāh (ﷻ). Surrender completely to Him. Thank Him.

Open your heart, open your spirit. This is the food of your spirit. Where is the divine singing? In His holy books, in His Qur'ān. If you read His words you will be alive.

The reading continues, "I ask Allāh (ﷻ) to give happiness in this life to all the beloveds, to all who are suffering, to all the sick people in this world. I ask Allāh (ﷻ) to send His mercy, and fill this life full with mercy, and I ask to see my beloveds as one nation and for them to return, as He said in His holy Qur'ān:

> This, your (human) nation, is one nation,
> and I am your Lord so worship Me (alone). (21:92)

Allāh (ﷻ), we have heard and we obey. So please, Allāh (ﷻ), forgive us, for we all return back to You. We promise You to keep the promise and to pay our souls, our spirits, our hearts, our bodies as a sacrifice to Your face. Please accept our sacrifice. It is pure, Allāh (ﷻ), it is just for Your face from us, for we are very poor. Help us in this life, accept our supplications. We are poor, Allāh (ﷻ). We need You and You said:

> Allāh (ﷻ) is rich and you are poor. (47:38)

My beloveds, this is the time for a very special promise. I want to help you to open your hearts to know the secrets of the love that I've talked about. I want you to make a special prayer to Allāh (ﷻ) and I want to help all my children know, in their hearts, this deep secret love that I talk about.

If you want to open your heart more, if you want to know how to give the love in the way of Allāh (ﷻ), in the way that Allāh (ﷻ) wants you to love, then this special promise will help you. It will help you open your heart to be able to give your beloved the real love in the way of Allāh (ﷻ), to love your children in the way of Allāh (ﷻ) and to be able to give your children what they need. It will help you love you parents in the way of the divine love, to love your brothers and sisters in the right way, and to love the earth and all of Allāh's creation in the way that Allāh (ﷻ) wants you to love them.

Come to me now if you're ready. If you're waiting for a beloved, come to me now and let me ask Allāh (ﷻ) to open your heart to be ready. If you want to help someone who is sick or needs help, if you want to help someone travel to Allāh (ﷻ) who has left the dunyā, if you want to help the poor and suffering, come to me now.

Come, my beloveds. Come for this very special holy promise. I have brought a very special gift that I am ready to give you after you've given your promise. I'm ready for you, my beloveds, come now."

Make the wedding between you and Allāh (ﷻ).

Sidi gives the promise.

Allah Opens His Door to the Sincere Ones (ﷻ)

Tawba Compilation from *The Traveler's Journey* and "The One Who Knows All the Secrets" and Music
Wednesday, July 28, 2010 AM, USHS Year 3

لا إله إلا الله – لا إله إلا الله – لا إله إلا الله – محمد رسول الله عليه صلاة الله
لا إله إلا الله – لا إله إلا الله – لا إله إلا الله – ابراهيم رسول الله عليه صلاة الله
لا إله إلا الله – لا إله إلا الله – لا إله إلا الله – موسى رسول الله عليه صلاة الله
لا إله إلا الله – لا إله إلا الله – لا إله إلا الله – عيسى رسول الله عليه صلاة الله
اللهم انت السلام ومنك السلام و إليك يعود السلام
تباركت ربنا وتعاليت يا ذوالجلال والإكرام

May peace and mercy be upon you, my beloveds. We are here in this holy place, and it is holy because it is a place of prostrating and following and remembering Allāh (ﷻ). We started to use this place years ago, so the angels (عليهم السلام) are here and the spirits of the prophets and messengers are here (عليهم السلام). It has become a holy location, a holy place by the will of Allāh (ﷻ).

This is a mosque. Allāh (ﷻ) allows us to mention His name in this home, so this home has become a mosque. We remember Allāh in this mosque and Allāh has allowed it to be a holy place of Allāh. It is holy by the name of Allāh and it is holy by the prophets and the messengers, and it is holy because we mention Allāh (ﷻ) here.

We ask Allāh (ﷻ) to give you all good things, and He is the healing for your hearts, for your spirits, for your selves and for your bodies. As one of the gnostics said, "There are special places and special times and special people for Allāh (ﷻ)," and this is a great thing. It is a great thing that Allāh (ﷻ) moved the University of Spiritual Healing and Sufism to this mosque. It is great that we don't give our lectures in hotels while people there drink alcohol. This is a holy place and this is a great thing, and Allāh (ﷻ) gave this to us.

When I mention that He wanted to move this university to the mosque, I know what I'm saying. Allāh (ﷻ) will give divine knowledge that He sent down to all of the prophets and messengers (عليهم السلام) to the people who graduate from this university. As you hold honesty and loyalty, you will succeed in your lives. This is one point.

The other point I'm seeing is very important for all our beloveds everywhere, at all the centers, to understand. The one who wants to join and receive knowledge from this university will be holy and, inshāʾa-llāh, blessed, and he will receive all good things. He will receive knowledge from the teachers, those who follow the orders of Allāh (ﷻ), and those who teach the orders that Allāh (ﷻ) sent down to all the prophets and messengers (عليهم السلام). I'm sure Allāh (ﷻ) will help them and that He will let healing come from their hands.

In the previous lesson, I spoke on how to heal yourself and others. This afternoon I will explain, in detail, many secrets of healing that I have never given before. I have received permission to give them now and I'm asking Allāh (ﷻ) for you to be able to understand this information and for it to enter your spirits and hearts. And, as usual, we should announce and admit our tawba from the bottom of our hearts.

I want to remind you to proclaim your tawba again, and you will give a promise again, inshāʾa-llāh. I will explain how tawba purifies the body. Human beings use their bodies to obey or disobey Allāh's orders and prohibitions. How do you use your body? To obey Allāh (ﷻ)? How do you use your hands, your legs, your eyes, your ears, your seeing and your heart?

You should repent to Allāh (ﷻ), and first, your tongue should repent. Then, your mind, your ears and your heart should repent. The mind should repent to Allāh (ﷻ) with an honest tawba. It should repent mentally and spiritually. Also, your genitals, your legs and your self should repent, because the self has ordered you to do bad things.

You should make tawba in your mind, in your eyes, in your ears, in your tongue, in your heart and in your spirit. First, make tawba in your spirit, then make it in your heart and then make it in your self.

You shouldn't eat anything ḥarām (forbidden); don't put anything ḥarām in your body. Don't steal and eat. Don't do forbidden things in order to eat. You will destroy your stomach because the forbidden money will go to the stomach and the stomach will work on it. Once the stomach processes it, it will go to every part of your body. You should take care not to eat food bought with money earned in forbidden ways and foods with a lot of chemicals.

Client Intake Interview Procedure

1. First, if someone visits you asking for healing, ask them, "What food do you eat? Do you eat food treated with chemicals or do you eat fresh, organic food?" The person came to heal his body, nafs, heart and spirit, so you should start by asking about his food. His food should be pure and it shouldn't be unnatural.

   Allāh (ﷻ) created all foods from the earth; people should only eat foods that are from the earth along with pure water, not water polluted with chemicals. If the body is healthy you will find the heart will be physically clean and his hearing and his eyes will be fine.

2. After that ask him, "How is your heart?" There is a special piece of your body, the heart. If the heart is healthy, everything else will be healthy. The heart holds your blood; one hundred twenty-five arteries come and go from your heart and it pumps blood to every part of the body. This is a basic thing and you should investigate it.

   If the visitor tells you, "I'm eating bad foods that have many chemicals in them," you should advise him to only eat fish from the deep oceans. Fish contains 125 minerals. He should eat clean fish from the deep ocean, not fish from the coasts. Allāh (ﷻ) created this in His wisdom and He gave us all of the medicine.

3. After that, start assessing the mind. You should be wise. Don't ask the client a question that allows him to feel bad or embarrassed, because the mind is a tool for thought. The mind takes orders from the heart and the heart should be clean.

> Note: Don't ask him, "How was your life before?" Don't ask him about his early life with his parents. First tell him, "Leave the past in the past! Don't talk to me about it!" Leave everything in the past and give him a new dress, because most diseases from childhood are from bad manners and from disobeying the orders of Allāh (ﷻ).
>
> If a woman's father or brother, for example, abused her...maybe they did many horrible things to her. You should integrate her heart to heal those horrible things. For this reason, we ask Allāh (ﷻ) to guide us on the straight path.

This is the way to succeed in your life. Don't think about the past. Don't think about the stories and the details of the past. It is finished! If you eat some bread, I shouldn't ask you what you ate; there is no benefit in asking you about something from the past.

You can heal a person by being merciful with him now. He needs love and mercy. Don't tell him, "Oh, you have a big problem!" You will destroy him and you will put other diseases inside his head. He came to you to receive healing, so do not give him other diseases. Our Master Muḥammad (ﷺ) said:

> Treat people with good manners. Be kind and sweet to them.

You should repent. Ask Allāh (ﷻ) for forgiveness for everything. Ask to be between His arms and in His place (ﷻ). Ask for His support (ﷻ) and call upon Allāh (ﷻ) by His name ash-shāfī. Do not call upon Allāh (ﷻ) using the names of other human beings—we should only call upon Allāh (ﷻ) by His names, including His name ash-shāfī, the Healer.

The healer should be humble and he should follow Allāh's orders. We should repent for all of our faults in all of our hearts. I will start to explain the meaning of tawba. Tawba means to not see anything except what Allāh (ﷻ) allows us to see. Tawba means to not listen to what other people are saying. Tawba of the mind is to not to think of anything that Allāh (ﷻ) has forbidden. Tawba of the emotions is very important. If you are honest, Allāh (ﷻ) will let you be a great healer, a wonderful healer.

Open your heart, please, and your spirit. Bismi-llāh.

This initial reading is comprised of excerpts from *The Traveler's Journey of Healing through Divine Love, Knowledge and Truth.*

"I ask Allāh (ﷻ) to make us steadfast in His way.
Make us firm in Your Way and forgive our faults.
Conceal our mistakes and bestow Your Mercy upon us.

Oh Allāh (ﷻ), I ask You by the reality of Your lofty essence
and by the reality of Your praiseworthy Prophet (ﷺ).
Please do not let any one of us be miserable or sad, or suffer.
And please do not forsake us
and put us in shame on the Day of Judgment,
but forgive us and bestow Your mercy upon us.
Grant us happiness, all of us.
Āmīn.

Know, my beloveds, that everything depends upon tawba. Tawba is your first step and it is a continuous step. It is like changing the oil in your car. Can you actually drive a car when it has no oil or when it has a different problem? No, you have to fix it in order to drive it. You are like this vehicle and you are full of things that need to be fixed and rectified and washed and cleaned in order to drive, to arrive at the divine presence.

The path to Allāh (ﷻ) is full of obstacles and danger and you must continue to purify yourself by walking this path until you become fully conscious of the divine presence. You must purify the body and the soul through tawba from their illnesses, because our bodies, hearts and souls accumulate dirt that causes illness. We must purify ourselves and truly follow the divine way by following His commands (ﷻ) and following His prohibitions (ﷻ).

Do not fear anyone except Allāh (ﷻ). Revere Allāh (ﷻ) and walk to Him through the essential gate, which is the gate of tawba.

Now we're going to hear some music called "The One Who Knows All the Secrets."

For this teaching Sidi had Ṣalīḥ Kent read an unpublished reading, "The One Who Knows All the Secrets" which is based upon the music of Shaykh Yasīn at-Tuhamī with Sidi's lyrics.

The lyrics of the music
are bold, italicized and indented.
The reading is in bold text.
Sidi's live commentary is in plain text.

Music plays.

> *You are He who answers our supplications.*
> *I carry my sins.*
> *You are the only One who answers me.*
> *I carry my sins.*
> *I'm walking to Your place.*

"I ask forgiveness from the only One who forgives sins.

Yā Allāh (ﷻ)! Oh Allāh (ﷻ), I am coming to You filled with all my sins, knocking on Your door and asking You to open it for me, please. Not only for my own sins, but I direct myself to You with all the sins of all the people on earth and on behalf of those who are suffering around the world for these sins. I ask You desperately, from the bottom of my heart, I make my supplication and I plead, Allāh (ﷻ), I plead for your acceptance, for I speak on behalf of all sinners; on behalf of all those who suffer. Now I come humbly to ask Your help and Your support.

They come to You with deep sincerity. They are honest and sincere and they are asking You to accept their tawba. They are longing, they are hoping, as they ask You for their tawba because they direct their faces to You, Allāh (ﷻ), to Your merciful face because You are the Most Compassionate and the Most Merciful (ﷻ).

So, my Allāh (ﷻ), open the doors, for You are the One who will answer our prayers and supplications. You are the One who forgives all sins. You are at-Tawwab. You say, "I am the Forgiver. I am the Merciful." For that reason, Allāh (ﷻ), I come to You with deep sincerity. Yes, I come to You with a clean heart, like what You say. And anyone who comes with a clean heart, and he is crying under Your throne, You say:

> If anyone asks Me for anything, if he is sincere, I will accept him, I will accept every word that he says.

For that reason, I carry all these sins to Your Garden. Like what You asked, I come to Your Garden. I choose You to rub out and erase all my sins, and to return me to be a real child between Your arms because You are My Lord. You are my Beloved in this life.

So, please, accept me in the right place. Give me real love in order to help me to be clean from every sin I made before. For that reason I ask You...I'm sure You do not discharge anyone who has the deep suffering because You contain everyone who comes like me."

When any person comes to Allāh (ﷻ), and he knows the door of Allāh (ﷻ), and he comes with the deep sincere, and his heart is crying inside, I am sure he will find the door open. For that reason, go ahead, if you have the deep sincere for that, go ahead. Allāh (ﷻ) says for you will come, but give the promise for Allāh (ﷻ), make more tawba than what you made before.

Allāh (ﷻ) is the Merciful, but it is very important to give your self and your heart mercy when you fall down. Maybe you die before you make tawba. Then the place for you is Hell. Help yourself now, not tomorrow.

Do not say, "Oh, maybe tomorrow. Maybe after tomorrow." You think you have time. You don't have another moment. Maybe before you make tawba you lose your life. How can you make tawba then? You will have lost your chance. Always, always, in everything say, "Astaghfirullāh al-ʿaḍẖīm" and stop your bad actions. Because if you don't stop, in one moment you will lose everything.

Don't say, "I am clean." No, you are not clean. Allāh (ﷻ) is the Clean. All of us except Allāh (ﷻ) need tawba. The Prophet (ﷺ) says, "Astaghfiri anbīk" (Ask forgiveness for your sins). All the prophets (ﷺ) said, "Astaghfiri anbīk."

The Prophet (ﷺ) always made tawba for everything, because maybe you forgot to say, "Lā ʾilāha ʾilla-llāh." Maybe you forgot to say "Astaghfiru-llāh." Then what happened? Allāh (ﷻ) said:

> If you give thanks, I will give you more;
> but if you are thankless,
> truly My punishment is indeed severe. (14:7)

When I want to make tawba, first I say, "Forgive me. I am a very poor slave between Your Hands (ﷻ). Forgive me. I am sorry." Don't be sorry like people who say it but don't mean it. Be sorry in your mind, in your heart and in every part of you. Be repentant in every part of your body. Your ears and your eyes have sinned, so every part of your body should say, "Astaghfiru-llāh." Every part of your body should ask Allāh (ﷻ) for forgiveness. Your hands should say, "Astaghfiru-llāh," your eyes should say, "Astaghfiru-llāh." Everything Allāh (ﷻ) gave you should say, "Astaghfiru-llāh," everything.

> *You are the only One who answers our supplications*
> *and solves our problems.*
> *You are the Owner of everything.*

The reading continues, "You contain everyone who comes like me, Allāh (ﷻ), and I am a very poor slave for You. I plead with You, for You are the One Who answers prayers and supplications.

Oh, Allāh (ﷻ), all the world is in Your Hands. No one else can change those who create suffering and sin without the deep sincere. There is no hope for the one who continues to create suffering for those who are crying everywhere. But I ask You to excuse anyone who holds out his hands and says, 'Allāh (ﷻ), I make tawba from my spirit. Āmīn.' There is no one who knows the secret in every heart of the human being, Allāh (ﷻ), only You.

I am sure that You will give everyone a chance to return under Your wing. For I know, Allāh (ﷻ), that You know all the secrets. You know and I know that You see all that people see, and You hear all that they hear, and You see the black ant on the black rock on the moonless night.

Because of that, there is no way for anyone who says, "You are not hearing or not listening," for You are the Seer, You are the Hearer. You see and You hear. You are the Creator, Allāh (ﷻ). You know the secret. You know what their selves say to them. Because of that we come to You. We are Your servants. We are Your slaves.

Don't despair, my beloveds, of the mercy of Allāh (ﷻ). Allāh (ﷻ) forgives all sins, for He is the Forgiver. He is the Merciful.

Allāh (ﷻ), we come humbly prostrated. We don't want anything but Your acceptance, Allāh (ﷻ), we only want Your forgiveness and we're not asking You for anything else, just Your mercy and Your forgiveness. For You are the Merciful, the Most Merciful. You are the Compassionate, the Most Compassionate. Allāh (ﷻ), there is nothing like You.

I come because everyone knows that You created us. Then, everyone throws his self and his heart and his spirit between Your Arms, my Beloved God (ﷻ).

The music is saying, "You are the only One who answers prayer," so I bring my sins and I come alone to Your tawba, knocking on Your door, voicing my regrets, expressing my sadness and my tawba. I ask You because You are the One who answers prayers. You are the One who helps those who are suffering.

You never allow them to be apart from Your mercy. You are the Owner of everything. We just need You to help us, for You are the Helper, You are the Owner of everything."

Music plays.

> *I am knocking on Your door.*
> *Please, Allāh (ﷻ), answer me; forgive me.*
> *You are the only One who knows my secrets.*
> *No one knows my secrets, just You.*
> *You are the only One who will give.*
> *Praise to You, Allāh (ﷻ).*
> *Praise belongs to You, Allāh (ﷻ).*

We never see You but we know You.

It is real tawba when you come to the door of your Lord (ﷻ) and you knock on the door. Don't go if the door is closed, but keep yourself near the door of Allāh (ﷻ), crying for His face truly from your heart. Be like Allāh (ﷻ) says in the Qur'ān:

> Say: "Oh My slaves who have transgressed against themselves!
> Do not despair of Allāh's mercy.
> (When a person with the deep sincerity comes to Me,
> crying with a broken heart, I will be close to him.)
> Truly, Allāh (ﷻ) forgives all sins.
> Truly, He is the one who is Often Forgiving, Most Merciful."
> (39:53 and tafsir)

Come to Allāh (ﷻ) and throw yourself between His hands with deep sincerity and tears. Make rakātayn (two rakʿāh) of ṣalāh, crying for Him. He will not discharge you from His ocean if you have the deep sincerity.

Music plays.

You are the only One who answers our supplication.
I carry my sins and I am walking to Your house,
knocking on Your Door, asking You to open Your Door.
I am waiting for You.
Please answer me. I am asking You. You are---

Give your self a chance, give your hands a chance, give everything a chance. Make real tawba about everything and cry for Allāh (ﷻ).

You are only One who forgives our sins
and You never discharge anyone. You accept us.
You are the only One.
You are the Owner of everything.
I ask just You. I need You.

He is your Beloved. He has waited for you to come. It is simple.

You are the Owner of everything.
You are the King of Kings.

I am asking Your help.
I am asking You to forgive my sins.
I am knocking on Your door.
I am awaiting Your answer.
Oh, my Lord, You are the Owner of everything.
I need Your help.
I am asking for Your support.
Please forgive me.
Yes, I am knocking on Your Door.
I am waiting.
You are the only One who knows everything.
You are the only One who accepts our tawba.
You are the only One.

The reading continues, "There is no one who knows the secret, Allāh (ﷻ). There is only You because You are Allāh (ﷻ) and You are my God (ﷻ). You know the secret that no one knows.

So, Allāh (ﷻ), I send my thanks to You, my Lord, and no one else can contain everything from all the people in this world because it is You who created everything. For that reason I send my voice for all the people.

This time is very short, beloveds. This life is very short, and so I send this message for everyone everywhere to stop sinning before he leaves this world, for he can only choose one---Hell or the Garden. The door of Allāh (ﷻ) is open, so do not lose your chance. This is a warning, a warning from my heart through Allāh (ﷻ): the door of Allāh (ﷻ) is open, so don't lose your chance.

This is not just from my heart. This is the voice of all the prophets (ﷺ) to everyone in this world. You can give mercy to everyone who's gone far away, and you can bring him and you can bring his spirit, whether he is your father or whether he is your beloved. You can do this for everyone who is crying from deep suffering before his time is finished.

Now, my children, in this time, my tears fall down. My heart is very, very sad for anyone who has not heard my message, but I am still in the deep praying for all of them. I say, 'Welcome' to everyone who has a special heart. I say, 'Welcome' to all those who are crying. I say,

'Welcome' to whoever accepts my voice and what I take from the holy books that Allāh (ﷻ) sent to the Prophet Ibrāhīm (Abraham) (ﷺ), the Prophet Mūsā (Moses) (ﷺ), the Prophet ʿĪsā (Jesus) (ﷺ) and the Prophet Muḥammad (ﷺ), and all those beloveds of Allāh (ﷻ) who send their voices for everyone that Allāh (ﷻ) created, from the beginning to the end.

My beloveds, open your ears to hear me. Wake up! The duration of this life is short for everyone. You were not told that you would live like Nūḥ (Noah) (ﷺ) for 1,000 years or more. So, please, I love everyone because His Prophet (ﷺ) said:

> All creatures are the children of Allāh (ﷻ).

I would like to give the mercy and the peace and the love and the justice and the freedom to every home. I would like to make all of them help each other, love each other and serve each other in the way of Allāh (ﷻ). Then everyone will see that in every home all people will be happy, for this is the message of Allāh (ﷻ) through His prophets (ﷺ)."

Music plays.

> *You know the secrets no one knows.*
> *You will praise the One who asks you by the name of Praise.*
>
> *You are the only One who knows all our secrets.*
> *No one knows our secrets.*
> *You will answer our supplications.*
>
> *We give our praise to You.*
> *Praise belongs to You, who knows everything.*
>
> *You will give the mercy and You will answer our supplication.*
> *You are the Giver.*
> *You will give us a hand.*
> *You will give us a place.*
>
> *I pay my praise to You.*
> *Praise belongs to You. You are the Giver.*

The reading continues, "Allāh (ﷻ), You give anyone who comes everything he asks for. But it is important, beloveds, to make deep tawba with deep sincerity. When He sees your tears come from your spirit, from your heart and from your tongue in the deep sincere, then surely Allāh (ﷻ) will give you what you ask.

Be ready by always being in deep gratitude. Always be in deep gratitude. Thank Allāh (ﷻ) for this holy gift of tawba. When you give thanks to Allāh (ﷻ) with real sincerity and you do not continue to do what you were doing wrong, then surely Allāh (ﷻ) will accept your tawba and not give any chance for Iblīs, pictures or illusion to stop you.

My beloveds, don't listen to just any voice; only listen to the voice of the prophets (ﷺ) because they speak from Allāh (ﷻ). Only listen to the voices of the prophets (ﷺ), and then I am sure Allāh (ﷻ) will change you."

Show the order of God (ﷻ). Show the order of God (ﷻ). The Prophet (ﷺ) does not come to you when you are not clean. You may see him in a dream, sometimes.

It is very important to pray and to follow the practices. When you make istikhāra then Allāh (ﷻ) gives to you in the deep sincerity.[17] Then you will see the answer very clearly. Some people can see lights, gardens and good things in their dreams. This means Allāh (ﷻ) accepts this matter, this issue, and you have received the answer.

Don't say, "I saw Allāh (ﷻ) and He talked with me!" What is the matter with you? You are full of dirt. It is important to be clean and have a clean heart, clean eyes, clean ears, clean everything. Then Allāh (ﷻ) opens the door for you and gives you a sign. Don't say, "This is the light of Allāh (ﷻ)."

Ṣalīḥ: Sidi was explaining in the car this morning that when you are clean in your heart and sincere in your being that then when you read

---

[17] In these two paragraphs Sidi is referring to the istikhāra, a practice where in order to receive guidance from Allāh (ﷻ) the petitioner does 2 voluntary rakʿāh (in addition to the obligatory ṣalāh) and recites a special prayer in addition to some other steps. For specific instructions contact the Shadhiliyya Sufi Center.

his teachings and when you read the Qur'ān and the Ḥadīth, treasures and treasures and treasures will open to you that will not open if you are not sincere.

Sidi: It is like a spring full of water that He gives you because you are thirsty. He gives you the clean knowing. This is Allāh (ﷻ), the Generous.

The reading continues, "So, clean your spirits, my beloveds. Clean your heart and clean your self and He will protect you from every bad thing to be a pure, pure beloved for Allāh (ﷻ).

Then He will take you between His arms and this is the real garden. For that reason, this is the message from Him, through what I've taken from the religion of unity, which is what Allāh (ﷻ) sent through all the prophets (عليهم السلام). But I start and I thank Allāh (ﷻ) first, and I thank, also, all the prophets (عليهم السلام) who give us this deep chance to always be connected with our beloved God (ﷻ)."

Only the holy people, the prophets, received the message from Allāh (ﷻ) through Jībrīl (Gabriel) (عليه السلام). This is a special thing to follow. It contains no teachings from any bad spirits or from Iblīs. No, they are only from Allāh (ﷻ). Allāh (ﷻ) opens them completely. Give what Allāh (ﷻ) asks; He gives you a blessing.

Music plays.

> *You accept our supplications.*
> *You are the only One who knows our secrets.*
> *You know all our secrets that no one knows about.*
> *And You are the only One who will answer our supplications.*
>
> *Praise belongs to You.*
> *Glory to You.*
> *We never see You, but we know You.*
> *We know You and We worship You.*
> *We worship You and just You.*
> *And we are yearning to see You, to meet You.*

The reading continues, "Oh, Allāh (ﷻ), I want all my beloveds to always be connected with You. Then surely the door of mercy will open for them.

He will open the door of divine love, the door of peace, which you will be able to carry, the door to real freedom. He will open the door to justice, for this is what all people need. There is no suffering after that, only heaven.

So understand this word that I speak to you all, my beloved children, from my deepest spirit and my deepest heart. In this moment I send my tears, for my holy heart is full of the suffering and sadness I see in the world. When I see all of the beloveds and all of these children that are sick and who can't find medicine or food, I ask Allāh (ﷻ) to send His mercy for all creation everywhere, without separation, for I carry the religion of unity that Allāh (ﷻ) sent through all His beloved prophets (ﷺ). I want you to praise Allāh (ﷻ), always praise Allāh (ﷻ).

Most of the people, Allāh (ﷻ), don't see You. But through a clean spirit and a clean heart they can know. With deep sincerity and an honest spirit, you will see that Allāh (ﷻ) is generous. When a person follows all the practices from Allāh (ﷻ) in the perfect way, he will come to know You. Allāh (ﷻ).

I say to you: be careful not to give your sins a chance to stop you from making tawba. Go ahead, my children, travel your road to the One who is merciful, for His door is open to everyone. He says on the tongue of His Prophet (ﷺ):

> If you did not sin, I would create others who did.

This means Allāh (ﷻ) is saying, "I won't allow him to suffer without accepting astaghfiru-llāh from him, for I created people to say to Me, 'I make tawba for Your Face, my Lord. I come to be cleaned from everything through my spirit, through my heart, through my self and through my body. I come to be cleaned and to carry Your message that you ask of us.'"

So help us, my Lord, make us Your heart and Your spirit and then You will see that I will follow all the practices that You send in order to be a complete beloved who follows what the Prophet (ﷺ) said when he declared:

> Oh Allāh (ﷻ), I promise to be a real slave for Your Face,
> to not look back,
> to not sin again after You accept me as a poor slave for You.

So, Allāh (ﷻ), please accept my duʿāʾ. No one who has sins can see Allāh (ﷻ), but when everyone cleans themselves then Allāh (ﷻ) gives us a very holy gift, like that that He gave Mūsā (ؑ), when he asked his Lord:

> Oh my Lord, show me Yourself that I may look upon You. (7:143)

Allāh (ﷻ) responds, "When you are in the material realm it is important to clean your heart first Then look to your heart and your spirit after you leave the material body. Begin to make a real prostration, a prostration that opens to Me, Allāh (ﷻ). Then, through your spirit, through your heart, you can see Me."

For that reason, when a person makes the real prostration, when he is absent from himself, when he is absent through al-fanāʾ, through al-baqāʾ, then he sees Allāh (ﷻ), and this is a very holy thing if you follow what Allāh (ﷻ) says in His Qurʾān. We worship You not because we are scared of Your Fire, not because we want to enter Your Garden. We worship You because of You, for we want to see You. We want to be with You, Allāh (ﷻ).

Music plays.

> *You are the only One who knows the secrets.*
> *We give you our praise and we praise You all the time.*
> *Praise be to You, Allāh (ﷻ). Allāh (ﷻ).*

Oh Allāh (ﷻ), accept all the prayers and all that my beloveds ask of You, because everyone promises You to keep themselves inside Your circle, inside Your world, Allāh (ﷻ), that is full of peace and love and mercy and justice. Āmīn.

I am sure that everyone heard my voice, for my voice carries tears and sadness. I ask Allāh (ﷻ) to keep my beloveds, to keep all the people who make real tawba in Your way, and everyone who likes to see all the people happy with Your help. Surely, everyone is working to keep the promise between You and them, Allāh (ﷻ). Āmīn, Āmīn, Āmīn."

So, my beloveds, it is now time to take your promise again, to take your promise in the deep, secret love for the face of Allāh (ﷻ). Come to me now, my children, and I ask Allāh (ﷻ) to accept your tawba. I have a very special gift for you to help you in your walking, to protect you, to keep you and your heart simple and pure. Come, my children. Now is your time. Āmīn. Āmīn. Āmīn. Do not lose your chance. The tawba is very deep.

A Drop of the Wine of the Deep Essence of Knowing

"Everything is from Love" and "A Drop of the Love" with music
Thursday, July 29, 2010 AM, USHS Year 3

لا إله إلا الله - لا إله إلا الله - لا إله إلا الله - محمد رسول الله عليه صلاة الله
لا إله إلا الله - لا إله إلا الله - لا إله إلا الله - ابراهيم رسول الله عليه صلاة الله
لا إله إلا الله - لا إله إلا الله - لا إله إلا الله - موسى رسول الله عليه صلاة الله
لا إله إلا الله - لا إله إلا الله - لا إله إلا الله - عيسى رسول الله عليه صلاة الله
اللهم انت السلام ومنك السلام و إليك يعود السلام
تباركت ربنا وتعاليت يا ذوالجلال والإكرام

As-salāmu ʿalaykum wa raḥmatu-llāhi wa bārakatuhu. Peace be upon you, my beloveds, my sons and daughters. I wish all the best for all of you. I am asking Allāh (ﷻ) for this on this holy day, on this holy morning, in this holy place.

Allāh (ﷻ) has allowed this to be a place of worship, remembrance and prayer. You will carry the flag of mercy, justice and freedom for all people, without discrimination. All of them are the children of Allāh (ﷻ) and they try to live in this life together.

I ask Allāh (ﷻ) to support you and to protect your hearts, your selves and your bodies. I ask Him to give you complete health and to heal you from all diseases, physical and spiritual, and to help you live in happiness with all of your beloveds and families. I raise my hands to protect and give mercy to all of the people who have passed away. He is the Merciful, the Compassionate. I am asking Allāh (ﷻ) to give His mercy and to accept our tawba. Āmīn.

Allāh (ﷻ) is capable of doing everything and He is the All-Knowing, the All-Hearing. It is my honor to be among you, to be a servant between your hands, as Allāh (ﷻ) wants me to be. I am just a poor servant. I do not want anything. I do not want any material things. We feed you just for the sake of Allāh (ﷻ); I do not want you to thank me. I just want you to know Allāh (ﷻ), to know the truth, to be good people, to follow the Messenger (ﷺ) and to let Allāh (ﷻ) send His mercy to all of you.

I direct my face toward Allāh (ﷻ) to pray for all people. I pray for the poor people who are suffering because of the horrible things others do to them, those who disobey Allāh (ﷻ) and the message of all the prophets (ﷺ). I am asking Allāh (ﷻ) to send His peace and happiness to the whole world.

I am asking Him to stop all wars and drive back those who destroy this world and take money from others and kill people just for ugly, material gain. Even if they obtain a lot of money they will die, and they will not take anything with them.

You should be satisfied with what Allāh (ﷻ) gives you. If you have enough food for the day, you should thank Allāh (ﷻ). If Allāh (ﷻ) sends health to your body and you have food, you are very rich. You have everything. If you have a lot, many jewels, do not take anything extra. Just take what you need. This is a very special thing. You only need clothing for winter and summer, not more than that, despite the fact that so many options are available.

We do not forbid others from wearing beautiful clothes or eating good food. Allāh (ﷻ) provides people with these good things. Just do not steal from others. Do not do bad things. When Allāh (ﷻ) provides you with beautiful things, you can enjoy them. You can receive your provision, but you should only depend upon Allāh (ﷻ). As Sayyidinā (our Master) Muḥammad (ﷺ) says:

> If you are honest with Allāh (ﷻ) and depend totally on Allāh (ﷻ), Allāh (ﷻ) will provide for you like He provides for the birds.

People are poor and they worry all the time about provision. Allāh (ﷻ) created you in the perfect shape and He decreed your provision.

Now I would like to say to you, in the final days in this university, that I wish you all the best. I wish for you to understand Allāh (ﷻ). I ask Allāh (ﷻ) to give you honesty and loyalty, inshāʾa-llāh. Allāh (ﷻ) says:

> And truly this is My straight path, so follow it. (6:153)

This is what Allāh (ﷻ) says and it is not from me. I am like you—I am a human being like you, even though Allāh (ﷻ) has given me divine knowledge in my heart and mind. This is a provision from Allāh (ﷻ). I do not have anything. Allāh (ﷻ) will choose certain people and send them His mercy.

Previously, I explained worship to you. Allāh (ﷻ) ordered and commanded us to participate in it. It is food for our spirits and our minds. It is a cure for your mind and your body. For example, I told you about and explained al-wuḍu' (ritual washing).

I would like to explain ṣalāh (the prayer we do five times a day). What is ṣalāh? Ṣalāh is the way you connect with Allāh and it establishes the relationship between you and Allāh (ﷻ).

The way of Sufism is to be pure and full of mercy. We are doing our best to let others know the way of Allāh (ﷻ). I have explained this thoroughly in the many books I've published about behavior and balance. I advise you to read these books and to write them in order to heal and to learn how to walk to Allāh (ﷻ).

Ṣalāh is the secret way to Allāh (ﷻ). For this reason, all of the messengers kept their prayers in order to purify their minds, their eyes, their ears, their spirits and their bodies.

How to Do Ṣalāh

In the first part of ṣalāh, you should say, "Allāhu Akbar!" What is the meaning of Allāhu Akbar? It is a promise. You are saying, "I will be between Your hands. I promise You that I will not be busy with anything other than You. Please, Allāh (ﷻ), let me know how to walk to You and give to me from Your knowledge." This is the beginning.

When you pray ṣalāh, you start by facing Allāh (ﷻ). Allāh (ﷻ) is the Greatest Thing. He is great. You direct your face toward Allāh (ﷻ). Do not be busy with anything else. Ask Him to support you and to let you be obedient. Ask Him to help you to be a servant and to use your provision, your heart, your eyes, your ears, your hands and your legs to do only good things, as He has ordered us.

Allāh (ﷻ) says on the tongue of His Prophet (ﷺ):

> My servant continues to draw near to Me with voluntary actions
> (extra ṣalāh)
> until I become the hearing with which he hears,
> the seeing with which he sees,
> the hand with which he strikes (and heals) and
> the foot with which he walks.
> (If he wants something, he will say, "Be" and it will be,
> because it is My wish.)

This is in the Ḥadīth Qudsī. Sayyidinā Muḥammad (ﷺ) narrated this ḥadīth for all the messengers.

First, purify your heart, body, hands and legs, and then all of your past will be clean. Allāh (ﷻ) created the five senses, which you know. There is also the sixth sense, which is hidden. It is a secret. When you reach the sixth sense, you will know by this sense what is good and what is evil. It will help you to walk to Allāh (ﷻ).

The ṣalāh (facilitates) your relationship with Allāh (ﷻ). If you want to travel, you get into an airplane, or a ship, or you your car. Your body is a vehicle like this. In the future, we will be able to use material vehicles for good things. They should use them for good things. One hundred years ago, we did not know about computers. You cannot see these new tools, these updated tools. Allāh (ﷻ) says to the jinn and the human beings:

> Oh assembly of jinn and men! If you have power to pass beyond the zones of the heavens and the earth, then pass! But you will never be able to pass them without My permission! (55:33)

You can reach Allāh (ﷻ) in the blink of an eye. This method is faster than a rocket. If you are pure and if you walk as our prophets (ﷺ) ordered us, you will reach Allāh (ﷻ) very quickly, as quickly as a blink or a kiss.

When you prostrate to Allāh (ﷻ) during ṣalāh, you are promising that Allāh (ﷻ) is your Lord. He is your creator and you are very close to Him when you are in this position.

The first station is to purify your body; you should purify your body. Allāh (ﷻ) gave you ṣalāh through our Prophet Muḥammad (ﷺ). He gave the Christians ʿĪsā (Jesus) (ؑ) and He gave the Jews Mūsā (Moses) (ؑ). There is no discrimination between the messengers. They are all the beloveds of Allāh (ﷻ). The one who carries the message of Allāh (ﷻ) should be honest.

During ṣalāh, behave yourself. First of all, know about your nafs (self), which has seven levels. When you prostrate, when you are bowing to Allāh (ﷻ).

When you start to recite, "al-ḥamdu li-llāhi rabbi-l-ʿālamīn," do not say or think, "He is the Lord of the Christians," "He is the Lord of the Jews," or "He is the Lord of the Muslims." Know that He is the Lord of all people, rabbi-l-ʿālamīn. Allāh (ﷻ) will say in response, "My servant praises Me."

When you say, "ar-raḥmāni-r-raḥīm," Allāh (ﷻ) says, "My servant knows I am the Lord of mercy. I will let him enter My mercy." When you say, "māliki yawmi-d-dīn" Allāh (ﷻ) says, "My servant admits that I am the owner of the Final Day," and, "My servant admits that I am the Lord of all the worlds." This is very beautiful.

You praise Allāh (ﷻ) by reciting the Fātiḥa. Each letter has its own meaning. The first letter in "al-ḥamdu" and the name of Allāh (ﷻ) is "alif." The sound of this letter is, "ah."

All religions say, "Allāh (ﷻ)." Some religions say, "God (ﷻ)." He is Allāh (ﷻ). Even if all of the people praying are of different races, in this station, all people behave themselves. Allāh (ﷻ) says, "By doing your prayers you will behave yourself, you will stay away from bad deeds. You will do good deeds." If you sin or make a mistake, Allāh (ﷻ) says, "He is the Merciful, the Compassionate." He will forgive you. He knows that He created the human being weak. If Allāh (ﷻ) does not support the human being, he will not be able to do anything.

The ṣalāh, in all of its stations, is food for your body. Wuḍuʾ is food for the spirit. By praying ṣalāh, you can walk through the seven stations:

1. al-amārra (the commanding nafs)
2. al-lawwāma (the blaming nafs)
3. al-mulḥamma (the inspired nafs)
4. al-muṭma'inna (the tranquil, secure nafs)
5. ar-rāḍiya (the satisfied or contented nafs)
6. al-marḍiya (the pleased nafs)
7. al-kāmila (the perfected nafs)[18]

While you are praying ṣalāh, you pass through these stations.

Allāh (ﷻ) ordered us to do ṣalāh as an exercise for our bodies. As I mentioned before, you know the meaning of this movement. During ṣalāh, the blood circulates throughout your body when you raise your hands and your legs. When you prostrate, there are different movements in your back and in every part of your body. When you pray ṣalāh in the correct way, as Allāh (ﷻ) ordered us, and when you bow as I mentioned before, you will know its meaning for your body. This is normal.

The divine issue is that you will walk quickly to Allāh (ﷻ) if you obey Allāh (ﷻ) and if you follow His orders. If you pray ṣalāh as Allāh (ﷻ) has ordered you, you will move to other stations. There are seven stations of the heart. Your tongue will remember Allāh (ﷻ) all the time and in this way you will walk to Allāh (ﷻ). When you reach the station where you purify your heart, Allāh (ﷻ) will let you enter the other stations. You can pray the five obligatory prayers, but you can add extra ṣalāh and pray more while people are sleeping. Allāh (ﷻ).

Sayyidinā Muḥammad (ﷺ) said:

> Be in thousand-fold peace.

Be in a good relationship with your relatives. Feed the poor and those who are needy. You will enter the garden of peace, the garden of knowledge, the garden of understanding Allāh (ﷻ). Pray when people are sleeping and you will be with Allāh (ﷻ). He says:

---

[18] Sidi has written about the stations in detail in several books, including *He Who Knows Himself Knows His Lord*, *The Path to Allāh, Most High* and *Music of the Soul.*

> Two of the worshippers will not be in the Fire:
> the one who prays while people are sleeping
> and those who are humble.

Following this will let you walk very quickly to Allāh (ﷻ).

Bring peace, feed people and pray ṣalāh while others sleep in the night. Then, you can leave the stations of the heart and you will be in a great station. If you want to be satisfied with Allāh (ﷻ) and happy, you should sacrifice yourself and your body as payment to Allāh (ﷻ). We do not want to stop in the station of fanāʾ. We want to be with Allāh (ﷻ). We want to be close to Allāh (ﷻ), sitting next to Him. This is the station of the spirit.

Because of this, I advise you all the time to write *He who Knows Himself Knows His Lord*. You know what I mean regarding this. You should write, read and follow the exercises in this book, and if you do you will find yourself with Allāh (ﷻ).

You should know that Allāh (ﷻ) is very close to you. He is with you all the time. He sees and He hears. This body is a holy body. This is why Allāh (ﷻ) forbids us from killing others. If you kill somebody, it is like you have killed all people.

I want to complete your knowledge of fasting. Allāh (ﷻ) has ordered all of the prophets (عليهم السلام) and all of the messengers (عليهم السلام) to fast. Sometimes, a prophet or messenger was asked to fast by the tongue, as Allāh (ﷻ) ordered Sayyidinā Zakariyā (Zachariah) (عليه السلام). Sayyidinā Zakariyā (عليه السلام) said, "I will fast and I will not talk to anyone." He would not say any bad things. He would not talk badly behind people's backs. He would not insult others. He would only use his tongue for good things.

Also, the eyes can fast. There is also the fasting of the mind. This is a very deep fasting. Do not use your mind for something Allāh (ﷻ) does not accept. Some people use their minds to plan how to kill people and how to do bad things. Allāh (ﷻ) created the mind for good things, not for bad things, so fast with your mind.

Allāh (ﷻ) gave you this fasting because He wants you to feel like the poor. They are needy and they are angry, so it is important to feel these same feelings. Besides this, there is mercy in fasting for your body. It keeps your body and your blood healthy.

Sayyidinā Muḥammad (ﷺ) said:

> The worst vessel to fill is one's stomach.
>
> We are people who do not eat until we are hungry.
> When we eat, we do not fill ourselves to the brim.
> We fill one-third of our stomach with food,
> we fill the second third with water,
> and we leave the third part for air.

Your stomach is a machine that works day and night and it should rest. It is a factory. Allāh (ﷻ) knows why He created the stomach and He ordered us to give the stomach rest. It is healthy to follow this order and it is part of healing. Excuse me, I gave you a long lecture, but this is what Allāh (ﷻ) wanted.

This reading is a combination
of a Portland teaching called,
"Everything is from Love" on page 133
and an unpublished reading,
"A Drop of the Love."
This is accompanied by the music
of Shaykh Yasīn at-Tuhamī.

The lyrics of the music
are bold, italicized and indented.
The reading is in bold text.
Sidi's live commentary is in plain text.

The reading begins, "On this holy day, I am among you. I am here in my form, in my body. But when I leave and return to the Holy City, al-Quds, Jerusalem, I want you to know that I will keep my heart and my spirit praying for you and for everyone who is crying from the deep suffering in this world. I cry from my deepest spirit. I ask Allāh (ﷻ) to send His

peace and His mercy and His love and His freedom and His justice to all people everywhere.

I ask that He help those who are crying from deep sickness everywhere. I ask that He send angel healers (ﷺ) for everyone who is crying from deep sickness, that He clean this heart, clean this land, clean all the earth everywhere from the bad sicknesses, from the bad diseases and from chemicals.

I pray for Allāh (ﷻ) to stop war everywhere and to send the wind of peace. I want to see His flag of unity go directly to every heart. I ask Him to stop those who play games and those who are not right, and I ask Him to help those who do walk though this order that helps people become pure and learn to help each other. I am sure of what He says:

> And when My slaves ask you concerning Me,
> then (answer them), I am indeed near.
> I respond to prayers when they call upon Me. (2:186)
>
> I am inside his heart.
> I hear everything he asks and I hear his crying.
> I accept him if he has a deep heart
> and if he makes the real prostration.
> I am inside everything, and everywhere he looks, he finds Me.

Raise your hands and ask Allāh (ﷻ), and then let Him answer your supplications. Āmīn. Be honest and ask with deep sincerity for Allāh (ﷻ), for He hears you, He sees you and He is listening to you, yā Allāh (ﷻ).

In this place, in this time, in this room, there are angels (ﷺ) listening to the teaching, praising Allāh (ﷻ) and remembering Allāh (ﷻ), helping to clean everyone who is honest and sincere. This is a very holy time. Say:

Allāhu, Allāhu, Allāhu, Allāhu, Allāhu, Allāhu, Allāhu, Allāh.

Lā ʾilāha ʾilla-llāh, Lā ʾilāha ʾilla-llāh, Lā ʾilāha ʾilla-llāh, Lā ʾilāha ʾilla-llāh,
Lā ʾilāha ʾilla-llāh, Lā ʾilāha ʾilla-llāh, Lā ʾilāha ʾilla-llāh.

Oh, Allāh (ﷻ),
You answer our supplications,
You Answer our questions and our needs.

We are knocking on Your doors,
so please, Allāh, answer us.
You are the Forgiver, so please, Allāh (ﷻ),
accept us and answer our supplications.
Allāh!

My Master,
You are the essence of our existence.
We are Your mirrors and we are knocking on Your door.
You know what is going on inside us.
You know everything.
We ask You and You are the Only One.
Please, please, Allāh (ﷻ), answer our supplications.
We are between Your hands.
We are Your poor servants.
We are praying for those poor, poor people.
They are praying for You, for Your essence.
for You created us and You provide for us.
We direct our faces toward You,
asking You to heal us, to heal our daughters
and our beloveds all around the world.
We complain of our weakness to You and our poverty, Allāh (ﷻ).
We take refuge in You.
You are the Only One.
Please, Allāh (ﷻ), answer our questions and our supplications.
Yā Allāh (ﷻ).
Āmīn.

Excuse me, my beloveds, my heart is crying for those who cry from the deep suffering in the whole world. Āmīn, Āmīn, Āmīn.

I start in this holy place at this holy time for everybody to cry to Allāh (ﷻ). So who will answer our supplications? You are the only One Who Answers Supplications. The honest worshippers should not have any fear in their hearts and they will never be sad. Āmīn.

Al-ḥamdu li-llāh, praise Allāh (ﷻ). Allāh (ﷻ) accepts our prayers and our supplications and He accepts us among His worshippers. Āmīn. So please excuse me. I did that obeying His order.

On this day, we will enter through a huge door, a big door: the door of love. Love is the first thing to enter to Allāh (ﷻ) and to knock on Allāh's doors. Allāh's doors are open to you. Allāh (ﷻ) told Hārūn (Aaron) (ع) and Mūsā (ع):

> I hear and see (everything). (20:46)

He hears our supplications and He sees us. Now we are in the ocean of the love of Allāh (ﷻ). Prepare your hearts. Be honest. Don't lose this chance in this time of mercy. The angels (ع) and the spirits of the prophets (ع) are around us.

Be with me and my heart and my spirit because I am with you. I will give everything as a sacrifice, just for you to solve your problem. Ask Allāh (ﷻ) to help you, to let you be stable in your religion, standing, praying, fasting and prostrating. Purify everything that Allāh (ﷻ) has provided to you.

I will start with love, al-maḥabba. What is maḥabba, love? It is the first degree. It is the degree to enter the presence of the Truth (al-Ḥaqq). First of all, you should clean your tongue, your hearts, your minds and your selves, because Allāh (ﷻ) says:

> ...except the one who brings Allāh a whole heart.
> And Paradise will be brought near to the pious. (26:89-90)

One of the gnostics (ق) said:

> You can find Allāh's existence everywhere,
> even if you escape somewhere deep within the earth.
> He will hear you and He will see you.
> He sees you and He knows what you are doing.
> He can see your hand and you can see.

I swear by His name that He loves you. Why do you turn away from His love? Why don't you listen to what He says? Why haven't you obeyed Him?

Come to the mercy of Allāh (ﷻ). Clean your hearts. Clean your spirits to be near Him in His place, to be in the ocean of love, the entire love.

He is the Manifester in everything and you are His mirror. So how can you be unable to see Him? You are the follower, the traveler to Allāh (ﷻ). He said on the tongue of His Prophet (ﷺ):

> I was a hidden treasure and I loved to be known.

By you, this manifestation, Allāh (ﷻ) revealed Himself in the human being. They know Him."

Music plays.

This is the food for your spirit.

("A Drop of the Love" begins here)

I would like to send the essence of the secret love through the essence of my holy spirit to explain to my beloveds the meaning of love.

> *Mention the name of my lover, even in my dream.*
> *The conversations between me and my Beloved are my wine.*
> *The conversations are wine for me.*
> *My ears will be my witnesses.*

To begin, I say, if you want to be with Allāh (ﷻ), then I would like to give you a special gift through this song. In the beginning, I give you a drop of this love. I give this in a special cup to make you absent, to change you from everything that you have, to leave the past and discharge it and to go deep, my children. Then I give you to drink from a drop of His love. Please do not go far away. Be ready."

Are you ready?

Yes!

Then I will give you a drop from the wine of Allāh (ﷻ) to be with Him, not with anything else. Then He will give you the real life.

The reading continues, "After you have all the sincerity, all the surrender, when you do not try to surrender to anything else or to your nafs, but you surrender completely to the One you love who created you to be pure, this is what I mean by 'be ready.' I would like to give you my cup, full of my essence of the deep secret love."

This is the deep secret life, to be with Allah (ﷻ) in the perfect way. If you are ready to take what He would like to give in the deepest way.

The reading continues, "Then Allāh (ﷻ) will change your eyes and your ears. He will change everything within you. He will change you and move you from this world to another world, the world of the love."

The world of the love means we would like to take you to a very deep station, the beginning of the station of al-fanāʾ. It is important to understand, to care about it and to be ready for everything. Allāh (ﷻ). Bismi-llāh.

The reading continues, "This means the world of the real life and this means to be with Him. So if you love Him, it is important to follow everything He says, because every beloved listens and obeys every order when He sends it. Are you ready for that?"

Group: Yes.

Sidi: Inshāʾa-llāh.

The reading continues, "If you are ready, then the water of His love is ready now. If you love me, follow me and listen. You have asked me many times, 'I would like to see Allāh (ﷻ).' Well, Allāh (ﷻ) is not absent, He is everywhere. He is in everything."

But you are absent! It is important to be ready for everything that He gives. Like what you give, He gives. Allāh (ﷻ) is the Generous.

The reading continues, "Do not keep your ears from hearing and your eyes from seeing. He wants you to follow Him and then you can understand everything. He always sends love. He is always sending love and He never stops. He opens His arms for you and His arms are open for eternity. He says:

> Come, my beloved.
> I am ready for everything that you give.
> Why do you go far away?
> You have been far away from your beloved God long enough."

Nʿam (Yes).

Music plays.

> *I want to see my Beloved even in my dreams.*

I want to see Him even if I am at work. I will follow Him.

> *I enjoy remembering Allāh in every time and in every picture.*
> *Even if people blame me, I do not worry, I do not care.*
>
> *My love, my Spirit, my Beloved.*
> *Mention the name of my Love.*
> *Let me hear His name even in my dreams.*

The reading continues, "My beloved is saying, 'Give me a drop of my Beloved.' This is not like a drop of the wine that people know. A drop of this wine is different. It makes you absent from this material world. Be ready, for this drop gives you the deep essence of knowing. It opens your eyes so that you can see what Allāh (ﷻ) wants to show you.

> *At the same time, you will be drunk with His love.*

This means that Allāh (ﷻ) changes this drop of wine to be water, to be life, to be the real life. This is what I mean.

The speech of my Beloved gives me life, it is like the water of the truth, it is like eternal life. I am happy when I mention the One that I fell in love with, my Beloved One, I am happy, even if I see Him only in my dreams. He is far away but He is everywhere.

Through your spirit you can see everything, but in reality, not as an image. When He talks with me, He gives me the gift of being with Him completely and understanding what He says. I am always ready to drink and I do not speak another word after that, for His word is enough for me. It comes from the One who loves me, who has cared about me all my life.

This is my situation. I am absent from everything that people see, because I am with Him in my body, heart, self and spirit. I have no choice. It is not easy to be in this situation if you do not surrender completely to your Beloved. He wants you to give a special sacrifice to your Beloved who created you. Listen to understand what He means. Allāhu Akbar.

The conversation between Him and His beloveds
are the cups of wine from Him.
Let my hearing be my witness.
I love my Beloved, even if He is away from me.
Let my hearing be my witness, I hear Him.
I hear my Beloved, even if He is far away.

My hearing witnesses that I love You. The dream that comes to my eyes, to my ears, to my heart, all of them witness that I love You. My ears, my eyes, everything that God (ﷻ) gave me witness that I love You. They witness that I do not return back. Always, I keep my deep spirit with my Beloved who loves me, Allāh (ﷻ). Even if I am far away and do not see Him, He does not go far away. He never leaves me, not for one moment. This is a chance for me to be with Him. This is the real wedding. It is my pleasure..."

This wine I mention here is the wine of eternity. Within this wine is the secret of existence; it helps you to be absent from this world, to be in the presence of Allāh (ﷻ). There will be no veils between you and Allāh (ﷻ). From this point on, your real life starts.

Oh human being, be ready to let Allāh (ﷻ) give you everything, even the secrets of the qualities of the name of Allāh (ﷻ), as He gave those secrets to your fathers, Ibrāhīm (Abraham) (ﷺ) and Ādam (ﷺ). He prepared you to be inheritors, khalīfāt, on this earth. He prepared you to carry the message of divine truth and use it with understanding. How will you use this message and how will you give it? How will you teach others about it to be a divine servant?

This is the wine of life. It is not wine as you understand it. He wants you to be full of hearing, understanding and seeing. He says on the tongue of His Prophet (ﷺ):

> Be to Me as I want you to be,
> and I will be to you as you want Me to be.

This will allow you to leave the worlds of illusion and pictures and arrive at the presence of divine truth. Your ears will hear with divine hearing, which will take you to the ocean of everything. This is the Garden. This is the Garden Allāh (ﷻ) described in His Qur᾽ān. Because you are honest, you love Him and you are sincere. Beautiful. You know the meaning when Allāh (ﷻ) says:

> He loves them, so they love Him. (5:54)

When you give your sacrifice as the Prophet Ibrāhīm (ﷺ) did, you will know the meaning of love. That will help you to walk to Allāh (ﷻ) without disobeying Him. Anyone who breaks the divine mercy and the orders of Allāh (ﷻ), Allāh (ﷻ) will send him a severe punishment. The Prophet Muḥammad (ﷺ) said:

> Do not cause harm to yourself or others.

It is forbidden for you to cause any pain or harm to others. He is the peace and He says, "as-salām, peace, for all."

We are asking Allāh (ﷻ) to let you be honest worshippers, honest lovers. Love everyone. Love your families, love yourselves. Love your Lord, the One who created you. Then you will put on the beautiful clothing of beauty and love. This is a very precious thing. These are the clothes of Allāh (ﷻ). If you put on these clothes, Allāh (ﷻ) will heal you. He will heal your body, your spirit and your mind. You will be now, this moment, in the Garden.

If you want to wait, you can wait. But if you want, you can enter the Garden now, in this moment. If you work for someone, you want to give him your best and Allāh (ﷻ) will give you everything immediately. He will let you be happy and you will be in the Garden. The Prophet's (ﷺ) companion ʿUmar ibn al-Khaṭṭāb (ؓ) said:

> Judge yourselves before you are judged,
> evaluate yourselves before you are evaluated
> and be ready for the greatest investigation
> (the Day of Judgment).

The reading continues, "It is my pleasure to hear remembrance within my witnessing and within my love. I am very lucky that Allāh (ﷻ) took me into His arms and that He supports me in obeying His orders and that He helps me to always be in His eternal world. This is my pleasure and this is my hope. This is my end and this is my goal, that He puts me in front of His eyes and takes care of me. Āmīn. It is my deep wish to see all of you who love Allāh (ﷻ), everyone, in this holy station. Āmīn.

I want to see the whole world dance with each other, to be real beloveds, to have a real wedding with Allāh (ﷻ). I want to see all of the beloveds who love Allāh (ﷻ) live in the ocean of His love. Āmīn. Āmīn.

I want them all to reach and to hear the divine station, for Allāh (ﷻ) wants to position all of His creatures in this station. If they obey His orders (ﷻ) and the orders carried out by all the prophets (ﷺ), and if they carry the message of unity through the love that Allāh (ﷻ) gifted us, they will be clean. To be clean gives life to you and to everyone who is in this state, in this place and everywhere.

He loved us, so He gave us the gift of His sharī'a, His rules, His orders. He taught us His prohibitions and what we should not do. It is Allāh's gift to us to clean us, to clean our hearts to know His love, because He loves you. He loves you and you love Him.

If you follow His orders, you will be in His loving presence all the time. There is no life except within Him, and this is why it is important to follow Him, to obey Him, and to be between His hands as He wishes. Because He said:

> I will be with you everywhere and anywhere. (20:46 and Tafsir)

My beloveds, this is the truth. How do you want to walk to Allāh (ﷻ)? This is the walking. I have explained it in all my books. This is what you need to know. If you speak from an ugly mind, you will not be able to reach Allāh (ﷻ). You will forget Him and you will turn away from Him.

You will leave His Garden and you will go into the material world, the rubbish world, the recycle bin.

Allāh (ﷻ) wants to give you sweets, but you do not want them. What are you trying to say? You claim that you are a slave, but you do not follow His orders. You do not follow the commands that He sent down to His prophets and messengers (ﷺ).

Some people say they are lovers but they kill others. They are killers. They break hearts. Some people say they are lovers but they are thieves. What is that? Return back to Allāh (ﷻ)! The cure, the healing, is in Allāh (ﷻ). He provides us with everything. After that, how can anyone disobey Allāh (ﷻ) and follow the shayṭān, Iblīs? Allāh (ﷻ) says:

> (Escape to) Allāh, the true Guardian-Protector. (Tafsir of 2:257)

Allāh (ﷻ) is the supporter of those who are honest. Allāh (ﷻ) will forbid those who disobey Him from tasting the love. They will not be able to taste the love. Those who love Allāh (ﷻ), those who follow His divine law, will be under the tent of Allāh (ﷻ). They will be in the Garden with spreading branches where you can always find His provision.

> Say: 'If you love Allāh (ﷻ) then follow me.' (3:31)

Music plays.

> *I enjoy mentioning His name in every way, in every picture.*
> *Even though people blame me, I do not care.*
> *I enjoy mentioning Him, I enjoy remembering Him.*
> *I do not care if anyone says stop;*
> *I will not listen to their blaming.*

Allāh (ﷻ) gives me this special gift, Allāh (ﷻ), the only truth, al-Ḥaqq, He gave me a message for those who have already heard the divine call, but disobeyed. I hope and I ask Allāh (ﷻ) to open their hearts, their spirits and their minds to be among those who receive His mercy and purification. His message is the message of the Most Compassionate, the Most Merciful.

When you mention the name of Allāh (ﷻ) with sincerity in your heart, it is not just your tongue that says the name. Every part of you is saying the name. Your trillions of cells are saying the name of Allāh (ﷻ) when you say it with sincerity. My love, my spirit, by mentioning the One I love, I will have eternal life.

My beloveds, keep repeating, keep mentioning and keep remembering. Keep giving the water of life to your hearts and your spirits so that you can continue to be in Allāh's order, the divine order in which He commanded us to reside.

It is the holy order to carry Your message and to save all people from suffering around the world, and not only this world, but in all of Your worlds that You created and gave the real life. You asked and ordered them to carry the flag of happiness, pleasure and spirit, which will send love to their hearts, for You are our love. You are our Lord (ﷻ). Oh, my Lord (ﷻ).

I will not listen to people who say many different things, who try to distort the orders of Allāh (ﷻ) or make the orders of Allāh (ﷻ) confusing. They live in illusion, in pictures that they talk about with false tongues. This is not what Allāh (ﷻ) wants. He wants you to throw your self, your heart and your spirit between the arms of Allāh (ﷻ) under His religion of unity. He wants you to follow everything that He says and then you will be a pure one.

Do not choose another way, my children. Do not choose dark and false ways. Be in the ocean of your Beloved, under His command, under what He says for you to do because He cares about you. He wants you to be and to live in the way that He wants for you. You will be in His ocean, full of love.

This is the life for you, my daughters, my sons, my children. I will open my life and my spirit to every one of you who wants life. This life has already been given by Allāh (ﷻ). The provision comes from Allāh (ﷻ).

Many, many thanks Allāh (ﷻ), for You gave me the water of mercy. I ask You to accept my supplication and to give this holy water of mercy to others, to all my children, and to allow them to live a good life.

Oh my beloveds, let's hear your beautiful melodies. Let all people hear this beautiful music. Allāh (ﷻ). These are the prayers that You command us to pray and we obey You, as You wish.

The one who blames me
gives me the good news that I am close to my Beloved.
I enjoy remembering Him. I enjoy mentioning Him.

I do not care about those who choose to disobey. They choose to be disobedient although Allāh (ﷻ) ordered them to hear Him and to treat others with love. Allāh (ﷻ) wants us to give mercy and love to others. What can I say? It makes me very sad and I hope they will open their ears and their hearts again, because Allāh (ﷻ) gave us a great, great gate, a large door. It is the door of tawba. He called to His creatures and said to them on the tongue of His Messenger (ﷺ):

Oh My worshipful slave,
if you did not make mistakes
I would create another creation that would make mistakes
and that would repent to Me,
and I would give them tawba and forgive their mistakes.

They will see all of His doors open, but only the ones who are honest, who make their real tawba and are willing to be guided, will enter. Allāh (ﷻ) will change those people. He will change their bad, offensive deeds into good deeds. Allāh (ﷻ) is the Forgiver, the Merciful, the Most Compassionate. This is the end of this talk, because for each article, every talk, there is a station."

Music plays.

It is more beautiful to remember my Beloved
than anything else.
I enjoy remembering Him.
It is very beautiful, more beautiful than anything else.
If anyone tries to stop me from loving my Beloved,
If anyone blames me and tells me to stop,
it is good news for me, because I will love Him more.

When someone tries to stop me from loving my Beloved
and tells me not to love Him like this,
it is good news to me that I am close to my Beloved.
I will soon be with Him.
I am with Him.
I do not care about those who try to stop me from loving Him.
With all my spirit, I have ruined my spirit with His love.
I want to die for Him; I love Him.

Because He gave me life.

Oh, my Love, Ḥabībī.
Now I recognize the good news.
People start to blame me, to ask why I love Him.
I do not care. I love Him and I will be with Him in every song.
I will be close to Him.

There is no way to live unless it is with Him. He gives me life. He gives me what I need completely, more than what I said. Allāhu Akbar.

You are within my spirit.

If I leave Him, I will lose everything. He is generous with me. He keeps my life between His hands. I am one of His children; He is not from me.

I speak about everyone who loves Allāh (ﷻ). Be one of His children and swim in His ocean. You will have the complete life and this is what people need. Allāhu Akbar. Be like the bird who sings the song of Allāh (ﷻ) everywhere. Then you will hear the music of Dāwūd (عليه السلام) who always lives in the real Garden, even now.

The reading continues, "I hope that my words enter your hearts, spirits and white minds. Keep the relationship and the love between you and Allāh (ﷻ) all the time. I hope that you will find that you live in Allāh (ﷻ), with Allāh (ﷻ) and for Allāh (ﷻ), and that you direct yourselves toward Allāh (ﷻ).

I wish for happiness in this life for all the beloveds, for all those who are suffering and for all of the sick people in this world. I ask Allāh (ﷻ) to send His mercy and to fill this life full of mercy. I ask to see my beloveds as one nation and for them to turn back toward Him, as He says in His Holy Qurʾān:

> This, your (human) nation, is one nation,
> and I am your Lord so worship Me (alone). (21:92)

Allāh (ﷻ), we heard and we obeyed.
Please, Allāh (ﷻ), forgive us, for we all return back to You.
We promise You to keep the promise,
to pay our souls, spirits, hearts and bodies as a sacrifice.
So, please accept our sacrifice.
It is pure, just for Your face, from us.
We are very poor, so help us in this life.
Accept our supplications.
We need You.

My beloveds, this is the time for a very special promise. I want to help you open your hearts to know the secrets of the love that I talk about. I want to make a special prayer for Allāh (ﷻ) to help all of my children know in their hearts the deep secret love that I talk about. If you want to open your hearts more and to know how to give the love the way Allāh (ﷻ) wants, this special promise will help open your heart."

The bayatu-l-kubra (great promise) is for all people to receive real healing and love from Allāh (ﷻ). I want everyone to promise Allāh (ﷻ) to be in the right way when giving healings, to follow what Allāh (ﷻ) says, and to give healings in the way that Allāh gives them to us through His beloved prophets. I do not want to have anyone heal from his mind, only from what Allāh (ﷻ) says. I am sure this will make me very happy.

I want to speak a message for all to hear. This is a message from my heart. I would like to see many people come to the University of Spiritual Healing because it is a special university. I am sure Allāh (ﷻ) will make this university bigger and bigger. If anyone has a friend or beloved, call him to take his chance, because he may not find another one.

Tawba is the Door to Goodness

Tawba Teachings from *The Traveler's Journey* and "The One Who Knows All the Secrets" and Music
Tuesday, August 4, 2010 AM, USHS Year 1 Spring

لا إله إلا الله - لا إله إلا الله - لا إله إلا الله - محمد رسول الله عليه صلاة الله
لا إله إلا الله - لا إله إلا الله - لا إله إلا الله - ابراهيم رسول الله عليه صلاة الله
لا إله إلا الله - لا إله إلا الله - لا إله إلا الله - موسى رسول الله عليه صلاة الله
لا إله إلا الله - لا إله إلا الله - لا إله إلا الله - عيسى رسول الله عليه صلاة الله
اللهم انت السلام ومنك السلام و إليك يعود السلام
تباركت ربنا وتعاليت يا ذوالجلال والإكرام

Peace be upon you, my beloveds. It is my honor to be among you today, to give you the message of Allāh (ﷻ) and of all the prophets (ؑ). The message has been sent by the Angel Jībrīl (Gabriel) (ؑ). These orders and commands are not from me—they are not from my head—they are from Allāh (ﷻ) to His angels (ؑ), and Jībrīl (ؑ) relayed them to all the prophets (ؑ).

No one knows about these commands and orders, just those who understand them through Allāh's holy books. These are the books that Allāh (ﷻ) sent to His prophets (ؑ), not from His self, not from His Heart, not from His spirit. Everything would not follow the orders from Allāh (ﷻ) if it were not for Allāh (ﷻ).

The one who is unable to understand the holy books will not be able to understand Allāh's orders. Allāh (ﷻ) created us and He created our minds, our hearts, our spirits and our selves. No one can understand all of that without divine knowledge. From this knowledge, you should know, is where Allāh (ﷻ) created you from clay. Allāh (ﷻ) created your mind and He created your heart and your body and your hands. He knows with absolute certainty if any part of your body has a problem, He created cures for pain. The Prophet (ﷺ) said:

> Allāh (ﷻ) has not sent any disease without sending a cure to it.

Who knows these cures? Allāh (ﷻ) taught all the prophets (ﷺ) about them. Those who disobey Allāh (ﷻ), the disbelievers, cannot understand and know the secret of what Allāh (ﷻ) sent. Only Allāh (ﷻ) knows the secret of what a human being might need if he is sick in his mind, heart and body. Physicians, when they do not have divine knowledge, will fail most of the time. Physicians need to have divine knowledge and follow the orders of Allāh (ﷻ).

If someone says that they want to learn about Sufism, but they do not want to learn about the divine law (sharīʿa)...the divine law was explained to you: the truth exists in the Qurʾān. It is in the sunna and the divine book. The Prophet Muḥammad (ﷺ) received the divine law from Allāh (ﷻ) through the Angel Jībrīl (ﷺ).

We believe in all the prophets (ﷺ). We believe in Mūsā (Moses) (ﷺ) as a prophet, we believe in ʿĪsā (Jesus) (ﷺ) as a prophet, and we believe in Ibrāhīm (Abraham) (ﷺ) as a prophet. We make no separation or discrimination between them. We are calling you to the message the unity, which we are following. Allāh (ﷻ) is the Only One. He created everything. He gave us life and He will let us die.

Previously I explained the way, the path to knowledge. First of all, you should follow His orders. Allāh (ﷻ) sent prayers (ṣalāh) as a mandatory order to all of the prophets (ﷺ). The final religion is Islām. What is the meaning of Islām? Islām is the way to divine peace. It is the way to keep your spirit and your heart safe, and Allāh (ﷻ) ordered us to carry the flag of peace, love, mercy and justice. This is the message of Allāh (ﷻ).

You should understand the divine law, but how can you understand it if you haven't learned to read and write Arabic? All secrets, all languages, are hidden within the Arabic letters. For example, the first letter in Arabic is "alif" which has the same sound as "a" in English. The letter "a" means that the language of the Qurʾān contains all languages.

If you look at ancient English you can see that English numbers are from Arabic numbers, and now you write them as Indian numbers. I do not want to go deeply into this subject.

Allāh (ﷻ) has just one language. He spoke to all the prophets (عليهم السلام) in just one language. Allāh (ﷻ) knows all languages and He taught the angels (عليهم السلام) to speak in Syriac and Arabic and other languages. I insist and advise that all my beloveds, all those who want to be healers, know that they can be healers just by embodying the message of unity. Any other science will not follow the order of Allāh (ﷻ) and will not help them.

Welcome, my beloveds, from the bottom of my heart. I wish you all success and I wish for your hearts and your spirits to hear this message. This university teaches the commands and orders of this type. There is no other university in the world like this. There are other universities. They started to teach the divine orders, but Allāh (ﷻ) selected you and Allāh (ﷻ) selected these teachers to give you divine knowledge. You will be a good healer by following these orders and commands, and you will know how to heal others when you learn these orders in the correct way, I am sure. I confirm that you will be a healer. This is a mercy from Allāh (ﷻ).

For example, someone will say, "I want to travel from the world of Malakūt or Jabarūt," and then they say, "I want to reach the worlds of fanāʾ and baqāʾ." This is beautiful, if you can understand how to do so.

For example, you must do your prayers (ṣalāh). When you stand to pray, your body will stand. While standing you are in the position of the world of Mulk. How do you pray? You should know how to pray and the physical benefits of these movements. There is exercise in these movements.

When you stand, you will stand facing Allāh (ﷻ) and not facing idols. You will say, "Allāhu Akbar (God is the Greatest)." What is the benefit of this movement? Your teachers will teach you this. When you are humble and you prostrate to Allāh (ﷻ), you will travel from the world of Mulk, this world, to the world of Malakūt, another world. However, it is important for you to know the meaning of these movements.

Do not let your mind be busy with the lower world while you are praying. You should only think about Allāh (ﷻ). Before prayer, you should announce the purification of your nafs, your spirit, your heart and your body. You should not use the mind as you like. There are many illusions and pictures. We believe in these material things; for example, a carpenter made this table. Who made the wood? Did Allāh (ﷻ) make the wood? Who allowed the wood to be here? Allāh (ﷻ). We do not believe in illusions.

We should follow the orders of Allāh (ﷻ). After that, purify your tongue. Purify your eyes. Purify your ears. If you have purified your body completely, you will be in the world of Malakūt, the pure world. After that, you will begin the journey of the nafs and you will walk through all the stations I mentioned in the book.

It is important to follow the prophets (ﷺ), so that we are all carrying the message of all the prophets (ﷺ) and al-Ḥaqq. This is the divine law and the truth that Allāh (ﷻ) sent down to all the prophets (ﷺ). Then, when you say, "Bismi-llāh," I will hear you and you will call Allāh (ﷻ), "Ash-Shāfī" the Healer, because you have purified your tongue, your heart and your self. My teachers will explain this to you, and I feel and I know that our teachers are honest, they love Allāh (ﷻ), and they can give you this clear message.

No one can say, "I see Allāh (ﷻ)" or, "I saw Allāh (ﷻ)." When you are a prophet then maybe you can say that. I do not want to go further into that subject. I want to encourage you to receive knowledge from the divine. This is a holy thing and this is a mosque.

There are special things for Allāh (ﷻ), special places, special times, special people. This is a special place. The people who try to carry the words of Allāh (ﷻ) and rate it highly. They are special and this is a place to pray. We do not want to be in hotels and other buildings, drinking alcohol and doing other bad things. We want our beloveds to receive the teachings in a holy place. They are holy and the place is holy for them.

In the beginning, all schools were in a mosque and in holy areas and Allāh (ﷻ) said, "Mention the name of Allāh (ﷻ) in these homes, schools and places." So you will say, "Allāhu Akbar."

We brought you here because this is a holy place. I ask Allāh (ﷻ) to support you and to give you all the best all the time. I want to explain tawba to you, which teaches how to be in this way.

This reading is comprised of excerpts on tawba from *The Traveler's Journey of Healing through Divine Love, Knowledge and Truth.*

"I ask Allāh (ﷻ) to make us steadfast in His way.
Make us firm in Your Way and forgive our faults.
Conceal our mistakes and bestow Your Mercy upon us.

Oh Allāh (ﷻ), I ask You by the reality of Your lofty essence
and by the reality of Your praiseworthy Prophet (ﷺ).
Please do not let any one of us be miserable or sad, or suffer.
And please do not forsake us
and put us in shame on the Day of Judgment,
but forgive us and bestow Your mercy upon us.
Grant us happiness, all of us.
Āmīn.

Know that everything depends upon tawba. Tawba is your first step and it is a continuous step. It is like changing the oil in your car. Can you actually drive a car without oil or when it has a problem? No, you have to fix it in order to drive it. You are like this vehicle and you are full of things that need to be fixed and rectified and washed and cleaned in order to drive, to arrive at the divine presence.

The path to Allāh (ﷻ) is full of obstacles and danger and you must continue to purify yourself by walking this path until you become fully conscious of the divine presence. You must purify the body and the soul through tawba from their illnesses, because our bodies and hearts and souls accumulate dirt that causes illness. We must purify ourselves and truly follow the divine way by following His commands and prohibitions."

For this teaching Sidi had Ṣalīḥ Kent read an unpublished reading, "The One Who Knows All the Secrets" which is based upon the music of Shaykh Yasīn at-Tuhamī with Sidi's lyrics.

The lyrics of the music
are bold, italicized and indented.
The reading is in bold text.
Sidi's live commentary is in plain text.

"I ask forgiveness from the only One who forgives sins. Yā Allāh (ﷻ)! Oh Allāh (ﷻ), I am coming to You filled with all my sins, knocking on Your door and asking You to open it for me, please. Not only for my own sins, but I direct myself to You with all the sins of all the people on earth and on behalf of those who are suffering around the world for these sins. I ask You desperately, from the bottom of my heart, I make my supplication and I plead, Allāh (ﷻ), I plead for your acceptance, for I speak on behalf of all sinners; on behalf of all those who suffer. Now I come humbly to ask Your help (ﷻ) and Your support (ﷻ).

They come to You with deep sincerity. They are honest and sincere and they are asking You to accept their tawba. They are longing, they are hoping, as they ask You for their tawba because they direct their faces to You, Allāh (ﷻ), to Your merciful face because You are the Most Compassionate and the Most Merciful (ﷻ).

So, my Allāh (ﷻ), open the doors, for You are the One who will answer our prayers and supplications (ﷻ). You are the One who forgives all sins (ﷻ). You are at-Tawwab (ﷻ). You say, "I am the Forgiver. I am the Merciful." For that reason, Allāh (ﷻ), I come to You with deep sincerity. Yes, I come to You with a clean heart, like what You say. And anyone who comes with a clean heart, and he is crying under Your throne, You say:

> If anyone asks Me for anything, if he is sincere, I will accept him,
> I will accept every word that he says.

For that reason, I carry all these sins to Your Garden. Like what You asked, I come to Your Garden. I choose You to rub out and erase all my sins, and to return me to be a real child between Your arms (ﷻ) because You are My Lord (ﷻ). You are my Beloved in this life."

When your Mother gave you birth to you, you were pure. Your hearing was pure. Your heart was pure. Your seeing was pure. All of your feelings were pure, clear. How much you cried and screamed! You were saying, "Aah aah," which is a name of Allāh (ﷻ), that greatest name. Allāh (ﷻ).

Oh Allāh (ﷻ), You let me be here. You let me be here in this world, the world of Mulk. When you were first born, your spirit was purified. You were invoking Allāh (ﷻ) to be pure. You were crying, asking Allāh (ﷻ) to let you be pure. Allāh (ﷻ) said:

> And (I have) shown him the two ways (good and evil). (90:10)

I give you two places, the breasts of your mother. Allāh (ﷻ) gave the mother this milk because Allāh (ﷻ) gave her pure love.

There are many evils in this country and in other countries, and I want to tell you about when your mother gave birth to you. Many mothers do not breastfeed their children, because they think that if they feed their babies from their breasts they will not be beautiful and they will have problems with their health. Allāh (ﷻ) created them and He sent milk through them for a reason.

Alternatives to breastfeeding will not be organic and natural and they will cause many diseases. There are 27 arteries in the breast. Allāh (ﷻ) taught the baby how to obtain food from breasts. Now the young ladies, the mothers, they stop giving milk in this way and breast cancer is widespread, because they stop following the order of Allāh (ﷻ). If you go to a Bedouin village, those mothers never feed their children except breast milk. None of those mothers have breast cancer. There is no concept of it there.

The reading continues, "You are My Lord (ﷻ). You are my Beloved in this life. So, please, accept me in the right place. Give me real love in order to help me to be clean from every sin I made before. For that reason I ask You...I'm sure You do not discharge anyone who has the deep suffering because You contain everyone who comes like me. I am a very poor slave for you."

Music plays.

> *You are the Owner of everything.*
> *You are the Only One we ask for help.*
> *You are the Forgiver.*
> *You forgive all our sins.*
> *I am knocking on your door.*
> *For those are the secrets, the secrets that no one knows.*
> *You are generous and You praise those who praise You.*
> *We don't see You but we know You.*

The reading continues, "Oh, Allāh (ﷻ), all the world is in Your Hands. No one else can change those who create suffering and sin without the deep sincere. There is no hope for the one who continues to create suffering for those who are crying everywhere. But I ask You to excuse anyone who holds out his hands and says, "Allāh (ﷻ), I make tawba from my spirit. Āmīn." There is no one who knows the secret in every heart of the human being, Allāh (ﷻ), only You.

I am sure that You will give everyone a chance to return under Your wing. For I know, Allāh (ﷻ), that You know all the secrets. You know and I know that You see all that the people see, You hear all that they hear and You see the black ant on the black rock on the moonless night.

Because of that, there is no way for anyone who says, "You are not hearing or not listening," for You are the Seer, You are the Hearer. You see and You hear. You are the Creator, Allāh (ﷻ). You know the secret. You know what their selves say to them. Because of that we come to You. We are Your servants. We are Your slaves.

Don't despair, my beloveds, of the mercy of Allāh (ﷻ). Allāh (ﷻ) forgives all sins, for He is the Forgiver. He is the Merciful.

Allāh (ﷻ), we come humbly prostrated. We don't want anything but Your acceptance, Allāh (ﷻ), we only want Your forgiveness, and we're not asking You for anything else, just Your mercy and Your forgiveness. For You are the Merciful, the Most Merciful. You are the Compassionate, the Most Compassionate. Allāh (ﷻ), there is nothing like You.

I come because everyone knows that You created us. Then, everyone throws his self and his heart and his spirit between Your Arms, my Beloved God (ﷻ)."

Music plays.

> *You are the only One who answers our supplications.*
> *I carry my sense in the walking.*
> *I am walking, asking Your forgiveness.*
> *I invoke You, You are the only One who helps. You accept. 3*
> *You are the Owner of everything.*
> *We are asking Your help.*
> *You are the only Forgiver.*
> *You forgive our sins.*
> *I am knocking on Your door,*
> *Oh You who knows all the secrets.*

Allāh (ﷻ) created you pure. Pure and clean, with a pure heart, a pure mind, pure seeing, pure hearing, a pure self and a pure body. Allāh (ﷻ) created you like this. All of us were born as children this way. We don't know more than to eat good food, not ḥarām food. We took food from our mothers. We took this life, step by step, day by day. If mothers follow the orders of Allāh (ﷻ) and teach her children what Allāh (ﷻ) taught her, babies will stay pure. The children will remain holy because Allāh (ﷻ) created the human being holy because his life is from Allāh (ﷻ). Allāh (ﷻ) says:

> I created the human being and his body from My spirit.

Parents now do not follow the orders of Allāh (ﷻ). They do not teach their children knowledge from Allāh (ﷻ). They try to destroy them by teaching them the other sciences which pollute themselves and their spirits. Allāh (ﷻ) taught Ādam (ﷺ) all the names.

You should teach your children politeness, how to be responsible, how to be loyal, and how to respect his parents, brothers and sisters. If we teach our children the divine orders, everything will be okay. This is our way. Do not let him be a killer, a thief, or a liar. Just be aware of the divine knowledge. Allāh (ﷻ) says:

> I created Ādam (ﷺ) like My picture,
> so all people would be brothers and love each other.

Be polite and full of love. This is the first thing to teach the child as he starts to speak. As you speak to him, he will speak. If the mother speaks Arabic, he will speak Arabic. So the mother is a school. She will be the school if she drinks from the holy water. If she follows the orders of Allāh (ﷻ).

The presidents and governments of Allāh cheated Allāh (ﷻ) and they don't follow the message of Allāh (ﷻ). We carry the message of Allāh (ﷻ). We should teach our children how to carry the message of Allāh (ﷻ), the message of love, justice and freedom. Our knowledge, our science, is full of politeness. There is no discrimination between black and white. This is our way to Allāh (ﷻ). This is the way of all the prophets (ﷺ). This is the truth.

If the mother follows the divine orders, she will teach her child how to be like an angel. The believers can teach their children how to carry the message of Allāh (ﷻ). They can teach them how to love each other. This is our way. This is the way we want to establish.

We ask all my beloveds to repent to Allāh (ﷻ): repent with your heart and repent with your spirit. This is the beginning of healing. After that you will enter the gates of Allāh (ﷻ). He does not say, "Who believes?" He says, "Who repents to Allāh (ﷻ)?" After repenting a person believes, and then he will be guided and Allāh (ﷻ) will open the gate. Allāh (ﷻ) will change the evil and bad deeds of these people into good deeds.

So who will repent an honest tawba? You will be like you were right after your mother gave birth to you. When we mention the beloveds who repent, we call them the children of Allāh (ﷻ) because they pay their tawba to Allāh (ﷻ).

Music plays.

> *You know all the secrets,*
> *You who accept our ablutions.*
> *You who know all of the secrets, all of our secrets.*
> *You who will give, praise to those who face You.*

The reading continues, "There is no one who knows the secret, Allāh (ﷻ). There is only You because You are Allāh (ﷻ) and You are my God (ﷻ). You know the secret that no one knows.

So, Allāh (ﷻ), I send my thanks to You, my Lord, and no one else can contain everything from all the people in this world because it is You who created everything. For that reason I send my voice for all the people.
This time is very short, beloveds. This life is very short, and so I send this message for everyone everywhere to stop sinning before he leaves this world, for he can only choose one---Hell or the Garden. The door of Allāh (ﷻ) is open, so do not lose your chance. This is a warning, a warning from my heart through Allāh (ﷻ): the door of Allāh (ﷻ) is open, so don't lose your chance.

This is not just from my heart. This is the voice of all the prophets (ﷺ) to everyone in this world. You can give mercy to everyone who's gone far away, and you can bring him and you can bring his spirit, whether he is your father or whether he is your beloved. You can do this for everyone who is crying from deep suffering before his time is finished.

Now, my children, in this time, my tears fall down. My heart is very, very sad for anyone who has not heard my message, but I am still in the deep praying for all of them. I say, "Welcome" to everyone who has a special heart. I say, "Welcome" to all those who are crying. I say, "Welcome" to whoever accepts my voice and what I take from the holy books that Allāh (ﷻ) sent to the Prophet Ibrāhīm (ﷺ), the Prophet Mūsā

(ﷺ), the Prophet ʿĪsā (ﷺ) and the Prophet Muḥammad (ﷺ), and all those beloveds of Allāh (ﷻ) who send their voices for everyone that Allāh (ﷻ) created, from the beginning to the end.

My beloveds, open your ears to hear me. Wake up! The duration of this life is short for everyone. You were not told that you would live like Nūḥ (Noah) (ﷺ) for 1,000 years or more. So, please, I love everyone because Allāh (ﷻ) and His Prophet (ﷺ) said:

> All creatures are the children of Allāh (ﷻ),

I would like to give the mercy and the peace and the love and the justice and the freedom to every home. I would like to make all of them help each other, love each other and serve each other in the way of Allāh (ﷻ). Then everyone will see that in every home all people will be happy, for this is the message of Allāh (ﷻ) through His prophets (ﷺ).

Allāh (ﷻ), You give anyone who comes everything he asks for. But it is important, beloveds, to make deep tawba with deep sincerity. When He sees your tears come from your spirit, from your heart and from your tongue in the deep sincere, then surely Allāh (ﷻ) will give you what you ask.

Be ready by always being in deep gratitude. Always be in deep gratitude. Thank Allāh (ﷻ) for this holy gift of tawba. When you give thanks to Allāh (ﷻ) with real sincerity and you do not continue to do what you were doing wrong, then surely Allāh (ﷻ) will accept your tawba and not give any chance for Iblīs, pictures, or illusion to stop you.

My beloveds, don't listen to just any voice, only listen to the voice of the prophets (ﷺ) because they speak from Allāh (ﷻ). Only listen to the voices of the prophets (ﷺ), and then I am sure Allāh (ﷻ) will change you.

So, clean your spirits, my beloveds. Clean your heart and clean your self and He will protect you from every bad thing to be a pure, pure beloved for Allāh (ﷻ).

Then He will take you between His arms and this is the real garden. For that reason, this is the message from Him, through what I've taken from the religion of unity, which is what Allāh (ﷻ) sent through all the prophets (عليهم السلام)."

Tawba is the door to goodness, and it is how to be in a good relationship with your beloved Allāh (ﷻ). One of the lovers of Allāh (ﷻ) said:

> I hope everything will be fine between me and You,
> I don't care if everything will be bad between me and others.
> Everything will be okay between me and You,
> if there is love between me and You,
> everything will be fine with me.

Everything upon this earth is dust. Are you ready to make this beautiful relationship between you and your Lord? He loves you. Allāh (ﷻ) says:

> He loves them, so they love Him. (5:54)

Allāh (ﷻ) loves you and He created you. He created you in the perfect shape. This is a sign that He loves you and that He will forgive you. He is the Forgiver. Come to Allāh (ﷻ) and do not hesitate. Come to pay your tawba.

The reading continues, "I thank Allāh (ﷻ) first, and I thank, also, all the prophets (عليهم السلام) who give us this deep chance to always be connected with our beloved God (ﷻ).

Oh, Allāh (ﷻ), I want all my beloveds to always be connected with You. Then surely the door of mercy will open for them.

He will open the door of Love, the door of peace, which you will be able to carry, the door to real freedom. He will open the door to justice, for this is what all people need. There is no suffering after that, only heaven.

So understand this word that I speak to you all, my beloved children, from my deepest spirit and my deepest heart. In this moment I send my tears, for my holy heart is full of the suffering and sadness I see in the

world. When I see all of the beloveds and all of these children that are sick and who can't find medicine or food, I ask Allāh (ﷻ) to send His mercy for all creation everywhere, without separation, for I carry the religion of unity that Allāh (ﷻ) sent through all His beloved prophets (ﷺ). I want you to praise Allāh (ﷻ), always praise Allāh (ﷻ).

Most of the people, Allāh (ﷻ), they don't see You. But through a clean spirit and a clean heart they can know. With deep sincerity and an honest spirit, you will see that Allāh (ﷻ) is generous. When a person follows all the practices from Allāh (ﷻ) in the perfect way, he will come to know You. Allāh (ﷻ).

I say to you: be careful not to give your sins a chance to stop you from making tawba. Go ahead, my children, travel your road to the One who is merciful, for His door is open to everyone. He says on the tongue of His Prophet (ﷺ):

> If you did not sin, I would create others who did.

This means Allāh (ﷻ) is saying: I won't allow him to suffer without accepting astaghfiru-llāh from him, for I created people to say to Me, 'I make tawba for Your Face, my Lord. I come to be cleaned from everything through my spirit, through my heart, through my self and through my body.'"

When you announce your tawba, you are a good man and a good woman. You should remember your parents. They were the reason you are here in this life. Ask Allāh's forgiveness for them, even if they pass away. You should ask Allāh's forgiveness for them. He is the Forgiver, He is the Most Merciful and Compassionate. Allāh (ﷻ) says that the a person will pass away but he will leave three things behind him.

The first thing he will leave behind is a good daughter or son. A good son or daughter will ask forgiveness for his parents and offer a continuous sacrifice for them after their deaths. This sacrifice will help them. The third thing is a good job, good work. For example, helping a school or a hospital or people. Those three things will continue to exist in this world and even after death.

The reading continues, "We are helpless, my Lord (ﷻ), and with my heart and my spirit You will see I follow all the practices that You send to make me a complete beloved who follows what the Prophet (ﷺ) sent. I promise You to be a real slave for Your face. I promise to not look back and to not sin again after You accept me as a poor slave for You."

You should keep your promise you made in your tawba. Do not go back to your mistakes. You should repeat your tawba every time and ask Allāh's forgiveness. Allāh (ﷻ) accepts your supplications and Allāh (ﷻ) wants for us to be honest and loyal.

The reading continues, "No one who has sins can see Allāh (ﷻ), but when everyone cleans themselves then Allāh (ﷻ) gives us a very holy gift, like that that He gave Mūsā (ﷺ), when he asked his Lord:

> **Oh my Lord, show me Yourself that I may look upon You. (7:143)**

Allāh (ﷻ) responds, "When you are in the material realm it is important to clean your heart first. Then look to your heart and your spirit after you leave the material body. Begin to make real prostration, the prostration that opens to Me, Allāh (ﷻ). Then, through your spirit, through your heart, you can see Me."

For that reason, when a person makes the real prostration, when he is absent from himself, when he is absent through al-fanā', through al-baqā', then he sees Allāh (ﷻ)."

When you purify your body, your heart and your spirit, then you will be among those people who are honest. Allāh (ﷻ) will let you see wonderful things that you have never seen before. He will let you hear beautiful things such as you have never heard before. If you are not polite, you will not be in this position, in fanā'u-l-baqā'.

The reading continues, "This is a very holy thing if you follow what Allāh (ﷻ) says in the Qur'ān."

Music plays.

Praise Allāh (ﷻ), we have never seen You but we knew.
You who accepts our excuses.
You are the Forgiver. You forgive us.
You who give praise to those who praise You.
Praise to Allāh (ﷻ), glory to Allāh (ﷻ).
We never have seen You but we know You.
We recognize You. We are longing to meet You.
We worship You not because we are scared of Your Fire."

Knowledge is the basis. You will not be able to know something just by walking to Allāh (ﷻ). You have to follow His orders, pay your tawba and worship the presence of Allāh (ﷻ). He is here, He is everywhere. He hears you and He sees you, He will never be absent. But if you disobey Allāh (ﷻ), you will be absent.

We worship You not because we are scared of Your Fire,
nor because we want to enter Your garden.
We worship You because of You.
We want to see You, Allāh (ﷻ), we want to be with You.

The reading concludes, "Oh Allāh (ﷻ), accept all the prayers and all that my beloveds ask of You, because everyone promises You to keep themselves inside Your circle, inside Your world, Allāh (ﷻ), that is full of peace and love and mercy and justice. Āmīn.

I am sure that everyone heard my voice, for my voice carries tears and sadness. I ask Allāh (ﷻ) to keep my beloveds, to keep all the people who make real tawba in Your way, and everyone who likes to see all the people happy with Your help. Surely, everyone is working to keep the promise between You and them, Allāh (ﷻ). Āmīn, Āmīn, Āmīn."

So my beloveds, come to take your promise again in the deep secret love for the face of Allāh (ﷻ). Āmīn, Āmīn, Āmīn.

My Lord, my beloveds and my children come to You, asking You for forgiveness. They announce their tawba. They will worship no one but You. And they will hear You. They came to follow the tawba. They are honest and loyal.

invoke You, Allāh (ﷻ) to purify their minds,
to purify their hearts,
their spirits,
their tongues,
their selves. Allāh (ﷻ),

I am asking You to wash their minds,
their hearts,
their spirits
with the holy, holy, repentant water,
and to let them be honest believers.

Allāh (ﷻ) I am asking You to accept their tawba.
Oh Allāh (ﷻ), do not let them be away from You.
Do not let them be miserable.
Teach them the knowledge You want them to know,
from Your divine knowledge.
Wash them with the holy water,
to let them be scientists and believers and loyal.

Alif Lāām Mīīm.
Kaf Ha ʿAyn Ṣāād.
Kaf ʿAyn Sin Khāāf
Hā Mīīīm.
Alif Lāām Ṣāād.

The Straight Path to Love

"My Heart Tells Me" and Music

Wednesday, August 5, 2010 AM, USHS Year 1 Spring

لا إله إلا الله - لا إله إلا الله - لا إله إلا الله - محمد رسول الله عليه صلاة الله
لا إله إلا الله - لا إله إلا الله - لا إله إلا الله - ابراهيم رسول الله عليه صلاة الله
لا إله إلا الله - لا إله إلا الله - لا إله إلا الله - موسى رسول الله عليه صلاة الله
لا إله إلا الله - لا إله إلا الله - لا إله إلا الله - عيسى رسول الله عليه صلاة الله
اللهم انت السلام ومنك السلام و إليك يعود السلام
تباركت ربنا وتعاليت يا ذوالجلال والإكرام

Oh Allāh, You are the Peace and peace returns to You. Peace is from You. Allāh (ﷻ), You are the Forgiver and You forgive us and You are able to do that.

Peace be upon you, my beloveds. I ask for all good things for you on this morning, in this holy place. I wish for this to be a place for light and justice and to be a place that Allāh (ﷻ) will accept all of you. All of the people who take care of this place need to remember that it exists for Allāh (ﷻ).

Beloveds. I worry about all of you and I want you all to be safe and happy in this place, I want there to be an easy way to reach it. I feel sad every year when I come to this land. I notice that when we come by car it is stony. If this were your house, you would not accept this road's stoniness.

I take care and I worry about my beloveds. I worry about accidents happening. Two years back I mentioned this and I said that you should take care of it. This will not cost much money. It doesn't cost $100,000. It is easy. It would take me six days to make an easy-to-drive road that would make all the people who come here safe. I just want to mention this issue to all of you. Don't say, "It would cost $20,000 or $50,000." It would take just six days.

I just want to mention this so that everyone stays safe. I hope you will listen and not let others be endangered. If you want to make this center safe, you should not spend a lot of money for no reason. That's what I want to mention this, so that you can make this center strong, easy to reach and safe.

Many people will come here. Many people will come to the center because we have added other sciences—the Qur'ān and Arabic—so we must prepare a safe road for them. You shouldn't say, "We don't have the money." You have the money and we can use this money with wisdom. Your people are kind and good people, as I know. I think they will agree with me.

We turn now to the true lesson and we will keep giving you knowledge about health, and we will explain it in detail to prepare the first year students, inshā'a-llāh.

As I said, the gate to knowledge is love. If you love something, you will give everything to be with it and to live with it. True love will give you that. You cannot be in a home without love. Lack of love is the opposite of the qualities of Allāh (ﷻ). When we give love, peace, justice and freedom to all people it is a sign of our faith in Allāh (ﷻ). Love should be in your heart and your spirit. A healthy heart can accept these principles. Life without love is nothing.

Love—you can find love in bears and trees and all of the creatures of Allāh (ﷻ). You can find a healthy mind, a pure mind, within a healthy body. Allāh (ﷻ) has ordered us, those walking the straight path, to have healthy minds. The straight path is the closest way to be with and arrive at Allāh (ﷻ). This is the main point I wanted to mention.

For this teaching Sidi used an unpublished reading, "My Heart Tells Me," which is based upon the music of Shaykh Yasīn at-Tuhamī with Sidi's lyrics.

The lyrics of the music are bold, italicized and indented. The reading is in bold text. Sidi's live commentary is in plain text.

Music plays.

> *My heart tells me that You will make me disappear.*
> *I sacrifice my spirit to You,*
> *whether You know that or You don't.*

"I knock on the door of love, asking for a drop of love. I ask Him to accept me. This is divine love, for He manifested Himself through the world of love.

Many praises to You, Allāh (ﷻ), You are the only One. You are the One who revealed Himself in a beautiful picture.

Beloveds, before you come to the land of Allāh (ﷻ), you should swim in the sea of love to know my story, to know my secret through my singing and my understanding. If this is the secret of life, then I will become absent in this secret. If this is the matter, then it deserves a sacrifice. I will give a sacrifice. I will give a sacrifice to receive just one drop. I will give a sacrifice to cease my existence. In order to deserve this love, I will die, I will pass away. I will die to live an eternal life.

This eternal life is from you, Allāh (ﷻ). You let me into Your divine world, Your holy world, in order to free me from imagination and illusion. I am just an atom of love and this love gives me life. Prevent me from dying for any reason except for the sake of the One I love (ﷻ).

Oh Allāh (ﷻ), you say, 'My follower, come, for My door is open to those who are honest and come directly to Me, without turning left or right.'

My beloved, you revealed yourself with the light from the Eternal (ﷻ), so spread your perfume and fragrance in the world. This fragrance is the secret of life given to all people who fall in love with You. Give them a taste if they will sacrifice their hearts to You."

My heart. My heart. My heart is telling me that you will...Why am I saying, "My heart?" Why do I mention my heart many times? The heart is the center of all the senses and it is the center for your spiritual life. It will give you a sign pointing you to the door that will guide you to spring. Allāh (ﷻ) says:

> My heavens and My earth cannot contain Me.
> Only the heart of My faithful, honest servant contains Me.

Because of that we should keep our hearts for Allāh (ﷻ) and we should not allow devils and bad people to enter the divine home of Allāh (ﷻ)—our hearts. We should not to allow anyone who disobeys Allāh (ﷻ) to enter our hearts. The heart is the center of love and love will guide you to real love, not love at the sensory level, or fantasies about love, or sexual love. The heart will lead you if you purify yourself. It will lead you to true love, and through this you will give love to everyone and bestow wisdom to others.

This is not like some of you who say, "I am seeing something in my heart. I can see you in my heart." What is your power to see another person in your heart? Your heart is for you. You cannot see what other people's hearts contain. You cannot see the hearts of others. The human being has a holy kingdom and this heart controls everything—all the parts of your body, the divine signs of your body. If your heart is pure, you can use all of your body's parts in a correct and precise way.

Allāh (ﷻ) says, "For those who have a heart or are listening with pure ears, these are My eyes." He will give those people the melody of His heart. This melody, this peace, is holy. This melody is in each of you with everyone.

Allāh (ﷻ) created this heart. Don't put dirt into this divine heart. Keep it pure. Don't use your heart to house bad thoughts and illusions and imaginations. Allāh (ﷻ) created your heart. The heart never stops; it works day and night. The heart is the king. The Prophet Muḥammad (ﷺ) said:

> There is a piece of flesh inside the body; it is the heart.
> If the heart is well, the whole body is well.
> If the heart is not well, the whole body is not well.

The truth moves from the heart to the spirit, and when it is healthy, the heart will be huge and the spirit will be big and they will be in contact with everything. They will both be one.

What feeds your heart? The heart needs food—and its is al-maḥabba, the love. The heart will achieve peace by following the orders of Allāh (ﷻ), and in this way the heart will be able to contain divine knowledge, al-Ḥaqq. This position is al-Jabarūt, which contains many things. The people need it, because the human being will continue to travel to world of al-Laḥūt if he is honest and if his knowledge is true and pure. How can we travel like this? By following Allāh (ﷻ).

Allāh (ﷻ) wants you to be His beloved, so your Lover will give you everything you need. We, as Sufis, follow this way, and we follow this way by true knowledge. We will be the children of this moment. We will not say, "Tomorrow." Today. Sayyidinā Muḥammad (ﷺ) says:

> You live, in this moment, in the Garden.

Why do you postpone this? Look in your heart and see what the problem is. The science of hearts is faster than rockets if you sit in your heart. If you have a healthy heart, it will display signs of its health everywhere. If you are honest and carrying the message of Allāh (ﷻ), your heart will be full of His lights. Allāh (ﷻ) says, "I will let you see all of My signs throughout world if you are honest, but if you are not speaking from your pure heart..."

My heart is telling me that the white mind, combined with the spirit, can be used to discern right from wrong by the one who the spirit knows. A car can't move without fuel. The real fuel for your heart is knowledge gained through following the orders of Allāh (ﷻ). As the song will tell you, by remembering Allāh (ﷻ), by purifying your heart, Allāh (ﷻ) will give you everything. If you say, "I emigrate to Allāh (ﷻ)," then Allāh (ﷻ) will guide you, because your heart has become pure and you are listening to your Lord (ﷻ) who created you in perfect shape.

My students, my beloveds who came to healing school: purify your hearts, your spirits and your minds and you will be a divine servant. Allāh says, "My servant comes close to me by praying more and more." The servant is honored and at the same time he is obligated, so you are the servant of Allāh (ﷻ). Allāh (ﷻ) gave you the order to follow, and He gave you an honor. I ask Allāh (ﷻ) for you to be like that.

The reading continues, "Oh Allāh (ﷻ), you say, 'My follower, come, for My door is open to those who are honest and come directly to Me, without turning left or right.'

My beloved, you revealed yourself with the light from the Eternal (ﷻ), so spread your perfume and fragrance in the world. This fragrance is the secret of life given to all people who fall in love with You. Give them a taste if they will sacrifice their hearts to You.

Your heart is the heart of Allāh (ﷻ); no one else can make a place in it. No one can know where or when. There is nothing like Him. Do you see?

My heart is absent..."

I am wondering why the human being doesn't open his heart to the One who loves him. Allāh (ﷻ) gave him everything. He gave him this heart. How can you break other people's hearts? Can you accept it if your lover breaks your heart? This is a crime. Breaking another's heart is the biggest crime a human being can perpetrate.

The life Allāh (ﷻ) gave you is very kind and gentle and nice. Do you accept someone coming and breaking your heart? How could someone do this? Why are isn't he kind and noble? This is what Allāh (ﷻ) tells us. This is the order.

The reading continues, "My heart is absent because my heart is the manifestation of divine truth. When I was a child, I drank a drop of Allāh's praiseworthy love. I will be drunk with Your love and I will sacrifice myself to give it to others who want to be with this love. This love is Your love, Allāh (ﷻ).

I will be drunk with Your love and I will sacrifice myself for Allāh (ﷻ) in order to give to other people who want to be with this love, who want to be with You. For this love is Your love, Allāh (ﷻ), and I cannot receive anything beyond what You give me. So, please, let me have love without beginning or end..."

You want love. You ask to have love, so ask yourself first. Can you protect this love? Can you save this love? If you are like that, Allāh (ﷻ) is the Generous and He will protect you.

The reading continues, "So, please, let me have love without beginning or end, for You are my eyes. You are always in my heart. Let me forever be in the spring of prostration."

It is important to speak honestly and not to lie, and then Allāh (ﷻ) will give to you.

The reading continues, "Allāh (ﷻ) says, 'Oh my friends, you are singing the song of the lovers. How can you reach if you will not give Me the things I gave you from the eternal life? Your life doesn't have a beginning. This contains the secret of eternity.'

Music plays.

> *I did not love You as You deserve.*
> *I did not suffer a lot in this love.*
> *I did not have anyone.*
> *I do not have any ...*
> *... my spirit and when I give myself for the one I love.*

Oh Allāh (ﷻ), You are the pleasure, You are the Giver, You give the whole world the melodies of prostration. You give them eyes that see everything and lights revealed upon them, and You give to them through Your existence.

Allāh (ﷻ) is the Generous. He is the Love. Only love Allāh (ﷻ), nothing else.

Oh Allāh (ﷻ), through Your existence You give them everything in this world. They become drunk from the wine of this knowledge and then they become absent. They witness You.

The lovers are absent from everything but the truth. There is no prostration if you don't know love.

Those who become absent from their selves into His self, let them know they shouldn't go beyond My borders. Don't stop following My commands and My prohibitions.

Beloveds, I send my voice to all those who search for the deep, secret love. I call all my children to come and knock on the door, to hear the song of the Holy Qur'ān, and I am sure that anyone who comes will come with a deep sincerity. He will be completely absent from the dense world to be inside the world of the truth. This is the world of the love.

Don't wait, my beloveds, time is very short. Really, the truth is that there is no time for anybody. Only this moment exists; this is the time of your beloved God (ﷻ). So listen for His flute; if you listen, you can remember, you can understand. If you like to be absent from everything, if you like to only be with your Beloved, then now is the time for you. This is the real time between you and Allāh (ﷻ). This is the time to be only with Allāh (ﷻ), to be in the arms of Allāh (ﷻ).

Don't lose your time, don't give it to anyone who doesn't understand, who doesn't follow Allāh (ﷻ) in everything. This is the real drink of the source of love. He will give you the real life, not a false life. I am a child from His children, and I like to sing what He wants from me."

Give me the time to swim all my life in the ocean of the essence of truth and to know You, Allāh (ﷻ), and to be with You and to carry what You want from me and to be a real, real slave for You.

Oh Allāh (ﷻ), teach me how to walk, show me where there is a holy door to cross to You..."

The way is very clear. Our Prophet Muḥammad (ﷺ) explained how and where to walk. He told us:

> I left behind me two things.
> If you keep those two things, you will never be lost.
> They are the Qur'ān and the sunna (the Prophet's example).

Everything, all knowledge, is in those two great things and he (ﷺ) encouraged you to be honest and loyal in everything. If you walk, Sayyidinā Muḥammad (ﷺ) will guide you, all doors will be open for you, and you will gain all of the divine knowledge. Allāh (ﷻ) created that knowledge for you and it will allow you to arrive to Allāh (ﷻ).

The reading continues, "Show me where there is a holy door to cross to You, for without You there is nothing. Take me from this material world to the world of Your essence, because You are my beloved. Destroy all of my humanity and return me to Your spirit, for my spirit comes from Your spirit.

You gave to the father of all human beings (ﷺ), and if I don't understand the meaning of this then I will lose everything, and I will be without Your help.

You told me, 'Read My Qur'ān and you will find and know the essence of the deep secret love, and you can drink. You will help yourself to remain always with Me and to listen to everything I say. For that reason, you can't take anything if you do not give Me the essence of your heart. This is the price. This is the sacrifice.'

This is like what the Prophet (ﷺ) said:

> Die before you die.

Oh Allāh (ﷻ), How can I reach You if you do not accept me? If You do not help me? If You do not give me a new life and a new creation? For this reason, I keep my heart behind Your door until I see Your door is open.

I searched for a long time to drink from the source of Your love, Allāh (ﷻ). Then You gave me the real life to be with You. For this reason I call to You, 'Oh my heart, my poor heart. Without Your love, Allāh (ﷻ), I am nothing.'

For this reason, I give myself completely, not only in my heart but in my spirit. I like to clean myself in the way that Allāh (ﷻ) wants. I like to purify myself, to be a poor slave for You. I don't want to travel unless

You show me how I can travel within the holy song of lā ʾilāha ʾilla-llāh."

Music plays.

> *I will be miserable if You will not support me,*
> *and I will be happy if You will support me.*
> *How miserable I will be if You do not accept me!*

I am sure that if you are honest, He will support you. He will keep you. He will give you His help in obtaining His knowledge. He will let you be happy and loved. The support of Allāh (ﷻ) is the most important thing, because it will keep you away from your thoughts. Don't look to those thoughts that are from the shayṭān. They will make you late in arriving to Allāh (ﷻ). If Allāh (ﷻ) does not support you, you will not be able to arrive.

The reading continues, "Sure, He knows everything, but it is important for everyone to be as Allāh (ﷻ) wants. Surrender completely and do not say 'I.' Only say, 'Allāh (ﷻ),' for He is the love.

He is the One of the truth, and for that reason He created everything. He gives and He puts the essence of all His knowing in everything. Then He puts us in the Garden through His way (ﷻ), not the way of those who do not how to walk to Him.

It is not easy for anyone to say 'I am.' It is forbidden for anyone to say 'I.'"

Many people say, "I," but they are nothing. They have nothing. They claim that they have something, but they have nothing. Divine knowledge has its own signs that appear on a person's tongue, in his behavior and in his hearing. If you are a merchant dealing with oils, signs of the oils you buy and sell will appear on your clothing. If you don't have love, how can others see its signs upon you? Love's signs should appear upon your tongue, in your behavior and in your feelings. You will be an angel if you are loyal and honest, not a liar, not a cheater.

If the eyes of Allāh (ﷻ) protect you, do not fear anything. Why are you given this protection? Because you follow His orders and you walk on the straight path. You say, "Guide us on the straight way, the straight path." You will speak the truth, because it is from Allāh (ﷻ). Allāh (ﷻ) will heal people through your hands, because you have proven that you are honest and loyal. This is the truth.

The reading continues, "I do not need even one moment to see the face, to see the light, of my beloved Laylā."

You just need one gaze and you will be in a beautiful relationship with Allāh (ﷻ). Allāh (ﷻ) will teach you what you have never known before, in just one blink of the eye. The lover will obey his Beloved.

The reading continues, "Then I throw myself into prostration between His arms (ﷻ) and drink from His water (ﷻ), for He gives me eternal life without death. This is al-baqāʾu-l-bi-llāh (subsistence in Allāh ﷻ).

For anyone that has heard my voice, there is permission to listen to the song of God (ﷻ) through my spirit, but it is important to be gentle and to be polite when you are around the Beloved. Āmīn.

> *Oh Allāh (ﷻ), I didn't pay you the rights of Your love.*

I spent all my time and You gave it to me without taking anything.
And for that reason I cry to You, "Give me just a drop from You" to give me the real life.

I have been waiting a long time to see with my real eyes, not my earthly eyes, the beauty You give to all that You have created, Allāh (ﷻ).

This is the real life.

> *I didn't give You the rights of Your love.*
> *There are no rights for love, and I didn't give anything.*

Allāh (ﷻ) says, 'My beloved, carry My love to help those who have been crying for a long time.' I answer, 'Yes, I will,' in my heart. There is no way to say, 'No, Allāh (ﷻ).' I listen for Your notes, for Your flute, and I follow Your words from when You said: 'Kun.'

This is the real life. I don't like to die in a way that people don't understand.

I don't like not giving people a chance to see Your face, because of all of Your beauty. Everyone is so thirsty for Your love, Allāh (ﷻ). You are the Merciful. Give a drop of this mercy to those who open their hearts in order to explain the real idea of love and how to love in the right way. I want my beloveds to love Your face, my Lord (ﷻ), as I love only Your face."

Oh Allāh (ﷻ), how can I leave Your love? How can I live without Your love? This is the love. This is the real life for everyone who wants to travel to reach Your real Garden. Oh my Beloved, keep me under Your foot to know how to make the real prostration to Your face. Please teach me, Allāh (ﷻ), how to thank You. Teach me how to serve You, and how to be the poor slave, the real slave, like what You want from me. Give me a chance to travel only for Your face, and for me to see the face of my Beloved who created me, and to be only for His face.

Oh my beloved children, follow me in this way to drink from the cup of Allāh (ﷻ). This is my voice submitting to the voice of the Greatest One who carries everything (ﷻ). Oh Allāh (ﷻ), give everyone a drop of Your love so that they can reach the real baqāʾ in the world of God (ﷻ).

My children, if you'd like to walk in a deep, deep way then be polite, open your heart, and leave everything to clean yourself. Be only spirit, for without Allāh's spirit you could not walk, because God (ﷻ) changes the heart to be His spirit.

Life without the essence of His love, beloveds, is nothing. This singer likes to explain this in the song, but he does not have the real words to explain it.

I am a very poor slave and I will try to explain it. I will make a real prostration for Allāh (ﷻ) in order to drink from His source, and I will not leave because He gave me this chance to explain this song of His love, to explain the real love of Allāh (ﷻ) to my children. Whoever takes the real love has the real life and he carries what Allāh (ﷻ) says.

Listen to His voice (ﷻ). Listen to His tone (ﷻ). He will teach you what you have never known before. This is just from obeying Him and following His orders and commands in this life. Without His help you can't do anything, not even walk.

If a person drinks from His love like He asks us to, then I'm sure he will sing His song. He will always dance and will not stop. He will not stop through his ṣalāh and he will say, 'Bismi-llāhi-r-raḥmāni-r-raḥīm.'

This is the key to the home of Allāh (ﷻ). For this reason, anyone who likes to come, to be and to follow—to see what He likes to give and to follow what He likes to say—I am sure Allāh (ﷻ) will give him a chance to know himself, to clean himself and to clean his heart. Then he will see that the Kaʿba is love and he will circumambulate it and kiss the stone that the Prophet Ibrāhīm (ﷺ) brought.

On Ḥajj

This stone is the center of divine love. A few people understand the meaning of what Allāh (ﷻ) says to Ibrāhīm (ﷺ), 'Build My home, the home of love. Make ṭawāf (circumambulation) around My home, the home of love. Here is the first home for everyone that likes to drink from the source of his beloved God's love.'

So why does He say, 'Throw the stones?'[19] It means to leave everything and to not listen to Iblīs. Throw the stone that Allāh (ﷻ) gave to Ibrāhīm (ﷺ) to discharge everything that is not from and for Allāh (ﷻ). Then, my children, you will have made the real Ḥajj, because you will say, 'labayk-allāhumma labayk.' Now, not tomorrow, my children.

You will say, 'Here I come, Allāh (ﷻ).' Then you will see that in the home of love, love walks around you. This is the real bride. It is the real wedding for you to dance around the Kaʿba.

---

[19] Sidi is referring to the part of Ḥajj where pilgrims throw stones at three walls called, "jamarāt" in the city of Mina just east of Mecca.

When you have the deep knowing of what Allāh (ﷻ) says in the Qur'ān, and when you know everything that He sends through His beloved prophets (ﷺ), you will know real love.

Don't search for false love, my children. You will lose your chance if you don't wake up. Excuse me if I give something of this secret, but I am nothing without Him. I am just a drop from His essence (ﷻ). He sent me to explain this song, the song of His deep praying. I will. Let us continue to see what He says."

Oh my beloved children, follow me in this way. Follow me in this way to drink from this holy cup from Allāh (ﷻ). This is my voice through the voice of the Great One (ﷻ) who carries everything. He wants to give everybody a drop of the love to reach the real baqāʾ in the world of God (ﷻ). This is the meaning of love. This is what we are crying for. I am sure everybody is hungry for this.

If you would like to walk deeper in the deep politeness, open your heart, clean your heart, and be only spirit. Be only a holy spirit, for without spirit you could not walk. Then, follow what He says. God (ﷻ) will change your heart to be His spirit, because He created you from His face, from His light. He gives everything light. Light without the essence of His love is nothing.

This is a divine matter—it is divine support. No one can stay away from it. This is an opening, a divine opening. If you open your hearing, if your hearing is pure and all of your feelings are ready, Allāh (ﷻ) is generous. If you keep His promise, He will keep you in His heart. You have never seen such things and you have never heard such wonderful music. This is a mercy, so you will be in the highest garden with beautiful clothes. The mercy of Allāh (ﷻ) is a very special gift. The mercy of Allāh (ﷻ) is for you and it will be for eternity.

When you trust a person who is not straight, he will take you and throw you in rubbish. This is not useful for you. If you want to live in the real life, follow peace and love and understanding, the real understanding. This is what Allāh (ﷻ) says.

Music plays.

> *I don't have anyone, Allāh (ﷻ), just You.*
> *I don't have anything except my spirit, and even this I sacrifice.*

The reading continues, "If Laylā asks me to give everything for her, then I give everything without asking why or what.

Why? Because I like to drink from His milk. I like to live a real life and return everything that He gives, and to live in the way He wants. I want to always be in the tajjalī al-jamāl (beautiful ongoing revelation) when He reveals Himself in beauty. Through His love I reach to be complete.

Then I begin to use the flute to sing, 'Oh Allāh (ﷻ). Oh Allāh (ﷻ).'

He gave me the flute of Dāwūd (David) (ﷺ) to send His voice to everyone, for every bird, for everything in creation to hear His voice. This is the flute of the prophets who love Allāh (ﷻ). My Master Muḥammad (ﷺ) who sent his voice to all people, said:

> Say: 'If you love Allāh then follow me.' (3:31)

He says, 'Follow me, for I am of the child of God (ﷻ). I have this flute through saying, "Allāhu Akbar" to carry His message.'

This is some of the deep meaning of what Allāh (ﷻ) has said.

> *The one who sacrifices himself for the sake of his Lover*
> *is not wasteful.*
> *The one that loves and spends his life sacrificing himself for*
> *his Lover did the right thing.*
>
> *Oh my Love, oh yes, my Love*
> *I did not suffer much in Your love.*
> *You are right, I should suffer, and I didn't suffer much.*
> *If you are the One then I will give my soul for You.*

This is my life. My Lover gave me this life, the life He wants me to have. It will not be as I want it to be, because I want His wish. There is nothing before or after His wish.

There is no place or time that is eternal. It is one. He created everything with beauty, as He wished. He gave me His love in every way. He let me be His lover, as He wished. He used me to be a lover. He gave me an atom of His love.

This atom contains the entire existence of humanity, the jinn, the plants and everything. This chair contains all of the skies. This is the earth in a small atom of what He created. So excuse me if I sing the song of the Eternal (ﷻ). Who initiated that? Who lit this song with His light and His love?

Oh my beloved, I am calling to all human beings, everywhere that you are, everywhere that you will be, in every time and place. My Beloved loves you, so love Him.

He gave you everything. You shouldn't prostrate just for His beauty, my beloved. Follow me everywhere I go, because I have no choice. I just want the beauty of His face and the wine that will give me eternal life. Recognize your life, my beloveds, my sons and my daughters, those who are thirsty and want to be full.

He gives you and your spirit life and then, through this spirit, you will speak with Allāh's tongue, with His words. You will be like a bird singing in al-Malakūt, al-Jabarūt and al-Lahūt. You will live the eternal life. There is no death, my beloveds, in this life.

If you understand what I am saying, then pray and prostrate to Allāh (ﷻ). I am nothing. I am nothing, but within Him I became everything. Can you understand what I am saying? Yes, you can. You can do it. You should forbid yourself to eat or drink from any other plate or cup; only drink from the cup of Allāh (ﷻ). Then, my children, you will be saved. If you are follow these instructions then you will hold a new creation. Allāh (ﷻ) said on the tongue of our Master Muḥammad (ﷺ):

> My servant continues to draw near to Me with voluntary actions (extra ṣalāh and worship)

> until I become the hearing with which he hears,
> the seeing with which he sees,
> the hand with which he strikes (and heals) and
> the foot with which he walks.
> I will be his life full of love.

This is the real life, the giving life.

My beloveds, you have a cure within you. You should give this cure to all who need it. How? Give it through sharing this divine medicine. When you give, you give to yourself, not to anyone else. You give to your life, to serve yourself, and for your Master (ﷻ). For this reason, always open your ears and your spirit. You should give this cure to all those who need it through what Allāh (ﷻ) has given you through Sayyidinā (our Master) Muḥammad (ﷺ).

This is just some of the meaning from the deep, secret garden that you all carry from your beloved God (ﷻ), so follow what He says.

> *I don't have anything, just my spirit.*
> *One who will give himself is not spending much,*
> *and he is not wasteful.*

What would you like to give? You do not have anything because You have not created yourself. For this reason it is important to make the real fanā' through the beloved rūḥ (spirit). He says, 'I give you this spirit' because He is generous. He gave you life, but He wants you to live a real life.

You are more holy than the angels (ﷺ). Why don't you sing like the angels (ﷺ) sing? He gave you the flag of love, so why do you hide it? Follow the flag and then you will see yourself in the complete walking. This is the real baqā', the real existence.

If a person has nothing and wants to visit his Lover (ﷻ), bringing a gift from himself, he will go to Allāh (ﷻ) who created him. What gift will he bring Him? The person doesn't have anything to give but himself. What can he make? The only gift Allāh (ﷻ) asks of you is to be pure, to clean your heart, to clean your spirit and to say, 'My gift is all that I can give You, which is everything I have, for without You, I am nothing. I would only like You to give me some light so that I can see Your robe in order to drink from the source of Your love, my Lord.'

This is the water and it gives real life, for without real life from God (ﷻ), full of love, then you can't be anything.

> *If You do not accept me I will be so miserable.*
> *I will live in deep suffering, deep sadness,*
> *because I will lose the sense of the deep, secret life.*
> *I only have a creation through You, Allāh (ﷻ),*
> *and without that I will lose everything.*
>
> *How can I live without Your love? I will suffer.*
> *If You accept my gift, I will give myself as a gift to you.*
> *If you accept it I will be the ransom, I will be the gift.*

The tongue of my Beloved says, 'When you give to those who are crying, for those who love Me, then you give My love to everyone and then I accept your giving.' This is what He wants from you, my children.

So when you give to those who are crying, who love Me, you give My love to everyone. This, I accept, and when you give you are only sharing a tiny portion of what I have given you.

My children, for this reason He wants you to be the tree of the love. He wants you to give the fruits from your tree to everyone, to help all voices sing the song of Allāh (ﷻ). Allāhu Akbar. This is the essence of the religion of God (ﷻ). for He is the Merciful, ar-raḥmāni-r-raḥīm. He contains everything."

The real beloved will always make the real tawba. Then, after that, you will see yourself. You are very holy and this is a sign. Would you like to swim in a dirty ocean? No. I like to drink. These secrets are from His heart and He gives everything to anyone who gives himself completely to Allāh. There is no separation between You and Him. Then you will say, "I am nothing without Allāh (ﷻ)." For that you can reach, but more than reach.

Oh people, you are poor for Allāh (ﷻ) and Allāh (ﷻ) is the Rich.

If you need any help, do not go to a person who does not have Allāh (ﷻ). Go to the door of Allāh (ﷻ) and He will give you everything. He created you and He gives you more than what you request from Him. Always be with Allāh (ﷻ).

Follow what He says. Be careful. Do not be with any human being who guides you to the rubbish way. Listen only to Allāh (ﷻ). Follow what He says and then He will protect you from everything. Āmīn.

The reading continues:

> *"How can I sleep deeply when I am suffering from Your love?*
> *If you refuse to give Your love to me, then how can I sleep?*
> *If you refuse to give me Your spirit,*
> *the essence of Your love, how can I sleep?*
> *How can I be in the real life?*
>
> *I will miss everything;*
> *I will lose everything without help from You.*
> *I will not be able to sleep.*
>
> *You will let me put on the clothes of suffering*
> *if You don't give me what I ask for—Your love.*

Without Your love there is no life!

> *My lusting for You will kill me,*
> *You will let me be nothing very soon.*
> *Please be kind to me, my Love.*
> *I am thirsty, so please give me a drop.*

I am very thirsty. If You don't give me the water of Your love then I will cry forever. I will cry all the time until I lose everything.

> *I am very weak.*
> *My body is very weak.*
> *Without the essence of the deep secret from You, Allāh (ﷻ),*

I could not walk,
I could not stop,
I could not give anything, and my heart would be sick.
Please give me the real medicine from the sweet bees,
from the source of Your life, because you are al-Ḥayy."

So, my beloveds, if you are ready, if you want to know how to open your heart, to be clean and pure, if you are ready to make a true sacrifice, come to me now and let me help you to open your hearts to help those who are poor and suffering. I have a special paper to protect you and to help you, but I want you to give. I want you to give with the deep sincerity to know that there are people in this life who are calling to you for help, for this is our religion. Āmīn. Āmīn. Āmīn.

Sidi gives the promise.

The Best of Allah's Creation (ﷺ) Are Those Who Make Tawba

"Complete Tawba" from *The Traveler's Journey of Healing*
Wednesday, August 19, 2010 AM, Sufi School East

لا إله إلا الله – لا إله إلا الله – لا إله إلا الله – محمد رسول الله عليه صلاة الله
لا إله إلا الله – لا إله إلا الله – لا إله إلا الله – ابراهيم رسول الله عليه صلاة الله
لا إله إلا الله – لا إله إلا الله – لا إله إلا الله – موسى رسول الله عليه صلاة الله
لا إله إلا الله – لا إله إلا الله – لا إله إلا الله – عيسى رسول الله عليه صلاة الله
اللهم انت السلام ومنك السلام و إليك يعود السلام
تباركت ربنا وتعاليت يا ذوالجلال والإكرام

May peace and mercy be upon you. Peace belongs to Allāh (ﷻ) and may peace be upon Sayyidinā (our Master) Muḥammad (ﷺ), his followers, his family (رضي الله عنهم), all the inheritors and the gnostics (رضي الله عنهم), and all of the messengers and prophets (عليهم السلام). We praise and thank Allāh (ﷻ) for giving us His mercy. We ask Him to let us be on this path of unity and not to discriminate between His prophets and messengers (عليهم السلام).

I am blessed to be His servant, to serve his message. Allāh (ﷻ) sent His message down to all of us, through our Prophet Muḥammad (ﷺ) and all the prophets, as sharīʿa and ḥaqīqa (divine law and divine reality) so that we may understand how to live this life, which is full of sorrow, sadness and suffering. Allāh sent down all the prophets (عليهم السلام) as mercy to all people. Allāh (ﷻ) says in the Qurʾān:

> We have not sent you (oh Muḥammad)
> but as a mercy for all the worlds. (21:107)

I'm grateful to Allāh (ﷻ) that He lets me be His servant, serving this sharīʿa and serving you. I will protect your faith as I protect my spirit and my heart because you are my beloveds. I am here to be your servant; I am just a poor slave. Allāh (ﷻ) says:

> Allāh (ﷻ) is rich and you are poor. (47:38)

We need Allāh (ﷻ). We love Him and we are longing to be between His arms. Our aim is to gain Allāh's acceptance and love. Allāh (ﷻ) says:

> He loves them and they love Him. (5:54)

This is the arrival. If Allāh (ﷻ) loves you, you will be happy. I am asking Allāh (ﷻ) by His greatest name—and if you ask Him by this name, He will answer you—I am asking Allāh (ﷻ) by this name to be among those people that Allāh (ﷻ) accepts. Who will be among them? Those who obey Him and follow His commands. Allāh (ﷻ) will accept those who follow His orders. This is the answer.

We are also grateful to Allāh (ﷻ) for letting us be in this holy month of Ramaḍān, the month of fasting. Keeping this holy month sacred has been obligatory for all the prophets before Sayyidinā Muḥammad (ﷺ) and prescribed to all of other prophets including: Mūsā (Moses) (عليه السلام), ʿĪsā (Jesus) (عليه السلام), and Zakariyā (Zachariah) (عليه السلام).

Fasting is a divine gift. Allāh (ﷻ) says:

> What! Did you then think that We had created you in vain
> and that you will not be returned to Us? (23:115)

Allāh (ﷻ) says, "We created you to take care of you, for you to be happy within yourselves and to give happiness to others."

You carry the color of Allāh (ﷻ). You are the creation of Allāh (ﷻ); you are the human being. Fasting doesn't mean you only stop eating—it is divine worship. Be assured that even the angels (عليهم السلام) are fasting for Allāh, the angels in the sky and the angels in the air. Fasting is a deep decree, a sacred one, and the human being carries its secrets within him. Most of the ignorant people do not know what fasting is.

If you look at it simply, the human being is like a tool. There are many things in this tool. I'm not a physician, but I know from what Allāh (ﷻ) taught me: the human being is a divine tool.

Allāh (ﷻ) has created the human being in the perfect way. If you search and investigate what is in the head, you will find that there are many arteries and extra details. Even if I know many things, I don't want to give you all the details. I'm worried about this human body, because Allāh (ﷻ) created you in the perfect picture.

I will give you an example: the stomach is a tool. Allāh (ﷻ) created the stomach and her job is to receive food and to work day and night. The first thing to understand about the stomach is that it needs rest. Another thing to understand is that when the stomach feels hungry it will search for food. Allāh (ﷻ) wants to give you a divine lesson through the stomach—you are the stomach. Allāh (ﷻ) wants you to know the meaning of hunger. He wants you to know how poor people are suffering, those who can't find food to eat and who are treated badly. You should pass through this period so that you can feel their suffering and you can help the poor people; this is a divine lesson.

You fast because you want to fast, not because you are in a prison. Allāh (ﷻ) doesn't want to put you in a prison like the corrupters do. Allāh (ﷻ) created us free. He gives us freedom, so we should follow Him.

I came in this holy month to be among all of you, to worship Allāh (ﷻ) together. I am sure this Ramaḍān is a holy month. Allāh (ﷻ) says:

> Truly, We have sent it (this Qurʾān)
> down in the Night of al-Qadr (decree) (97:1)

So, if you attend this month, fast. We should prepare ourselves for this month. I don't mean that we should just stop eating and drinking. Fasting in Islām means that first we should repent, because we should travel to Allāh (ﷻ) in our bodies. Allāh (ﷻ) will guide you.

This is a great journey because it is a journey to Allāh (ﷻ), to our creator. Allāh (ﷻ) will reward us with many wonderful gifts, the likeness of which we've never imagined.

Ḥadīth of the Three Āmīns

Allāh (ﷻ) says that Sayyidinā Muḥammad (ﷺ) was talking to people in Ramaḍān in Jumʿa prayer. When he was in the first stage, the Angel Jībrīl (Gabriel) (ﷺ) spoke to him, saying, "Oh Muḥammad (ﷺ), say, 'Āmīn,'" Sayyidinā Muḥammad (ﷺ) said, "Āmīn."

When Sayyidinā Muḥammad (ﷺ) was in the next step, Jībrīl (عليه السلام) said, "Yā Muḥammad, say, 'Āmīn.'" And he said, "Āmīn." When he (ﷺ) was in the third stage Jībrīl (عليه السلام) said, "Say Āmīn," and he said, "Āmīn."

When he (ﷺ) finished his speech, his followers and friends said, "Sayyidinā Muḥammad, we saw you say 'Āmīn' three times. Why was that?"

Sayyidinā Muḥammad (ﷺ) told them, "Jībrīl (عليه السلام) told me that the one who fasts for the month of Ramaḍān will be successful. That's why he told me to say 'Āmīn.'"

"Then he told me that everyone who does not believe in the one God (ﷻ) will be in Hell and will be a loser."

"And for the third 'Āmīn,' Jībrīl told me that a person will be a loser if he attends Ramaḍān without fasting and if he disobeys his parents."

Ramaḍān is a holy month. The first part is for mercy, the second part is for forgiveness, and in the last days of Ramaḍān, Allāh (ﷻ) grants us freedom from the Fire. Because of this, it is mandatory for us to fast during the month of Ramaḍān.

This journey will last for one month and it is a holy journey. The angels (عليهم السلام) of the sky will be sent down, and their spirits are within this holy month. There is the night of decree, Laylātu-l-Qadr, and this holy journey is healing for the mind, the spirit, the hearts and the bodies.

Before you start this journey you should make your tawba, and we call the big one "the greatest tawba." We are the people of tawba. We should not promise Allāh (ﷻ) that we will abstain from food and drink from dawn to sunset, but rather, we should admit our sins and promise our tawba in front of Allāh (ﷻ).

Allāh (ﷻ) is hearing and listening all the time, and He is very close to you. We should give our promise to Allāh (ﷻ); the tawba of mind, and direct our faces to Him, asking Him to clean our minds and to fill our minds by His divine knowledge, and to help us to clean our spirits, and we are asking Him to purify our spirits by His divine knowledge.

We should make our tawba and ask Him to give us the tawba of the hearts. We ask Him to purify our hearing by His divine knowledge. We ask that He purify our vision, our seeing and our eyes; we should make tawba for them to Allāh (ﷻ). We ask Him to purify our selves, our hands, our legs, our feelings and our senses—this is the real tawba.

So if you want to travel to Allāh (ﷻ), you should make the real tawba, not just by the tongue or in your speaking, but in all of your senses and every part of your body.

Every part of your body will be judged. Your eyes will be judged, your seeing and your hearing will be judged. Your heart will be judged. Your mind, which thinks evil thoughts, will be judged. And your mind, which thinks good thoughts, will be judged, so this is the greatest tawba.

Sidi gives the promise and then, "Complete Tawba" from *The Traveler's Journey of Healing* is read from the beginning.

"As-salāmu ʿalaykum, my beloveds. As-salāmu ʿalaykum, all you present spirits—those who came to us to bless our gathering. My beloveds here came knocking on Your doors and all the doors are closed, but with Your bounty, benevolence and mercy, You open the door of tawba to those who have made mistakes. Here they are coming to You and they enter the door of mercy and tawba. I ask You to benefit them from this tawba in the name of Your angels (ﷺ) and the spirits of Your prophets (ﷺ).

All of the prophets (ﷺ) said, "All the doors we knocked on were closed. There is only one door that stayed open and that is the door of piety and surrender, filled with lights. That is the door of tawba, tawba." Allāh said in a ḥadīth̲ qudsī:

> Oh My worshipful slave,
> if you did not make mistakes
> I would create another creation that would make mistakes
> and that would repent to Me,
> and I would give them tawba and forgive their mistakes.
>
> Oh son of Ādam, were you to come to Me with sins

> nearly as great as the earth
> and were you then to face Me,
> ascribing no partner to Me,
> I would bring you forgiveness nearly as great as it.

Oh worshippers of Allāh (ﷻ), if any of you come to Allāh (ﷻ) replete with sins that could fill the entire earth and make an honest, true tawba...if you come to the mercy of Allāh (ﷻ) with a pure, sincere intention and a clear heart and pure senses, He will open to the door of tawba and the door of mercy to you. He will come to you with the lights of His divine lights equal to that which would fill this earth. He will give you a tawba that will purify you.

One should not be stopped from coming forward toward Allāh (ﷻ) by something that he or she did, because Allāh (ﷻ) says:

> Say: "Oh My slaves who have transgressed against themselves!
> Do not despair of the mercy of Allāh.
> Truly, Allāh forgives all sins.
> Truly He is Often-Forgiving, Most Merciful." (39:53)

At this point, my children and my beloveds, Allāh (ﷻ) has made me a servant serving my children, my sons and daughters, and all those who love Allāh (ﷻ). All those who come forward through the door of tawba and regret what has happened in the past and who promise they will not return to what they have done before will be forgiven.

If a person who repents returns to do what he was doing before, it is as if he had been dishonest with his Lord (ﷻ). For this reason, when you declare your tawba to your Lord (ﷻ) do not deceive yourself and think that you can repent and go back to that wrong action. Do not think, "As long as this door is open we can make mistakes and come back and repent." No, this is not how it works. When you take this promise, it is a solid oath. If you break it, it is as if you broke your promise with Allāh (ﷻ), so do not go back to what you have done before.

All of the prophets (ﷺ) and the Prophet Muḥammad (ﷺ) said:

> I ask for forgiveness seventy times a day.

Are you ready for true tawba? If this is the case, Allāh (ﷻ) says:

> ...unless he repents, believes and works righteous deeds,
> for Allāh will change the evil of such people into good,
> and Allāh is Often-Forgiving, Most Merciful (25:70)

This is a small tradition to explain to you how great the door of tawba is. This is the door of the poor who are returning to Allāh (ﷻ). "The poor" here are the ones who are in need of divine mercy and divine love and it refers to the state of those in complete surrender to Him (ﷻ)."

Allāh (ﷻ) will forgive your sins and He is the Merciful. Don't let your sins stop you from worshipping Allāh (ﷻ). To make your tawba is to be in obedience. An honest tawba will let you out of your sins and return you back to the state you were in when your mother gave birth to you. A false tawba will not do this.

You should be honest when you speak. To say that you repent is not enough. You should repent with your heart, your spirit and your self. Then Allāh (ﷻ) will take you from the station al-lawwāma (the blaming/still questioning nafs) to a different station like ar-rāḍiya or al-marḍiya (the satisfied nafs or the pleased nafs). Allāh (ﷻ) will call those selves and say: "Enter My paradise and come to worship Me."

So do not believe those who tell you that you are in the station of ar-rāḍiya. If you lie and don't follow His orders, how can you be satisfied in the nafs? How can you be in ar-rāḍiya? You are in the station of al-amārra because you are still disobedient. This path is not traveled by talking, it is traveled by walking to Allāh (ﷻ) with honesty and loyalty.

Allāh (ﷻ) will judge you even for your bliss. Do you mention Allāh (ﷻ) when you take a breath—are you thanking Allāh (ﷻ) for that? Are you grateful for letting Him give you all those things without having to ask? You cannot give Him the sufficient and exact thanks that are appropriate.

Allāh (ﷻ) gives us everything without asking Him and He doesn't ask us to pay Him. It is free, and He wants us to live in this world happily, not to kill each other or cause harm and pain to others.

When Allāh (ﷻ) created Ādam (عليه السلام), the angels (عليهم السلام) asked:

> "Will You place upon the earth
> those who will make mischief and shed blood,
> while we glorify You with praises and thanks and sanctify You?"
> He (Allāh ﷻ) said: "I know that which you do not know." (2:30)

Allāh (ﷻ) created you in order to let you know that those who repent and do good deeds are the best of creation. Yes, He knows we are weak, but He put tawba in front of our eyes and He said:

> Say: "Oh My slaves who have transgressed against themselves!
> Do not despair of the mercy of Allāh.
> Truly, Allāh forgives all sins.
> Truly He is Often-Forgiving, Most Merciful." (39:53)

He sent His orders to us through the tongues of all the prophets (عليهم السلام), Ibrāhīm (Abraham) (عليه السلام), Mūsā (عليه السلام), ʿĪsā (عليه السلام), Sayyidinā Muḥammad (ﷺ) and all of them. They were all asking for the message of unity.

There is nothing like Allāh (ﷻ) and He is the All-Hearing, the All-Knowing. He is hearing us, listening to us and seeing us. Allāh (ﷻ) sees the black ant on the black rock on the moonless night. He sees us and He provides for us.

What would happen if there were no rain for just two years? Imagine—what could people do? What would happen to life? What would happen if there were volcanoes and floods? This is a simple thing.

Five days ago in Pakistan, 15 million human beings lost their homes, and many people passed away because of the floods (that occurred after monsoons). What if Allāh (ﷻ) wanted to judge the corrupters and the thieves who eat the money and wealth of others?

His name is the Merciful, the Compassionate. We cannot say why He created these floods. Judge yourself before the Day of Judgment. Judge yourself and ask yourself: are you polite? Have you done good deeds?

Allāh (ﷻ) is the Creator and His creation is perfect. He creates and He provides life, and because of that tawba should be continuous.

Allāh (ﷻ) says there are certain days that are best for tawba; there are special days, special people, special months, special times and special places. All of these holy lands, all the prophets and gnostics (ﷺ) are servants for the human being.

Story of Mūsā, the Transgressor and the Real Gnostic

Sayyidinā Mūsā (ﷺ) says that there was a man who transgressed against himself. He was a thief; he did every bad deed and he killed 99 human beings. So this man went to a gnostic and judged himself.

The transgressor said, "I will stop those bad actions; I am sorry for all of it. I want to make an honest tawba—but I want to understand first if Allāh (ﷻ) will accept my tawba."

So he went to a gnostic and told him, "I did all of these bad things and I am here now. I want to make my tawba." The gnostic told him, "How can you do that? You are late; the train has passed."

The transgressor asked him, "Are you Allāh (ﷻ)? Are you God (ﷻ)?" The gnostic answered, "No," but still this gnostic told him, "Go, for I know Allāh (ﷻ) will not accept your tawba."

Then the transgressor cut off the gnostic's head. He said, "I killed you because you put yourself in the position of Allāh (ﷻ). You are not the Creator. Allāh (ﷻ) is the Doer, not you."

Then the transgressor went to another gnostic and he asked him, "This is my situation, what do you think?" This man was a real gnostic; he told him, "I can't do anything. I'm like you; I'm a slave. My advice is to direct your face to Allāh (ﷻ) and ask Him for tawba. Don't go to people.

Allāh (ﷻ) says:

> And when My slaves ask you concerning Me,
> then (answer them), I am indeed near.
> I respond to prayers when they call upon Me. (2:186)"

The gnostic said, "You have travelled from a land of trouble where you disobeyed Allāh (ﷻ), to another land where you never disobey Allāh (ﷻ)

and you are honest and loyal." As Sayyidinā Mūsā (عليه السلام), the Prophet of Allāh (ﷻ), narrated, he went from a land where he did many bad deeds to this other land.

The former transgressor passed away while in this new land. When he died, the angels of punishment (عليهم السلام) came down to take his spirit, and the angels of mercy (عليهم السلام) also came down. The angels of punishment (عليهم السلام) said, "He goes to the Fire because he disobeyed Allāh (ﷻ)." But the angels of mercy (عليهم السلام) said, "He is travelling to Allāh (ﷻ)."

Then a great angel came down to tell them, "Just measure the distance between those two lands. If he is closer to the land of disobedience, he will be in the Fire. If he is closer to the land of obedience, he will be in the Garden." And when they measured the lands, they found that he was closer to the land of the pure people—so Allāh (ﷻ) will accept his tawba.

That does not mean that we can sin and make mistakes and say, "We will give our tawba later," because we don't know when we will die. We don't know if it will be today, tomorrow, or the day after tomorrow.

You don't know, so you should make your tawba and be honest, because you don't know in which land you will die. Everyone will pass at an exact time, and if the time comes, a person cannot postpone that hour by a single moment. You should be in a hurry to make your tawba.

If your spirit goes and you pass away, we are asking Allāh (ﷻ) for a true tawba and His mercy.

The reading continues, "'The poor' here are the ones who are in need of divine mercy and divine love and it refers to the state of those in complete surrender to Him, those who put themselves in a place of humility. The poor come promising Allāh (ﷻ) that they are giving everything to Him so that He can purify them with the water of mercy.

This is the meaning of tawba.

This day that I am here with you is blessed. I came here carrying love for you and also carrying pain, crying for the pain in my heart for the world because people are suffering all over the world, especially in the

Holy Land. The Holy Land is the heart of the world. Jerusalem is the holy heart of the world. It is the city of all of the messengers and prophets (عليهم السلام) in their manifested right creeds and beliefs and their need to be one hand and one heart.

Now, I would like to start to explain how to purify your bodies, selves, souls and hearts, and also how to purify your spirits and intellects so that we can continue our walking toward Allāh (ﷻ) within the boundaries of His law. This walking is not in accordance with illusion, ignorance and fantasy, because we want to be true children of Allāh (ﷻ) who sit around His table.

Allāh (ﷻ) does not want us to continue to live in the illusions of those who claim to know the truth but never know the divine reality because they were raised and trained by Iblīs and his followers. We do not want to follow this. We want to be as Allāh wants us to be—one nation. As Allāh (ﷻ) says in the Qurʾān:

> Truly! This, your religion (or nation) is one religion (or nation), and I am your Lord; therefore, worship Me. (21:92)

Today I would like to explain the meaning of tawba. Tawba has steps. The steps begin with repenting physically, which is the tawba of the material realm. The next step is the tawba of the heart. Following this comes the tawba of the spirit and the tawba of the secret. Then, you learn how to arrive at the divine presence and be conscious of the divine presence.

In this way, we become true worshippers and believers in Allāh and we learn how to travel from this material lower realm to the realm of divine dominion, al-Malakūt.

We want you to repent so that you can return to the divine presence and become a true child in the divine presence, conscious of the divine presence. In this way you will be happy, you will be more alive, more peaceful and in continuous prayer. You will witness Allāh (ﷻ) in the witnessing station. This is an allusion to the deep and real meaning of tawba.

You move forward after you purify and repent with your body and you purify your heart. You purify your body and your heart with tears of regret, promising your Lord (ﷻ) that you will not return to what you have done, and you promise an absolute promise that you will not return to what you have done before. You purify this body so that it comes back to the point where Allāh (ﷻ) said:

> Truly, I am going to create a human being from clay. (38:71)

Allāh (ﷻ) created this body, the human being, with His divine light and put in it a divine light of love, peace, mercy and unity. For this body to be beautifully pure it must contain only purity within it, so do not put anything in it that will bring impurities. Then you will be pure in your body and pure from all that Allāh does not want you to be or to have in your body. At that point, Allāh (ﷻ) said:

> He loves them and they love Him. (5:54)

Allāh (ﷻ) loved you before you loved Him when He created you and filled you with His divine fragrance. Allāh (ﷻ) is very eager to care for you. Allāh (ﷻ) wants you to be with Him—that is why He gave you this light within you and perfected your creation.

Do you not see how He created you and perfected you in the perfect picture that He wanted for you? Has anyone created a hand or an eye or an ear or a leg of yours? No, it is only Allāh (ﷻ); He is the great beloved, the one who loves you and who put a great love within you. You can never put a limit on that love. How do you contain and care for that love? You have to be honest and sincere. Do not lie, do not kill, do not hate. Be the soft ground. There are tools that Allāh (ﷻ) gave in the s̲harīʿa, the divine law, to His prophets (ﷺ).

What is the body? The body is the vessel in which Allāh (ﷻ) has manifested Himself with His name "the Manifest." He has manifested within it His names "the Love" and "the Beautiful." He manifested within it His names "the Clement" and "the Subtle." How can you destroy these qualities of the divine? Do not be one who is destroyed for not knowing these qualities. It is not lawful for you to destroy these qualities.

Do not transgress the divine boundaries and destroy people's homes. They are divine jewels; there is nothing equal to them. When you steal, you destroy that jewel. When you commit adultery with someone else, you destroy the love and you destroy its container. When you hurt others, you also destroy the divine creation.

Tawba, or repentance, is a mirror that reflects the purity of this light. Our Prophet (ﷺ) said to us:

> Allāh (ﷻ) is beautiful and He loves beauty.

He is beautiful; He loves what is beautiful. Beauty is what the pure divine qualities have manifested in you. Allāh (ﷻ) has provided this pure water of love, of life, for you. He gave you this creation and He has also prepared a reward for you, as He says through the tongue of His Prophet (ﷺ):

> I have prepared for My righteous servants
> what no eye has ever seen,
> and no ear has ever heard,
> nor has it occurred to the human heart.

Allāh (ﷻ) has manifested in you and He loves to see His manifestation in you. This is a divine mirror, so do not destroy it and ruin it with wrong actions. If you truly smelled the fragrance of the sins in your body, you would see that they smell worse than anything. Sin has a fragrance, a very nasty fragrance that, if you can smell it, is worse than smelling a dead animal that has been dead for some time. If you are a person of intellect, you will not accept this."

The complete ones, the good people, those people who know Allāh (ﷻ), and spend their lives worshipping Allāh (ﷻ), and are humble and know Him—when such a one walks, you can feel his beautiful fragrance and it is sweeter than any other perfume because it comes from his worship of Allāh (ﷻ). Allāh (ﷻ) is beautiful and He loves beauty. We should take care of those qualities.

Sayyidinā Muḥammad (ﷺ) said:

> Purification is from faith.

He asks us to purify our bodies, our hearts, our spirits and our minds. He is the Beautiful and He is the Lord of Beauty (ﷻ). So we should obey Allāh (ﷻ) and what Sayyidinā Muḥammad (ﷺ) said to us.

No one can keep a person at home for 1-2 days after his death. No one. Why? Because of the bad smell. This one was a good man and he was your beloved, so why not? Because the smell will offend them; this is the truth. We should be pure and the one who has a real tawba—if death comes to him, his fragrance will be very beautiful. It will be more beautiful than musk. Tawba is the principle. Āmīn.

The reading continues, "Your body is the divine mirror of Allāh (ﷻ). Allāh (ﷻ) wants you to exist in a purified state; He wants to keep you clean. We have to be very careful with our bodies because they are the vehicles Allāh (ﷻ) created. He ordered you to use your vehicle properly and He taught you how to use it, how to be in it and how to walk in this life. He taught you how to use this vehicle to serve you. He taught you how use your hands, your eyes, your legs and your hearts. This is the true meaning of the tawba of the body.

Allāh (ﷻ) said in the Torah, "First, worship Me and do not associate others with Me. Do not kill, steal or commit adultery. Do not lie. Do not betray. Be honest and be truthful." These are holy words and these words are also confirmed in the Qur'ān. There He said, "Worship Me and establish ṣalāh. Avoid all sins and do not steal. Fulfill My promise, and I will fulfill your promise." It is also there in the Injīl (Gospel of ʿĪsā). It is all one message.

For every soul that Allāh (ﷻ) created...the prophets (ﷺ) are from the light of Allāh (ﷻ) and Allāh (ﷻ) has bestowed those lights upon you. Allāh (ﷻ) said in His Qur'ān:

> Allāh is the light of the heavens and the earth. (24:35)

His light fills the seven earths, the seven heavens and the whole divine world. You carry those seven heavens and seven earths in your body. Why do you want to spoil your body with sins and mistakes? Allāh (ﷻ) has sent divine commands and He is very eager for you to keep your body pure. He created everything in a precise measure.

As I said before, the sinner, or the disobedient one, has a very nasty fragrance. When he makes a mistake and sins, we smell it and we know it even if he wears the best of clothes and washes with the purest water. We have a deep sense of smell and we have eyes—not the eyes you are looking at. We can see what he has done.

If there was permission to tell him what he has done we would tell him, but Allāh (ﷻ) has commanded us to protect him and to advise him with politeness and kindness. We will speak to him with a tongue full of love and mercy and advise him with all we have because we are the servants of the divine presence.

We care for this divine body much more than a mother cares for her child. If we are far from your body we pray for your body, we pray for your self, we pray for you, and we pray for the whole world. However, we have a purpose with you. This is the meaning of tawba: tawba is the return to Allāh (ﷻ), the return to the Beloved. What would you do? If you were a woman with a beloved and you gave him your body and you did not know anyone but him, what would you do if that person was not there for you? Allāh (ﷻ) says:

> Oh human being. (49:13)

He did not say, "Oh man" or "Oh woman." Allāh (ﷻ) has responded and told him that He would not lose track of any of your good actions. Allāh (ﷻ) created Ādam (ﷺ) and from His divine light He created Hawwā' (Eve) (ﷺ). Thus, Hawwā' (ﷺ) is Ādam (ﷺ) and Ādam (ﷺ) is Hawwā' (ﷺ).

Be careful when you see illusions or pictures—they are not from Allāh (ﷻ). They are from the s̲hayṭān, from Iblīs. In the world of divine truth there is no Iblīs. There is only the one who says, "Lā 'ilāha 'illa-llāh," which means, "There is no deity worthy of worship except Me." Allāh (ﷻ) said to the People of the Book (Christians, Jews and Muslims):

> Say: "Oh People of the Book!
> Let us agree that we worship none but Allāh (ﷻ)." (3:64)

These are the meanings of tawba and the secrets of tawba, I say this to you and I explain this more deeply for the first time so that you can:

- understand the meaning of the tawba of the body,
- understand how to carry yourself from the purity of the body to the world of complete purity,
- understand how to heal your body and your self, so that you pass forward and start healing with the name of Allāh (ﷻ),
- and so that your prayers are answered.

If you are sinning and killing and stealing and you say, "I see what you mean," then you do not see. You are blind; you do not understand. You have betrayed Allāh (ﷻ) in the body He gave you. You have betrayed this mirror of Allāh (ﷻ). Is not He the Manifest and the Hidden? Are these not His qualities? Why did you destroy the divine home Allāh (ﷻ) created in the perfect manner?

Remember, if you defy the orders or commands of Allāh (ﷻ), nothing will be accepted from you. Immediately ask for tawba and forgiveness; I pray to Allāh (ﷻ) for Him to accept your tawba. You have to leave the realm of illusion, fantasy, ignorance and confusion that you have learned through others. Throw it away. Then really see the divine reality and live in accordance with it and within the natural laws Allāh (ﷻ) created.

We are commanded to help others return to the Garden of Allāh (ﷻ), in which there is no suffering for anyone and no separation from the divine presence. Allāh (ﷻ) says through the tongue of His Messenger (ﷺ):

> Be to Me as I want you to be,
> and I will be to you as you want Me to be.

He opened the door for all those who make mistakes, commit sins and suffer a life of misery, disease and pain. Do you see how many new diseases appear today? These diseases did not exist in the past. Our ancestors did not suffer from these diseases and they were healthier. Why? They were healthier because they were living more in accordance with the way of the prophets and messengers (ﷺ).

We must also purify the heart, the self and the intellect. If we would like to completely travel in this pilgrimage to Allāh (ﷻ), then we must follow the way of the Prophet Ibrāhīm (ﷺ) who said:

> I am emigrating to my Lord. He will guide me! (37:99)

We must follow the steps of tawba. Physical tawba starts with purifying the limbs and the senses that Allāh (ﷻ) gave you. The first sense is seeing. Then there is tasting, hearing and touching. All of these senses must be purified. In addition, smelling must be purified.

You have to be responsible for how you use your senses. The person who backbites, lies, speaks badly about others, refrains from speaking good about others, spies on people and/or ruins people's reputations by speaking badly about them, is not following Allāh's order. Know that Allāh (ﷻ) says:

> Not a word does he (or she) utter
> but there is a watcher by him ready (to record it). (50:18)

There are two angels: one to the right of you and one to the left of you, and they record everything you say (see 50:17).

There is also the sense of hearing. Hearing could be used to listen to gossip, but this deviates from Allāh's way. Also, seeing can be used in the wrong way if you look at what people have and envy them, which deviates from Allāh's commands. The envious one looks at what people have and thinks, "Look at what they have. They have so much," and he envies them. This envy hurts people.

An envious one might be driving and see a person who has a better car and think, "Look at what he has. Why can I not have this? It is not fair." He has envy in his heart. The polite way to handle a situation in which you see something you admire is to say, "Mā s̲h̲āʿa-llāh," which means, "Allāh (ﷻ) willed it." Mā s̲h̲āʿa-llāh is said to acknowledge that Allāh (ﷻ) gave that person a gift.

Be conscious of Allāh (ﷻ). When you see a gift or a talent someone else has say, "Mā s̲h̲āʾa-llāh." Say, "It is Allāh's will, may Allāh bless him." In this way you will always be grateful for that person, wish him well and pray for Allāh (ﷻ) to bless him. Want for your brother what you want for yourself.

Anything the hand does for evil will be brought to account. If the hand does anything that deviates from Allāh's command, it will be brought to account. Whoever wants to walk toward Allāh (ﷻ) must repent a sincere, honest tawba, and he must never commit those past actions again. He must purify his senses. As mentioned in the Qur'ān, Nūḥ (Noah) (ؑ) said to his people:

> Ask forgiveness from your Lord, for He is Often-Forgiving;
> He will send rain to you in abundance,
> give you increase in wealth and sons
> and bestow gardens and rivers upon you. (71:10-12)

This means that you have to purify your senses and you cannot return to committing wrong actions. Allāh (ﷻ) will not accept tawba from someone who harms others, someone who steals, or someone who deceives people and takes their money without right. Allāh (ﷻ) will not accept tawba just given on the tongue. He must take action; he must return the money he took from the people he wronged.

If you backbite someone and you want your tongue to repent, it is not enough to say, "Forgive me, Allāh (ﷻ)." You must go to the person and say, "I mentioned you in a way that I should not have. Please forgive me." Whenever a person does something that harms another, he must go to that person and ask for forgiveness. Then he must go to Allāh (ﷻ) and ask for forgiveness and he should ask for Allāh (ﷻ) to help him sincerely repent."

I am sure everything is very clear to you. I am sure you understand everything and the meaning of tawba. And you understand that tawba means travelling to Allāh (ﷻ). Travel in your bodies and in your hearts, in your spirits and in your minds. This is the real journey. It will give you real life in your body, and it will give you divine light. It will open the doors of Allāh (ﷻ). And Allāh (ﷻ) is the Wise, and He is the Forgiver, and He is the Merciful. And I am asking you to come to me and take the tawba of the spirits. Come to me.

The Emigration to Allah (ﷻ)

"Oh Lord, Guide Us" and Music

Wednesday, August 19, 2010 PM, Sufi School East

لا إله إلا الله – لا إله إلا الله – لا إله إلا الله – محمد رسول الله عليه صلاة الله
لا إله إلا الله – لا إله إلا الله – لا إله إلا الله – ابراهيم رسول الله عليه صلاة الله
لا إله إلا الله – لا إله إلا الله – لا إله إلا الله – موسى رسول الله عليه صلاة الله
لا إله إلا الله – لا إله إلا الله – لا إله إلا الله – عيسى رسول الله عليه صلاة الله
اللهم انت السلام ومنك السلام و إليك يعود السلام
تباركت ربنا وتعاليت يا ذوالجلال والإكرام

As-salāmu ʿalaykum to all those who are gathered here. Peace be upon you, all my beloveds. I wish you all good things for your beloveds and your families. I wish all of you and all those around the world peace, justice, freedom and love. Āmīn.

We will start now. Sayyidinā (Master) Muḥammad (ﷺ) says:

> Our deeds are judged by our intensions.

If you intend trouble for Allāh (ﷻ) and His Prophet (ﷺ), so your journey will be to your Prophet (ﷺ) and your Lord (ﷻ). If your journey was not to Allāh (ﷻ) but to a lady to get married or to commerce to receive benefit, so you will experience trouble in those areas.

If we want to travel to Allāh (ﷻ), our journey should be to Allāh (ﷻ). We want to travel to Allāh (ﷻ) in our selves in this holy month. This month the angels (ع) are happy and the poor people are also happy this month. This is the month of poor people and they are happy during this month because they will receive a lot of mercy and help from others who love Allāh (ﷻ). They await the sacrifice; those poor people are waiting for your help. The sacrifice that you give will purify you from all your sins. Allāh (ﷻ) says:

> Take ṣadaqa (voluntary charity) from their wealth
> in order to purify them. (9:103)

This holy month, Ramaḍān, is a generous month. Why is it a generous month? This is the month the poor people will receive help and you will also receive help as will those people who spend their money for the sake of Allāh (ﷻ). It is like a plant and in each plant there are hundred seeds and Allāh (ﷻ) will multiply these seeds for whom He wants. We want you to be as Sayyidinā Ibrāhīm (Abraham) (عليه السلام) because Sayyidinā Ibrāhīm (عليه السلام) said:

> I am emigrating to my Lord. (37:99)

He did not say, "I am traveling to the dunyā or to the lower world." We are the son of Ādam (عليه السلام), our race counts on us; the angels (عليهم السلام) will count that for us and we will be judged for every minute.

There are two angels (عليهم السلام) with you all of the time, one on your right side and one on your left side. The one who receives the book containing the record of his deeds in his right hand will be happy and the one who receives his book in his left hand will be the loser. We do not want to receive our records in our left hands.

This holy month is the month of emigration. You should know that the emigration of Sayyidinā Ibrāhīm (عليه السلام) to the Holy Land happened on the ninth day of Ramaḍān. Sayyidinā Mūsā (Moses) (عليه السلام) and the miracle of parting the Red Sea was after this on the tenth day of Ramaḍān. All of the prophets (عليهم السلام) made their emigrations during the month of Ramaḍān.

We ask Allāh (ﷻ) to let us make our real emigration to Him and to let us obey His orders and to follow all the messages that have been sent by all the prophets (عليهم السلام). We ask Allāh (ﷻ) to purify our minds, our spirits, our hearts, our selves and our bodies and to help us be honest and sincere. We are asking Allāh (ﷻ) this.

There is music and it is food for your spirit; the spirit need food. If it is a divine melody it will feed your spirits. The singer is a servant of Allāh (ﷻ) and I know him personally.

Below is, "Oh Lord, Guide Us," a teaching based upon the music of Shaykh Yasīn at-Tuhamī with Sidi's lyrics.

The lyrics of the music
are bold, italicized and indented.
The reading is in bold text.
Sidi's live commentary is in plain text.

"This is a letter, a holy message to my beloveds and to those who love Allāh (ﷻ) and to those who want to know Him. I want to explain how they should walk to Allāh (ﷻ) and how they may arrive at what Allāh (ﷻ) wishes. If they want to walk like the prophets (ﷺ) and to carry His message, the message He sent down to them. Allāh (ﷻ) said on the tongue of Sayyidinā Ibrāhīm (ﷺ):

> I am emigrating to my Lord and He will guide me!
> He will help me to carry His message
> after I become like Him and carry His qualities within me.
> (37:99 and Tafsir)

Allāh (ﷻ) said, 'I am calling all people who want to arrive to Him and to know Him.' He said:

> And take a provision (with you) for the journey,
> but the best provision is at-taqwā (piety, reverence, awe). (2:197)

The food that Allāh (ﷻ) was referring to in this verse is to follow His orders completely and to forbid anything that He does not allow. First of all, you should purify your heart, because the heart is the place of the Lord. Then, purify your mind. Allāh (ﷻ) says, 'Don't those with minds remember?' He meant the white mind, not the black mind.

He wants all people to purify their souls and their selves and to take the holy water and to get holy food to purify their tongues and their senses and their hands, their feet, their hearing, their vision, their seeing and their eyes for Allāh (ﷻ). He created all those things. Allāh (ﷻ) said to all the people:

> **And I did not create the jinn and human beings**
> **except they should worship Me. (51:56-57)**

'I only created them to worship Me and to know Me. When they know Me they will worship Me and I am the Only One. There is no Lord with me because I am the Giver and I am the Creator and I am the Generous.'

My beloveds, I send this message to all of you from the bottom of my heart and soul."

This is a responsibility and I give to it from the bottom of my heart and my spirit; I am crying for those who are suffering and asking Allāh (ﷻ) to help them. Allāh (ﷻ) is the Greatest Creator and He is the Generous and He gave us life and He says:

> And I did not create the jinn and human beings
> except they should worship Me. (51:56-57)

He created us to be one nation and He says:

> Truly! This, your religion (or nation) is one religion (or nation),
> and I am your Lord; therefore, worship Me. (21:92)

There is no difference between black or white and there is no difference between rich or poor. Our father and mother are the same, Ādam (عليه السلام) and Hawwā᾿ (Eve) (عليها السلام). We are all created from clay and we are the sons of one father, Ādam (عليه السلام). Allāh (ﷻ) ordered the angels (عليهم السلام) to prostrate to Ādam (عليه السلام); not just to Ādam (عليه السلام) but to all of humanity.

The human being is the human being, with no discrimination between female and male, He called us all, "human being." The gender human being is not female and is not male, but Allāh (ﷻ) created the husband from his wife and the wife from her husband, and this is the will of Allāh (ﷻ).

Allāh (ﷻ) put everything in order and it is the divine wisdom. Allāh (ﷻ) created all of us from dust, from clay. This earth is clay and we have been created from it; it is our mother who is waiting for us and we will return back to her.

This is life. Live as you want you to live, but you will die someday. We should emigrate to Allāh (ﷻ); we should travel and make the divine emigration in this month, the month of emigration, the month of obedience. No shayṭān can affect worshippers in this month. Allāh (ﷻ) says:

> Remember Me, I will remember you,
> and be grateful to Me and never be ungrateful to Me. (2:152)

We should give everything to Allāh (ﷻ) because we are nothing. You were nothing and you became everything just by Allāh (ﷻ). Therefore, prove that you know this and emigrate to Allāh (ﷻ), obey His orders, follow His commands.

Don't just fast from food and drink; true fasting means to stop doing every evil deed. Just be with Allāh (ﷻ); the only the emigration is to Allāh (ﷻ). You should fast, you should remember Him and praise Him, glory to Him.

He is seeing you, and if you want the real emigration, if you want to ravel from this world of Mulk to Malakūt to Jabarūt to Laḥūt in order to travel to Allāh (ﷻ)...He is waiting for you. We should strive to achieve this; we should do it as all the prophets (ﷺ) and all the honest and sincere worshippers have done.

When we achieve our goal we can plant the divine tree—the tree of divine knowledge, the eternal tree, the tree of unity. All the prophets (ﷺ) planted this tree and sit under her shade. Allāh (ﷻ) is the light of the heavens and the earth. This is the divine tree of blessings. This is the tree of Mūsā (ﷺ), the tree of ʿĪsā (Jesus) (ﷺ) and the tree of Sayyidinā Muḥammad (ﷺ) that carries the peace, love and justice to all people.

Why do you turn away from Allāh (ﷻ)? Allāh (ﷻ) is calling you. Come to Allāh (ﷻ). Allāh (ﷻ) is the all knowing.

The reading continues, "These divine orders have been sent to our Prophet (ﷺ) and all the prophets before him (ﷺ). These orders will help you and they help me, as well. Following His orders helps us all to know Allāh (ﷻ) and to receive His love. For as Allāh (ﷻ) said:

> He loves them and they love Him. (5:54)

So, my beloveds, are you ready for this divine emigration?

Group answers: Yes!

Then I want you to listen to this song. The phrases repeat many, many times. The first one says:

> *Yes, my Lord, You are my direction*
> *and wherever I face, Your face is in front of me."*

Wherever you direct your face, there is the face of Allāh (ﷻ). You should be sincere and honest. This is the real emigration; you will die one day and there is nothing you can do afterwards. If you want, you will be in a divine wedding and you will be with all the prophets (ﷺ) and with Allāh (ﷻ). The gates of the Gardens will be opened and the guards of the Garden will say:

> As-salāmu ʿalaykum!
> You have done well, so enter here to abide (for eternity).(39:73)

Oh human being, return to Allāh (ﷻ) in peace. Bismi-llāh.

The reading continues:

> *"Yes, my Lord, You are my direction*
> *and wherever I face, Your face is in front of me.*
> *Wherever I direct my face,*
> *You are my direction, my qibla,*
> *and wherever I am this is my qibla, my place of prostration."*

Music plays.

The one who carries the message of unity is carrying the Muḥammadan (ﷺ) message. The angels (ﷺ) first built this Kaʿba and then Sayyidinā Ibrāhīm (ﷺ) led his family there to worship Allāh. Allāh (ﷻ) says in the Qurʾān:

> And (remember) when Ibrahim and Ismāʿīl (Ishmael)
> were raising the foundations of the House (the Kaʿba) (2:127)

Sayyidinā Ibrāhīm (ﷺ) said to Allāh (ﷻ), "Oh my Lord, let other people...be kind to them, even the birds will emigrate to them from, every species." Allāh (ﷻ) accepted his supplication; this is holy emigration. It is just for Allāh (ﷻ) and Allāh (ﷻ) ordered us to mention His name in the houses of Allāh (ﷻ). Therefore, Allāh's name will be mentioned in your house; your heart should be the house of Allāh (ﷻ). Allāh (ﷻ) says:

> My heavens and My earth cannot contain Me.
> Only the heart of My faithful, honest servant contains Me.

The reading continues, "Anyone who does not worship and direct his face toward Him will be a loser. For there is no one to worship except Allāh (ﷻ) is al-Ḥaqq (the True, the Real).

> ***You are my cup, You are my wine.***

You are the real water for me, the real life for me. These are your beloveds and they are walking to You, yes.

> ***They are a group and they are Your beloveds***
> ***and were walking to You,***
> ***and they believed in You,***
> ***and they believed in al-Ḥaqq.***
> ***Those beloveds believed in the Lord of this world***
> ***and they purchased Paradise."***

Allāh (ﷻ), these are my beloveds who come to be always with You, they give everything like Ibrāhīm (ﷺ) who gave his son as a sacrifice for Your face. For that reason, give mercy, give peace, give love, give mercy and give justice to those who believe in You. Yā Allāh (ﷻ), Allāh (ﷻ). Bismillāh.

The reading continues, "Sell yourselves and get rid of the trial of your sons and your wealth.

Give yourselves, my beloveds, give yourselves as a sacrifice for Allāh (ﷻ), for the one who sells all of himself to Allāh (ﷻ) will receive the love of Allāh (ﷻ), and he will be His beloved. Allāh (ﷻ) will love the one who emigrates to Him and then He will give him His love.

> *Those beloveds, when they answered the call, it was a promise.*
> *Every sign I send down to you is a call.*
> *Every sign from Allāh (ﷻ) is a call.*

These are signs and these are directions to You, because You are the Greatest Beloved, You are the One who created us and so it is an honor for us to receive Your love. You were calling us when You took the promise from us in the pre-eternal world and You asked us:

> 'Am I not your Lord?' And they said, 'Yes.' (7:172)

We answered, 'Yes, you are our Lord and You are our creator and we replied to You and we will return to You.'

Give us Your love, Allāh (ﷻ), we are always in Your place. We ask you to let us be in this way and on this path. Please give us knowledge. Please, Allāh (ﷻ), accept our supplications and answer us, for one of Your qualities is that You are the Giver. You never say no to the one who asks You with sincerity, for You are the Generous and You open doors and You open your heart. We will keep the promise while we live in this dunyā, in this witnessed life. We will meet You, inshā'a-llāh, and You will accept us. You ask us if You are our Lord and we say, 'Yes!' You are the witness and we will keep our promise, the promise between us and You,

I am wondering how people can break the promise and stop worshipping and following His orders. They don't follow God, the Lord (ﷻ), but they turn away and leave the promise and the order of Allāh (ﷻ). They became corrupters of this earth and they break the love and the peace. They ruin things and they destroy the love and the peace and the mercy after they broke the promise. They have become the soldiers of Iblīs.

We invoke You to not let us be among those people Allāh (ﷻ), keep us on the straight path and give us life, the true life, the real life so that we can have eternal happiness in this world and in the final world. We ask to be with You, Allāh (ﷻ), in Your Garden, and You are Allāh (ﷻ).

When you arrive to Allāh (ﷻ) and you follow His orders honestly, at that time you will have the divine meeting that Allāh (ﷻ) has promised us. We will meet Him, we will meet our Beloved, the Greatest One. Allāh (ﷻ) will gift us and allow us to enter the eternal place without punishment, for Allāh (ﷻ) says:

> Allāh is the light of the heavens and the earth (24:35)

Allāh (ﷻ) sent His books and all the prophets (ﷺ) and the martyrs (ﷺ) who have been guided. Come, for this is the divine wedding for all beloveds, all those lovers who divorced this lower world. They divorced the life of the lower world but they were mercy for other people. They were the mercy for those who were suffering everywhere, for they carried the love and the peace and the justice and the freedom to all people who were suffering in this earth. They followed the order of their Master, the Beloved, Allāh (ﷻ).

This is the message, this is the message. I repeat: this is the message. So my beloveds, hurry, hurry to this message, come to this message and complete your emigration to Allāh (ﷻ) in order to arrive at your knowledge and be happy for your entire life. Do you want that?

The crowd responds: Yes!

Allāh (ﷻ) is warning us: don't look to anyone except Him. He said:

> Do not turn left or right.

So, wherever you direct you face you will see Him and you will hear Him because He loves you more then you love yourself."

Allāh (ﷻ) has bought the worshipper's selves. Allāh (ﷻ) is the Buyer and Allāh (ﷻ) is the Creator. You are dear and holy because Allāh (ﷻ) created you with His hands and He blew within you from His spirit and you are honest and sincere and you travel to Him and you believe in Him. You sold yourself to Allāh (ﷻ) by obeying His orders and you think about Him all the time. Your work will be worship. You should be honest, sincere and love all good deeds so that you will be the servant of Allāh (ﷻ).

This matter is a divine order. When you are honest and you carry the divine orders, you don't want anything from anyone. You just want His face. This lower world has nothing and you have left this dunyā to her people. We do not say, "Do not enjoy this dunyā." No one can forbid you to enjoy this dunyā, beautiful things and to eat good food. But don't cause pain to other people. You should know how to use this dunyā, how to use this earth, how to be able to support yourself and to support others. This emigration means to follow Allāh's orders (ﷻ).

The reading continues, "Allāh (ﷻ) wants to make you happy while you are in His station of existence, prostrating in His mosque, in His place of prostration. As the Prophet Muḥammad (ﷺ) once said:

> You are very close to Allāh (ﷻ) when you are in prostration.

Therefore, you are with Allāh (ﷻ) all the time."

The closest position you will be in to Allāh (ﷻ) is when you are in the position of prostration.

The reading continues, "You will be very close to Allāh (ﷻ) when you are in the position of prostration. Do you love this position? This is the divine wedding for you, because you are in the position of remembrance and at this point as the Qur'ān says:

> And wait patiently for the judgment of your Lord, for surely you are before Our eyes. (52:48)
> You are in a holy position in front of your Lord, Allāh. (tafsir)

He is seeing you and hearing you and He provides for you and He will give you the divine gift. This gift places you among the winners, for the lover is invoking Allāh (ﷻ) and he never says, 'You did not do this and You did not do that," because he came to You humbled and surrendered. His heart and his spirit are open and in great politeness and Allāh (ﷻ) is hearing and seeing everything. Just as the human being does, when the lover makes mistakes he comes to the Beloved gently. Thus the lover comes to his Lord humbly; he does not want anything from Allāh (ﷻ) except His forgiveness and acceptance. The beloved comes to Allāh (ﷻ) humbly, full of humility. He gave his whole self to be in the presence of his Master, his Lord. He is invoking Him and he admits all of his mistakes. He comes with tawba, humble and very polite, to receive the forgiveness and acceptance of his Lord."

Beloveds of Allāh (ﷻ), to those who mention Allāh (ﷻ) and remember Allāh (ﷻ); those who carry the ḥaqīqa (divine reality) of Allāh (ﷻ) and the sharīʿa (divine law) of Allāh (ﷻ), the doors of Allāh (ﷻ) are open. The doors of Allāh (ﷻ) are open to all people. There is no discrimination, there is no separation; we are all servants of Allāh (ﷻ) and we prostrate one prostration. We go to Allāh (ﷻ) and we worship just Allāh (ﷻ).

The reading continues, "My breath is rising up to You. I am not here to ask You, 'Allāh (ﷻ), why have You done this or that.' You know that is hidden in my self. I do not need to talk for You to know everything about me, for You are the Forgiver and I feel myself between Your arms, safe.'

When the secrets appear,
when the secrets appear,
the secrets are the letters.
I am wondering: is there any answer
for the letters of the lover?
The secrets, the secrets are the letters.

These letters in our souls are letters of love and they are the admission that You are our Lord (ﷻ), that we worship only You and that You are our lover. We are poor and we come to You with humbleness, with our tears that witness that we are coming to You, that we are prostrating to You. Our tears prove that we are obedient and that we are lovers.

We do not have anything, but we are between Your arms. We know You are able to do everything that You want and we accept Your wish as it is, for no one can stop Your wish. Please Allāh (ﷻ), give us Your love, give us Your mercy, give us Your peace."

They obey You, because I'm dying; even when I die they obey You. What is death? Death is to be between His arms; this is the real life because He is the Greatest Beloved.

No one came before Him and no one will come after Him, because He is Allāh (ﷻ) who created everything. He carries all of the qualities. He is the Kind, the Wise, the All-Knowing, the Forgiver, the Love: all ninety nine qualities. Allāh (ﷻ) wants us to be like Him and to live this life with divine politeness. We are asking Allāh (ﷻ) to give to us, to provide us with divine politeness.

The reading continues, "Oh Allāh (ﷻ), please give us the peace that makes our hearts and spirits and selves happy. Don't just give it to us, please give it to all people, because Your name is the Peace, Your name is the Merciful, Your name is the Compassionate. This, Allāh (ﷻ), is what we want, for You to let us know the truth and to let us know the truth of what You want from us. You sent that truth down to all the prophets (ﷺ) and we will follow it as we followed it before, honestly. We will be honest, we will be loyal, we will keep Your promise, for You are the Greatest Lord. You are our Lord, al-ḥamdu li-llāh, all praise belongs to You, Allāh (ﷻ) because we depend upon You and You are the best one to depend upon.

I ask You Allāh (ﷻ),
I ask You Allāh (ﷻ) to make me feel more than sweet
for all of my life, to make my life full of happiness,
full of mercy, full of peace;
Do not make my life bitter, difficult and full of suffering,
full of bad things that come to the people in this life.
Make my life full of happiness and love and good deeds;
for this is the happiness of the life Allāh (ﷻ), if You accept me.

Even if my life is filled with difficulty,
I will be happy if You accept me.
For the most important thing is that You accept me,
and it is important to accept Your love to make me pure,
for any other thing I do not care about.

If You accept me that will be enough for me,
even if other people are angry at me.

Only Your acceptance is everything for me.

I do not care,
I do not care what other people who do not follow You think,
all I care for is that I want You.
I want to accept the life that You want for me,
full of peace and love and mercy and justice and freedom,
for me and for all people everywhere."

Therefore, remember to say what Rābiʿa (ﷺ) says:

> I never worship You because I am afraid of Your Fire
> and not because I want Your Garden.
> I worship You because You deserve to be worshipped.

This is Rābiʿa (ﷺ), this is the lady who lived for Allāh (ﷻ) and she gave Allāh (ﷻ) what He wanted. She was divine, she arrived to Allāh (ﷻ), she reached Allāh (ﷻ).

One day Rābiʿa went on pilgrimage and a man who was a gnostic met her. He was walking around the Kaʿba and she told him, "What is wrong with you? You are walking around the Kaʿba,"
He told her, "Yes."
She told him, "I am wondering, it is acceptable to walk around the Kaʿba when, though unbelievable, the Kaʿba will walk around me?"

This is because she became divine. I am telling you, if al-Ḥaqq is what you believe, al-Ḥaqq is what you will follow. Crush yourself, do not allow your nafs (lower self) to control you. Crush it. Do not follow the nafs to disobedience, because the nafs will order you to disobey Allāh (ﷻ) every time. Crush and destroy every bad thing and then you can know al-Ḥaqq. Thus, you will be purified and your body will be pure, your heart will be pure, your senses will be pure and your feelings will be pure. Then your heart will be the place of Allāh (ﷻ) and you will be a divine manifestation. There is a ḥadīth qudsī where Allāh (ﷻ) says:

> I was a hidden treasure and loved to be known.
> Therefore, I created the creation so that I might be known.

Look to yourself you will see yourself in the mirror.

The reading continues:

> *If those do not accept what I have,*
> *then this is from those people who do not follow You.*
> *If You give me Your love, it means You give me Your life.*
> *Then You put me in the real wedding*
> *from what You have given me,*
> *because You give the essence of the deep secret water.*
>
> *This is the real life,*
> *and after that I do not care,*
> *because You accept me and You give me what I want,*
> *and for that reason I come to knock on Your door.*
>
> *You keep me always in the real life with You.*
> *What do I need, nothing after that.*
> *Everything over the dust is the dust and I know what happens after that;*
> *if you accept my ḥijra, my emigration,*
> *for that you accept my pilgrimage*
> *the real pilgrimage*
> *and I see everything around me is full of the love everywhere..."*

Many people ask me about going to Mecca on pilgrimage. I used to reply to them, "You can do pilgrimage (within yourself) before you do pilgrimage." When you obey Allāh (ﷻ), when you purify your heart and your spirit, when you are on the straight path, you are on Ḥajj. You will see yourself everyday and every minute in Ḥajj because you are remembering Allāh (ﷻ). You can see yourself on Ḥajj, in reality, because you will get real knowledge of Allāh (ﷻ).

Now you start to understand how you can go and visit your Beloved without traveling anywhere. If you are a liar, if you disobey your Beloved, how can you go to see Him? He will not want to see you if you eat the money of others, if you belittle and break the hearts of others, or if you kill someone and after that want to go to Ḥajj. Do Ḥajj now, before you go to the real Ḥajj. Purify yourselves.

The reading continues, "I see everything around me as full of love, everywhere. This is a drop from Your love, Allāh (ﷻ), that I like to give. For that reason, this is the real, complete sacrifice of yourself, like Ibrāhīm (ﷺ) gave in his pilgrimage. Keep me with You all the time, Allāh (ﷻ), for this is the real life that I am waiting for.

This is what Rābiʿa (ﷺ) says. 'If things between You and me are good I do not care if the relationship between me and the others is bad.'"

All that I ask is to be always with You, to be a real beloved who follows everything that You say. After that, I do not need anything, only Your face, ar-riḍā, satisfaction, acceptance. This is the real life for me.

Oh my beloveds, come to me and make al-ḥijra-l-ḥaqīqa (emigrate to the reality of Allāh). Give me a real, true emigration to Allāh (ﷻ). Follow the divine orders, for this is the path of the love, this is the path of the real life. Always be obedient and loyal and always follow Allāh (ﷻ). Follow Allāh's order, for He is the one who loved you first and then you loved Him, inshāʾa-llāh.

I wonder when there will be no difference between me and You and no suspicion? The most important thing is my hope that there will be no sins between me and my Lord so that when I come to Allāh (ﷻ), I will be pure.

The most important thing is to not carry mistakes and sins. Try to go to Allāh (ﷻ). This is how to be pure and a lover all the time until the end, for if You gave me everything, if You gave me jewels, if You gave me wealth, if You gave me money, if You gave me palaces, if You gave me everything from this material rubbish world and they kept me away from You, then life would be full of suffering, it would be a painful thing. I do not need all those things Allāh (ﷻ), I just need Your love. I pray for You to not give me anything, for everything material will take me far away from You and that will put me in the Fire. I do not need any of the things, like wealth or money, that will let me turn away from You.

For that reason my Lord, my Greatest Beloved, I love You with two kinds of love. I love You with the love as love and with the other kind of love, the love that You deserve. You deserve this love, You gave me the love and I am in all my times, and all of my times are Your times. In all of my stations I am between Your arms, whether standing or prostrating or bowing to keep me in a station of witnessing, a station of absence. I do not want anything else, just Your acceptance. Your acceptance, Allāh (ﷻ), will give me existence. My promise will be real with You and I will complete my emigration, my journey to You.

This is the message of Your beloveds, my Lord. Give them the happiness of being in Your station of prostration in Your existence. Please give peace and love and mercy and justice to all of this world which is full of suffering, and let their emigration be guided so that they come back to You as You wish them to.

Allāhumma anta-s-salām, You are the Peace,
wa minka-s-salām, from You is the Peace,
ya'ūdu-s-salām, to You is the peace,
tabārakta rabbanā wa taʾalayt, glory to Allāh (ﷻ),
yā dhū-l-jalāli wa-l-'ikrām, oh Lord of Majesty and Bounty.

My beloveds, if you would like to make the holy journey like Ibrāhīm (ﷷ) made, the door is open to you. This is a special time, this is a holy month, this is a special day and we are in a special place. Come and take your chance. Are you ready to make this holy journey? Come to me, come ready to give what Allāh (ﷻ) wants from you, to give like Ibrāhīm (ﷷ) gave.

Come, my beloveds, for I have a special protection prayer for you if you take this promise. Come now to make this special promise in this special time and in this special month so that I can give you this special protection, Āmīn.

Sidi gives the promise and the protection paper.

How to Travel in the Deep Way Like the Prophet Ibrahim (عليه السلام)

"Prophet Ibrāhīm (عليه السلام)" from *Stories of the Prophets*
Saturday, August 22, 2010 AM, Sufi School East

لا إله إلا الله - لا إله إلا الله - لا إله إلا الله - محمد رسول الله عليه صلاة الله
لا إله إلا الله - لا إله إلا الله - لا إله إلا الله - ابراهيم رسول الله عليه صلاة الله
لا إله إلا الله - لا إله إلا الله - لا إله إلا الله - موسى رسول الله عليه صلاة الله
لا إله إلا الله - لا إله إلا الله - لا إله إلا الله - عيسى رسول الله عليه صلاة الله
اللهم انت السلام ومنك السلام و إليك يعود السلام
تباركت ربنا وتعاليت يا ذوالجلال والإكرام

...to know that Allāh (ﷻ) is the only God (ﷻ). He created the human being to live the secret of the beauty within him. So He will reveal Himself by His name al-Kāmal (the Perfect) within this manifestation, the human being. They didn't know, and so they started to look to idols and they thought this was their existence and they became deaf and blind. They couldn't understand. But we live in the presence of our Lord (ﷻ).

Allāh (ﷻ) taught us and He taught our Prophet Muḥammad (ﷺ). He said to the Prophet (ﷺ): "Read." (96:1) Sayyidinā (our Master) Muḥammad (ﷺ) replied, "I can't read." But He told him, "Read, in the name of your Lord."

This is an example of Him teaching us what we have never known, by the grace of Allāh (ﷻ). He gave you excellent vision and good hearing. The human being, by himself, is a jewel, but he doesn't know what he is. The human being is a jewel in the divine world. His tongue speaks by the tongue of al-Ḥaqq, Allāh (ﷻ).

If he directs himself totally to Allāh (ﷻ), Allāh (ﷻ) will give him the divine knowledge He has already given to the beloveds. He will give him the divine knowledge He sent out to all the prophets and messengers (عليهم السلام). I don't want to go in detail on this subject. This subject could not be completed even after days and days of speaking. This is the garden of knowledge. We will take something from this garden to give you this knowledge. Its fragrance is very beautiful and it is from

Allāh (ﷻ), not from His servant, His slave. Allāh (ﷻ) will give this knowledge to the hearts who are totally directed toward Allāh (ﷻ).

Wherever you direct yourself, there is the face of Allāh (ﷻ). There is no face except the face of Allāh (ﷻ). But it is the will of Allāh (ﷻ). He created everything in perfection. Allāh (ﷻ) created the skies, the airs, the birds, and different worlds. And the divine inheritor is within the human being. And just a few people will praise and thank Allāh (ﷻ).

I would like to start this morning by asking forgiveness and permission from Sayyidinā Ibrāhīm (Abraham) (عليه السلام), and asking Allāh (ﷻ) to give me His support, to explain to you the emigration of Ibrāhīm (عليه السلام) to Allāh (ﷻ). I want you to understand from this journey how we should travel, how we should achieve our journey to Allāh (ﷻ). This teaching, inshāʾa-llāh, will help you understand how he traveled, how he walked to Allāh (ﷻ), and became the Shaykh of the Prophets (عليهم السلام).

Allāh (ﷻ) ordered us to pray upon Sayyidinā Ibrāhīm (عليه السلام) in our prayers. Allāh (ﷻ) prayed upon Sayyidinā Ibrāhīm (عليه السلام) and so he is a teacher for the whole universe along with Sayyidinā Muḥammad (ﷺ).

Let us learn from Sayyidinā Ibrāhīm (عليه السلام). The word "khilla" means friendship, it means to become His friend. It is a kind of friendship unique to those who will walk like them. If we walk we will receive knowledge from our emigrations to Allāh (ﷻ); there will be spiritual lessons which give our spirits the capacity to continue walking and to understand.

You can learn from the prophets of Allāh (ﷻ), and we are children sitting next to the tables of the prophets (عليهم السلام). Allāh (ﷻ) will place who will sit next to the tables of the prophets (عليهم السلام), and we will sit next to Sayyidinā Ibrāhīm's table (عليه السلام). Oh, be polite, and open your heart to him. He will tell you his story and how he arrived at the station of the divine presence.

"Prophet Ibrāhīm (ﷺ)"[20] begins at the beginning, "Bismi-llāhi-raḥmāni-r-raḥīm. The Prophet Ibrāhīm (ﷺ). Now, I would like to speak about the Prophet Ibrāhīm (ﷺ)."

I'd like to speak about the emigration of Sayyidinā Ibrāhīm (ﷺ). Ibrāhīm (ﷺ) is a wide world, because his spirit from Allāh (ﷻ).

The reading continues, "He was the second father of all the prophets (ﷺ). Most of the prophets after him came from his body. First, Ismā'īl (Ishmael) (ﷺ) and Isḥāq (Isaac) (ﷺ) came from Ibrāhīm (ﷺ). Then, from Isḥāq (ﷺ) came Ya'qūb (Jacob) (ﷺ) and from Ya'qūb (ﷺ) came Yūsuf (Joseph) (ﷺ). From the blood of Yūsuf (ﷺ) came the Prophet Mūsā (Moses) (ﷺ), and from the blood of Mūsā (ﷺ) came 'Īsā (Jesus) (ﷺ). From Ismā'īl (ﷺ) came the Prophet Muḥammad (ﷺ).

Ibrāhīm (ﷺ) had twelve sons and each one was a prophet. He carried the religion of the unity. He was the second father of all the prophets (ﷺ), and this gave him a special station with Allāh (ﷻ).

The name Ibrāhīm (ﷺ) in the Arabic language has a special meaning. The first three letters are 'alif,' 'bā,' and 'rā.' In Arabic his name has two parts: 'Ibrā' and 'hīm.'"

What is the meaning of "hīm?" It means that he carried the divine meaning, that he carried it, he was honest by it, and he was standing in Allāh (ﷻ) as His divine servant. He was a real servant and he was in the ocean of love. Allāh (ﷻ) let him know the meaning, not other than that. He was not lost. He is the peak of the love by knowing the secrets of al-Ḥaqq in His existence.

The reading continues, "Ibrā means that your body, heart and soul are completely healthy. The one who reaches this station begins to be in the essence of the reality of love. He is absent from everything, and his food is always the love. He drinks from the love and lives for the love. There is no space for anything else in his heart. His love is the love of Allāh (ﷻ). And this is the meaning of 'Ibrā.'

---

[20] *Stories of the Prophets*, p. 86.

Anyone who reaches this station is like Ibrāhīm (ﷺ) in every station. All the beloveds who are in this rank can travel through all the stations, to reach the higher stations that Ibrāhīm (ﷺ) reached. Allāh (ﷻ) says, 'Ibrāhīm (ﷺ) carries the essence of the reality of the religion of the unity,' and for this reason Allāh (ﷻ) said to the Prophet Muḥammad (ﷺ) in Sūratu-l-Ḥajj:

> **And strive for Allāh (ﷻ) with the endeavor which is His right.**
> **He has chosen you**
> **and has not laid any hardship on you in religion.**
> **The faith of your father Ibrāhīm (ﷺ) is yours.**
> **He has named you Muslims. (22:78)**

Ibrāhīm (ﷺ) was born in al-Iraq about 3,500 years ago near the old city of Ur of the Caldeas."

He was born near Ur, Babel, in Iraq. I visited his home in Iraq. The home of Ibrāhīm (ﷺ) is still there now! It is in the city of Ur, near the city of Babel. Yes, ok...

The reading continues, "It was in a place in the lower reaches of the Euphrates, about 160 kilometers from the Persian Gulf. Today, this city is called Moeyrr (Here Sidi, Ṣalīḥ and Hadeel consult about spelling. Ṣalīḥ spells out the word but seems to be told that this spelling is a mistake. The correct word is pronounced like the English word, 'more.'"

Jerusalem means, "Ur Salām." It means, "Mountain of Peace." Salām was a Canaanite king. Canaan is the Arabic word for the area modern-day Israel is located.

Ibrāhīm (ﷺ) came to the Holy Land and he sent a message to, "Ur Salām." He came to be one who believed in the origin of Allāh (ﷻ). Ur Salām. This is "Ur."

The reading continues, "...between the two rivers Didla and al-Farat. After his birth, Ibrāhīm (ﷺ) traveled with his father to the city of Farūn in western Iraq. Some people say that he was born in Babel, which was near the city of Ur.

In that time, like today, the people of the country knew many things about the material world. This area was an important center for human civilization. They knew about agriculture and ships and they had knowledge of the stars and the heavenly bodies."

They had more knowledge than we have in this time.

The reading continues, "Worship of the sun and the moon and the stars was the prevalent religion. When Ibrāhīm (☉) was still young, very young, he saw that his people prayed to something that was not right. His people prayed to stone and wood idols that represented the heavenly bodies."

This is exactly like in this time. People pray to idols, but in different faces. Some people pray to a king. Some people pray to their leaders, because a leader might make a law forbidding people to speak anything otherwise. The king would say, "This is my law. I am king, I am the leader." All of these laws are not what Allāh (☉) wants. For that reason you see so much suffering. You see bad things and people living bad lives.

All of these laws are for the corrupt leader, the thief, so that he can use his people. If you do not pray for this law and he catches you, he'll punish you. The way the people fought Ibrāhīm (☉) at that time is like the case of this time. For that reason, there is no peace. There is no love. There is no mercy. Look at his story, yes.

The reading continues, "Ibrāhīm (☉) saw this and he also saw that, in that time, the king guided people to pray to these idols. From the time Ibrāhīm (☉) was a child, Allāh (☉) gave him the chance to be the real beloved for Him. Allāh (☉) cared about his heart and his soul, and Ibrāhīm (☉) looked with the deep eye, and he knew what the people prayed to was not right.

He knew this because the idols couldn't do anything. They couldn't care for themselves. So he refused what his people prayed to, knowing that it was not right. Allāh (☉) opened his heart, and opened his heart to what He wanted from him.

Allāh (ﷻ) said in the Qur'ān:

> **And indeed We bestowed upon Ibrāhīm his (portion of) guidance,**
> **and We were well-acquainted with him.**
> **When he said to his father and his people, 'What are these images to which you are devoted?'**
> **They said, 'We found our fathers worshipping them.'" (21:51-53)**

"What you are worshipping, oh people?" Allāh (ﷻ) lit his heart and He lit his mind. He sent down a divine preparation to him, so he carried the message of unity. He was a child but his mind, divine mind, contained knowledge of the skies and the earth.

When Ibrāhīm saw what he saw, he asked them, "What are you doing? Does this idol eat, drink, or move? This idol can't understand, can't hear. So how can you worship those idols as if they give you your needs, your provision? Why do you hang upon them all that gold? They told him, "Our forefathers worshipped them and we worship them." So he told them, "I will talk to them, but they will not answer me."

The reading continues:

> **"He (Ibrāhīm ﷺ) said,**
> **'Indeed, you and your fathers have been in manifest error.'**
> **They said, 'Have you brought us the truth,**
> **or are you one of those who play about?'**
> **He said, 'No, your Lord is the Lord of the heavens and the earth who created them**
> **and to that I am one of the witnesses.' (21:54-56)"**

In fact, in this scene Sayyidinā Ibrāhīm (ﷺ) realized that people worshipped the material world, and so they considered those idols holy because they think idols will answer their supplications, as we do in this world. We followed other idols in the picture of the human being in the pictures of the presidents and those who lead the world. They are idols.

The human being is a human being and he can be kind if he believes in the orders of our Lord. This is the beginning of the emigration of Ibrāhīm (ﷺ). He will teach us how we can travel and start our journey from the darkness to the light. He is our teacher. Allāh (ﷻ) gave him the divine knowledge of the divine sciences. We should be like him, carry the freedom and justice and love without discrimination in this world that is from one father and one mother and looks like one body.

The reading continues, "They said that they prayed to that which their fathers worshipped. Ibrāhīm (ﷺ) answered them, 'If your father followed something that was not right, it is important to look inside your heart, and to open your heart to see to whom he prayed. Was this form of worship useful to him? Did it listen when he spoke? When he did something for the idol did it answer him or not?'

But Ibrāhīm's people said to him, 'What truth do you come to us with to make us leave praying to our idols? These are the real beloveds for us.' This meant that the idols were the masters of his people.

But Ibrāhīm (ﷺ) said to them, 'It is so important. If you open your heart to Allāh (ﷻ) and to the truth, then you pray to the One who created the heavens and who created the earth and who created you and who created everything. If you pray to the Lord of the worlds, then you can understand what I mean. So Ibrāhīm (ﷺ) was called khalīlu-llāh, the friend of Allāh, because he was more than the friend of Allāh (ﷻ).

He carried the reality of the existence of Allāh (ﷻ) completely inside himself. I mean, there was no Ibrāhīm (ﷺ) and Allāh (ﷻ), but just Allāh (ﷻ), in this case."

Yes, sure. He returned every quality to Allāh (ﷻ) in perfect surrender to Him.

The reading continues, "For that reason he said to his people, 'Look deeper within yourself and you can find everything inside yourself. You will begin to touch the truth through yourself.'"

Yes.

The reading continues, "How, if you do not know yourself, can you know who created you, or where you came from? Your body..."

Many times I have told my sons and daughters...and I have explained this a lot. I have asked them to write the book *He Who Knows Himself Knows His Lord*. First of all, everyone should write it and then read it. Then, work the exercises. In this way you will start to emigrate to Allāh (ﷻ). The doors will open for you and you will understand. You will surrender completely in your emigration to Allāh (ﷻ), and you will realize and you will understand how Sayyidinā Ibrāhīm (ﷺ) traveled before you. IN this way you will see the secrets and the facts with your own eyes. Inshā'a-llāh.

The reading continues, "Your body is the real place to know, through yourself. Allāh (ﷻ). Allāh (ﷻ) judges us by our selves. You could say we judge our selves by our selves, but through Him.

When Ibrāhīm (ﷺ) showed his people that it was important to break the idols he meant two things: 1. He meant the idols that his people spoke about and prayed to, and 2. He meant the idols that were inside his people, inside their bodies. He gave an outside and an inside meaning.

Allāh (ﷻ) is not recognized until His beloved removes all the veils. He who knows himself, knows his Lord. Because the reality of his existence is the hearing of his Beloved. If you look deeply, you will see Allāh (ﷻ) inside you. You do not need to look outside. But if you put very thick things around you, how can you know who created you? For that reason He says: first of all, break everything. Break everything. Break everything that you see. They are all illusions. They are nothing. They are veils. It is important to remove all veils from everything that you see.

Then Allāh (ﷻ) said by the tongue of Ibrāhīm (ﷺ) in the Qur'ān:

> He (Ibrāhīm ﷺ) said:
> 'Do you observe that which you have been worshipping,
> you and your ancient fathers?
> Truly, they are enemies to me, except for the Lord of the alamīn
> Who has created me.
> and it is He who guides me.
> And it is He who feeds me and gives me to drink.
> And when I am ill, it is He who cures me.
> And who will cause me to die, and then will bring me to life.
> And who, I hope, will forgive me my faults

on the Day of Recompense.' (26:75-82)"

This means that there is no end for you. There is no beginning for you. But in the real meaning, you see yourself. You are the human being, but really you are the light of God (ﷻ). If you go deeper, you will see that you are a very holy one, and He cares about you and wants you to understand how to reach for what Allāh (ﷻ) wants for you, for why Allāh (ﷻ) created you in His image. This is a deep meaning. Ibrāhīm (ﷺ) is his name, there is a special meaning. "Ibrā" "hīm" means it is important to heal yourself, to not have any sickness—outside or inside. There is no outside, in the deep meaning, and there is no inside. But you are He, no one else! Go ahead and search to see who you are! There is no beginning to Allāh (ﷻ) and there is no end. He said in His Qur'ān (ﷻ):

> But We have made it (this Qur'ān) a light (42:52)

This is secret. But this is real. You are very special. Why do you throw yourself in the trash? You are very special. Talk into Allāh (ﷻ) directly! He is not far away. He is with you, anywhere, everywhere.

Open your eyes, then you will see. Now, now you are in the Garden. Why? The door of the Garden is open for you through the deep knowing. Not through the deep thinking. Tap into Allāh (ﷻ). From the first moment your mom gave birth to you, you said, "Allāh (ﷻ)!" The first voice for you is Allāh (ﷻ)!

This is the truth. For that reason I want you to travel like Ibrāhīm (ﷺ) traveled. He explained how to travel into light, how to always be in the real life. Excuse me, my language is very weak.

The reading continues, "You need to look deeply at to whom you pray and to whom your father and forefathers prayed to know where they took the praying from. If anyone from anywhere prays and does not know Allāh (ﷻ), he is not my Beloved."

Sure.

The reading continues, "Only my beloved Allāh (ﷻ) is the real Beloved for me."

Oh yes. Sure.

The reading continues, "Because He created me..."

Āmīn.

The reading continues, "He guides me to the straight path..."

Āmīn.

The reading continues, "He feeds me..."

Āmīn.

The reading continues, "He gives me what I need for my body and for my heart and for my soul. He gives me the real water to drink."

Sure. And water is the water of the love, it is the water of life. Continue.

The reading continues, "The beloved Prophet Ibrāhīm (ؑ) said, 'If I am sick, Allāh (ﷻ) makes me healthy.' This has a very deep meaning. He said, 'If I am sick.' He did not say, 'If Allāh (ﷻ) makes me sick.' He does not attribute sickness as coming from Allāh (ﷻ); he attributes the cause of sickness to himself.

Yeah, sure. This is the deep politeness. He is very polite. This is Allāh (ﷻ). He created Ibrāhīm and Allāh (ﷻ) cares about His picture. You carry His picture. But He wants you to move and to share, He wants you to know how to heal, but in the right way. Sure. Yes.

The reading continues, "He does not attribute sickness as coming from Allāh (ﷻ); he attributes the cause of sickness to himself."

Many people misunderstand politeness. When they say sickness or diseases are from Allāh (ﷻ) they misunderstand. Allāh (ﷻ) will not send down sickness and diseases. Allāh (ﷻ) created you in the perfect way, but you didn't follow His orders. He didn't tell you make chemicals and put them in your plants to let the plants be poisoned. He didn't tell you that. You did that. This is what you did.

Allāh (ﷻ) created everything in the perfect way, clean from any sickness or disease. He created the animals. He created the air pure. But people destroyed the weather and built their factories and everything else they are doing. Allāh (ﷻ) created everything in a complete shape, pure and clear, and people created dirtiness, and so insects have begun to spread infections. Purification is from your beliefs and Allāh (ﷻ) is beautiful; He loves beauty. Why do you change that, oh human being?

The reading continues, "In the outside meaning this is because in the eyes of the people, sickness is bad, and they ask, how can Allāh (ﷻ) make something bad for the people? He is merciful. See, my beloved, when a person is veiled he says to his beloved God (ﷻ), 'Why did You do this?' or, 'Why did You do that to us?'

Beloved Ibrāhīm continues; he attributes death to Allāh (ﷻ), because no one can do anything, or do anything to anyone, if there is no water from Allāh (ﷻ). He said, 'After I die, He gives me the real life.' For that reason he says, 'Die before you die. If you do not die now, you cannot take the real life.'

For that reason, beloved, I always say, be absent from this world. Which means that I say, die to everything around you. Do not give anything around you any chance, which means, break all these presences, break all these pictures, break all these idols, all the thick veils and the material things."

Go ahead to Allāh (ﷻ)! Don't stop for one moment to be between the rubbish, no! Go ahead to Allāh (ﷻ). Swim in the ocean of your beloved God (ﷻ). This is what he means. Yes, continue.

The reading continues, "Change all these things to be for Allāh (ﷻ). Then, you will see that He gives you the real life. For that reason He said in His Qur'ān:

> Had He so willed, He would, indeed, have guided you all. (6:149)

Beloved Muḥyi-d-dīn ibn al-ʿArabī (ﷺ) said, 'Allāh (ﷻ) did not will "if," but He willed everything as it is.'"

Sure.

The reading continues, "For that reason, beloved, I say remove all those veils, and then you will see that He guides you."

Be careful not to stop with images or pictures or anything like that. Be careful to not put yourselves in the knot of the pictures or illusions.

The reading continues, "Then you will see that Allāh (ﷻ) gives you the real life, and you will always be in the real Garden between the arms of Allāh (ﷻ), and He is the Giver."

Sure.

The reading continues, "This is the way of the Prophet Ibrāhīm (ﷺ), may peace and blessings be upon him. He completely surrendered everything that he had. He did not surrender only his body, he completely surrendered everything he had. That is, if he had anything, which he didn't, because everything is from Him.

For that reason Ibrāhīm (ﷺ) did not say, 'I have,' he said, 'I haven't anything to give,' for Allāh (ﷻ) is the Giver. He surrendered completely and trusted God (ﷻ) completely. If someone does not trust and surrender completely to God (ﷻ), then how can he receive from Him? If he does not surrender this means that he lives in an illusion. He lives in the shadows, he lives with the pictures, and this is the real Fire for him because he is still with these pictures.

Ibrāhīm (ﷺ) wanted to say, "Travel from this world now, before you leave your body." He carried the real love for his people. He loved his parents, he loved his people, everything. And he did not like to see anyone sad, suffering or sick. The work of Ibrāhīm's father..."

This is the message of all the prophets (☼), the noble prophets (☼), and the beloveds who followed the prophets (☼), who want to see the whole world full of mercy and love. All of them gave their selves and their spirits as sacrifices to Allāh (☼) for people to be happy and full of kindness and mercy. We bow before them with our heads to keep their nobility and holiness, because the happiness came through them from Allāh (☼) to this world, the world of suffering. We can't achieve peace if we don't return back to the orders of Allāh (☼). Allāh (☼) says that He will not change the qualities within your self if you do not change yourself. This is what Sayyidinā Ibrāhīm (☼), Sayyidinā Mūsā (☼) and Sayyidinā ʿĪsā (☼), the messengers of good deeds, say.

The reading continues, "The work of Ibrāhīm's father was to make idols from wood and then to sell them. When they were made, he would give them to Ibrāhīm (☼) to sell for him. When he was still a youth, Ibrāhīm called to his people and said, 'Who wants to buy these things, who wants to buy these things?' And then he would tell them, 'It's important to know that these things are not useful.'

This is true, the Prophet Ibrāhīm (☼) could speak only the truth.

The reading continues, "Ibrāhīm would say, 'Not only are these things not useful, they can't do anything for you. If you want to buy them you can, but I want to tell you they are nothing. They do not feed themselves, and anyone who wants to can steal them.' When the people heard what Ibrāhīm (☼) said they refused to buy idols from him, so he returned the idols to his father.

His father said to him, 'Why don't you sell the idols? Our fathers gave these idols to their children to sell and they sell them. You are the only one who doesn't sell anything.' Ibrāhīm (☼) said to his father, 'How can I lie? Allāh (☼) did not teach me to lie to the people. I could not sell anything that is not useful.'"

Honesty should be anywhere and everywhere, in the child and in the big one. If a person is not be honest, whether he is a president or he is poor, his final situation will be one of destruction and you will have ruined yourself.

The same thing is happening now. Who can believe a liar? A liar can believe a liar. At the end, he is the loser. It is enough to simply call him a liar. But we will not put an announcement on his back stating that he is liar. Even animals they know he is liar. People are hungry and children are suffering and all people know he is a liar.

The reading continues, "I could not sell anything that is not useful, so how could I sell something that is full of darkness and sickness. How could I sell anything to people that does not guide the heart to Allāh (ﷻ)?"

Yes.

The reading continues:

> "And mention in the book, Ibrāhīm.
> Truly, he was a man of truth, a prophet.
>
> When he said to his father, 'Oh my father!
> Why do you worship that which hears not,
> sees not and cannot avail you in anything?
> Oh my father! Truly, there has come to me of knowledge
> that has not come to you.
> So follow me, I will guide you to the straight path.
> Oh my father! Worship not shayṭān.
> Truly, shayṭān has been a rebel against the Most Gracious.
> Oh my father! Truly, I fear that a torment from the Most Gracious should overtake you, so that you become a companion of shayṭān.'
>
> He (the father) said, 'Do you reject my gods, oh Ibrāhīm?
> If you don't stop, I will indeed stone you.
> So get away from me safely.'
> Ibrāhīm said, 'Peace be on you!
> I will ask forgiveness of my Lord for you.
> Truly, He is ever Most Gracious to me.
> And I will turn away from you
> and from those whom you invoke besides Allāh.
> And I will call upon my Lord and I hope that I will not be unblessed in my invocation to my Lord.'

> So when he had turned away from them and from those whom
> they worshipped besides Allāh,
> We gave him Isḥāq and Yaʿqūb
> and each one of them We made a prophet. (19:41-49)

Ibrāhīm (؏) explained the truth to his people. He explained the straight way, the right religion to them, because he wanted to help them to be people who follow the straight path of Allāh (ﷻ). If they had followed the path of the devil, the devil would have guided them to the Fire. This means that you put yourself in the Fire. For this reason, do not make the devil your beloved, but leave everything completely. Leave everything, like I said, and take the real Beloved. Allāh (ﷻ) is the real Beloved for you, because He gives you what you need. He is inside you. Make your heart special only for Him.

Ibrāhīm (؏) said, 'Oh, my beloved people, do not give space for anything but Allāh (ﷻ),' and he told his father, 'If you do not listen to my words, I will say "astaghfiru-llāh" for you and ask God (ﷻ) to forgive you, because I love you.'

This is from the deepest courtesy. You see, he doesn't want to leave his father. He carries not only love for his people, but he lives in the world of the unity. He loves all people because everyone is a part of him. He is the real father for all of the people in his time.

For that reason, he was very careful about everyone. He wanted his children to be with him and did not like to see anyone go far away. He wanted to see everyone inside the heart of his beloved Allāh (ﷻ). His calling to the people was the voice of Allāh (ﷻ) calling to every heart, asking them to open their hearts to the word of Allāh (ﷻ). He continued calling and calling and he didn't stop, even when he saw that a person's heart, or the hearts of the people were closed. He didn't stop talking or giving mercy to them. From his religion he said, 'When the people are sick, they need the real medicine.'

Some people are very sick. They are crying about the pain that they feel. If you give them medicine they may refuse to take it, but it's better to try to give it because if you don't that person might go away and die. For that reason, the beloved Prophet Ibrāhīm (؏) gave mercy to his

people even though they always refused his message. They even threw stones at him; they tried everything to make him stop, but he didn't listen. If a person gave him something strong, he did not return the stone but was patient; more than patient."

He gave love. He gave mercy, because he was the mercy. He was the real medicine for every heart who cried and didn't have mercy.

The reading continues, "He was more than patient because his heart contained everyone."

Sure.

The reading continues, "This is the way of the beloved Prophet Ibrāhīm (ع) who contains all of his children. If he had children, how could he leave any of them? He always cried in the night and in the day for everyone to open their ears to his words."

Prophets (ع) advise their followers and the ones who carry the message like them, and hold their qualities. All of a prophets' followers should be patient and generous or Allāh (ﷻ) will punish him and ask him, "Why were you not polite with others?"

Allāh (ﷻ) said to Sayyidinā Muḥammad (ﷺ):

> And had you been severe and harsh-hearted,
> they would have broken away from about you. (3:159)

Among Sayyidinā Muḥammad's people a man asked, "Where is Sayyidinā Muḥammad (ﷺ)?" because Sayyidinā Muḥammad (ﷺ) was sitting on the ground with his people—and not only Muḥammad (ﷺ), all the prophets (ع) were like that. All of them were in complete adab (courtesy, politeness).

The prophets (ع) are the people of politeness, the people of generosity; they are the most generous, the most kind. They carry the qualities of Allāh (ﷻ). The one who claims to be a guide but is not kind and full of mercy is a devil. Do not listen to such a person. But if you see one who is polite with everyone—the young people and old people—and he serves at their feet, believe him and follow him. This is the healing, full of love. He loves everyone.

The reading continues, "If he had children, how can he leave any of his children? He always cries in the night and in the day for everyone to open their ears to His words. Ibrāhīm (ﷺ) continued, but his father told him, after he had talked to him many times, that he wanted his beloved son Ibrāhīm (ﷺ) to return to praying to his idols. His father became very angry with him, threatening to throw stones at him and to kill him if he did not listen. Ibrāhīm (ﷺ) returned his father's strong words with words of compassion. He was always very soft and very polite to his father, and also to his people. 'I give you my life,' the Prophet said, 'to return to the real life and to be one of the children of Allāh (ﷻ). I give my life to sit around His table to help you feed yourselves.' But his father and his people refused everything he said.

See, my beloveds? Do you see the way of the Prophet Ibrāhīm (ﷺ), how he gives in his religion? He doesn't listen o any voice, only to the voice of Allāh (ﷻ). After the strong words that came from his father, Ibrāhīm (ﷺ) began to pray for his father and for Allāh (ﷻ) to forgive him, and it says in the Holy Qur'ān..."

Because he was completely full of mercy for all people. He was polite with all people. Those are the qualities for those good people. He forgot his human body, so he was kind in his heart and his body. His message was to make others happy, not to complicate their lives.

The belief of unity is very simple. It is not complicated, but scientists now, those who claim that they are scientists, never talk to the spirits and they don't give mercy. This religion is easy. Our religion is easy. Don't complicate it for people. This religion is established in justice and love and mercy. The human being is noble and we should keep his dignity to keep him dear, and his position aligned with Allāh (ﷻ).

Those scientists—the people who speak in the name of our religion—are not from Islām. They are from devil. Those who complicated people's lives and try to make Islām very difficult for people...they changed the words. They call themselves scientists but they are not from us. They are not from Allāh (ﷻ).

We, in our religion, the religion of Allāh (ﷻ) and the prophets (ﷺ)—Mūsā (ﷺ), ʿĪsā (ﷺ), Muḥammad (ﷺ), Ibrāhīm (ﷺ)—believe in one religion. There is one religion. The prophets (ﷺ) came with this message from Allāh (ﷻ), not from stupid, foolish, corrupt people. They tried to change a lot, but this is not our issue now. I just wanted to give a brief speech about it.

The reading continues, "It says in the Holy Qurʾān:

> And Ibrāhīm's invoking for his father's forgiveness
> was only because of a promise he had made to him.
> But when it became clear to him that he (his father)
> was an enemy of Allāh, he dissociated himself from him.
> Truly, Ibrāhīm was one who invokes Allāh with humility,
> glorifies Him and remembers Him much and was forbearing.
> (9:114)

After his father refused to be one of the children of Allāh (ﷻ), Ibrāhīm (ﷺ) said, 'I cannot be with my father any longer,' but he did not give his father anything bad or strong. He didn't leave him or throw stones at him. He said, 'You have a chance and you have a choice. If you return to Allāh (ﷻ), this is from you. If you do not return to Allāh (ﷻ), this is also from you.'

He gives you the choice and everything is from you, not from any other. If you knock at His door, you will see that His door is open to you.

One day after his people and his father had refused to listen to his words, Ibrāhīm (ﷺ) took a big axe and went to the place where the people kept their idols. There were eight of them, with beautiful things around their necks. Before he broke the idols he brought them food and said to them, 'Will you not eat?' No one answered him. He brought hem water and said, 'Maybe you are thirsty?' but the idols did not answer him.

This was a teaching for the people to help them open their ears to understand the One who created everything. Then he reduced the idols to fragments, all save the chief of them, that happily they might have recourse to it. When the people saw the destruction of their idols they said, 'Who has done this to our Gods? Surely it must be some evil-doer.'

This is in the Qur'ān. Ibrāhīm (ﷺ) took an axe to all the idols except the biggest one, and then he tied the axe around its neck. When the king and the people came to pray, they found their idols broken and asked, 'Who did this to our beloved Gods?' They knew that Ibrāhīm (ﷺ) had refused to pray to their gods, so they went to him and asked, 'Who did this?' Ibrāhīm (ﷺ) told them to ask the biggest one, and then pointed with his finger. He said, "The biggest one did it."

He was not lying because what he said carried two meanings. When he pointed he meant that the finger was responsible, but they thought, of course, that he meant the biggest idol. They replied, 'How can that idol break them? It can't do anything.'

Then Ibrāhīm (ﷺ), may peace and blessings be upon him, said to them, 'Then why do you pray to idols if they can't do anything for you and they can't forbid anyone to break them or their brothers? Why do you pray to these things when they are of no use to you?'

Ibrāhīm (ﷺ) also saw with certainty that their idol-worship of the stars was not right, and that it was important to see Allāh (ﷻ) behind these phenomena. In the Qur'ān Allāh says:

> When the night covered him with darkness he saw a star.
> He (Ibrāhīm ﷺ) said, "This is my Lord."
> But when it set, he said, "I don't like those (things) that set."

He wanted to teach the people some understanding of God (ﷻ).

> When he saw the moon rising up, he said, "This is my Lord."
> But when it set, he said,
> "Unless my Lord guides me,
> I will surely be among the people who went astray."
>
> When he saw the sun rising up, he said,
> "This is my Lord. This is greater."
> But when it set, he said, "Oh my people!
> I am indeed free from all that you join as partners."
> (6:76-78)

God (ﷻ) is not absent in any moment. He is always present."

Sure. Lā ʾilāha ʾilla-llāh.

The reading continues, "If he were absent there would be no heaven, no earth, and no humanity; there would be no life. So it is important to pray to He who created all of these things."

Sure.

The reading continues, "For Allāh (ﷻ) wanted to teach Ibrāhīm's people what they did not understand. But see, my people, he was the mercy for them. Some of them listened to Ibrāhīm (ؑ) but were afraid to follow him, because if they followed Ibrāhīm (ؑ) there was a sword that awaited their necks. Their king was very strong.

The king and most of the people were very angry with Ibrāhīm (ؑ). They tried to think of a way in which they might get rid of him. Then Iblīs came to them in the form of a human being and began to speak to them."

Iblīs came to give a teaching for the leaders everywhere. He is the guide for all those who make things dangerous everywhere. He is bad, he is Iblīs. He drives them to kill and to destroy everything. He is the enemy of the human being who came from Ādam (ؑ).

The reading continues, "They took Ibrāhīm (ؑ) to court and the judge began to ask him questions about the destruction of the idols. Ibrāhīm (ؑ) answered as he had answered before. Then the judge asked him directly, 'Are you the one who broke the idols?' Ibrāhīm (ؑ) answered, 'Yes. I wanted to help all of my people leave these idols and return to Allāh (ﷻ).'

If the people did not return to Allāh (ﷻ), there was still a chance. Still, they refused to listen to his word. So they put Ibrāhīm (ؑ) in prison and discussed various ways of killing him. Someone said to leave him in a dark prison until he died. Some said to put him in a well. Others said to put him in some situation until he died. Then Iblīs said, 'Burn him and stand by your gods.'

While the people gathered wood and anything that would burn, Ibrāhīm (ﷺ) surrendered to what they wanted to do, because he knew that Allāh (ﷻ) would not leave him. For that reason, he said he did not care what people wanted to do to him.

He was a prophet and a mercy for the people. Allāh (ﷻ) can change anything at the perfect time. Ibrāhīm (ﷺ) contained a lot of water—it was part of his quality. One drop from the water he had was enough to change the fire into a garden for him.

When the fire was ready, and it was very large, they sent Ibrāhīm (ﷺ) into the middle of the fire with a catapult.

> When they propelled him toward the fire,
> but before he reached the fire,
> the Angel Jībrīl (Gabriel) came to him and asked him,
> 'Ibrāhīm, do you want anything? Do you need any help? '
>
> He told Jībrīl, 'I do not need anything from you.
> Allāh knows my state and He knows what I need. '
>
> We (Allāh) said: 'Oh fire! Be cool and safe for Ibrāhīm.'
> (21:69)"

Ibrāhīm (ﷺ) told Jībrīl (ﷺ), "I don't need anything from you. Allāh (ﷻ) knows my situation and He is rich; He doesn't need to hear my request. I will not even ask Allāh (ﷻ) because He is seeing me and hearing me. This is Ibrāhīmic faith. He believed that Allāh (ﷻ) is the doer; he does everything. Allāh (ﷻ) called to the fire, talking to the fire, "Oh fire, be cool and peaceful for Ibrāhīm (ﷺ)."

Then the fire changed into a garden. The fire that was burning changed into a garden, and underneath this garden was water. Some gnostics say that the Euphrates river flows from the time of Ibrāhīm (ﷺ), when Allāh (ﷻ) transformed the fire and led the water underneath this garden. The people looked at Ibrāhīm (ﷺ). They saw him sitting under the trees in the garden. He was eating and drinking from the water and the fire couldn't reach his body.

The exact same fire, the same people who disbelieve in Allāh (ﷻ)—Allāh (ﷻ) will eat them in this world and in the next world. For the people who are full of mercy, Allāh (ﷻ) will send down His mercy. The Prophet Muḥammad (ﷺ) said:

> Have mercy on the ones on earth
> and the One in heaven will have mercy upon you.

Sayyidinā Ibrāhīm (ﷺ) paid himself a sacrifice to Allāh (ﷻ) for the sake of Allāh (ﷻ), for the sake of belief, and for the sake of humanity. This is the master of all the prophets (ﷺ). This is the khalīlu-llāh (ﷻ), the lover of Allāh (ﷻ), and more than a friend to Allāh (ﷻ). If a person doesn't believe in Ibrāhīm (ﷺ) as a prophet, how could he say he believed in God (ﷻ)?

One day I was talking to the Pope and I said, "Why do you hoard gold here in church when so many people are suffering everywhere from hunger and sickness? Why?" He didn't reply. Because he is Iblīs.

Sure. Listen what I say. Many, many millions of people are crying from sickness. And they keep more than 20 tons of gold inside the church? This is not right. You are not a holy one. If you were a holy one you would use it for the poor and suffering people. What good can you do when you keep it in a cave? Nothing. I gave him the message. I did not care. Bismi-llāh. Yes, continue.

The reading continues, "Anyone, my children, who loves Allāh (ﷻ), Allāh (ﷻ) loves him."

This means the first one who gives a sacrifice for himself and his heart gives a sacrifice for Ibrāhīm (ﷺ).

Anyone who believes in God (ﷻ) and walks straight and has a clean heart, I am sure that God (ﷻ) helps him and He does not let anyone do anything bad to him, for He cares about him.

This man carried all the mercy, all the love, and all the justice in his heart and in his spirit, and he prayed for all of the people who were suffering. He is the first one who gave his spirit and self as a sacrifice for all people. He teaches them how to deal with each other with politeness and mercy and how they should deal with others. They should carry the divine qualities and they should give this holy body as a sacrifice for all people. This sacrifices helps all people to live in happiness and peace, not suffering from hunger and many sicknesses.

This is the way of the Prophet Ibrāhīm (﵇). He put himself in the fire for the people and he was never scared, because he was sure that this is the right way. He had faith and belief.

His message was to let all other people be happy. Sayyidinā Ibrāhīm (﵇) was not for only a certain group of people; he was a prophet for all people. No one can say, "Ibrāhīm (﵇) is from Israel, from ʿĪsā (﵇), or from another religion." He was a human being. Allāh (ﷻ) created him and gave him the general message to give to all people, without discrimination. I have read all of the scriptures of Ibrāhīm (﵇) and his message is universal. It is the message of unity; there is no discrimination between nations and races. Ibrāhīm (﵇) is the prophet of the one nation and the human being is one nation. He gave himself as a sacrifice for all of you, for all people.

After Allāh (ﷻ) exchanged the fire for the garden for the Prophet Ibrāhīm (﵇), He sent down peace. This is part of the message for the other prophets (﵇). Their job was to exchange the fire for gardens. It meant their jobs were to save people, because they were working for the benefit of all people, for all good things. They sacrificed themselves for you, for all people, from the time of Ibrāhīm (﵇).

The reading continues, "Allāh (ﷻ) helped Ibrāhīm (﵇) because he loved Allāh (ﷻ)."

Sure.

The reading continues, "Anyone, my children, who loves Allāh (ﷻ), Allāh (ﷻ) loves him. Anyone who believes in God (ﷻ) and walks straight and has a clean heart, I am sure God (ﷻ) helps him.

The king sent an order for him to leave the country, but before Ibrāhīm (﵇) left, Allāh (ﷻ) sent something to King Nimrūd. He sent a very small animal that crawled inside his nose and into his brain. The king cried all night because of this small animal and he couldn't sleep. Then he

went to every doctor for help, and one of the doctors came to Ibrāhīm (ؑ) for help."

(To much laughter, Sidi says:) Sure, if Wadude were there, he would have come to Wadude, and what would Wadude have made for him? Now, this is what Ibrāhīm said to him.

The reading continues, "One of the doctors came to Ibrāhīm (ؑ) and asked him if he knew of the best thing to help the king sleep. Ibrāhīm (ؑ) told him to take his shoes—Ibrāhīm's—or the shoes of someone who believed in him, and to hit the king three times in the head. When the animal hears something, it will stop moving and the king will be able to sleep.

So the king found people who believed in Ibrāhīm (ؑ) and in the God of Ibrāhīm (ﷻ) and he brought their shoes. He took them and gave them to one of his chamberlains. When the king would cry out from the gnat in his head, the chamberlain would hit him in the top of his head. After he had hit him six or seven times with the shoe, the gnat would be quiet. Allāh (ﷻ), praised and exalted is He, kept him in this situation until he left the dunyā. He killed him with the shoes of holy feet."

This is example for anyone who is not straight. This is the end for everyone who is not straight, who does not have mercy for people, who does not make all of the people happy. If a person does not give love to every human being, then there will be a bad, bad end to his life. Look everyone! You see that Allāh (ﷻ) sends very strong things, send sickness and disease. Allāh (ﷻ) is the Justice. Allāh (ﷻ) is the Justice and He is Allāh (ﷻ). He wants to see all of creation full of peace and love and mercy. Allāh (ﷻ), yes, He is aṣ-Ṣabūr.

The reading continues, "He killed him with the shoes of holy people, and with a gnat, a little insect."

The king who had everything died from being hit with shoes. He told him, "The medicine for you is to leave the dunyā by means of the shoes of a poor slave." Allāhu Akbar. Allāhu akbar. Allāhu akbar.

The reading continues, "This is for everyone who does not walk straight, for everyone who does not help people, and for everyone who makes bad things for people. This is a deep lesson for any king or anyone who Allāh (☆) puts here to care about people, give them mercy, and give them love. To anyone like that, Allāh (☆) sends many lessons like those of Nimrūd, the king of the people of Ibrāhīm (☆).

Ibrāhīm (☆) left his country, went to the Holy Land, and continued his message there. He went with his wife Sāra, who was the real beloved for him and the real mirror for him, and a few others who followed him, including Lūṭ (Lot) (☆), who was the son of his brother. Lūṭ stayed in Canaan and was sent to the cities of the plains, Jericho, east of the Dead Sea, to give the message to the people. He continued to give it in the same way as his uncle, Ibrāhīm (☆).

The people who followed him came to be known as the Abranian people, which comes from the word 'crossing,' because they crossed trans-Jordan to the Holy Land. They were not Jews, nor were they Christians—they were real Muslims and followers of the religion of divine unity. Ibrāhīm (☆) sent the religion of Allāh (☆) everywhere throughout all of this country. This country has always been the country of the message of Allāh (☆).

Ibrāhīm (☆) lived like the Bedouin people when he first came to this land. He took care of sheep until he reached Jericho, and then he travelled and remained near the town of Hebron. The Arab people at that time were known as the Canaanites and the name of their king was Salām. He was the first person to build the holy city, Jerusalem, and he called it, "Ur-Salām," Mountain of Peace.

When the king met Ibrāhīm (☆) he opened his heart to him. The king worshipped the sun and the stars, but Ibrāhīm (☆) taught him to Whom he should pray, and he surrendered to the religion of Ibrāhīm (☆) and became a real Muslim. The king gave land to Ibrāhīm (☆) from Hebron the Red Sea.

Ibrāhīm (☆) sent his message everywhere. He had left his people and his father because the truth was more important to him. He surrendered

completely to Allāh (ﷻ); he trusted Allāh (ﷻ) completely. For that reason, he became the second father of all the prophets (عليهم السلام).

I want to read you a really special thing. Last night, Sidi was..."

Allāh (ﷻ). Before you finish, I want you tell you how Allāh (ﷻ) told Ibrāhīm (عليه السلام) in a dream to kill his son as a sacrifice for the face of Allāh (ﷻ). This was a great test, a great exam for Sayyidinā Ibrāhīm (عليه السلام).

He loved his son and Ismāʾīl (عليه السلام) was his only son at that time. Allāh (ﷻ) told him to slaughter his son as a sacrifice to Allāh (ﷻ). So Ibrāhīm (عليه السلام) told his son, "My son, I'm seeing to slaughter you by the order of Allāh (ﷻ)." His son accepted this and he told Ibrāhīm, "Because the order of Allāh (ﷻ) wants that, do what Allāh (ﷻ) wants, my father."

Then, when Ibrāhīm (عليه السلام) put the knife on Ismāʾīl's neck, the knife became water. It didn't do anything. He tried again and the knife couldn't do it again. Then the third time the same thing happened.

Allāh (ﷻ) sent down the Angel Jībrīl (عليه السلام), carrying a sheep, a big one, and he told him, "Ibrāhīm (عليه السلام), you are honest. Instead of giving your son as a sacrifice, We give you this sheep. Kill this sheep and give the meat to the poor people instead of killing your son. This sacrifice will help you to walk."

This is the message from my heart to all my beloveds.

The Table of Divine Love

"Everything is from Love" and "A Drop of the Love" with music
September 23, 2010 AM, Austin

لا إله إلا الله – لا إله إلا الله – لا إله إلا الله – محمد رسول الله عليه صلاة الله
لا إله إلا الله – لا إله إلا الله – لا إله إلا الله – ابراهيم رسول الله عليه صلاة الله
لا إله إلا الله – لا إله إلا الله – لا إله إلا الله – موسى رسول الله عليه صلاة الله
لا إله إلا الله – لا إله إلا الله – لا إله إلا الله – عيسى رسول الله عليه صلاة الله
اللهم انت السلام ومنك السلام و إليك يعود السلام
تباركت ربنا وتعاليت يا ذوالجلال والإكرام

This evening, I would like to give you a noble gift; I would like to tell you about the table of the love, which is full of beautiful, delicious meanings. I would like to explain the reason for our creation.

The love is food for our spirits and for all of His creation, It is not just for human beings, but for all of His creation, for all of the different worlds, the divine worlds. The love is food for the fish, the animals in the oceans and in the trees.

This existence has been built on love. The love is in the divine water. Allāh (ﷻ) says:

> And We have made every living thing from water. (21:30)

This is the secret of water. And Allāh (ﷻ) says:

> I was a hidden treasure and loved to be known.
> Therefore, I created the creation so that I might be known.

He let the human being know Him. The sound of the love is music on the tongues of the birds, the tongues of the camels. When Allāh (ﷻ) sent down His order to the camels, they were shaped. The mountains were shaped and water came out from them. Allāh (ﷻ) sent down His love to all of His creation. He said to the mountains:

> And indeed We bestowed grace upon Dāwūd (David) from Us:
> "Oh you mountains, glorify (Allāh) with him! And you birds!
> And We made the iron soft for him." (34:10)

He ordered the mountains to sing and pray with Sayyidinā Dāwūd. Allāh (ﷻ) says:

> Each one (of His creatures) knows its ṣalāh
> and its glorification (of Allāh). (24:41)

Not just you, but everything in existence praises the name of Allāh (ﷻ). All of the honest worshippers who carry the love in their souls all of the time are in a deep prayer. Their souls are alive and the skies, the heavens and the earth will be happy. Allāh (ﷻ) says:

> It is He who sends ṣalāh (prayers) upon you,
> and His angels, too. (33:43)

They will ask Allāh (ﷻ) and they will make supplications for you if you are honest, if you are a real, loyal worshipper. If you are a criminal or corrupter, the angels will ask Allāh (ﷻ) to send...

Allāh (ﷻ). Allāh (ﷻ). He is praying. What does this mean? It means that He is will send down His mercy if you are pure, if you are a real worshipper, if you are with His love, the divine love. If you walk in the streets you can hear the melodies of the water. These melodies are alive. They carry life to you and to the plants and to all of creation. The sounds of the trees are melodies. This is the love.

Why are you trying to ruin the love, cutting down trees and destroying the seas and the oceans and causing pollution? Who is doing this? They are the enemies of love. We are the children of the truth and we are the soldiers of Allāh (ﷻ). We spread love to all people. This is our way; this is our path. We love all of the people Allāh (ﷻ) created, regardless of religion. Allāh (ﷻ) created us to be lovers and He says:

> Oh people, We have created you from a male and a female,
> and made you into nations and tribes
> so that you may know (and love) one another. (49:13)

And our beloved Prophet (ﷺ) said:

> All people are the children of Allāh,
> and the most noble are the ones who help others.

The love is from Allāh (ﷻ) to Allāh (ﷻ) to His people, those who are kind and full of mercy, regardless of whether they are rich or poor, black or white. Their father is Adam (ﷺ) and their mother is Hawwā' (ﷺ). We should all bow to all human beings. You should respect others and all of Allāh's creation. Allāh (ﷻ) says:

> He created you and fashioned you in the best mold. (95:4)

No one can create anything, not even an ant. Allāh (ﷻ). You are holy because Allāh (ﷻ) created you. You shouldn't belittle others. You think you are a small star, but you contain all of the worlds within you. You are the smallest planet in this world and He is the king of the planets. He created you in the perfect shape.

Why don't you carry the love? Why do you turn away from His love? You can't achieve anything by hating others. Don't hate anyone, it's not from Allāh (ﷻ). Allāh (ﷻ) says:

> He loves them, so they love Him. (5:54)

This is the law of Allāh (ﷻ), not the law of shayṭān. Allāh (ﷻ) created all people to be lovers and beloveds. I want to talk about love.

This reading is a combination of a Portland teaching called, "Everything is from Love" on page 133 and excerpts of an unpublished reading, "A Drop of the Love." This is accompanied by the music of Shaykh Yasīn at-Tuhamī.

The lyrics of the music are bold, italicized and indented. The reading is in bold text. Sidi's live commentary is in plain text.

The reading begins, "Bismi-llāhi-r-raḥmāni-r-raḥīm. I am here in my form, my body, but I keep my heart and my spirit to pray for you, to pray for everyone who is crying from the deep suffering in this world. I

cry from my deepest spirit. I ask Allāh (ﷻ) to send His peace and His mercy and His love and His freedom and His justice to all people everywhere. Āmīn.

I ask that He help those who are crying from deep sickness everywhere. I ask that He send angel healers (ﷺ) for everyone who is crying from deep sickness, that He clean this heart, clean this land, clean all the earth everywhere from the bad sicknesses, from the bad diseases and from cancer.

I pray for Allāh (ﷻ) to stop war everywhere and to send the wind of peace. I want to see His flag of unity go directly to every heart. I ask Him to stop those who play games and those who are not right, and I ask Him to help those who do walk though this order that helps people become pure and learn to help each other. I am sure of what He says:

> And when My slaves ask you concerning Me,
> then (answer them), I am indeed near.
> I respond to prayers when they call upon Me. (2:186)
>
> I am inside his heart.
> I hear everything he asks and I hear his crying.
> I accept him if he has a deep heart
> and if he makes the real prostration.
> I am inside everything, and everywhere he looks, he finds Me.

So raise your hands and ask Allāh (ﷻ) and then let Him answer your supplications. Āmīn. Be honest and ask with deep sincerity for Allāh (ﷻ), for He is hears you, He sees you and He is listening to you, yā Allāh (ﷻ).

In this place, in this time, in this room, there are angels (ﷺ) listening to the teaching, praising Allāh (ﷻ) and remembering Allāh (ﷻ), helping to clean everyone who is honest and sincere. This is a very holy time. I begin in this holy place at this holy time for everybody to cry to Allāh (ﷻ). So who will answer our supplications? Allāh (ﷻ)! You are the only One who answers supplications. The honest worshipper should not have any fear in his heart and he will never be sad. Āmīn.

Al-ḥamdu li-llāh, praise Allāh (ﷻ). Allāh (ﷻ) accepts our prayers and our supplications and He accepts us among His worshippers. Āmīn. So please excuse me. I did that obeying His order.

For this day, we will enter through a huge door, a big door: the door of al-ḥubb, the door of the love. Love is the first thing to enter to reach Allāh (ﷻ) and to knock on Allāh's doors. Allāh's doors are open to you. For Allāh (ﷻ) told Hārūn (Aaron) and Mūsā (ﷺ):

> I hear and see (everything). (20:46)

He hears our supplications and He sees us."

He sees and hears the black ant on the dark, moonless night on a black rock. Allāh (ﷻ) is the Hearing. Even this small ant spoke to the other ants when Sayyidinā Sulayman (ﷺ) was approaching.

> Oh ants! Enter your dwellings, in order to avoid Sulayman and his troops crushing you while they do not see us. (Qurʾān 2:18)

This ant warned them because she already carried the love.

Story of Sulayman, Hudhud and Bilqīs

Sayyidinā Sulayman (ﷺ) was able to talk with insects, birds and animals. One of his soldiers was a beautiful bird, called Hudhud (Hoopoe). One day, the bird was distant from Sayyidinā Sulayman (ﷺ) and Sulayman (ﷺ) asked, "Where is Hudhud?" When Hudhud returned he told Sulayman (ﷺ), "I was flying and I saw a beautiful woman (Bilqīs, the Queen of Sheba ﵂), but she was worshipping the sun instead of worshipping Allāh (ﷻ)."

Sulayman (ﷺ) said, "We will figure out if you are honest." Then, one of the believing jinn told him, "I will bring her kingdom to you before you stand up." So very quickly, a thousand times faster than an airplane, in the blink of an eye, the jinn came and put her kingdom in front of Sayyidinā Sulayman (ﷺ). Sulayman (ﷺ) said, "Alḥamdu li-llāh."

Then, Bilqīs (﵂) was brought forward and Sayyidinā Sulayman (ﷺ) asked her what she was doing. She figured out that Sulayman was carrying the message of peace, love and mercy. She believed in him. Bilqīs (﵂) said, "Oh my Lord, I witness that He is Your messenger carrying the message of love and peace without discrimination." She believed in him. She was a believer. She found faith, peace, love and mercy. Her story is a lesson for all princes and kings.

This is the woman. The woman, in our way, is a jewel. She is a daughter, a mother and a wife. You have a mother. From where did you come? Your mother gave birth to you. So, establish your love, and this love should be pure. Life in this dunyā cannot be quiet or full of peace except through divine love, loving your brother as you love yourself. Don't kill each other; respect each other so that the earth can be full of love. Listen to the melodies of love. It has very high, beautiful, divine melodies. Allāh (ﷻ) sent down this music.

One of our beloveds told me, "Sidi you teach about love all of the time." What do you want me to teach? The message of rockets, death and wars? My message is love. I want to teach you how to love others, how to love plants, animals and the earth and sky. You shouldn't be away from the sky and you shouldn't pollute the sky. Allāh (ﷻ) didn't ask you to pollute the sky. The one who does this is a corrupter. Why is the atmosphere damaged? Why have the oceans moved forward? Why are the seasons changing? Now summer is winter and winter is summer.

In Pakistan, monsoons destroyed 25,000 homes and 25 million people don't have anywhere to live because of the corruption, the gases in the atmosphere. I'm telling you the truth. I'm ready to tell you the exact numbers. You didn't hear about this?

We should stop the corrupters and stop corruption in order to guide people in how to love each other. We do not need rockets and bombs. We need calm, peaceful lives. I will keep singing for peace and love and mercy and justice to let people live beautiful lives.

We believe in one God and we love all of the prophets without discrimination, all of them. They are the beloveds of Allāh (ﷻ). This is our goal. We shouldn't hate others. This is the music of love.

The reading continues, "Now we are in the ocean of the love of Allāh (ﷻ). So prepare your hearts, my children, and be honest. Don't lose this chance in this time of mercy. The angels (ﷺ) and the spirits of the prophets (ﷺ) are around us.

Be with me and my heart and my spirit, because I am with you. I will give everything as a sacrifice, just for you to solve your problems. I ask Allāh (ﷻ) to help you, to let you be stable in your religion, standing, praying, fasting and prostrating. Purify everything that Allāh (ﷻ) has provided to you.

I will start with love, al-maḥabba. What is maḥabba, love? It is the first degree. It is the degree to enter the presence of al-Ḥaqq (ﷻ). First of all, you should clean your tongue, your hearts, your minds and your selves, because Allāh (ﷻ) says that He loves those who come to Him with healthy hearts. Allāh (ﷻ) loves them and they love Him.

One of the gnostics (ق) said:

> Allāh's existence?
> You can find it everywhere,
> even if you escape somewhere deep within the earth.
> Allāh (ﷻ) will hear you and Allāh (ﷻ) will see you.
> He sees you and He knows what you are doing.
> He can see your hand.

I swear by His name that He loves you. So why do you turn away from His love? Why don't you listen to what He says? Why don't you obey Him?

Come, my children. Come to the mercy of Allāh (ﷻ) and clean your hearts. Clean your spirits to be near Him and to be close to Him in His place, to be in the ocean of love, the entire love. He is the Manifester in everything and you are His mirror. So how can you be unable to see Him? You are the follower, you are the traveler to Allāh (ﷻ). He said on the tongue of His Prophet (ﷺ):

> I was a hidden treasure and I loved to be known.

Allāh (ﷻ) revealed Himself in the human being. They know Him. Open your ears, listen to hear this song of Dāwūd (David) (ع).

This is called "I am Revealing My Secrets to You." This is the food for your spirit.

I would like to send the essence of the secret love through the essence of my holy spirit to explain to my beloveds the meaning of love.

> ***Mention the name of my lover, even in my dream.***
> ***The conversations between me and my Beloved are my wine.***
> ***The conversations are wine for me.***
> ***My ears will be my witnesses.***

To begin, I say, if you want to be with Allāh (ﷻ), then I would like to give you a special gift through this song. In the beginning, I give you a drop of this love. I give this in a special cup to make you absent, to change you from everything that you have, to leave the past and discharge it and to go deep, my children. Then I give you to drink from a drop of His love. Please do not go far away. Be ready."

It is very important to taste. If you don't taste what will happen to you? You will lose yourself. It is important—this is the real truth for you to always be happy, to keep your heart full of happiness and full of the love. It needs love. Don't break any heart. For this reason, listen to the music of the beloved of Allāh (ﷻ). If you like to clean your heart and you soul...bismi-llāh.

Music plays.

> ***In the name of love, my love.***
> ***It is my drink.***
> ***Mention His name.***
> ***I will accept it even in my dreams.***

I want to be absent. I want to be absent from this awful existence, full of pain. The corrupters cause it. I want to emigrate to the melodies of mercy, so I need a glass of divine water. I am absent now. I am with Allāh (ﷻ) and His angels (ﷺ). This is what I want. I wish for you the same; you are my beloveds. You love Allāh (ﷻ).

All of us are thirsty and hungry. We need the divine meanings, the divine melodies. This is the real food, and we will be absent within Allāh (ﷻ), with Allāh (ﷻ), and you can find healing for your spirits, your souls and your bodies here. You can see, even the earth will give you beautiful, beautiful plants. Allāh (ﷻ) sent down water from the sky. It is a sign of love. Allāh (ﷻ) sends this water as a sign of love. You can find different colored flowers. These are divine signs.

The reading continues, "To begin, I say, if you want to be with Allāh (ﷻ), then I would like to give you a special gift through this song. In the beginning, I give you a drop of this love. I give this in a special cup to make you absent, to change you from everything that you have, to leave the past and discharge it and to go deep, my children. Then I give you to drink from a drop of His love. Please do not go far away. Be ready."

Don't drink dirty water. It's very important to be careful and to choose the water of life. When you feel it, then you make a real prostration for Allāh (ﷻ). Then you see yourself in the real Garden between the arms of God! Don't be far away, between the shoulders of those who don't know Allāh (ﷻ)! Don't try to eat any food that isn't clean. This is what I mean.

The reading continues, "You are ready after you have all the sincerity, all the surrender, when you do not try to surrender to anything else or to your nafs, but you surrender completely to the One you love..."

Be careful with your nafs, your self. It will push you to sin. Allāh (ﷻ) wants you to live a beautiful life. Emigrate to Allāh (ﷻ). Travel to Allāh (ﷻ). Sayyidinā Ibrāhīm (ﷺ) says:

> I am emigrating to my Lord. He will guide me! (37:99)

Die in Allāh (ﷻ). You will be alive for eternity in Allāh (ﷻ).

You have to know this divine knowledge. Allāh (ﷻ) gave this knowledge to all of the prophets and messengers. Sayyidinā ʿĪsā (ﷺ) is the prophet of love. Sayyidinā Mūsā (ﷺ) is the prophet of dignity and justice. Sayyidinā Ibrāhīm (ﷺ) was the father of all the prophets. He contained the whole world and he was the father of the whole world. He was the shaykh of all the prophets. Allāh (ﷻ) sent Sayyidinā Muḥammad (ﷺ) as a mercy to all people.

Now can we know if those who claim they are with Allāh (ﷻ) are honest? We want signs. Many people claim that they fall in love with Laylā, and Laylā is innocent; she doesn't have anything to do with them. So observe those who make this claim: do they put on beautiful garments or garments from the foxes? What do you see?

I am asking Allāh (ﷻ) not to be among those bad people. I am asking Allāh (ﷻ) to let you be divine worshippers. I'm quite sure Allāh (ﷻ) will protect your hearts and your intellects. Allāh (ﷻ) loves you and you love Him.

Look, look at your holy books. You carry these books and what can you find within them? Do you want to see Allāh (ﷻ)? You should obey Him. You have to obey Him. He is ar-Raḥmāni-r-Raḥīm, the Merciful, the Compassionate. You are kind, you are gentle, you are merciful, you love people. If you says, "Yes" it is nothing. A lot of people say, "Yes." You can hear a lot of people talking on television. Many people say they will bring peace. They say this on their tongues while they are inventing rockets. Where is the love? Where are those who say, "We are good people and we love others?" Do they help the poor and needy people? Where is the love?

Allāh (ﷻ) created this love and Allāh (ﷻ) created the supporters of this love, those who will carry His message. They are crying for others, the ones who are in need. They are the people of love. This message of love is full of music and beautiful melodies. The soul is crying. It needs love. It needs to support the needy people. Are you able to hear my voice? This is the soul, and the soul will repeat and repeat the melodies of love. Allāh (ﷻ) will not look at what you say or at your faces, He will look at your hearts.

He is very close to you. He is closer than the space that was between you and your mom when you were in the womb. Don't ask, "Where is my Lord?" Ask yourself: where are you? Ask yourself if you are in the trash. Allāh (ﷻ) says:

> He is with you wherever you are. (57:4)

He knows everything. He knows what you hide and what your leaders hide. There are no games. Allāh (ﷻ) is the truth. Do not try to play games. Wake up! This is what He says.

Music plays.

> ***This is the name of my lover in my dreams.***
> ***The conversations between us are my wine.***
> ***My hearing is my witness. I love Him.***
> ***Even if He is far away, I love Him in my dreams, in my reality.***

The reading continues, "Oh, Allāhu Akbar. I just want to be alone with my beloved God (ﷻ) in this life. This is the life I am waiting for—to not look left or right but to be only between His arms. Yā Allāh (ﷻ). Yā Allāh (ﷻ).

That is what I wait for. I wait to drink from His source and to swim in His ocean. Because of this I follow his commandments. Yes, yes, I follow what He says. When I mention the one I fall in love with, my beloved one, I am happy if I see Him only in my dreams."

Music plays.

> ***I enjoy mentioning His name.***

Allāh (ﷻ) says on the tongue of His Prophet (ﷺ):

> Oh My worshipper, be to Me as I want you to be
> and I will be to you as you want Me to be.

These are the words of Allāh (ﷻ) in the Bible, in the Qur'ān and in the book of Ibrāhīm.[21] Allāh (ﷻ) says to all the beloved prophets, "Beloveds, give Me everything and I will give you everything."

---

[21] The Scrolls of Ibrāhīm are also known as the "Forty Scrolls" and the "Suḥuf Ibrāhīm wa Mūsā." They are a lost scripture and are generally attributed to Ibrāhīm (ﷺ) and Mūsā (ﷺ). They are referred to in the Qur'ān in two places. "Indeed, this is in the former scripture—the scripture of Ibrāhīm and Mūsā," (87:18-19) and, "Or is he not informed with what is in the pages of Mūsā and of Ibrāhīm, (they) who fulfilled/conveyed all that (Allāh ordered)." (53:36-37).

Allāh (ﷻ) says two words, "Follow Me!"

> If you love Allāh then follow me. (3:31)

"Then," He says, "you will find Me. You will be happy and you will not need anything. Everything is with My hands."

The reading continues, "Oh, Allāhu Akbar. I just want to be alone with my beloved God (ﷻ) in the real life."

This is the real wedding. Allāh (ﷻ) makes everything for all people a real wedding, but most of them are blind. They can't hear. What will happen to those people?

The reading continues, "This is the life I am waiting for—to not look left or right but to be only between His arms. Yā Allāh (ﷻ). Yā Allāh (ﷻ)."

Are you waiting for Allāh (ﷻ) to give you the Garden after you die? This is a long time to wait. Now! Be in the Garden of Allāh (ﷻ). You are in the Garden when you carry His message. You will love for Him and live for Him. This is the Garden now, not tomorrow. You'd like to see the garden full of vegetables full of everything. You will be waiting a long time. He says, "Enough." Bismi-llah.

The reading continues, "That is what I wait for. I wait to drink from His source and to swim in His ocean. Because of this I follow his commandments."

If you follow Allāh (ﷻ), you are in the Garden now. But if you don't follow Allāh (ﷻ), you are in Hell—direct—if you do not make the real tawba and walk straight. After you die, how many years? Allāh (ﷻ) knows. But Allāh (ﷻ) changes everything in one moment when you give, and Allāh (ﷻ) will make it a garden for you if you are straight. This is in all of the holy books.

Music plays.

> ***My love, my spirit.***
> ***Mention the name of my love, my soul.***
> ***Mention the name of Allāh (ﷻ), of my Lover.***

The reading continues, ““When I mention the one I fell in love with, my Beloved One, I am happy, even if I see Him only in my dreams.”

If you want to see Him in your dreams, you will be happy if you see Him in your dreams. What would you think if you saw Him in your reality?

He is with you. Don’t lie. He can hear you. Don’t say, “Allāh (ﷻ) spoke to me.” Are you Sayyidinā Mūsā (عليه السلام)? He was a noble prophet and Allāh (ﷻ) spoke with Him. You think you can say, “Allāh (ﷻ) spoke with me,” no. Or, “I can see Him.” You should be absent from your humanity and you will be in a witnessing station, in the station of life.

Allāh (ﷻ) speaks to you through His holy books, al-Qurʾān, at-Tawrā (Torah) and al-Injīl (Gospel). This is the speech of Allāh (ﷻ). He is speaking to you through these books. He has sent them down through Jībrīl (عليه السلام). So when you read Qurʾān or you pray and you ask Allāh (ﷻ) to answer your supplications, Allāh (ﷻ) will say, “I will answer your supplications. Don’t worry about that.”

Sayyidinā Mūsā (عليه السلام) asked Allāh (ﷻ):

> “Oh my Lord, show me Yourself that I may look upon You.”
> Allāh told him, “You cannot see Me, but look at the mountain.” (7:143)

What is the meaning of the mountain? The mountain here is the heart. Look to your heart. The heart isn’t just a piece of meat, no. Allāh (ﷻ) says:

> My heavens and My earth cannot contain Me.
> Only the heart of My faithful, honest servant contains Me.

We should study the Qurʾān because this enables us to speak to Allāh (ﷻ). We should understand the holy books and their secrets. Then Allāh (ﷻ) will open the doors for us.

The reading continues, “It is my pleasure to hear My remembrance within My witnessing and within my love.”

Ask Allāh (ﷻ) for forgiveness; He is the Forgiver. Talk to Allāh (ﷻ). When you ask Him for forgiveness, when you praise Him, when you glorify Him, you are speaking with Him and He hears you and your supplications. There are no borders between you and Him and Allāh (ﷻ) says:

> And when My slaves ask you concerning Me,
> then (answer them), I am indeed near.
> I respond to prayers when they call upon Me. (2:186)

This is the truth.

The reading continues, "My hearing witnesses that I love You. The dream that comes to my eyes, to my ears, to my heart, all of them witness that I love You. My ears, my eyes, everything that God (ﷻ) gave me witness that I love You. They witness that I do not return back. Always, I keep my deep spirit with my Beloved who loves me, Allāh (ﷻ). Even if I am far away and do not see Him, He does not go far away. He never leaves me, not for one moment.

This is my chance. This is my chance to be with Him. This, my beloveds, is the real wedding. It is my pleasure to hear my remembrance within my witnessing, to hear and feel my remembrance within my love."

Music plays.

The reading continues, "Oh, I am so lucky that He took me in His arms, that Allāh (ﷻ) took me into His arms and that He supports me in obeying His orders and that He helps me to always be in His eternal world. This is my pleasure and this is my hope. This is my end and this is my goal, that He puts me in front of His eyes and takes care of me. Āmīn. It is my deep wish to see all of you who love Allāh (ﷻ), everyone, in this holy station. Āmīn.

I want to see the whole world dance with each other, to be real beloveds, to have a real wedding with Allāh (ﷻ). I want to see all of the beloveds who love Allāh (ﷻ) live in the ocean of His love. Āmīn. Āmīn. I want them all to reach and to hear the divine station, for Allāh (ﷻ) wants to position all of His creatures in this station. If they obey His orders (ﷻ) and the orders carried out by all the prophets (عليهم السلام), and if they carry the message of unity through the love that Allāh () gifted us, they will be clean. To be clean gives life to you and to everyone who is in this state, in this place and everywhere.

He loved us, so He gave us the gift of His sharīʿa, His rules, His orders. He taught us His prohibitions and what we should not do. It is Allāh's gift to us to clean us, to clean our hearts to know His love, because He loves you. He loves you and you love Him. If you follow His orders, you will be in His loving presence all the time. There is no life except within Him, and this is why it is important to follow Him, to obey Him, and to be between His hands as He wishes. Because He said:

> I will be with you everywhere and anywhere. (20:46 and Tafsir)

My beloveds, this is the truth. How do you want to walk to Allāh ()? This is the walking. I have explained it in all my books. This is what you need to know. If you speak from an ugly mind, you will not be able to reach Allāh (). You will forget Him and you will turn away from Him. You will leave His Garden and you will go into the material world, the rubbish world, the recycle bin."

I'd like to speak a word for two or three minutes. I'm very blessed by this center and the people who work here, Abdullah and his wife and all of his brothers and sisters.

I have corrected many of the things that were taught in the Sufi University. I have established the university's teachings in divine knowledge, not from myself. I'm not a creator of science and knowledge. I received this knowledge through the knowledge of the prophets, and some of this knowledge is from 800 years ago.

This healing knowledge is very deep knowledge. Some of this is from Sayyidinā Ibrāhīm () and some is from other prophets. When Allāh () created a plant He taught the prophets what disease it could cure. These six healing books are from old, old, old ancient books. Those books took 37 years from my life. I worked day and night to give humanity their benefit. They are from me and I'm from them, and they are from Allāh (), regardless of religion and race.

These books have been translated into English, Spanish and other languages. I accept these books with my tears, giving many herbs, for all of humanity. These herbs have been tested and you can find Sufism in those books, the path of Allāh (ﷻ), and how to behave in your hearts and souls.

I am lucky to be able to tell you that Allāh (ﷻ) sent us my daughter to teach you Arabic and Qur'ān in the University and the secrets of the letters. She was teaching at what was the greatest university in the world 900 years ago—Baghdad University. I'm asking Allāh (ﷻ) to help her to do her best and to give her heart and self as a sacrifice to our beloveds.

It is not acceptable for you to go to other universities to obtain knowledge instead of joining the University Spiritual Healing and Sufism. if you have a university full of divine fruits and you are thirsty, and then is it right for you go to other universities to get knowledge when the divine fruit is right in front of you? Divine knowledge is a fruit.

I encourage all of you to take the opportunity to study and attend the University of Spiritual Healing and Sufism. It will give you certifications. All of the teachers are scholars and they are qualified to teach. No one can teach anything there except what is from divine knowledge. This is not from my head. I wish for all of you to have access to this. It is important for me to say this to you, this is what He wants from me.

The reading continues, "Allāh (ﷻ) wants to give you sweets, but you do not want them. What are you trying to say? You claim that you are a slave, but you do not follow His orders. You do not follow the commands that He sent down to His prophets and messengers (ﷺ). So how, then, are you a slave?

Some people say they are lovers but they kill others. They are killers. They break hearts. Some people say they are lovers but they are thieves. What is that? Return back to Allāh (ﷻ)! The cure, the healing, is in Allāh (ﷻ). He provides us with everything. After that, how can anyone disobey Allāh (ﷻ) and follow the shayṭān, Iblīs? Allāh (ﷻ) says:

> (Escape to) Allāh, the true Guardian-Protector. (Tafsir of 2:257)

Allāh (ﷻ) is the supporter of those who are honest. Allāh (ﷻ) will forbid those who disobey Him from tasting the love. They will not be able to taste the love. Those who love Allāh (ﷻ), those who follow His divine law, will be under the tent of Allāh (ﷻ). They will be in the Garden with spreading branches where you can always find His provision.

> Say, 'If you love Allāh (ﷻ) then follow me.' (3:31)

Allāh (ﷻ) gives me this special gift, Allāh (ﷻ), the only truth, al-Ḥaqq, He gave me a message for those who have already heard the divine call, but disobeyed. I hope and I ask Allāh (ﷻ) to open their hearts, their spirits and their minds to be among those who receive His mercy and purification.

Music plays.

His message is the message of the Most Compassionate, the Most Merciful.

> *I remember His name.*
> *I enjoy remembering Him, even if all of you blame me.*
> *It doesn't matter, I love Him.*
> *Yes, I love Him.*
> *Ḥabībi, my love, my spirit.*
> *Mention my Lover, mention His name,*
> *Even in my dreams, mention His name.*

My love, my spirit, when you mention the name of Allāh (ﷻ) with sincerity in your heart, it is not just your tongue that says the name. Every part of you is saying the name. Your trillions of cells are saying the name of Allāh (ﷻ) when you say it with sincerity. My love, my spirit, by mentioning the One I love, I will have eternal life.

My beloveds, keep repeating, keep mentioning and keep remembering. Keep giving the water of life to your hearts and your spirits so that you can continue to be in Allāh's order, the divine order in which He commanded us to reside.

It is the holy order to carry Your message and to save all people from suffering around the world, and not only this world, but in all of Your worlds that You created and gave the real life. You asked and ordered them to carry the flag of happiness, pleasure and spirit, which will send love to their hearts, for You are our love. You are our Lord (ﷻ). Oh, my Lord (ﷻ).

I will not listen to people who say many different things, who try to distort the orders of Allāh (ﷻ) or make the orders of Allāh (ﷻ) confusing. They live in illusion, in pictures that they talk about with false tongues. This is not what Allāh (ﷻ) wants. He wants you to throw your self, your heart and your spirit between the arms of Allāh (ﷻ) under His religion of unity. He wants you to follow everything that He says and then you will be a pure one.

Do not choose another way, my children. Do not choose dark and false ways. Be in the ocean of your Beloved, under His command, under what He says for you to do because He cares about you. He wants you to be and to live in the way that He wants for you. You will be in His ocean, full of love.

This is the life for you, my daughters, my sons, my children. I will open my life and my spirit to every one of you who wants life. This life has already been given by Allāh (ﷻ). The provision comes from Allāh (ﷻ).

Many, many thanks Allāh (ﷻ), for You gave me the water of mercy. I ask You to accept my supplication and to give this holy water of mercy to others, to all my children, and to allow them to live a good life.

When you love Allāh (ﷻ), when you trust Allāh (ﷻ), when you remember Allāh (ﷻ), then in one moment you can be in His Garden. If you taste, you know what I mean. I am going to open the door for you. This is what Allāh (ﷻ) says:

> Come, come to My paradise!

He opens the door to be in the Garden now. So do not wait, my beloveds. Your Beloved is waiting for you. He wants to make a real wedding for you. This is the real life and there is no doubt.

This is the real life. There is no death, only life. This means to follow what He says. If you listen and follow what comes from the dirty water, how can you be in the real life? No one can do this. This is the real death. Drink the water of Allāh (ﷻ), my beloveds, the tawḥīd, the unity.

I hope that my words enter your hearts, spirits and white minds. Keep the relationship and the love between you and Allāh (ﷻ) all the time. I hope that you will find that you live in Allāh (ﷻ), with Allāh (ﷻ) and for Allāh (ﷻ), and that you direct yourselves toward Allāh (ﷻ).

I wish for happiness in this life for all the beloveds, for all those who are suffering and for all of the sick people in this world. I ask Allāh (ﷻ) to send His mercy and to fill this life full of mercy. I ask to see my beloveds as one nation and for them to turn back toward Him, as He says in His Holy Qur'ān:

> This, your (human) nation, is one nation,
> and I am your Lord so worship Me (alone). (21:92)

My beloveds, this is the time for a very special promise. I want to help you open your hearts to know the secrets of the love that I talk about. I want to make a special prayer for Allāh (ﷻ) to help all of my children know in their hearts the deep secret love that I talk about. If you want to open your hearts more and to know how to give the love the way Allāh (ﷻ) wants, this special promise will help open your heart."

I will give you a protection for your soul, for your family, for your heart. It will help you protect your soul from all of the jinn and shayaṭīn. And it will keep you, inshā'a-llāh (ﷻ), safe. This is very holy and it protects them in their lives and even after their deaths. If your parents have passed away it will even help them, too.

Sidi makes du'ā' and gives the protection paper and the promise.

The Light of Isa and Maryam (ؑ)

"True Spiritual Sustenance: The Table of ʿĪsā (ؑ)"

from *A Righteous Word is Like a Righteous Tree*

July 24, 2010 AM Austin

لا إله إلا الله – لا إله إلا الله – لا إله إلا الله – محمد رسول الله عليه صلاة الله
لا إله إلا الله – لا إله إلا الله – لا إله إلا الله – ابراهيم رسول الله عليه صلاة الله
لا إله إلا الله – لا إله إلا الله – لا إله إلا الله – موسى رسول الله عليه صلاة الله
لا إله إلا الله – لا إله إلا الله – لا إله إلا الله – عيسى رسول الله عليه صلاة الله
اللهم انت السلام ومنك السلام و إليك يعود السلام
تباركت ربنا وتعاليت يا ذوالجلال والإكرام

On this holy day, in this holy hour, on this holy night many spirits visited me, full of love, full of divine knowledge. They were complaining, crying because many people claim to be followers of the pure spirits, like Sayyidinā ʿĪsā (ؑ) (our Master Jesus Christ) and his holy mother Maryam (ؑ) (Mary), this noble one. They visited me and I am one of their children. I carry their spirits and their message and their stations.

I announce and admit in front of all those who claim they love ʿĪsā (ؑ) and his mother. I will tell you that our holy book, al-Qurʾān, mentioned them: Mūsā (Moses) (ؑ), Ibrāhīm (Abraham) (ؑ) and all the prophets. This holy, great lover, this noble one, Sayyidatunā (our Lady) Maryam, Allāh created her from the divine secret and Allāh (ﷻ) made her and her son great signs for all people. She is a gift to the earth.

The liars who say they are following ʿĪsā (ؑ) didn't understand the message of al-Masīḥ (the Messiah). Allāh (ﷻ) sent His spirit down as a human being (through Jībrīl ؑ) and she was a holy woman. This was the holy spirit that was sent down. Many, many times in my life, up until this moment, I have prostrated in front of the light of Maryam (ؑ) and ʿĪsā (ؑ). He is carrying the message of love, peace, mercy, justice and freedom. I'm carrying the same message.

I'm humble and I walk in front of their feet. When I see those who are glorifying Allāh (ﷻ), praising Allāh (ﷻ), loving Allāh (ﷻ) and loving Sayyidinā ʿĪsā (ؑ), and they start to lie and lie and lie and steal and kill and betray the message of Sayyidinā ʿĪsā (عليه السلام)...this is a sign. This is a very big lesson for all of us. There are a lot of liars, a lot of hypocrites. They are lying about Sayyidinā ʿĪsā (عليه السلام) and Sayyidatunā Maryam (عليها السلام). Because of that I would like to talk with you about the station of their walking to Allāh (ﷻ) and why Allāh (ﷻ) selected her as a noble jewel, a pure mother, an eternal one.

Maryam (عليها السلام) carried the spirit of Allāh (ﷻ). She was a pure, holy one and she carried a holy, holy spirit. The liars don't respect Allāh's signs and they are distant from the commands and orders of Sayyidinā ʿĪsā (عليه السلام). They kill a lot, they steal a lot, they cause corruption and they claim to be the children of Sayyidinā ʿĪsā (عليه السلام), the children of Sayyidatunā Maryam, the Virgin.

Allāh (ﷻ) sent down His spirit to her. This means that the divine spirit was sent down to her and she saw Jībrīl (عليه السلام) as a human being.

> And she who guarded her chastity (Maryam): We breathed into her and We made her and her son a sign for humankind and the jinn. (21:91)

You are pure and you are noble. You are not like other women. You are divine beauty and the divine beauty revealed Himself within you.

> And (remember) when the angels said: "Oh Maryam! Truly, Allāh has chosen you, purified you and chosen you above the women of the humankind and the jinn." (3:42)

So she carried Sayyidinā ʿĪsā (عليه السلام) and he was like Sayyidinā Adam (عليه السلام), neither of them had a father. ʿĪsā (عليه السلام) had a mother but Adam (عليه السلام) was from dust, from clay. He said:

> I (shaped him and) breathed into him of My spirit. (see 15:29 and 38:71)

Then:

> When Allāh said to the angels, "Prostrate to Ādam"
> and all the angels prostrated except Iblīs
> Allāh asked him, "Oh Iblīs, why did you not prostrate?"

> He said, "I am better than him. You created me from fire and you created him from clay." (38:72-38:76)

Allāh (ﷻ) was saying, "Don't prostrate to Adam but to My divine spirit manifesting within Adam (عليه السلام)." And Allāh (ﷻ) told Iblīs, "This was not the point. Prostrate or don't. I am the Lord, Allāh (ﷻ). I created you and you should follow My orders. So get out from Our divine presence. You are nothing."

You should follow Allāh's orders. Sayyidinā ʿĪsā (عليه السلام) is like Sayyidinā Adam (عليه السلام). Adam (عليه السلام), also, was from the spirit of Allāh (ﷻ).

We do not worship al-Masīḥ (the Messiah) and his mother. We respect and honor them; we love them because they are holy people. This holy, noble lady carried the holy prophet Sayyidinā ʿĪsā (عليه السلام) and his holy spirit is in the earth and the sky, everywhere. This is not just true for Sayyidinā ʿĪsā (عليه السلام)—the spirit of Allāh (ﷻ) is in all of His prophets (عليهم السلام). From this holy spirit Allāh (ﷻ) can remove disasters from you. This is not illusion and this is not imagination or a lie. It is the truth.

People are sleeping. They carry dead hearts, except those whose vision Allāh (ﷻ) has opened and those who use the name of Allāh (ﷻ) and became one of those who can see and understand. Open your hearts and your souls and your eyes to receive His message and to hear it through the holy book, al-Qurʾān al-Karīm (the Noble Qurʾān).

Your mother Maryam (عليها السلام) was a good lady, a pure one. She was pure. She came to her people pregnant and they told her, "What's that? How did you make a child?" She was carrying a baby in her womb and she was 16 years old. When the time came to give birth she went to the date palm tree. There was no water or food near there. She hung from the branch of the date palm. Maryam was very beautiful, the most beautiful woman on the earth, a pure virgin. She felt her birth pains and she heard a voice say, "Shake the date palm and it will give you fruit." In this way Allāh (ﷻ) sent Maryam fresh dates. This was a miracle.

We love Maryam (عليها السلام) and we honor her. Islām has honored and loved her. And we love Sayyidinā ʿĪsā (عليه السلام). He is the messenger of peace. He is still alive and he will come carrying the message of peace.

Those who claim they are under 'Īsā's tent, that they are his followers, in churches or anywhere...the Hour will come assuredly and Allāh (⌘) will let all of the people wake up by the...of Sayyidinā 'Īsā (⌘) and Sayyidinā Mahdī. They will both come, despite all of the criminals you see. They are the saviors and I am carrying their message, we are carrying their message, because we love those who are suffering, needy, sick and poor everywhere. Our hearts and our bodies, everything we have, we give to all of those poor and needy people. This is the message of Sayyidinā 'Īsā (⌘). There is no end to this message.

One of Allāh's names is as-Salām, the Peace. His names are al-Muhyamin, ar-Raḥmān, ar-Raḥīm. We are His children and we will carry the message. Yes, we come in different shapes, different faces and we are needy, but we are rich. We don't need anything from anyone! We don't want anything. We just want a pure heart. We will be happy when the poor and needy are happy and crying when they are crying.

Allāh (⌘) taught us through the prophets and messengers (⌘). We don't have any knowledge. knowledge is from Allāh (⌘), through all of the prophets and messengers. Allāh (⌘) sent down this knowledge. Allāh (⌘) says:

> Fear Allāh, (and guard yourselves against evil), if you have faith." (Qurʾān 5:112)

This is the beginning of the message. When Maryam (⌘) was carrying 'Īsā (⌘) they asked her how she became pregnant. They said, "Your father was a noble and honest person." Maryam (⌘) was a good and polite lady. They said, "This is sinful," and Maryam (⌘) said:

> Then she (Maryam) pointed to him ('Īsā).
>
> They said, "How can we talk to a child in the cradle?"
>
> He ('Īsā) said, "Truly! I am a slave of Allāh,
> He has given me the scripture and made me a prophet.
> And He has made me blessed wherever I am,
> and has enjoined on me prayer (ṣalāh), and zakāh (charity)
> for as long as I live,
> and (to be) dutiful to my mother,

and make me not arrogant, unblessed." (Qur'ān 19:29—19:32)

ʿĪsā (ﷺ) said, "He let me be a prophet and carry the message, the message of love, the message of unity, the message of peace, the message of justice." ʿĪsā (ﷺ) carried this message from his first breath.

All people, fear Allāh (ﷻ)! Fear Allāh (ﷻ) and prepare yourself for the Hour. When it comes everything will be overwhelmed and no one will be able to tolerate the fear.

ʿĪsā (ﷺ) is the slave of Allāh (ﷻ) and He let him be a prophet. He said, "I am to be good and righteous to my mother." ʿĪsā (ﷺ) didn't have a father, so Allāh (ﷻ) he told them to be good to his mother, to help her.

He said, "Allāh (ﷻ) made me a prophet. There is nothing like Allāh (ﷻ). He doesn't have a son, He doesn't have a wife, He doesn't have anyone." This is what all of the prophets say. This is what Allāh (ﷻ) says. We prostrate our heads and bodies before his words.

What did the people do for Sayyidinā ʿĪsā (ﷺ)? They tried to kill him. He suffered a lot but the word of Allāh (ﷻ) has been spread. His followers carried the message after him. Most of the people at that time were disobedient, so they followed Sayyidinā ʿĪsā (ﷺ) and believed inbthe word of Allāh (ﷻ) and they said, "We are your supporters. We are your soldiers. We will carry the message of love, peace and freedom. We will carry the message of tawḥīd (unity) on this earth." Then people tried to kill ʿĪsā (ﷺ). Allāh (ﷻ) says in the Qur'ān:

> And because of their saying, "We killed al-Masīḥ ʿĪsā, son of Maryam, the Messenger of Allāh (ﷻ),"
> But they did not kill him or crucify him, but it appeared so to them. (4:157)

They didn't kill him. Allāh (ﷻ) sent someone who looked like him, so they saw his picture. ʿĪsā (ﷺ) is still alive. Allāh (ﷻ) raised him up to heaven and he is still alive. No one can reach Sayyidinā ʿĪsā (ﷺ) to kill him. They are very weak. Allāh (ﷻ) protected ʿĪsā (ﷺ). Who can reach the spirit of Allāh (ﷻ)? This is the reality, the truth. You can find this story in Injīl Barnaba (the Gospel of Barnabus), a very old and true gospel; its truth hasn't been changed. Few people saw this gospel and the spirit of Sayyidinā ʿĪsā (🙼) in the earth and in the sky.

Twenty-one of ʿĪsā's followers carried his message. They suffered a lot and were in a lot of pain. They were beaten and were thrown in the fire, but they were strong and Allāh (🙼) protected them from others. They escaped to a cave that protected them from the corrupters and bad kings and leaders. Those followers tried to carry the message to let people live in a world full of happiness, not full of pain.

Allāh (🙼) created all people free. When your mother gave birth to you, she gave you this life in order for you to be free, not a slave, a follower of the shayṭān. The followers of Sayyidinā ʿĪsā (🙼) suffered a lot. Their path was very hard, full of fire, full of difficulty, but they carried the message. They gave themselves as a sacrifice for all people, all human beings. Each prophet was like this; this was their walking.

You ask me, "How can I walk? What is the walking? How can I understand and know Allāh (🙼)?" If you understand how Sayyidinā ʿĪsā (🙼), Sayyidinā Mūsā (🙼), Sayyidinā Ibrāhīm (🙼) suffered...even Sayyidinā ʿĪsā's dog refused to leave him.

Hadeel's feed is inaudible for several minutes.

I visited them (the sleepers in the cave). They entered the cave south of Jordan. Its name was Maʿtaba and its village name is ar-Raqīb (the Watcher). The name of their dog was Qatmīr. This is the story of al-Kahf (the cave).

Fifty-one years ago I went and visited them in Jordan and their dog. They stayed in this cave for 309 years. After 309 years they woke up. Allāh (🙼) sent them their lives back. One of them asked how many years they had slept. He thought maybe they had slept for one day. The angels told him they had been there for 309 years. This was a miracle.

Now the people have heard about Sayyidinā ʿĪsā (🙼), al-Masīḥ. We honor him and we honor his mother. We call this station al-ʿĪsawī. It's a station. If you want to reach and you want to walk further in this path, do as they did—they gave their lives as a sacrifice.

Sayyidinā ʿĪsā (ﷺ) and his followers lived for other people. He is beloved to all of us and his real followers were real believers, real worshippers. They did good deeds. We are the son of the truth and we carry the message of Sayyidinā ʿĪsā (ﷺ), Sayyidinā Mūsā (ﷺ), Sayyidinā Ibrāhīm (ﷺ) and all of the prophets (ﷺ). This is the way, this is the path, carrying the message of unity and freedom and peace without separation, without discrimination. They never belittle or hurt others and they always say the same words (ḥadīth):

> All creatures are the children of Allāh (ﷻ),
> and the most beloved to Him
> are the ones who are most beneficial to His children.

If you want to believe, believe. If you want to disbelieve in Allāh (ﷻ), this is your issue. We have Allāh (ﷻ) and His beloveds. This is the beginning. This is a sign.

The reading "True Spiritual Sustenance: The Table of ʿĪsā (ﷺ)" from *A Righteous Word is Like a Righteous Tree*[22] is read from the beginning,

My beloveds and my children, I have come to you from the Holy Land, from the holy city, which is the heart of the world. It is the main city in the world. Because I live in it, I am carrying its fragrance, I am carrying its spirit and I am carrying its reference to the whole world's need for peace, mercy, love and justice, without discrimination. We need these qualities without discriminating between gender, color or race.

I carry this message. It is the message of ʿĪsā (Jesus) (ﷺ), who carried the message of unity and offered everything for humanity. He offered everything so that people could be loving toward one another and live in peace and mercy for one another. This was also the message of all of the prophets, starting with Ibrāhīm (ﷺ), Mūsā (ﷺ) and the Prophet Muḥammad (ﷺ).

---

[22] Sidi Muhammad, *A Righteous Word is Like a Righteous Tree*. Pope Valley: Shadhiliyya Sufi Center, 2009, pp. 81-95.

This is a blessed day on which I come to you, carrying my heart and my spirit for you. I came on behalf of all of the prophets (ﷺ). I live for their message. I live to carry their message. I pray that a day will come when I will see all people singing the song of love, the song of life and the song of justice and mercy. This day has illuminated my spirit and heart and inspired me to send you a message that was sent by all of the prophets and messengers (ﷺ).

The lover ʿĪsā (ﷺ) sent this message. We need to pray as his disciples prayed with him for Allāh (ﷻ) to send signs from Heaven, to prove the message of unity to those who deny it. Those who denied the message in the past did not listen to ʿĪsā's voice (ﷺ), and many claimed to carry his message after him. But he has nothing to do with them, because in his name they kill children, destroy houses and destroy trees. Even the earth and nature are not safe from their cruelty. These people pollute the earth's resources, its water and its air. They work to destroy the world.

Allāh (ﷻ) sent us His message through the voices of all of the prophets and messengers (ﷺ). They prayed and asked Him to save the earth from the evil ones and to protect it, because Allāh (ﷻ) created the earth for all people. Allāh (ﷻ) created everything in the earth and in the heavens and what is between them to be filled with love, beauty, peace, freedom and justice for all people and all creatures. Allāh (ﷻ) says:

> I will be creating a human being out of mud.
> When I finish forming him and fashioning him
> and breathe into him out of My spirit (My own light)
> prostrate yourselves to him. (38:71)

Since that time, the message has been one. Look at al-Masīḥ ʿĪsā (ﷺ) (the Messiah Jesus). Look at how he lived and devoted himself to the message until he died. He brought the message of truth and justice to everyone. He carried the message of love, because no one can live without love. I am with you and all kind people like you holding the olive branch, which is a symbol of peace. Allāh (ﷻ) mentions it in the Qur'ān when He says:

> God is the light of the heavens and the earth.
> His light is like this:
> there is a niche and in it a lamp,
> the lamp inside a glass, a glass like a glittering star,

fueled from a blessed olive tree from neither east nor west. (24:35)

This verse describes the divine light that reaches all hearts and lights them with love, peace, mercy and justice.

The world was not created to be burned by those who invent weapons of mass destruction and destroy humans and animals alike with their weapons. The earth was not created for this. It was created to spread the message that the children of purity, the Sufis, are carrying after the prophets and messengers (s).

This message is like a firm tree, a blessed tree. Its roots are firmly established in the earth. Its branches reach up to the heavens, producing all kinds of fruits all of the time (14:24-25). Doves of peace rest on its branches, chanting the song of peace. The people who keep and preserve the purity in which they were created and carry the message of peace are there, too.

As beloveds of al-Masīḥ ʿĪsā (s), we want to live close to him, just as his disciples did in the past. They lived with him and listened to his message of al-Ḥaqq. After that, each of them carried the message of freedom, peace and justice. I pray that you will become a child of his and a lover of his, just as all of the disciples did before you. Listen to them in this story, when they asked him for a favor from Allāh (s). They said, according to the Qurʾān:

> (Remember) when the disciples said:
> 'Oh ʿĪsā (s), son of Maryam (s)!
> Can your Lord send down to us a table spread from Heaven?'
> ʿĪsā (s) said: 'Fear Allāh (s), (and guard yourselves against evil),
> if you have faith.' (5:112)"

This question is from the beloveds. They were full of love for Sayyidinā ʿĪsā (s). They carried his message. They were not hankering for food or bread as you understand it. They asked for a table full of divine meanings, love, unity, peace, justice, mercy. They were crying and asking Sayyidinā ʿĪsā (s) to send a table full of love and justice. Every day you eat and drink, you are full of food, but they were asking for different food from Sayyidinā ʿĪsā (s), our prophet.

He is the beloved of Allāh (ﷻ). Ask Allāh (ﷻ) to send down this table full of divine meanings and justice. Ask Him to be able to carry this table and to spread it throughout the world. The divine knowledge is on this table.

After they made this request ʿĪsā (ﷺ) asked the disciples, "Are you still in doubt?" They said, "No, we don't need food for our stomachs, we need spiritual food, divine knowledge, mercy of Allāh (ﷻ)."

> We wish to eat (of that spiritual sustenance)
> and satisfy our hearts (so that they can be at rest and content).
> (5:113)

Look to those holy students. Allāh (ﷻ) sent them with the message. The disciples were the followers of all the prophets: Mūsā (ﷺ), Ibrāhīm (ﷺ) and ʿĪsā (ﷺ). They didn't just follow one prophet.

Don't think that the table was full of bread and meat and chicken. The prophets carried the spiritual, divine food and asked Allāh (ﷻ) for His blessings. ʿĪsā (ﷺ) asked them, "You do not believe that I'm your prophet?" They said, "Yes, we believe you're our prophet and we believe in you and that you will return to us."

This is the message of the divine spirit. They did not carry money, they carried divine beauty. They carried divine wisdom.

The reading continues, "They were faithful disciples. They felt they needed sustenance from Heaven, and Allāh (ﷻ) inspired them to ask for it. Through ʿĪsā's heart (ﷺ), they felt the future suffering of the earth and they felt they needed spiritual sustenance. They did not ask for a table full of physical food and drink; they felt they needed spiritual sustenance directly from Allāh (ﷻ) —sustenance that was made of divine light."

You can go to a restaurant and get any food you want, but you cannot find spiritual food on the menu of a restaurant. This is free food, no money is needed. You cannot pay Sayyidinā ʿĪsā (ﷺ) for the food at his table. You need this spiritual food. It is life, love.

The reading continues, "Thus the disciples said to ʿĪsā (ؑ), 'Oh Spirit of Allāh,[23] ask Allāh (ﷻ) on our behalf, for He is the One who created you without a father and put you in the womb of your mother. Your mother Maryam (ؑ) was an innocent and chaste woman.'

Maryam (ؑ) was pure and clean and she devoted herself to prayer. Then, the Angel Jībrīl (Gabriel) (ؑ) appeared to her in human form. He told her that Allāh (ﷻ) would give her a pure and intelligent son, innocent and free of all human blemishes. He came directly from the spirit of Allāh (ﷻ), from His light. But this does not mean that he was a son of Allāh (ﷻ) and that she was Allāh's wife, like in human terms. No, because Allāh (ﷻ) says in the Qur'ān:

> Say: He is Allāh, the One and Only.
> He does not beget (children), nor is He begotten. (112:1, 112:3)

Allāh (ﷻ) is not like a human being. He is beyond human beings. He is transcendent. Allāh (ﷻ) is the Most Powerful. He made the Angel Jībrīl (ؑ) appear in human form as an image to Maryam (ؑ), because Allāh (ﷻ) can create anything from nothing.

Allāh (ﷻ) is transcendent. He is beyond a creature made of mud. He is free of all physical attributes. The divine light is unlimited. It cannot be limited by shape, form or gender. It is limitless. It is transcendent and beyond everything.

Allāh (ﷻ) sent ʿĪsā al-Masīḥ (ؑ), son of Maryam (ؑ), to be a noble man, a great man, a generous man, a pure man. Allāh (ﷻ) taught him of that which he had no knowledge. It was Allāh's decree (ﷻ) to send him into the world without a father. Maryam (ؑ) only carried him like sparks. Allāh (ﷻ) says in the Qur'ān:

> The example of the creation of ʿĪsā
> is like the example of the creation of Ādam. (3:59)

Ādam (ؑ) had no father and no mother, either. Allāh (ﷻ) says:

> I will be creating a human being out of mud.
> When I finish forming him and fashioning him
> and breathe into him out of My spirit

---

[23] Allāh refers to ʿĪsā as Rūḥi-llāh, which is translated at "the Spirit of Allāh."

> (you angels) prostrate yourselves to him. (38:71)

All of the angels saw a human being. I will not say, 'a man.' I say, 'a human being.' They saw a person—genderless, formless. Allāh (ﷻ) wanted him to be in that form. Then Allāh (ﷻ) said to the angels (عليهم السلام):

> Prostrate yourselves to him. (38:71)

ʿĪsā (عليه السلام) was created in the same way Ādam (عليه السلام) was created. The first words ʿĪsā (عليه السلام) uttered were, 'There is no God but One. Glory to You. You created me and I am Your worshipful slave. There is no benefit or harm that comes from myself. I am between Your hands. I listen and I obey, and for You I listen and I submit.' This is the example of ʿĪsā (عليه السلام).

After Maryam (عليها السلام) gave birth to him, she came home carrying the little infant to her people. That glorious holy one, who is a spirit from Allāh (ﷻ), came carrying him. The people said, 'How did you bring this child to life?' All of the rabbis and people gathered and said, 'What did you do?'

> Then she (Maryam) pointed to him (ʿĪsā).
>
> They said, "How can we talk to a child in the cradle?"

He speaks more than they do.

The reading continues:

> "He (ʿĪsā) said, 'Truly! I am a slave of Allāh,
> He has given me the scripture and made me a prophet.
> And He has made me blessed wherever I am,
> and has enjoined on me prayer (ṣalāh), and zakāh (charity)
> for as long as I live,
> and (to be) dutiful to my mother,
> and make me not arrogant, unblessed.' (Qur'ān 19:29—19:32)

He did not say, 'and dutiful to my father,' He said, 'and dutiful to my mother.' He also said, 'Allāh (ﷻ) made me a prophet. He created me and I am a worshipful slave and servant to Him.' He did not say, 'I am a king,' and he did not say, 'I am a boss.'

ʿĪsā (ﷺ) said, 'I am a slave, a servant, a worshipper of Allāh (ﷻ). He created me as a blessed worshipper. Wherever I am, I will be blessed. My spirit arrived here in this world by the command of my Creator and my Lord (ﷻ) who created me out of mud and made me a complete human being. He did not create me in the way that some may claim.'

The noble prophet is not as many people think of him. He was a spiritual and godly messenger. Allāh (ﷻ) brought him to earth so that he could blow life into the earth and he could distribute love, peace, mercy, justice, freedom and complete perfection, for Allāh (ﷻ) created him in the perfect form."

He is the perfect one. There is a deep meaning in these words, to be a poor slave only for Allāh (ﷻ). Yes.

The reading continues, "As Allāh (ﷻ) says in the Qur'ān:

> He created you and fashioned you in the best mold. (95:4)

Allāh (ﷻ) is speaking about the divine human being who blew life into the world. This world was screaming in pain, suffering and struggling, and that is why messengers were sent to it, just as ʿĪsā (ﷺ) was sent.

ʿĪsā (ﷺ) invited people to come to Allāh (ﷻ). He said to people, 'I am a worshipful slave and servant of Allāh (ﷻ). I am a noble messenger and He asked me to be good to my mother.' Because he did not have a father, Allāh (ﷻ) asked him to be benevolent to his mother. Allāh (ﷻ) says:

> He is a spirit from My command. (17:85)

He did not say, 'He is God.' He said, 'He is a spirit from Allāh (ﷻ),' just as He said of the other prophets and messengers (ﷺ).

We believe that Allāh (ﷻ) is absolutely One and that the entire world is declaring, 'There is no god but the One, and He has no partner. All dominions are His. All life belongs to Him.'

Allāh (ﷻ) never dies. Allāh (ﷻ) cannot die. Allāh (ﷻ) is beyond everything. He is transcendent. He is always alive. He is the Creator; He creates. He is not created; He creates. He originates things from nothing. We all have one father and one mother, and so we are inside Allāh's system (ﷻ) of creation. We all came from a mother and a father.

This is the belief of the people of unity. It is also the belief of those who realize the truth and believe in the truth, who respect humanity and who care for humanity. It is the creed of those who care for the lives of people and spread love, mercy, compassion, justice and freedom to all. Life cannot continue without true, pure love, true peace, true mercy and true justice for all, regardless of color or ethnicity. This is our belief; it is the belief of the people of the Sufi way, the way of purity.

We respect all people and we treat them equally. We love them all, regardless of their states and regardless of what they look like. In a ḥadīth the Prophet (ﷺ) said:

> He said, 'Be.'

Allāh (ﷻ) said, 'Be,' and the human being became. This is why we respect all of humanity. We had a beginning, but Allāh (ﷻ) has no beginning. He has always been and He will always be. We are His servants and we serve all people and care for them. We are no different from them.

Allāh (ﷻ) said to those who walk arrogantly on earth, 'Look, you have been created out of the earth, you will return to the earth. You will be resurrected from the earth again. You will keep traveling from one realm to another.' Life will continue, but we need life to be continued with peace, ease and truth.

Listen to the Divine narration, for I am only a vessel who conveys the message, the message that came on the tongues of Ibrāhīm (ﷺ), Mūsā (ﷺ), ʿĪsā (ﷺ) and Muḥammad (ﷺ). Allāh (ﷻ) says in the Qurʾān:

> We make no distinction between any of His messengers.
> (2:285. Also see 4:150 and 4:152)

We say, 'We listen and we obey,' to the message that came from their lips. When corruption had spread far and wide over the earth, and some people had begun to act like beasts and monsters, violating the rights of others, destroying the earth, killing, murdering and hurting

others, Allāh (ﷻ) inspired ʿĪsā's disciples (رضي الله عنهم) to ask Him to send the nourishing table humanity needed."

This holy table carries many divine meanings. The secrets of this life and the secrets of the soul and the body and the secrets in this spiritual food, the real food...how does this food support your soul to live in peace, love and justice? Through this table, ʿĪsā (عليه السلام) taught them how to give themselves, their souls, as a sacrifice and to keep those principle, spiritual foods within them. He taught them how to use those qualities to help the poor, needy and sick people. This is from al-Qurʾān al-Karīm (the Noble Qurʾān).

We are the children of Allāh (ﷻ). We are following Him. All of the prophets...Sayyidinā Ibrāhīm (عليه السلام) gave his son as a sacrifice. There's no discrimination, no separation. All of the prophets had to pay a sacrifice. I'm trying to help you to understand the meaning of giving a sacrifice. I want to tell you that this sacrifice will protect you because through it you are supporting the needy and poor people. This is the way of way of safety and peace. This is the real meaning.

Allāh (ﷻ) says:

> Who is he that will lend Allāh (ﷻ) a goodly loan
> so that He may multiply it for him many times?
> (2:245 and see 57:11, 5:2, 57:18, 64:17, 73:20)

Amin.

The reading continued, "What they asked for was a mercy for the people, because the disciples felt the suffering on earth. They asked ʿĪsā (عليه السلام) because ʿĪsā (عليه السلام) is the Spirit of Allāh (ﷻ) and His messenger.

Listen to their words as they spoke to him. They said in a clear tongue, 'Oh ʿĪsā (عليه السلام) son of Maryam (عليها السلام).' They did not even address him as 'Messenger.' They related him to his mother. This is how they addressed him, because he had no father.

Allāh (ﷻ) is transcendent, far beyond comparison to any physical form. They asked him, 'Can your Lord bring a table full of peace, mercy, complete justice, complete freedom, complete beauty and complete perfection? Can He bring a nourishing table available to all people, so

that they can offer their sacrifices on it in order that humanity might survive?'

They asked for an table spread that gathered all good things together. However, it was not a table of material food and drink, as people might think. They were asking for spiritual sustenance. ʿĪsā (ﷺ) answered them:

> Be conscious of Allāh (ﷻ) and guard yourselves,
> if you have faith. (see 5:112)

He asked them, 'Don't you believe that Allāh (ﷻ) is the Creator, the Originator, the Doer and the Capable? He is the One who created you, your ancestors, all of the worlds and the unknown invisible realms.' Allāh (ﷻ) says that He created one thousand worlds resembling ours. The disciples answered ʿĪsā (ﷺ), saying:

> We wish to eat (of that spiritual sustenance)
> and satisfy our hearts (so that they can be at rest and content).
> (5:113)
> And know that you have indeed told us the truth
> (through the certainty of tasting)
> and (so) that we ourselves (can) be its witnesses. (5:113)

The disciples answered ʿĪsā (ﷺ), 'We would like you to ask for this table of sustenance so that we can taste and hear and see. We want to hear this table chant its praises of Allāh (ﷻ).'

For the messengers are the lovers of Allāh (ﷻ) and their tables are full of glorification and praise. The disciples said, 'We will be your witnesses and only then will we know for certain that you are the messenger of Allāh (ﷻ). We will taste.'"

Enough for this taste. This is my message to all of you, to all those who have hearts. I carried this message before I came to this world. I carried this message through all of the prophets and messengers and it's in all of the holy books. I'm trying to give you this message...part of this message, because I give just a little bit from this divine knowledge. This is my duty and I'm a poor slave.

I want you to drink from the same spring of peace, mercy, love, justice and freedom and to drink from the prophets and messengers (ﷺ). For this reason I come here from my country, the House of Allāh (ﷻ), al-Quds, to fulfill this duty, this responsibility. I have lived in Jerusalem for 46 years and I have been carrying this message for a long, long, long time. I am still strong. I am like a bee and it is my honor to serve your shoes, because you love Allāh (ﷻ) and the Messenger of Allāh (ﷺ).

All of us should pay our sacrifice like Sayyidinā ʿĪsā (ؑ), Sayyidinā Mūsā (ؑ), Sayyidinā Muḥammad (ﷺ) and Sayyidinā Ibrāhīm (ؑ) to help those who are crying and suffering, who are needy, poor and sick, who have lost their homes, who are unable to obtain their medicine. If you help them you are following Allāh's orders and helping and supporting the needy. This is the order of Allāh (ﷻ).

If you can, pay a sacrifice. The door is open to protect yourselves, your houses, your families. Allāh (ﷻ) will protect you from disasters and volcanoes, and I'm encouraging you all of the time to make a sacrifice because it will help you a lot. Allāh (ﷻ) is the Generous.

As-salāmu ʿalaykum. Peace be upon you. Āmīn.

How to Care for Your Body

Remedies for Physical Healing and "The Rituals of Worship Commanded by Allāh are for Spiritual and Physical Healing" from *The Migration of the Truthful Traveler*

Saturday, October 9, 2010 AM, USHS Year 4

لا إله إلا الله - لا إله إلا الله - لا إله إلا الله - محمد رسول الله عليه صلاة الله
لا إله إلا الله - لا إله إلا الله - لا إله إلا الله - ابراهيم رسول الله عليه صلاة الله
لا إله إلا الله - لا إله إلا الله - لا إله إلا الله - موسى رسول الله عليه صلاة الله
لا إله إلا الله - لا إله إلا الله - لا إله إلا الله - عيسى رسول الله عليه صلاة الله
اللهم انت السلام ومنك السلام و إليك يعود السلام
تباركت ربنا وتعاليت يا ذوالجلال والإكرام

Peace be upon you, my beloveds. Peace be upon all of you. You are blessed worshippers. You are carrying the message of mercy and justice and love. I am here among all of you to serve you.

You gave your promise to be the children of our beloved Allāh (ﷻ) and to carry the real message; the same message all the prophets and messengers (ﷺ) have carried before. Your existence in this Sufi university means that you are carrying the message, and this university teaches you the orders of Allāh (ﷻ). It is my honor to serve this Sufi university, to serve all the students, and to serve the teachers.

I send my voice to all people, everywhere; not only in America, but to all people around the world. The way to save yourselves, the way to bring the love, is to follow the orders and the commands of Allāh (ﷻ) through our Sufi university, which follows the orders of Allāh (ﷻ). These orders and commands have been sent to all the prophets (ﷺ)—they are not from me—and we are slaves and students of Allāh's orders.

Following Allāh's orders, it looks like we are children and we sit next to His table. I urge you to follow His orders. Don't say "I see Allāh (ﷻ)," or, "Allāh (ﷻ) tells me something." Don't say such things. Receive Allāh's orders through the orders of the prophets (ﷺ). This is a holy university and it will provide you with Allāh's real orders and commands.

I will give you a gift this holy morning: how to heal yourself and others.

Sidi produces a document.

I will explain how you can use this letter. I'll translate it into English for you and you will receive two copies: one in Arabic and one in English, to let you know how to heal and depend totally upon Allāh (ﷻ).

I would like to give you some treatments for certain diseases. You cannot find these treatments in my book. They are true treatments and many people have been healed through them, both children and the elderly. Prepare yourselves and write what I explain to you. I will give you the chance to write what is in my heart. Don't lose your chance. Prepare yourself and write what I will give and explain to you.

First of all, I send my prayers to all the prophets and messengers (ﷺ), asking Allāh (ﷻ) to give me the strength—and to give you the strength—to help people and to heal the people who need it.

The first thing I want to explain is the sexual relationship; how to strengthen this intercourse so you will not need to take chemicals like Viagra. This is very dangerous. Viagra can kill you because it can affect the heart and cause sudden death.

First of all, use black seed. If you need to strengthen your sexual life, your general vitality, your body, your blood, and if you want to be healthy, then use the black seed that the Prophet Ibrāhīm (Abraham) (ﷺ) and the Prophet Muḥammad (ﷺ) urged you to use. Follow this treatment. The Prophet Muḥammad (ﷺ) ﷺ says that black seed is food for everybody and it treats every disease. It is especially helpful for those who want to have a baby. This treatment can stop viruses and diseases in your body.

Treatment to Purify the Blood: Black Seed

1. Crush a big tablespoon of black seed—it is better to take two—and mix it with 1 tablespoon of honey.

2. Mix them together and eat the mixture before you eat breakfast.

3. Take those two tablespoons of black seed and honey every day and you will purify your blood and get rid of any bad, black blood.

4. At the same time, you should do cupping. Why? Because cupping will remove black blood and clots in your blood, both of which weaken your blood. If you keep bad blood in your body, you will expose your body to other diseases. This is the first thing; this is the first treatment.

Treatment for Mouth, Tongue and Lip Inflammation: Egg Whites

If you have inflammation in your mouth, in your tongue and in your lips, then you can use this formula for children and the elderly.

1. Take 5 egg whites per day for 3 days, using a spoon.

2. Try to put one spoon inside the mouth of the patient for three days.

3. If his voice is not clear or he has problems speaking, you can use this. Physicians do not know the real medicine for this problem.

You can also heal a baby with this treatment. This condition will cause heat and for the baby who cannot eat or drink, there is no treatment except this treatment. They say, "this is virus" and I'm telling them no, how can a baby wait for few days without water and food? He will die. It will cause many problems in his body and his stomach to wait like that.

I have used this many times. After one day of this treatment, the baby will be feeling better and will start to drink water. After three to four days, the baby will be perfect and there will no longer be a virus.

This is a tested treatment; I have used it many times. I used it for my grandson when he could not eat or drink. After four days he started to walk. This is from the Prophet Ibrāhīm (ﷺ), who was the first one to use it and other prophets and gnostics. This is the second one.

Treatment for Poor Memory: Olive Oil

Many people have a hard time remembering things and they don't know why. Some of them are old, and they say "He is old, he can't remember." I'm telling you, no. I am 77 years old and I use this treatment. The one who forgets things used to eat unhealthy food; unhealthy, non-organic chicken, non-organic fruits, polluted with chemicals.

In the center of the intellect there are important arteries. These arteries heat the different organs. This problem does not just affect old people; even young people can feel they are forgetful if they eat this kind of food. It causes imbalance. What is the healing for that?

Allāh (ﷻ) says:

> God is the Light of the heavens and the earth.
> His Light is like this: there is a niche and in it a lamp,
> the lamp inside a glass, a glass like a glittering star,
> fueled from a blessed olive tree from neither east nor west,
> whose oil almost gives light even when no fire touches it (24:35)

This oil heals your arteries in order to heal your intellect. It is what you need for your body when you need oxygen. If there is a shortage of oxygen, first it will affect the arteries in your brain. Then it will affect the arteries in your heart.

Olive oil is the treatment, I am sure. Science proves that and we discovered it before the scientists, through the Qur'ān. Olive oil is from a holy tree, the olive tree.

I told Rifka when she had problems to drink olive oil. You need oxygen. She couldn't move, she couldn't walk, and she used it as I prescribed it to all of the other beloveds. You can see her: she's smiling and laughing. This is divine medicine.

- Every day drink two tablespoons of olive oil.

You can add this oil into your salads. Don't put any chemicals in your salads. This is healing for you. If you have enough oxygen you will never, ever forget. And you will heal the arteries in your brain and purify your blood. You will be young forever. If you want, when you are 70 or 77 or 100 years old you will still be young. Many of our gnostics, our shuyukh, ordered us to drink it in the early morning, and this keeps us satisfied even if we don't want to eat.

This is the healing I wanted to let you know about. If someone comes to you and tells you, "My body is weak, fatigued, tired" it is because he needs oxygen. The arteries in his brain are very weak; they cannot work correctly and that will cause problems in the heart. The heart will be weak, so maybe he will get a blood clot and die. This healing is for many things. This is from the Qur᾿ān. This is the holy tree, the light, as Allāh (ﷻ) says in His Qur᾿ān.

Oxygen shortage can cause many different diseases: depression, frustration, fatigue. This is a treatment for many diseases and this oil will kill viruses, the worst ones, and will provide you with strength.

Sayyidinā (our Master) Muḥammad (ﷺ) says eat olive oil. Eat it, put it on your skin like a cream when you take a warm bath. You can use it when giving a massage. Why? Because your skin needs the oxygen and needs the olive oil. It will penetrate and enter into your body and keep your organs healthy. So by using it in a massage you will clean them.

Treatment for Cancer and Its Prevention: Garlic and Onion Oil

The fourth thing I want to tell you about is garlic oil and onion oil. This is very important to fight and prevent cancer. It stops cancer cells. This garlic oil and onion oil can prevent cancer and kill existing cancer cells. Yes, this oil is very strong, but it is healing treatment and it has 100 percent complete results. The natural chemicals in garlic oil will kill those cells, especially if you recognize that you have cancer in an early stage. You should use it twice a day, morning and evening. This is a great thing.

- Before breakfast, take 1 tablespoon of garlic oil and 1 tablespoon of onion oil.

You can also add them to your food and to your salads. Don't add spices. That will affect your intestines and stomach very much. Don't add salt. You can use rocky salt.[24] You can add rocky salt to food because it is natural from the earth. This is Allāh (ﷻ), He created it. We did not create it. It is natural, healthy.

Treatment for Skin Disorders: Rocky Salt

Use rocky salt in a bath to get rid of many problems in your skin. If you have problems with your skin, this will clean it. Don't add any shampoo or chemical things to this salt.

- Add rocky salt to a bath and stay in the water for 30 minutes.

Don't add any shampoo or creams or chemicals. You can use only olive soap. Don't try to use any other soap with chemicals, because that will stop the healing. That will cause disease to your skin, and even if you have many problems inside your skin you will stop them and get rid of all the problems. This is what I would like to tell you.

Treatment for Hair Loss: Onion Oil

These are essential things. These are very important things. Many people have problems when they lose their hair. The healing for that: onion oil.

1. Put onion oil on the root of your hair and massage it in.

2. Sit under the sun for 30 minutes in the early morning, around 7 o'clock.

3. After 30 minutes take a bath and wash your head with olive soap.

That's all. So if you lose your hair, that's what you need to do.

[24] We're not sure if this refers to kosher salt or a type of large grain sea salt.

- f you have already lost your hair and there is no hair, you can use garlic oil, the same way. Use it for one week and you will see the result.

In one week, you will see your hair begin to grow. This is magic medicine! This is also not from me, but from the holy people who have used it and I recommend it to many people. This is very holy gift for everybody to know.

Treatment for Impotence and Infertility: Luqmān Pill
I make this pill with my own hands and I give it for the people, because it is completely natural. It is not like Viagra or something. Viagra is very dangerous.

Physicians have figured out that Viagra is very dangerous. Many people have passed away because of Viagra, even young people. This is not medicine, because of chemicals. This Luqmān medicine is natural.

If you use it to improve sexual ability, use it in this way:

1. First of all, take one pill.

2. After three minutes, drink hot tea or mint, or something hot to let it melt. This is before the wife and the husband get together.

3. After you finish the love you can drink a glass of cold water. I'm sure about that.

We have given this medicine to many people and they have had wonderful results and had many babies. This is a very important issue, the relationship between the wife and her husband; it is very important to have a good relationship. This is a jalāl thing and we should try to help them. We are trying to help our beloveds using the knowledge I got through my shaykh, the gnostics and all the messengers.

But be careful about using these healings. I urge you to read my books. You will find different kinds of healing, different kinds of treatments. My beloved teachers and university read and teach. They come to me with questions and for explanations, so you will never ever obtain this knowledge from any other university.

Treatment for Weight Loss: Good Eating Habits and Clean Water

The 7th treatment is for fat. Many people are suffering and are asking to lose weight. This happens because they have been eating unhealthy food.

Our Prophet (ﷺ) says:

> The worst vessel to fill is one's stomach.
>
> We are people who will not eat until we are hungry.
> When we eat, we do not fill ourselves to the brim.
> We fill one-third of our stomach with food,
> we fill the second third with water
> and we leave the third part for air.

This is healing for the stomach.

The stomach is a divine tool that works all the time. If you fill this pot, how can you digest everything? This tool needs space to work.

Seventy percent of your body is water and it will provide you with all that you need. Especially pure water, clean water.

How can you drink clean water? Many viruses and germs are inside water, but you cannot see them. How can you obtain clean water? How can you purify this water? Boil your water. You might not like, but I am telling you the truth.

Yes, this is the truth, because you don't know what is in your water. You can find in water many types of bacteria and many unbelievable germs, so I'm telling you, boil it for minutes, only long enough to kill everything.

(An audience member asks if water that has been processed through reverse osmosis, or is otherwise purified or supposed to be pure, is OK.)

If you are sure, yes. If you know the source of water with a special name, you can drink it. It is important to see for yourself the source of the water and what it looks like. This is very important; water carries many, many things. If it is clean, you can use it. Allāh (ﷻ) knows. Be sure to know which company you are getting your water from.

I know what I am drinking because I see the water go from the lakes, through pipes, to my home. So try, my love. If it is clean, Bismi-llāh, but if it is not clean, it is very important to know this.

These things I give in order to protect your health, to protect your families and to protect the health of your beloveds. I urge you to read my books and to ask the teachers about the healing. Allāh (ﷻ) says:

> Say, "Are those who know equal to those who don't know?" (39:9)

Ask the knowledgeable people and ask the teachers. All the teachers in the University will help you. The door of Allāh (ﷻ) is open, and I'm ready to answer all of your questions by using the divine knowledge I received from all the prophets (ﷺ) and the gnostics. I will try not to waste your time, I will try to help you and to answer your questions. I am here to serve you, the students and the teachers.

I encourage all people to join this university. It is the source of the real life, the source of healing for the people, the source to let you walk in this path and reach the stations in order to be close to Allāh (ﷻ). It will teach you many different ways to walk to Allāh (ﷻ).

I encourage you to learn Arabic and Qur'ān to understand its meaning, and I recommend that Dr. Wadude establish a department to teach Qur'ānic Arabic. He can prepare a room, for example, just for Arabic and the Qur'ān like other universities. Many universities now teach Arabic, because they figured out that there are secrets in the Qur'ān. This is the divine knowledge, this is not our knowledge. In order to give wisdom to the people who ask for wisdom, most universities in America and Europe have a special department for Arabic and the Qur'ān. They even have this in Hebrew Universities.

I suggest that my son Wadude open a special department for Arabic and Qur'ān. It is not enough to have just one class each month. In order to learn the language you need to practice it, and after three months if there is a real department, you can learn Arabic and Qur'ān.

Audience question: Many of these medicines have to be taken on an empty stomach in the morning. What do you recommend if you want to do two or three of the remedies at the same time?

If there are, for example, three diseases and you want to heal them, I may tell you to start one healing treatment for a certain number of days and then to follow this with another remedy. Sometimes you can mix them. Do as I advise. My love, it is very important to follow what I say.

As Sayyidinā Muḥammad (ﷺ) says, I mentioned before, "The worst thing to fill is your stomach." Be careful. Don't eat processed foods or foods with many chemicals in them. Eat organic food. This is the cause of all diseases. Why? There are different kinds of chemicals and many are present in high levels.

I do not go to the store for different brands of an herb. I like to take it directly from the plant—nature! Every natural brand, Allāh (ﷻ), created. Allāh (ﷻ) knows the person who makes food without nature and what he needs. Allāh (ﷻ) created your body. You need the right food for your body. You understand? Many companies like to engineer plants or create things synthetically, but Allāh (ﷻ) knows more than them! From where did He create you? From the earth! Yes or no?

Allāh grows everything from the earth without chemicals. Your father, your grandfather—did they know chemicals? No. And do you see how long they lived, maybe 100 years, maybe 113 years, or more. My grandfather lived for 113 years. He did not eat anything if he did not plant it. His last words to me were, "My son, do not try to eat anything if you did not grow it from the earth, without anything else (fertilizers, additives, chemicals, etc.). Leave it for Allāh (ﷻ). Allāh (ﷻ) sends the rain.

Allāh (ﷻ) sends rain down to the earth, full of many medicines, through the water. Sidi's grandfather was one of the gnostics. He never ate meat except the meat he obtained from his sheep. Allāh (ﷻ) created all of the fruits. This is very important. The capacity of your stomach is limited, one pound is enough, and you want to add some water or something.

When you sleep, sleep on your right side. It helps the stomach to work properly. Also, it is not right to eat only 30 minutes before you sleep. This is a bad thing.

Treatment for Weight Loss: Apple Cider Vinegar

If a person is very fat, here is something very major and very important. Take apple cider vinegar, the real one, the pure one from the apple, not the one you get from the supermarket.

- Before you eat anything, take 2 Tbsp. apple cider vinegar mixed with 3 Tbsp. water.

This vinegar destroys food that is not right if there is a lot of fat in your body. Try this experiment. Take some fat and put it in a dish. Add some vinegar to the fat. After 30 minutes the fat will be melted. It will be gone. The apple cider vinegar takes all the fat from food and makes it like water. Then, when you go to the bathroom, you will lose it. (Sidi smacks his hands to indicate "instantly, totally.")

Drink this before you eat food, every time. You will see, all the fat will go. After two to three weeks, depending on your body, you will lose 20 pounds. This is the medicine. The vinegar should be natural, from the apple. Yes, my love.

Question: Is it OK to do this when you're nursing a baby?

Sidi: A baby, my love, how old is he?

Questioner: Two years old. I'm weaning him now.

Sidi: Yes, you can do this. In the Qur᾿ān it says you have to feed him from your breast for two years. It's OK to wean him now.

This is a very important thing to all of you. For every lady who has children, be careful. Only give your child milk from your body, not from a cow or a goat. Allāh (ﷻ) created this thing here to give the child the food from her, not from a cow, not from a goat. This is very important. If the lady does not like to give something from herself because the man likes to see her body looking beautiful, then something is wrong.

These are divine orders. Allāh (ﷻ) sent this milk for the baby. You are his mother, not the cow or the sheep. Allāh (ﷻ) created us and He knows what is wise. He knows what to teach us. Your grandmother gave her food to her children, not from the cow or from anything else, only from her. Allāh (ﷻ) is the Wise.

You can feed him for two years from your body. If you feed him from cows and sheep it will be harmful milk. This is how the prophets (ﷺ), all of them, lived.

The mother of Sayyidinā Mūsā (Moses) (ﷺ) put him in a box and put him in the river. You know the story. Pharaoh's wife, Asiya, found him and said, "I'd like to feed him from my body," but she could not give him milk. She found another woman to feed him.

This was a miracle. She was searching for someone to feed him, and the people told her about a lady who could feed him. They brought his mother to feed him. Children inherit the qualities of the mother from the breast milk they receive.

These are the things I would like to give to you. Worship, prayer and how to purify ourselves through the ṣalāh, through the divine practices.

Allāh (ﷻ) ordered us to establish ṣalāh, and we should do as He ordered. This will help you to walk to Allāh (ﷻ). Your body needs spiritual food. Your self, your heart, your spirit, needs this spiritual food.

Following His orders, establishing the prayer as a regular practice, is an exercise. It is full of sharīʿa and ḥaqīqa, divine law and divine reality, and it will help you. I am asking my wife to read you the spiritual ritual of worship. She knows the secret of what I write. Open your eyes, open your hearts, open your soul and open everything. Give your senses a chance to drink from what I write.

"The Rituals of Worship Commanded by Allāh are for Spiritual and Physical Healing" from *The Migration of the Truthful Traveler*[25] is read.

"Bismi-llāhi-r-raḥmāni-r-raḥīm. The rituals of worship commanded by Allāh (ﷻ) for spiritual and physical healing. Oh seeker, know that if you continue to perform the rituals of worship and follow the commands of Allāh (ﷻ), you will find physical and spiritual healing that protects you from every disease. When you continue your practices, you will find the healing of yourself, your heart and your spirit, and you will continue to enjoy physical and spiritual wellness.

Allāh (ﷻ) orders these rituals because of His care for this holy form. He says in His Qur'ān:

> Safeguard the ṣalāh, and especially the middle ṣalāh,
> and stand before Allāh (ﷻ) in utmost obedience. (2:238)

And He speaks to you about what He sent to the messenger of Allāh (ﷺ):

> There has come to you a messenger from among yourselves.
> Grievous to him is what you suffer.
> (He is) full of concern for you, for the believers,
> kind and singularly compassionate. (9:128)

Al-wuḍu' prevents skin diseases. Allāh (ﷻ) says:

> Oh you who believe,
> when you rise up to ṣalāh, wash your face and hands
> up to the elbows, and wipe your head and feet up to the ankles
> and if you are in a state of janaba, purify yourselves.
> But if you are ill or traveling,
> or if one of you comes from the answering a call of nature,
> or has had sexual intercourse and can find no water,
> then seek clean air and wipe your face and hands with it. (5:6)

---

[25] Sidi Muhammad, *The Migration of the Truthful Traveler*. Petaluma: Sidi Muhammad Press, 2010, pp. 121-123.

Allāh (ﷻ) does not wish to make a hardship for you, but rather He wishes to purify you and perfect His grace upon you so that you might give thanks.

The āyah I mention right now points to cleaning the body, especially the parts exposed to the outside which are often used in work and in dealing with daily tasks. Al-wuḍuʾ is important because His companions made prayers five times a day, keeping these body parts always clean. If we reflect deeply, we see that it is also included in the medicine of the Messenger (ﷺ) for the following reasons:

- It detoxifies the body, helping to remove harmful salts that exist on the pores of the skin. Leaving these harmful salts to accumulate can block the pores and disrupt the many functions of the skin. Therefore, we should always clean our body, especially the exposed areas, which are cleaned with performing the ritual wuḍuʾ.

- The skin has many functions. It protects against pollutants and serves as a general protector of health, as a protective membrane. The skin protects the body from excessive moisture from the outside and from germs from the outside. The skin contains pain sensors which inform the person to remove themselves from harm's way.

- The skin also assists in body temperature regulation. For example, during hot weather, the skin's glands secrete sweat, which plays a vital role in protecting the body from heat. And when the weather is cold, secretion of sweat decreases, preserving the body and the heart. Likewise, when one is ill and has a fever, the skin produces sweat which cools the body as it dries.

- The skin receives vitamin D from the sun for calcium absorption, which is important for bones and teeth. The skin's response to sunlight also helps regulate the daily diurnal cycle, allowing for proper balance of rest and activity. Its excretion of toxic substances through the skin and other organs of the body helps the body balance fluids and get rid of harmful substances.

- Recent scientific research recommends cleaning the skin to open the pores, especially for those who work in the oil industry and mines. Cleaning helps all the body's organs to renew blood circulation. Cold water is preferred because it stimulates the kidneys and nervous system.

Ṣalāh is a physical exercise. Allāh (ﷻ) says:

> Oh you who have come to believe, bow and prostrate yourselves,
> and worship your Lord, and do good,
> so that perhaps you may prosper. (22:77)

The entire community of believers is obliged to perform the obligatory prayers once they attain puberty, and that includes the elders.

Ṣalāh benefits everyone. Every human being has to train his body, and to move it in certain ways to be healthy. Jobs do not necessarily provide this kind of exercise. Each job may involve certain movements, but not other movements. A job may involve movement, moving the legs, and another may involve moving the hands, while another involves no movement at all.

For example, a clerk may sit at a desk for 8 hours a day, or someone may work in a factory even longer hours. Prayers are greatly beneficial for them. They are also beneficial to those whose work is exacting, such as work on construction job, or a teacher, or who works long hours in a school or college. This is why to have fitness you must move the limbs that you not often move the right way by performing regular exercise which involves the whole body. Ṣalāh provides the opportunity for us. They are an exercise for physical fitness and mental acuity."

Now, my beloveds, this is book (*The Migration of the Truthful Traveler*) you can read completely and you can follow. It is very important to read this book.

The Story of ʿIsa (ؑ)

"True Spiritual Sustenance: The Table of ʿĪsā (ؑ)"
from *A Righteous Word is Like a Righteous Tree*
Saturday, October 16, 2010 AM, Florida

لا إله إلا الله - لا إله إلا الله - لا إله إلا الله - محمد رسول الله عليه صلاة الله
لا إله إلا الله - لا إله إلا الله - لا إله إلا الله - ابراهيم رسول الله عليه صلاة الله
لا إله إلا الله - لا إله إلا الله - لا إله إلا الله - موسى رسول الله عليه صلاة الله
لا إله إلا الله - لا إله إلا الله - لا إله إلا الله - عيسى رسول الله عليه صلاة الله
اللهم انت السلام ومنك السلام و إليك يعود السلام
تباركت ربنا وتعاليت يا ذوالجلال والإكرام

Praise belongs to Allāh (ﷻ), and peace be upon Sayyidinā (our Master) Muḥammad (ﷺ), the messenger of Allāh (ﷻ). Peace upon all the prophets, all the messengers (ؑ). Peace upon all the beloveds of Allāh (ﷻ). Peace upon all the angels (ؑ). Peace upon all the gnostics, those who carry the message of unity and peace and freedom to all the people. It is my great honor to be among you in order to give you this message.

The message on this blessed day is the message of Sayyidinā ʿĪsā (Jesus) (ؑ)—and Sayyidatunā (our Lady) Maryam (ؑ), the Virgin Mary who received the divine light. She is a holy lady. She (ؑ) carried in her womb divine light. When Sayyidinā Jībrīl (Gabriel) (ؑ) was talking to Sayyidatunā Mary (ؑ), the holy Maryam (ؑ), he told her, "I am a messenger from Allāh (ﷻ)." He came to her in the shape of a human being, and by the order of Allāh (ﷻ) he brought within her from the spirit of Allāh (ﷻ), and this is the light, the divine light. It is a gift for all the people all over the world.

This is the birthday of Sayyidinā ʿĪsā (ؑ) who carries the message of peace and love and mercy and freedom to all the people. This is a divine sign. Allāh (ﷻ) announced to all the people, to all the angels (ؑ), to His beloveds, to His children, to those who know and love Allāh (ﷻ). This message is to all those good people. This message is also for all those who disobey Allāh (ﷻ), all of the corrupters. Sayyidinā ʿĪsā (ؑ) is a miracle from Allāh (ﷻ). Allāh (ﷻ) says that Sayyidinā ʿĪsā (ؑ) is like Ādam (ؑ). Allāh (ﷻ) created both of them.

On this blessed morning, we will tell you the story of Sayyidinā ʿĪsā (ﷺ). He carried the flag of peace, love, mercy, justice and freedom. He came to teach us how to heal ourselves by the order of Allāh (ﷻ). We are lucky that we are carrying the message of Sayyidinā ʿĪsā and the message of all the prophets (ﷺ) and that we can give the message to our sons and daughters. We can teach them how to walk, how to live a life full of peace, mercy and justice.

Allāh (ﷻ) sent our Sayyidinā ʿĪsā (ﷺ) down and He taught him how to heal the sick, how to help the blind to see, how to heal diseases and how to revive the dead, with the permission of Allāh (ﷻ). He could not do any of this by himself, but with the permission Allāh gave him and the knowledge that Allāh (ﷻ) sent down to him, he could. Allāh says:

> And when Allāh (ﷻ) will say (on the Day of Judgment):
> "Oh ʿĪsā, son of Maryam!
> Did you tell men, 'Worship me and my mother
> as two gods besides Allāh?'"
>
> He will say, "Glory be to You!
> It was not for me to say what I had no right.
> Had I said such a thing, You would surely have known it.
> You know what is in my inner self,
> though I do not know what is in Yours.
> Truly, You, only You,
> are the All-Knowing of all that is hidden. (5:116)

From here, I ask for Allāh's permission to tell you the story of Sayyidinā ʿĪsā. When he was a baby in one hour he appeared to this world, so he was the Spirit of Allāh (ﷻ) (rūḥi-llāh). He was the light of Allāh (ﷻ). He was a noble man, a worthy man. No one can imagine the boundaries of his nobility. Those who claim, "We follow ʿĪsā (ﷺ)" often disobey his orders.

Peace be upon you, Sayyidinā ʿĪsā (ﷺ). We send our prayers upon Sayyidinā ʿĪsā (ﷺ). You are the complete man. I fall in front of you. I am one of his children and I am carrying his message.

Sayyidatunā Maryam (☺), the holy virgin, carried this light, this baby, Allāh (☺) created. He was not a normal baby. He was the father of peace. He was the father of love. He was the love and the unity. So she went away and isolated herself in a place where there was no one close to her

You know about what the corrupters do in the Holy Land all the time. But Allāh (☺) will save this land. This land is the land of Sayyidinā ʿĪsā (☺). It is the land of all the prophets (☺), and it is the land of all people who believe in ʿĪsā and all the prophets (☺), from Ādam (☺) to Sayyidinā Ibrāhīm (Abraham) (☺) to Sayyidinā Ismāʿīl (Ishmael), to Sayyidinā Muḥammad (☺). It is the land of love, the throne of Allāh (☺). Allāh (☺) wants it to be a holy land forever.

In a ḥadīth qudsī Allāh talks about Jerusalem, saying:

> You are My heaven, from My countries.
> You are the place of gathering and scattering.

Allāh (☺) says:

> In the Hereafter, on the Day of Judgment, you will be the bride.
> And you are holy by My light.
> And woe, woe to all those corrupters.
> Anyone who will live in you,
> I will be blessed with him.

One prayer on earth equals thousands of prayers in other places. So if you want to live in this land, give it oil. What is the meaning of giving this land oil? The people over there are suffering all the time. You have to help this land. You have to help the people, the children, live over there. You have to help the old people live there.

The oil you can offer this land is your help: help all of the people who are suffering all the time. You can light a candle in this oil, give the light, and when you give your help you are giving the light to them. They are the children of Sayyidinā ʿĪsā (☺) and they are the children of all the prophets (☺). We have to make every effort to keep this land holy, full of peace and love and freedom and mercy. Look to this land.

Sayyidatunā Maryam (☙), Holy Mary, was there in this land. She was
outside of al-Quds (Jerusalem), a short distance between her place and
al-Quds. She directed her face toward this land because she did not
have a husband and she had a baby by herself. Those who came there
were carrying the message of Allāh (☙).

She went to this land and she took a place under a date palm tree, and
she had nothing: no food, no shelter, nothing. There was an angel that
spoke to her, saying, "Shake this date palm, without branches or fruits,
just open the tree."

This is the miracle of Sayyidinā ʿĪsā (☙) and Sayyidatunā Maryam (☙):
the while Sayyidatunā Maryam (☙) was giving birth the palm tree
started to grow and give fruit. The tree was not dead, and the dates
were very soft. Dates are very good for ladies giving birth. Even today,
while giving birth women should eat this kind of soft date. And the date
contains all the essential nutrients for a woman and her baby. This is a
miracle, because during the birth a woman will lose blood, and this will
help her so much. This was a miracle from Allāh (☙).

Sayyidatunā Maryam (☙) carried her baby and her people asked her,
"How did you become pregnant?" She answered:

> Then she (Maryam) pointed to him (ʿĪsā).
>
> They said, "How can we talk to a child in the cradle?"
>
> He (ʿĪsā) said, "Truly! I am a slave of Allāh,
> He has given me the scripture and made me a prophet.
> And He has made me blessed wherever I am,
> and has enjoined on me prayer (ṣalāh) and zakāh (charity)
> for as long as I live,
> and (to be) dutiful to my mother,
> and make me not arrogant, unblessed." (19:29—19:32)

He said, "Allāh (☙) gave me the book of peace and mercy and justice and
freedom, Allāh (☙) gave me the Injīl (Gospel) and He made me a
prophet. He made me a messenger to carry the message to all people."

That's what happened. This is the miracle of Sayyidinā ʿĪsā (ﷺ) and the miracle of Sayyidatunā Holy Maryam (ﷺ).

Sayyidinā ʿĪsā (ﷺ) was to fulfill the peace, to achieve the message, and we praise Allāh (ﷻ) because we are the sons of this message. Allāh (ﷻ) taught us this message through Sayyidinā ʿĪsā (ﷺ). This is ʿĪsā (ﷺ). He is calling and he is trying to let people come to carry this flag, the same flag, the same message you are carrying now.

We love all people without discrimination. Allāh (ﷻ) says:

> Oh people, We have created you from a male and a female,
> and made you into nations and tribes
> so that you may know (and love) one another.
> Truly, the most honorable of you with Allāh (ﷻ)
> is that who has taqwā.
> Truly, Allāh is all-knowing, all-aware. (49:13)

This is the message of the prophets (ﷺ), this is the message of Sayyidinā Mūsā (Moses) (ﷺ), this is the message of Sayyidinā Ibrāhīm (ﷺ), this is the message of Sayyidinā Muḥammad (ﷺ). It is the real message, the real divine message.

Allāh (ﷻ) says of Sayyidinā Muḥammad (ﷺ):

> We have not sent you but as a mercy for all the worlds. (21:107)

This is a brief introduction to let you feel the spirit of Sayyidinā ʿĪsā (ﷺ), and to live these moments with him and all the prophets (ﷺ). If you want, I will explain all of that in detail to you, so that you are sure about this message and can follow the message of Sayyidinā ʿĪsā (ﷺ), Sayyidinā Ibrāhīm (ﷺ) and Sayyidinā Muḥammad (ﷺ). The messengers believe in Allāh (ﷻ) and the angels (ﷺ) and all the holy books. There is no discrimination between all the prophets (ﷺ).

This is a brief introduction. This is the message of Sayyidinā ʿĪsā (ﷺ); this is the message of love. All humankind needs the love, needs this message. Peace upon all of you. Peace upon Sayyidatunā Maryam (ﷺ), holy Maryam. Peace upon Sayyidinā ʿĪsā (ﷺ) and peace be upon all the prophets and messengers (ﷺ). We are asking Allāh (ﷻ) to let us be among their children, to let us be among those who carry their message. Āmīn.

We are asking Allāh (☼) to help us and al-Masīḥ (the Messiah 'Īsā ☼) will come very soon. Al-Mahdī will come with him, inshā'a-llāh. Then you will see love and peace in the whole world, Āmīn.

The reading "True Spiritual Sustenance: The Table of 'Īsā (☼)" from *A Righteous Word is Like a Righteous Tree*[26] is read from the beginning,

My beloveds and my children, I have come to you from the Holy Land, from the holy city, which is the heart of the world. It is the main city in the world. Because I live in it, I am carrying its fragrance, I am carrying its spirit and I am carrying its reference to the whole world's need for peace, mercy, love and justice, without discrimination. We need these qualities without discriminating between gender, color or race.

I carry this message. It is the message of 'Īsā (Jesus) (☼), who carried the message of unity and offered everything for humanity. He offered everything so that people could be loving toward one another and live in peace and mercy for one another. This was also the message of all of the prophets, starting with Ibrāhīm (☼), Mūsā (☼) and the Prophet Muḥammad (☼).

This is a blessed day on which I come to you, carrying my heart and my spirit for you. I came on behalf of all of the prophets (☼). I live for their message. I live to carry their message. I pray that a day will come when I will see all people singing the song of love, the song of life and the song of justice and mercy. This day has illuminated my spirit and heart and inspired me to send you a message that was sent by all of the prophets and messengers (☼).

The lover 'Īsā (☼) sent this message. We need to pray as his disciples prayed with him for Allāh (☼) to send signs from Heaven, to prove the message of unity to those who deny it. Those who denied the message in the past did not listen to 'Īsā's voice (☼), and many claimed to carry his message after him. But he has nothing to do with them, because in his name they kill children, destroy houses and destroy trees. Even the earth and nature are not safe from their cruelty. These people pollute the earth's resources, its water and its air. They work to destroy the world.

---

[26] *A Righteous Word is Like a Righteous Tree.* pp. 81-95.

Allāh (ﷻ) sent us His message through the voices of all of the prophets and messengers (عليهم السلام). They prayed and asked Him to save the earth from the evil ones and to protect it, because Allāh (ﷻ) created the earth for all people. Allāh (ﷻ) created everything in the earth and in the heavens and what is between them to be filled with love, beauty, peace, freedom and justice for all people and all creatures. Allāh (ﷻ) says:

> I will be creating a human being out of mud.
> When I finish forming him and fashioning him
> and breathe into him out of My spirit (My own light)
> prostrate yourselves to him. (38:71)

Since that time, the message has been one. Look at al-Masīḥ ʿĪsā (عليه السلام) (the Messiah Jesus). Look at how he lived and devoted himself to the message until he died. He brought the message of truth and justice to everyone. He carried the message of love, because no one can live without love. I am with you and all kind people like you holding the olive branch, which is a symbol of peace. Allāh (ﷻ) mentions it in the Qurʾān when He says:

> God is the light of the heavens and the earth.
> His light is like this:
> there is a niche and in it a lamp,
> the lamp inside a glass, a glass like a glittering star,
> fueled from a blessed olive tree from neither east nor west. (24:35)

This verse describes the divine light that reaches all hearts and lights them with love, peace, mercy and justice.

The world was not created to be burned by those who invent weapons of mass destruction and destroy humans and animals alike with their weapons. The earth was not created for this. It was created to spread the message that the children of purity, the Sufis, are carrying after the prophets and messengers (عليهم السلام).

This message is like a firm tree, a blessed tree. Its roots are firmly established in the earth. Its branches reach up to the heavens, producing all kinds of fruits all of the time (14:24-25). Doves of peace rest on its branches, chanting the song of peace. The people who keep and preserve the purity in which they were created and carry the message of peace are there, too.

As beloveds of al-Masīḥ ʿĪsā (ﷺ), we want to live close to him, just as his disciples did in the past. They lived with him and listened to his message of al-Ḥaqq. After that, each of them carried the message of freedom, peace and justice. I pray that you will become a child of his and a lover of his, just as all of the disciples did before you. Listen to them in this story, when they asked him for a favor from Allāh (ﷻ). They said, according to the Qurʾān:

> (Remember) when the disciples said:
> 'Oh ʿĪsā (ﷺ), son of Maryam (ﷺ)!
> Can your Lord send down to us a table spread from Heaven?'
> ʿĪsā (ﷺ) said: 'Fear Allāh (ﷻ), (and guard yourselves against evil),
> if you have faith.' (5:112)

They were faithful disciples. They felt they needed sustenance from Heaven, and Allāh (ﷻ) inspired them to ask for it. Through ʿĪsā's heart (ﷺ), they felt the future suffering of the earth and they felt they needed spiritual sustenance. They did not ask for a table full of physical food and drink; they felt they needed spiritual sustenance directly from Allāh (ﷻ) —sustenance that was made of divine light.

Thus the disciples said to ʿĪsā (ﷺ), 'Oh Spirit of Allāh,[27] ask Allāh (ﷻ) on our behalf, for He is the One who created you without a father and put you in the womb of your mother. Your mother Maryam (ﷺ) was an innocent and chaste woman.'

Maryam (ﷺ) was pure and clean and she devoted herself to prayer. Then, the Angel Jībrīl (Gabriel) (ﷺ) appeared to her in human form. He told her that Allāh (ﷻ) would give her a pure and intelligent son, innocent and free of all human blemishes. He came directly from the spirit of Allāh (ﷻ), from His light. But this does not mean that he was a son of Allāh (ﷻ) and that she was Allāh's wife, like in human terms. No, because Allāh (ﷻ) says in the Qurʾān:

> Say: He is Allāh, the One and Only.
> He does not beget (children), nor is He begotten. (112:1, 112:3)

Allāh (ﷻ) is not like a human being. He is beyond human beings. He is transcendent. Allāh (ﷻ) is the Most Powerful. He made the Angel Jībrīl

---

[27] Allāh refers to ʿĪsā as Rūḥi-llāh, which is translated at "the Spirit of Allāh."

(☙) appear in human form as an image to Maryam (☙), because Allāh (☙) can create anything from nothing.

Allāh (☙) is transcendent. He is beyond a creature made of mud. He is free of all physical attributes. The divine light is unlimited. It cannot be limited by shape, form or gender. It is limitless. It is transcendent and beyond everything.

Allāh (☙) sent 'Īsā al-Masīḥ (☙), son of Maryam (☙), to be a noble man, a great man, a generous man, a pure man. Allāh (☙) taught him of that which he had no knowledge. It was Allāh's decree (☙) to send him into the world without a father. Maryam (☙) only carried him like sparks. Allāh (☙) says in the Qur'ān:

> The example of the creation of 'Īsā
> is like the example of the creation of Ādam. (3:59)

Ādam (☙) had no father and no mother, either. Allāh (☙) says:

> I will be creating a human being out of mud.
> When I finish forming him and fashioning him
> and breathe into him out of My spirit
> (you angels) prostrate yourselves to him. (38:71)

All of the angels saw a human being. I will not say, 'a man.' I say, 'a human being.' They saw a person—genderless, formless. Allāh (☙) wanted him to be in that form. Then Allāh (☙) said to the angels (☙):

> Prostrate yourselves to him. (38:71)

'Īsā (☙) was created in the same way Ādam (☙) was created. The first words 'Īsā (☙) uttered were, 'There is no God but One. Glory to You. You created me and I am Your worshipful slave. There is no benefit or harm that comes from myself. I am between Your hands. I listen and I obey, and for You I listen and I submit.' This is the example of 'Īsā (☙).

After Maryam (☙) gave birth to him, she came home carrying the little infant to her people. That glorious holy one, who is a spirit from Allāh (☙), came carrying him. The people said, 'How did you become pregnant?' All of the rabbis and people gathered and said, 'What did you do?'"

He was the son of one hour.

The reading continues:

> "Then she (Maryam) pointed to him (ʿĪsā).

They said, 'How can we talk to a child in the cradle?'

> He (ʿĪsā) said, 'Truly! I am a slave of Allāh,
> He has given me the scripture and made me a prophet.
> And He has made me blessed wherever I am,
> and has enjoined on me prayer (ṣalāh) and zakāh (charity)
> for as long as I live,
> and (to be) dutiful to my mother,
> and make me not arrogant, unblessed.' (19:29—19:32)

He did not say, 'and dutiful to my father,' He said, 'and dutiful to my mother.' He also said, 'Allāh (ﷻ) made me a prophet. He created me and I am a worshipful slave and servant to Him.' He did not say, 'I am a king,' and he did not say, 'I am a boss.'

He is ʿĪsā (ﷺ), not more than that. He was a human being carrying a message of God. He is clean from every slander that people taught about him. He is not Allāh (ﷻ). He is slave.

He didn't have a father, only a mother. He had a holy mother who contained the light and the love and the mercy and everything. She was the real mother. She did not know anything before it happened, but in one moment He give her the complete gift, a holy gift. For that reason it is a very holy gift and it is important for everyone who believes and who understands the meaning of the word, ʿĪsā (ﷺ).

ʿĪsā (ﷺ) carried the spirit, the light of Allāh (ﷻ), to give to all people without separation. This is what Allāh (ﷻ) wanted. What is the answer from everyone who carries the message of Allāh (ﷻ)? The answer is what He sent through His holy beloved, the Prophet ʿĪsā (ﷺ) the son of Maryam (ﷺ). ʿĪsā (ﷺ) did not call himself the son of Allāh (ﷻ)! He called himself the slave of Allāh (ﷻ)! He carried the message. For that reason, it is important for everyone to open his heart.

Anyone who claims that ʿĪsā (ﷺ) said, "I am the son of Allāh (ﷻ)" (is lying). Sayyidinā ʿĪsā (ﷺ) said, "I am the slave of Allāh (ﷻ)," he never said,

"I am the son of Allāh (ﷻ)." We have to follow his words in order to carry his holy message to all humankind, to all people without discrimination between male and female.

This is very holy. Do not use the word, "woman." Do not use the word "man." You are the mirror of this man and the man is the mirror of you. You carry the mirror of Allāh (ﷻ). Why do you like to make separation, because Allāh (ﷻ) says that every human being is very holy. He says:

> If anyone kills a person or spreads mischief in the land
> it is as if he has killed all humankind,
> and if anyone saves a life
> it is as if has saved the life of all humankind. (5:32)

This is the sense of the deep meaning of the message ʿĪsā (ﷺ) carried. All the prophets (ﷺ) said the same. Nothing! There is no separation between any of the prophets (ﷺ). These brothers carried the same message, the message of unity. Lā ʾilāha ʾilla-llāh. There is nothing else but Allāh (ﷻ). Allāh (ﷻ) is the creator of all people.

The messengers and prophets (ﷺ) said, "Lā ʾilāha ʾilla-llāh." This is what they said, so why do we go to liars and corrupters? Go to Allāh (ﷻ), return directly to Allāh (ﷻ), carry the message of Allāh (ﷻ). Not one of them worshipped an idol; all of them offered their selves, their hearts, their bodies, as a sacrifice to Allāh (ﷻ). All of them paid their souls as a sacrifice to Allāh (ﷻ) for all people; but the liars, the corrupters—they claim something different.

I am asking Allāh (ﷻ) to be among the chosen of all the prophets (ﷺ). I am asking Allāh (ﷻ), and I wish, for all your daughters and sons to be among those who follow the prophets and the messengers. I am a poor slave. I have nothing to do for myself; no benefit, no harm. Everything is from Allāh (ﷻ). I was carrying this message while I was a child. This is the message of Allāh (ﷻ), and I want you to carry this message.

I informed you, I told you. I told all of the people, and I'm telling all people all the time, whether they are in Africa, in America, or in other places: this is the message and I will continue to carry this message until my death.

The reading continues, "ʿĪsā (ﷺ) said, 'I am a slave, a servant, a worshipper of Allāh (ﷻ). He created me as a blessed worshipper. Wherever I am, I will be blessed. My spirit arrived here in this world by the command of my Creator and my Lord (ﷻ) who created me out of mud and made me a complete human being. He did not create me in the way that some may claim.'

As Allāh (ﷻ) says in the Qurʾān:

> We have certainly created the human being in the best mold. (95:4)

Allāh (ﷻ) is speaking about the divine human being who blew life into the world. This world was screaming in pain, suffering and struggling, and that is why messengers were sent to it, just as ʿĪsā (ﷺ) was sent.

ʿĪsā (ﷺ) invited people to come to Allāh (ﷻ). He said to people, 'I am a worshipful slave and servant of Allāh (ﷻ). I am a noble messenger and He asked me to be good to my mother.' Because he did not have a father, Allāh (ﷻ) asked him to be benevolent to his mother. Allāh (ﷻ) says:

> He is a spirit from My command. (17:85)

He did not say, 'He is God.' He said, 'He is a spirit from Allāh (ﷻ),' just as He said of the other prophets and messengers (ﷺ).

We believe that Allāh (ﷻ) is absolutely One and that the entire world is declaring, 'There is no god but the One, and He has no partner. All dominions are His. All life belongs to Him.'

Allāh (ﷻ) never dies. Allāh (ﷻ) cannot die. Allāh (ﷻ) is beyond everything. He is transcendent. He is always alive. He is the Creator; He creates. He is not created; He creates. He originates things from nothing. We all have one father and one mother, and so we are inside Allāh's system (ﷻ) of creation. We all came from a mother and a father.

This is the belief of the people of unity. It is also the belief of those who realize the truth and believe in the truth, who respect humanity and who care for humanity. It is the creed of those who care for the lives of people and spread love, mercy, compassion, justice and freedom to all.

Life cannot continue without true, pure love, true peace, true mercy and true justice for all, regardless of color or ethnicity. This is our belief; it is the belief of the people of the Sufi way, the way of purity.

We respect all people and we treat them equally. We love them all, regardless of their states and regardless of what they look like. In a ḥadīth the Prophet (ﷺ) said:

> He said, 'Be.'

Allāh (ﷻ) said, 'Be,' and the human being became. This is why we respect all of humanity. We had a beginning, but Allāh (ﷻ) has no beginning. He has always been and He will always be. We are His servants and we serve all people and care for them. We are no different from them.

Allāh (ﷻ) said to those who walk arrogantly on earth, 'Look, you have been created out of the earth, you will return to the earth. You will be resurrected from the earth again. You will keep traveling from one realm to another.' Life will continue, but we need life to be continued with peace, ease and truth.

Listen to the Divine narration, for I am only a vessel who conveys the message, the message that came on the tongues of Ibrāhīm (ﷺ), Mūsā (ﷺ), ʿĪsā (ﷺ) and Muḥammad (ﷺ). Allāh (ﷻ) says in the Qurʾān:

> We make no distinction between any of His messengers.
> (2:285. Also see 4:150 and 4:152)

We say, 'We listen and we obey,' to the message that came from their lips.

When corruption had spread far and wide over the earth, and some people had begun to act like beasts and monsters, violating the rights of others, destroying the earth, killing, murdering and hurting others, Allāh (ﷻ) inspired ʿĪsā's disciples (ﷺ) to ask Him to send the nourishing table humanity needed. What they asked for was a mercy for the people, because the disciples felt the suffering on earth. They asked ʿĪsā (ﷺ) because ʿĪsā (ﷺ) is the Spirit of Allāh (ﷻ) and His messenger.

Listen to their words as they spoke to him. They said in a clear tongue, 'Oh ʿĪsā (ﷺ) son of Maryam (ﷺ).' They did not even address him as

'Messenger.' They related him to his mother. This is how they addressed him, because he had no father.

Allāh (ﷻ) is transcendent, far beyond comparison to any physical form. They asked him, 'Can your Lord bring a table full of peace, mercy, complete justice, complete freedom, complete beauty and complete perfection? Can He bring a nourishing table available to all people, so that they can offer their sacrifices on it in order that humanity might survive?'

They asked for an table spread that gathered all good things together. However, it was not a table of material food and drink, as people might think. They were asking for spiritual sustenance. ʿĪsā (ﷺ) answered them:

> Be conscious of Allāh (ﷻ) and guard yourselves,
> if you have faith. (see 5:112)

He asked them, 'Don't you believe that Allāh (ﷻ) is the Creator, the Originator, the Doer and the Capable? He is the One who created you, your ancestors, all of the worlds and the unknown invisible realms.' Allāh (ﷻ) says that He created one thousand worlds resembling ours. The disciples answered ʿĪsā (ﷺ), saying:

> We wish to eat (of that spiritual sustenance)
> and satisfy our hearts (so that they can be at rest and content).
> (5:113)"

Everybody needs to eat from this holy table. Allāh (ﷻ) is always the Provider, the Giver. He sends the good deeds. You can find the secret of this life by following His orders and by carrying the message as all the prophets (ﷺ) did. All the prophets (ﷺ) paid their souls, their selves, as a sacrifice to Allāh (ﷻ) to save all the people, to save the world. They are the group of Allāh (ﷻ), full of peace and mercy and love. They came to help us understand how we can live in this life happily.

I'm pretty sure that all the prophets (ﷺ) sat crying out for this world, and they are invoking Allāh (ﷻ) to permit the whole world to carry the message of peace and love and mercy. I am encouraging you to carry this message all the time. Help others and to let all people live a happy life so that you can really be one of the children of the prophets (ﷺ).

And Allāh (ﷻ) says:

> Oh people, We have created you from a male and a female,
> and made you into nations and tribes
> so that you may know (and love) one another.
> Truly, the most honorable of you with Allāh (ﷻ)
> is that who has taqwā (piety).
> Truly, Allāh is all-knowing, all-aware. (49:13)
>
> And truly, this is My straight path, so follow it. (6:153)

Lā ʾilāha ʾilla-llāh (ﷻ). Lā ʾilāha ʾilla-llāh (ﷻ). There is no Lord except Him. There is no one next to Him. He is the only God (ﷻ).

The reading continues:

> **"We wish to eat (of that spiritual sustenance)**
> **and satisfy our hearts (so that they can be at rest and content).**
> **(5:113)"**

Allāh (ﷻ) gave us this message for free, without any payment. It is the message of love and unity. The one who follows this message is the winner. I hope that all of you will be among the winners. Āmīn.

The reading continues:

> **"And know that you have indeed told us the truth**
> **(through the certainty of tasting)**
> **and (so) that we ourselves (can) be its witnesses. (5:113)**

The disciples answered ʿĪsā (ﷺ), "We would like you to ask for this table of sustenance so that we can taste and hear and see. We want to hear this table chant its praises of Allāh (ﷻ)."

The first Sufi university here in the United States carries the message of all the prophets (ﷺ). This university is carrying the message. I established this university and I put within it the message of all the prophets (ﷺ). I encourage all of you to be among the students who will teach the message and carry the message. I renew it and purify it by the order of Allāh (ﷻ), so anyone who wants to join this university, yes, I encourage them. This is holy food for your spirits, for your souls, for your bodies, for your intellect. Join this university to carry the message. This is the second message for you today.

The reading continues, "...For the messengers are the lovers of Allāh (ﷻ) and their tables are full of glorification and praise."

And I warn all the teachers not to give any knowledge except from the message of Allāh (ﷻ). The teachers should be honest, loyal, sincere, full of love, mercy and politeness. They should be polite. The teachers should be polite. Āmīn.

I know they are polite, al-ḥamdu li-llāh, because they know the orders of Allāh (ﷻ). Maybe some of you think I'm saying the teachers are not polite (laughter)—no, these are the teachers' ethics.

The reading continues, "The disciples said, 'We will be your witnesses and only then will we know for certain that you are the messenger of Allāh (ﷻ). We will taste and we will know that Allāh (ﷻ) is love, Allāh (ﷻ) is peace, Allāh (ﷻ) is beauty and Allāh (ﷻ) is justice and perfection.' At this point ʿĪsā (عليه السلام) said, asking Allāh (ﷻ):

> Oh Allāh, our Lord (ﷻ). (5:114)

He did not say, 'Our Father,' he said, 'Our Lord, our God, our Master, our Creator (ﷻ).' He said:

> Oh Allāh, our Lord (ﷻ)!
> Send us from Heaven a table spread that there may be for us—
> for the first and the last of us—
> a festival and a sign from You;
> and provide us sustenance, for You are the Best of sustainers.
> (5:114)

ʿĪsā (عليه السلام) asked, 'Oh please, Allāh (ﷻ), send Your sustenance down on a table from Heaven.' ʿĪsā (عليه السلام), the divine spirit, spoke to his Lord. He said, 'Send down to us this nourishing outspread table, a table that is full of goodness, a source of true life.'

He did not ask for a table full of bombs and weapons of mass destruction. He did not ask for poisons and pollution to kill plants and animals. No, he asked for true sustenance.

ʿĪsā (ﷺ) asked, 'Oh please, Allāh (ﷻ), send down this table as a feast for us. We need divine sustenance to have a feast,' which means, 'Make us always happy, as if we were at a festival. Make us always safe, always secure and always at peace and in love with You.' This is the true table Allāh (ﷻ) wants for us."

This table is only for the followers of Sayyidinā ʿĪsā (ﷺ). This table exists now. It is a message for all people. Yes, Allāh (ﷻ) has sent down what they need: food, fruits and drinks. Through this table you can find abundant peace, love and mercy. That's what I want to explain to you.

This has been sent down to all the prophets (ﷺ). It exists right now. It is a divine mercy. Allāh (ﷻ) sent down all of His orders, all of His instructions, for how to follow Him. He sent food for our bodies, food for our souls, food for our intellects in order to let life continue.

A car with no oil can't move; you can't drive it. Allāh (ﷻ) said:

> I will be creating a human being out of mud.
> When I finish forming him and fashioning him
> and breathe into him out of My spirit
> prostrate yourselves to him. (38:71)

He gave the human being life. This holy table exists now. Allāh (ﷻ) sent it down and it is forever, and it will feed all people who are searching for truth through the message of all the prophets (ﷺ). This is not from me. I am a poor slave. This is the message of Allāh (ﷻ).

The reading continues, "The table full of material fruits, food and drink is nothing compared to this, because animals eat the same thing. What he was asking for was spiritual sustenance—not a cheap, perishable thing. He was asking for that which is eternal, that which carries the secret of life and the secret of happiness.

ʿĪsā (ﷺ) said, 'Our Lord, send for us a nourishing, table spread from Heaven as a feast for us, for the first of us and the last of us,' which means for all of humanity, from beginning to end.

ʿĪsā (ﷺ) wanted love, peace, mercy and justice for all people, from the first human being to the last human being. He wanted healing for us.

He wanted to destroy barriers and discrimination. He wanted to destroy racism and hate. He wanted a complete, perfect table full of sustenance that contained the qualities of God. In response, Allāh (ﷻ) sent it down to him. He sent a holy table that was full of that which no human mind had ever conceived. He sent gifts that no eyes had ever seen and no ears had ever heard.

Today, people hear the sounds of airplanes and bombs; they hear screaming and cries of hunger. This is what they hear today, ʿĪsā (ﷺ) did not ask for this. He asked for life. He asked for life for people so that they could celebrate their existence.

How can people be always festive while there is destruction, war, pollution and disease? People do not need this; they need what ʿĪsā (ﷺ) asked of our Lord. He asked for a nourishing table so that we could live in continuous celebration, in a festival full of joy. He wanted this table to be free of pollution, poison, suffering and disease. He wanted it to be free of pain. He wanted it to be granted to all human beings, for he is a noble prophet, a beloved of Allāh (ﷻ) and a lover of humanity.

When ʿĪsā (ﷺ) asked Allāh (ﷻ) he said, 'Please send us a divine table of sustenance that will be a feast for us, from the first of us to the last of us.' This means, 'We want pure sustenance, a pure, eternal meal that is not perishable, that is good for all of humanity. We want it to be free from disease and disasters.' This is the divine prayer ʿĪsā (ﷺ) prayed for all people.

He said, 'We want it to be a sign from You. We want a sign, a mark from You that will always remain on earth, despite the corrupters, murderers and destroyers. This divine sign will always remain on earth.' As Allāh (ﷻ) says:

> They (those who cover up the Truth)
> want to extinguish Allāh's light (ﷻ) with their mouths,
> but Allāh (ﷻ) will not allow anything
> except that His light will be perfected
> even though the disbelievers hate (it). (9:32)

Allāh (ﷻ) sent this table full of spiritual sustenance to ʿĪsā (ﷺ) and his disciples. In reality, it is full of whatever people may need. Anything that crosses your mind that you feel you need, you will find it there. It is full of everything, physically and spiritually. Where is it? Here, on earth. It exists. Everything still carries the traces of the table that was sent to ʿĪsā (ﷺ), because ʿĪsā (ﷺ) was the messenger of love, the messenger of peace. It was a pure meal and it still is.

You can fulfill your needs by receiving from this table in accordance with divine, natural law. You do not take that which is illegal for you to take, or violate someone else's rights. Allāh (ﷻ) wants your needs to be met in a pure way, according to His natural law. This is an eternal sign, an eternally sustaining meal that will remain forever and never perish.

ʿĪsā (ﷺ) prayed to Allāh (ﷻ), 'Provide for us, for You are the best of Providers.' He understood that people need provision, that they need pure drink, pure food and pure sustenance, like vegetables that are free from chemicals, hormones and pollution. He wanted our physical and spiritual food to be pure so that people would not be hurt, but would preserve His purity and reflect the divine qualities.

This is the message of the prophets and messengers. This is what they brought in their holy scriptures. Allāh taught them how to use this sustenance, how to use the resources of the earth. He taught them how to plant and keep everything pure, and how to preserve its original purity.

Yet there are people who deviate from the divine, natural law. What do they do? They follow another messenger, an evil messenger, Iblīs, the accursed devil and his followers. He whispers to them and makes things appear good for them that are not good. He says that is all right to kill. Those who do this deviate from divine commands and do not surrender to the divine, natural law. Allāh (ﷻ) will question them about everything. On the Day of Judgment, He will ask them about every minor and major action they carried out.

I seek refuge in Allāh (ﷻ) on your behalf. May He protect you, so that you will not listen to the s̲hayṭān and you will not be a tool or an instrument in its hands. May He protect you so that you will not submit your children to be followers of those who deviate from the divine commands.

Allāh (ﷻ) answered ʿĪsā's prayer (ﷺ), saying:

> I am going to send it (the table) down to you... (9:33)

'I will send down this sustaining table, this blessed table, which is the table of eternal life. It is granted for the faithful believers who follow the guidance of the prophets and messengers (ﷺ).'

When the prophets die they do not die as all others do. At death they are transferred from the physical, metaphorical, perishable world to another realm that is spiritual. They move from the realm of material possessions and indulgence, the dense realm, to a realm that is subtle, that is eternal, and that is pure and full of love and peace. This is the secret of that nourishing table Allāh (ﷻ) sent.

For that reason, Allāh (ﷻ) ordered the angels (ﷺ) to prostrate to the human being in his original form, which is made after the divine image. This means that Allāh (ﷻ) provided human beings with a spirit from Him, a hearing from Him, and the ability to see from Him. He is a holy being. The human being is a holy being in his origin. Allāh (ﷻ) wants us to preserve that purity, to remain in His image, to preserve the trust with which He entrusted us (33:72). This trust must be preserved and kept pure because it is a divine mirror. It is a reflection of the divine, so it must be kept pure, clean and polished.

Imagine you are carrying this mirror. When you look in this mirror you see your true image. You see your true image, but can you touch your picture there? You cannot, but it is there. It is a subtle, transparent, spiritual image, not a material one. If you see your true image and know who is carrying it you will be in great joy, because you will see yourself dressed in a divine garment."

Ḥayy!

The reading continues, "At night, in the dark, you cannot see this image, but in the morning you can see your shadow on the ground, can't you? If you are looking at the seashore and the water is pure and you look, you can see your own image. But can you touch it physically? No, you can't. This is an allusion, an indication, to help you know what the subtle spiritual world is. This indication appears through signs given to us in the physical world.

The same thing happens during your sleep. During your sleep you see a lot of things. You are physically still here, but you are asleep. Your sister could be sleeping beside you, another sister could be sleeping beside you, and you all are asleep. Then you see a shadow. You see in your imagination the images of people that you sometimes know.

For example, suppose a woman is living in America and her sister is living in Jerusalem. During sleep she can see her sister in Jerusalem and they speak. They converse together and they both understand each other despite the language they speak in the dream. Or, someone can be in Texas and someone else in New York, but they can still converse. During your sleep you can do a lot of things. Sometimes you can see someone beating you up, and you will be screaming, but the one lying beside you does not hear your screams, is that not right? The dream state is called divine spontaneous imagination, and it is a true realm.

When this human body perishes, you will go and live in this subtle, spiritual realm. That is why Allāh (ﷻ) says:

> Do they not reflect within themselves
> (so that they may understand)? (30:8)

Allāh (ﷻ) says that within yourselves, inside yourselves, you can find the truth.

This dense metaphorical, physical realm is not eternal. The body is perishable. Why is the body perishable? Because it belongs to this lower realm, the dense realm. Humans are heedless of their reality. They think they will live forever, and they live as if they will be eternal in this world. However, no matter how long you live, 70 or 100 years, you will die and leave everything physical behind.

Will you be able to take anything physical with you when you pass away?"

No.

The reading continues, "No, you will not. You will leave everything. Even if a human being has tons of gold and is very wealthy, he will not take a penny with him. When you die and you are in your coffin and they search your pockets you will not have a cent. You do not take anything with you. No one takes any physical things with him. If anyone claims that this is not so, show me. Show me proof of that. Is he different? Can he really take things with him physically?"

No.

The reading continues, "No, the body will go back to dust. Then seeing and hearing will pass away to another realm.

Allāh (ﷻ) manifested Himself with His names "the Hearer" and "the Seer." He also manifested His name "the Living," and gave you life. You can see a human who is strong and healthy suddenly die. A minute ago he was talking. You can say, "Wake up. Can you talk?" You can bring all of the physicians of the world to him; can they bring him back to life? Can anyone bring him back to life? There is a secret, a secret that was taken from him—the secret of life. Inventors have done a lot for us in the physical world but they still cannot create a machine which can make him breathe and come to life again. Can you bring him to life after a few years of death?"

No.

The reading continues, "No, you cannot bring him back to this physical realm. No one can say how or why. They cannot do it because this is not his location anymore.

It is like when you travel from place to place in an airplane. At your destination you have to get off of the airplane, and then you are in a vehicle. This body is like a vehicle; when your station comes, you leave. You must leave. Then the angels (عليهم السلام) will take you and you will travel to another realm, because Allāh (ﷻ) decreed a lifespan for every human, a journey that he goes through. When the journey ends, you go back to the spiritual realm."

This is the end of the reading, but I would like to say something. There is a very important secret. All the prophets (عليهم السلام) and Sayyidinā ʿĪsā (ﷷ) carry this secret. Sayyidinā ʿĪsā's secret is healing: he knows how to heal people. He knows how to heal blind people, how to give life to those who have passed away, by the permission of Allāh (ﷻ). He taught people how to heal others. He taught healing. He taught people how to do good.

So I have prepared a healing paper for you, and this paper will protect you from jinn and devils and all the liars. It will protect your and your family. You can use this healing the correct way. It is āyah from al-Qur'ān al-Karīm (the Noble Qur'ān). You can see the letter from Sayyidinā Muḥammad (ﷺ) and I prepared it for you in Arabic and in English. I will teach you know how to use this protection, and I encourage you to pay a sacrifice to help the needy people and poor people. I encourage you to follow his message and pay a sacrifice for yourselves and your families.

Anyone who wants to get this protection paper has to pay a sacrifice as he can. And Allāh (ﷻ) is generous, so be generous to help yourself. All of the sacrifices will go to those who are suffering greatly all over the world.

Come all beloveds who would like to take the sacrifice. This is important. Come here. Anyone who can, come to see Dr. Wadude and I read it. I will read it in Arabic and he read it in English.

They teach the healing method and then Sidi gives the promise.

The True Meaning of Hajj

The Life of the Prophet Ibrāhīm (عليه السلام) and "The True Beginning of Healing" from *Secret of the Spirit*

Sunday, October 17, 2010 AM, Florida

لا إله إلا الله - لا إله إلا الله - لا إله إلا الله - محمد رسول الله عليه صلاة الله
لا إله إلا الله - لا إله إلا الله - لا إله إلا الله - ابراهيم رسول الله عليه صلاة الله
لا إله إلا الله - لا إله إلا الله - لا إله إلا الله - موسى رسول الله عليه صلاة الله
لا إله إلا الله - لا إله إلا الله - لا إله إلا الله - عيسى رسول الله عليه صلاة الله
اللهم انت السلام ومنك السلام و إليك يعود السلام
تباركت ربنا وتعاليت يا ذوالجلال والإكرام

Peace be upon all the messengers and all of the prophets (عليهم السلام). Peace upon all the beloveds and all the followers of Allāh (ﷻ). I am asking Allāh (ﷻ) for all of you to be stable and firm on this path and to love all the prophets (عليهم السلام). I am asking Him to provide you with love and mercy for the whole world, your families, your sons and your daughters. It is my great pleasure to be among you.

This is the last day with you. I will not leave you. My spirit is with you. My supplications are always for you. I can feel all of the people who are suffering and who need prayers. I am asking Allāh (ﷻ) to send happiness to everyone. I direct my face to Allāh (ﷻ), asking Him to protect our world from the hurricanes, volcanoes and disasters. This is a great year with many events in the world. We are asking Allāh (ﷻ) to protect all people, all children and to heal the sick. He is the Healer, the Knower.

We talked yesterday about the journey of Sayyidinā ʿĪsā (our Master Jesus) (عليه السلام). Today we will talk about the father of all the prophets (عليهم السلام), Sayyidinā Ibrāhīm (Abraham) (عليه السلام). He was also a father to his sons, Isḥāq (Isaac) and Ismāʿīl (Ishmael). He is the friend of Allāh (ﷻ), the khalīlu-llāh, the friend of Allāh (ﷻ) who carried the message of unity. He suffered a lot.

Sayyidinā Ibrāhīm (عليه السلام) was born in Ur, Iraq close to (Badin) Babel. When this noble prophet was twelve years old, his father would take him to his workshop. His father was a carpenter. The king at that time was named Nimrūd. He was a bad king who treated people like slaves without any mercy. Sayyidinā Ibrāhīm (ﷺ) was thinking a lot about who provided for him and who gave him life. Could those idols do this? In the Qur'ān Allāh (ﷻ) tells us:

> When he (Ibrāhīm) saw the moon rising up, he said,
> "This is my Lord."
> But when it set, he said, "Unless my Lord guides me,
> I will surely be among the people who went astray."
>
> When he saw the sun rising up, he said,
> "This is my Lord. This is greater."
> But when it set, he said, "Oh my people!
> I am indeed free from all that you join as partners." (6:76-78)

Allāh (ﷻ), my Lord, is alive forever and never disappears. He is greater than any other thing you can imagine. After that he started to think that Allāh (ﷻ) was not like the human being because He created everything— the heavens, the skies, the animals and humankind—so how could He disappear? He said, "My Lord, guide me to the right way." Sayyidinā Jībrīl (Gabriel) (ﷺ) came down to him and told him, "Allāh (ﷻ) keeps within you the true words of Allāh (ﷻ) who created the skies and the heavens."

Ibrāhīm's father told him (ﷺ) to take the idols he made and to try to sell them. He took the stones and idols and started to call to the people, "Who can buy something that will not do anything to them? They will not give you any benefit and they will not even harm you." So no one bought anything from him.

He told his father that the people would not buy a god that would never help them or even cause harm to them. His father was angry with him and told him, "You stopped our provision, how can I offer you food? You are not a good son." He talked badly about him and told him he was a disobedient son. Ibrāhīm (ﷺ) told his father, "No I cannot do that." He was very polite. He asked his father, "How can you worship something that cannot give you anything or cannot help you? This is an error, a mistake, an illusion. No one with an intellect can accept this."

His father was angry with him and told him to get out of his place. Ibrāhīm (عليه السلام) told him that our creator is Allāh (ﷻ). The people heard about this story. Ibrāhīm (عليه السلام) was thinking about how he could help those people. He was brave and bold. He wanted to make a change. He was a strong young man.

One day his king, Nimrūd, entered the place and worshipped the idols. Ibrāhīm (عليه السلام) was very intelligent and after they left, he took the axe and began ruining the idols. He left the big idol and hung the axe on its neck. In the early morning they went to pray and saw that their Gods were ruined. Who did that? They heard that it was Ibrāhīm (عليه السلام) who did it.

Nimrūd sent his soldiers to get Ibrāhīm (عليه السلام). They asked Ibrāhīm (عليه السلام) who did it. He pointed to the biggest idol with the axe and said, "This one, the great one. The god with the axe around his neck did it. Look at him." Nimrūd and the soldiers said to Ibrāhīm (عليه السلام), "How can we talk to the idol? He cannot talk." Ibrāhīm (عليه السلام) asked, "Then how can you worship him? This god cannot defend himself. What kind of god is this?"

God (ﷻ) is strong, God (ﷻ) is great, God (ﷻ) is the Creator. This is the issue of Sayyidinā Ibrāhīm (عليه السلام) and all of the prophets (عليهم السلام). In spite of Nimrūd, Ibrāhīm (عليه السلام) was strong. He knew that Nimrūd could kill him but Ibrāhīm (عليه السلام) did everything for the face of Allāh (ﷻ). Sayyidinā Ibrāhīm (عليه السلام) lived to be 175 years old.

We return back to our story. They asked him, "What should we do to Ibrāhīm (عليه السلام) who destroyed our Gods?" The devil, Iblīs, came looking like a man to the horrible king Nimrūd and said, "I will tell you what to do with Ibrāhīm (عليه السلام). Gather a lot of wood, light the wood and put him in the fire." This was the judgment of Iblīs.

Here was the miracle and the greatness of Allāh (ﷻ). Here you can see the nobility and how Sayyidinā Ibrāhīm (عليه السلام) was great. This is faith. The son of the truth will never be frightened. They do not fear anyone except Allāh (ﷻ). They believe Allāh (ﷻ) will defend them. The corruptors are weak. An insect, an ant is stronger than the corruptors, the criminals and the oppressors.

All the prophets (ﷺ) pay their selves, their souls and their hearts as a sacrifice for Allāh (ﷻ). This is the mercy of Allāh (ﷻ). They are strong and brave. This station, the son of the truth, does not fear anyone except Allāh (ﷻ). They are sure that Allāh (ﷻ) will send His victory to them. They are the winners and the corruptors are the losers.

The prophets are the link to Allāh (ﷻ). Allāh (ﷻ) has everything. He has soldiers of this earth and of the heavens. The soldiers of the heavens are the angels (ﷺ) and the soldiers from the earth are the good doers. Sayyidinā Ibrāhīm (ﷺ) is the perfect pattern, the example for all of us in order to teach us.

Allāh (ﷻ) does not accept the weak. You should keep your religion and protect the poor and needy people; then they will never fear kings, criminals and corruptors. What did Allāh (ﷻ) do to Hitler? He was great but Allāh (ﷻ) took him. Allāh (ﷻ) will send His angels (ﷺ) for all those corruptors who do not follow the order of Allāh (ﷻ). Allāh (ﷻ) will destroy all of them sooner or later. Everything will have its time.

They gathered a mountain of wood and they brought Sayyidinā Ibrāhīm (ﷺ) there. This is an example and a lesson for all people. He never feels frightened. They put him in a catapult and threw him into the fire. Look at how great Sayyidinā Ibrāhīm (ﷺ) was. When they put him in the catapult, Ibrāhīm (ﷺ) began to smile and ask them why they put him here. He said, "Do you think Allāh (ﷻ) will leave me by myself?" They asked him, "Who is your Lord, your Allāh (ﷻ)?" He told them, "He is my creator. He will defend me and you will see by your eyes what Allāh (ﷻ) will do for me."

Then they threw him and he was between the sky and the earth. Look at the son of the truth—Sayyidinā Jībrīl talked to him and asked him, "Ibrāhīm (ﷺ), do you need anything? Do you need any help? Ibrāhīm answered, "I do not need anything from you because Allāh (ﷻ) knows my situation. Allāh (ﷻ) does not need me to ask anyone except Him." Ibrāhīm (ﷺ) was brave and bold. He is the father of all the prophets (ﷺ). He is khalīlu-llāh (ﷻ), the close friend of Allāh (ﷻ).

Ibrāhīm (⌖) went into the fire but Allāh (⌖) ordered the fire to be cool and peaceful for Ibrāhīm (⌖). Before his body touched the fire, the wood changed into trees and green plants. There were different and beautiful trees, some fruitless and others with fruit like apples. Ibrāhīm (⌖) was in a paradise full of flowers, watching the birds singing with happiness that Allāh (⌖) saved Sayyidinā Ibrāhīm (⌖). This is Sayyidinā Ibrāhīm (⌖), al-khalil (the friend of Allāh). Many people believed in Ibrāhīm (⌖) and his message and in the message of Sāra and Lūṭ (Lot) in Iraq and Palestine.

Then Nimrūd was sent a trial. It was his first punishment and it was a hard punishment. Allāh (⌖) wanted to prove to all people that Ibrāhīm (⌖) was not coming from himself, that he was carrying the message of Allāh (⌖). Nimrūd started to have a lot of pain and he started crying out and screaming, "Where is the physician?" The physicians told Nimrūd, "No one can heal you except Ibrāhīm (⌖)."

One of Nimrūd's guards came to Ibrāhīm (⌖) and explained that Nimrūd was suffering and could not sleep. Ibrāhīm (⌖) said that he would help him. He called one of his followers, a poor man, full of faith, whose name was Rafed. Ibrāhīm (⌖) told him to take his shoes and hit Nimrūd on the head. The poor man said, "How can I do that?" Ibrāhīm (⌖) said, "Allāh (⌖) will be with you. Go." Through this Allāh (⌖) will let you see a picture of how He can belittle the corruptors.

Sayyidinā Ibrāhīm (⌖) was the messenger of Allāh (⌖) and he spoke the truth. Therefore, the poor man took his shoes and said to Nimrūd, "Your medicine is here." This is the wisdom of Allāh (⌖). Allāh (⌖) will make the poor and weak people strong, brave and bold by His permission. He told Nimrūd, "This is the physician." He was very poor.

All of the people gathered to see the healing. They came to see how he would heal Nimrūd. He said to take away Nimrūd's throne full of gold, jewels and diamonds and throw it to the earth. Nimrūd took it all and threw it to the ground. Then the poor man took his shoes out and put them next to the throne of the king. Look at this picture. This is a poor, honest believer. He began to hit Nimrūd. After the second time, Nimrūd began to feel pain in his head. Sayyidinā Ibrāhīm (⌖) told the poor man to sit down when he was finished hitting him.

After one half hour Nimrūd started to scream out that he had severe pain. What was the matter? It was an insect that had entered through his nose, crawled into his brain and started to eat it. Nimrūd started to scream. This is the miracle. It is a very small insect. Allāh (ﷻ) judged Nimrūd. There are many killing insects that you can see with your eyes.

Welcome to all the corruptors and others who do not follow Allāh's orders. I am asking Allāh (ﷻ) to keep you and to guard you and to let you to be honest with Allāh (ﷻ), the God (ﷻ) of all the prophets and messengers (عليهم السلام). This insect killed him. He was dead now and their custom was to put him into the earth, into dust.

After this, Sayyidinā Ibrāhīm (عليه السلام) went to Palestine, the Holy Land. It is the throne of Allāh (ﷻ). It is the first Qibla, the direction toward which the Prophet Muḥammad (ﷺ) and all of us were told to pray. Ibrāhīm (عليه السلام) traveled from Ur, the land of Padanine in Iraq to Canaan, the Holy Land, to Ur-Salām (Jerusalem), the land of peace.

No one can change Jerusalem. It will be the land of peace, despite everything. It is peaceful for everyone without discrimination. In a ḥadīth qudsī Allāh (ﷻ) said:

> Yā Quds (Oh Jerusalem).
> You are honored by My light and you are My heaven.
> You are the land of gathering and suffering.
> In the Hereafter it will be as if you were a bride to your groom.
> Whoever caused you pain will receive My anger and punishment.

Sayyidinā Ibrāhīm (عليه السلام) had two sons. He had his first son, Ismā'īl (عليه السلام), when he was 86 years old and he had his second son, Isḥāq (Isaac) (عليه السلام), when he was 100 years old. Sayyidinā Ismā'īl (عليه السلام) was a prophet and his mother, Hajjar (عليها السلام), was the daughter of the king from Habasha. When Sayyidinā Ibrāhīm (عليه السلام) and Sāra (عليها السلام), his first wife, traveled to Egypt, Pharaoh gave Hajjar (عليها السلام) as a gift to serve Sāra (عليها السلام). Sayyidinā Ibrāhīm (عليه السلام) and Sāra (عليها السلام) did not have a son at the time. He asked Allāh (ﷻ) for a son, and so he married Hajjar (عليها السلام) and they had a son, Ismā'īl (عليه السلام). However, Sāra (عليها السلام) felt jealous and she asked Allāh (ﷻ) for a son. This is human nature. She loved her husband. How can another women come and share her husband? It was a normal thing to feel this way. Could you bear to see your husband with other women?

Sayyidinā Ibrāhīm (﵇) sent supplications to Allāh (ﷻ) to send Sāra (﵈) a son. She had her son when Sayyidinā Ibrāhīm (﵇) was 100 years old. It is a miracle of Allāh (ﷻ). She had Sayyidinā Isḥāq (﵇) and after Sayyidinā Isḥāq (﵇) came Yaʿqūb (Jacob) (﵇). Yaʿqūb (﵇) had eleven sons and one of them was Sayyidinā Yūsuf (Joseph) (﵇). All of them were holy and noble.

There was a problem with jealousy between Sāra (﵈) and Hajjar (﵈). By the order of Allāh (ﷻ), Sayyidinā Ibrāhīm (﵇) took Hajjar (﵈) and his son Ismāʿīl (﵇) on al-Ḥijra (emigration). Why? The first house of Allāh (ﷻ) had been built in Mecca: the Kaʿba. Who built the Kaʿba? The first person to build it was Ādam (﵇) with the help of the angels (﵊). Allāh (ﷻ) says in the Qurʾān:

> And (remember) when Ibrahim and Ismāʿīl
> were raising the foundations of the House (the Kaʿba), saying,
> "Our Lord! Accept (this) from us.
> Truly! You are the All-Hearer, the All-Knower." (2:127)

Hajjar (﵈) and Ismāʿīl (﵇), who was an infant, were in this place with no food or water, but Ibrāhīm (﵇) knew that Allāh (ﷻ) would be with them. Hajjar (﵈) began to walk back and forth looking for water. The baby began hitting the earth and the water came out from under his feet. This was another miracle. Hajjar (﵈) saw the water and she started to drink it. The Bedouin people asked her if they could have some water. She (﵈) said, "This is the water of Allāh (ﷻ)."

Later Sayyidinā Ibrāhīm (﵇) returned to them. He knew that they would be fine and that Allāh (ﷻ) would take care of them. This was the order of Allāh (ﷻ). Allāh (ﷻ) had prepared something. There is an āyah in the Qurʾān describing the beautiful picture of how Sayyidinā Ibrāhīm (﵇) had strong faith and that he told Allāh (ﷻ) about leaving his wife and his son in this desert where there was no water or plants. There was nothing. He prayed, "Please Allāh (ﷻ), let the people love them and let the House be close to them." The Ḥajj (pilgrimage) started here.

At this moment you can still find the water that appeared for Hajjar (☻) and Ismā'īl (☻), this miracle, and drink from it. The name of this water is Zamzam. If you drink this water with the intention for Allāh (☻) to heal you, Allāh (☻) will heal you. This water of Zamzam is different than any other water on this earth. Geologists and scientists have tested it and taken samples of it and they found out that it contains more than twenty elements and that it is different than any other water on earth. The scientists made their reports and now you can find the water of Zamzam everywhere. This is a divine issue. Now I will ask my son to read to you.

The reading, "The True Beginning of Healing" from *Secret of the Spirit*[28] is read from the beginning.

"Who is Ibrāhīm (☻)? Ibrāhīm (☻) is the father of all the prophets. He is the father of all the prophets and Allāh (☻) once inspired him in his sleep. Ibrāhīm (☻) explained to his son that he saw a vision in which he was slaughtering him. He did not see him in a dream or vision, but it was a true state of seeing. He said, 'I see that I am slaughtering you,' but it did not mean slaughtering in the way that people think. It had a deep meaning. It had a very deep meaning, which meant, 'I am slaughtering all of the animal qualities within myself. I am slaughtering the physical diseases; I am slaughtering the psychological diseases and all the selfish and non-godly qualities.'

> And, when he (Ismā'īl ☻) was old enough to walk with him,
> he (Ibrāhīm ☻) said, 'Oh my son! I have seen in a dream
> that I am slaughtering you (offering you in sacrifice to Allāh),
> so look what you think!' (37:102)"

When Sayyidinā Ibrāhīm (☻) said, "I saw in my dream," it was not a dream. For a prophet (☻) it was real, not an illusion, because he was seeing by the light of Allāh (☻). Allāh (☻) let him see beyond what normal people see, for he was a prophet and messenger. He was a noble one. He saw by His eyes and he heard by His ears this divine order. He said, "I have seen." He did not say, "I had a dream" but he said, "I see with my eyes that I am slaughtering you." His son Ismā'īl (☻) told him, "Please, my father, do what Allāh (☻) has commanded you to do. This is a divine order."

---

[28] *Secret of the Spirit*, pp. 419-435.

The reading continues:

> "He (Ismāʿīl ﷺ) said, 'Oh my father! Do that which you are commanded, inshāʾa-llāh (if Allāh wills),
> you will find me to be one of the patient ones.'

The child of Ibrāhīm (ﷺ) was also a prophet. He was around nine years old and he said to his father Ibrāhīm (ﷺ), 'Oh my father, do as you were commanded,' because he understood that what Ibrāhīm (ﷺ) was telling him was, 'I want to purify you.' So he said, 'Purify me; do as you were commanded,' because he believed that the one who commanded his father was Allāh (ﷻ). Because the prophet's vision is a godly vision, it is direct knowledge from Allāh (ﷻ). He knows that Ibrāhīm (ﷺ) was his father, biologically speaking, but he was Ibrāhīm's very soul when we talk from the spiritual perspective.

When Ibrāhīm (ﷺ) took his son to the mountain of Arafat...this mountain is where Muslims go for pilgrimage and there is a belief that all of the prophets (ﷺ) went to this mountain. Mūsā (Moses) (ﷺ) went to this mountain and all other prophets (ﷺ) went there, as well. It is not as some ignorant Muslims and other ignorant people understand it. I also visited that mountain for seven years and I saw divine visions in it, scenes in it, in a true way of seeing.

Going back to our story, Ibrāhīm (ﷺ) took his son and put him on the altar and took the knife in his hand. People thought that he was truly going to kill his son, but who could ever kill his son? What happened to the sharp knife at this point? It became water. It was moving as water moves. It was a purification operation, it was not a true killing. He kept trying to use the knife, but it turned to water. When the knife turned to water, it could not really slaughter his son.

Ibrāhīm's name (ﷺ) has two syllables. Ib-rāhīm. It means to become the merciful father, which means to become absent from everything except Allāh. It means to be absent from your animal self and to get in touch with your divine essence. The divine essence is far from the animal essence; it is the godly essence. In this instance Ibrāhīm's hand (ﷺ) was a divine hand. His hearing, his seeing, all of his senses were luminous. He was full of light. All of his senses were full of light and he was a

luminous being. Ismāʿīl (ﷺ), his son, was also full of luminous light. Can a knife really slaughter light? It cannot go through light and hurt it. So they became light, and that is why the knife couldn't slaughter him.

Do you truly want to be like that, to be an Ibrāhīmic being or an Isḥāq-like being or an Ismāʿīl-like being? Do you want to be like those beings, to be one with them? So, do what Ismāʿīl (ﷺ) did. He said, 'My father, I surrender fully to you. Do as you are commanded by Allāh (ﷻ).' Therefore he surrendered to all of the commands of Allāh (ﷻ)."

The meaning of this sacrifice was as one of the gnostics says: there are special people, special places and special times for Allāh (ﷻ). Allāh (ﷻ) guided Ibrāhīm (ﷺ) who was a special person. A special place was Mecca because it was the first place to worship Allāh (ﷻ). The angels (ﷺ) felt this place. The special time was the time Allāh (ﷻ) stated to do your pilgrimage, and Sayyidinā Ibrāhīm (ﷺ) was the first one to establish the pilgrimage. All the prophets (ﷺ) made pilgrimage. Allāh (ﷻ) ordered the people to make Ḥajj (pilgrimage) at a special time. This is an exact time which is 10 Ḥijja. No one can change it. Allāh (ﷻ) fixed this date. Therefore, for Allāh (ﷻ) there are special people, special places and special times.

When you go on Ḥajj, Allāh (ﷻ) will remove all of your sins. This is a new birth for you. You will feel the jalāl (majesty) of Allāh (ﷻ). Everyone puts on white clothes, the clothes of death, to gain admittance and announce that, "We are Your servants." All people are the same. No one is better than any other. No one can say, "I am king." Men and women are all together and are the same. There is no difference between them. You will see all people in the same clothes, the clothes of death, the white clothes.

Who will gather the people? The voice of Sayyidinā Ibrāhīm (ﷺ). If you could see the Ibrāhīmic view over there...it is unbelievable. Your heart will be absent when you see the view of Sayyidinā Ibrāhīm (ﷺ) calling the people to come. The gnostic does not think of anything except Allāh (ﷻ) and they call, "Yā Allāh (ﷻ)." There are no other words except Yā Allāh (ﷻ) and fear and jalāl. Hearts will be humble and with Allāh (ﷻ), never looking right or left, so that Allāh (ﷻ) will send His mercy.

As I mentioned, there are special places and special times. This is the will of Allāh (ﷻ). When the divine order was sent down to Sayyidinā Ibrāhīm (عليه السلام), he told Ismāʿīl (عليه السلام), "I am seeing in my dream that I am slaughtering you." Yawm al-Arafat is the slaughtering day, the pilgrimage day. What is the wisdom in this? They will not arrive to Allāh (ﷻ) unless they are absent from this existence, not of this place or of this time. Allāh says, "If you really want Me and you are honest, then come to Me as I wish and you can fulfill this wish by obeying My orders. Do not disobey Me."

The son is very appreciative to his parents. Allāh told Ibrāhīm (عليه السلام) to kill his son. It meant: give the dearest thing to you for the face of Allāh (ﷻ). In giving a sacrifice Allāh (ﷻ) does not want you to kill your son. He wants you to give Him the dearest things to your heart.

Allāh (ﷻ) is the Rich. Allāh (ﷻ) wants you to walk from the world of al-fanāʾ, annihilation into God, to the world of al-baqāʾ, subsistence in God, and to be with Allāh (ﷻ) and nothing else. Behave yourself and carry the qualities of Allāh (ﷻ). Do not be attached to this dunyā. Be straight and be honest and do not lie. Do not kill. You should walk and obey Allāh (ﷻ) in your eyes, in your intellect, in your heart and in your spirit. This is the meaning of the pilgrimage, the Ḥajj. Leave everything behind and remember Allāh (ﷻ).

You must give a sacrifice. What is a sacrifice? It is to slaughter a sheep, which means to behave well in your self, your heart and your soul. Come humbly toward Allāh (ﷻ) and carry the message of Sayyidinā Ibrāhīm (عليه السلام) and the message of peace and mercy. Do not cause any pain to anyone. Then you will establish your pilgrimage.

If you go on Ḥajj 100 times, Allāh (ﷻ) will not accept any of them if you cause pain to others upon your return. Allāh (ﷻ) will not accept your offering. Allāh (ﷻ) will not accept it. Purify yourself from all your sins and give your heart a sacrifice, your soul a sacrifice and your body a sacrifice. Giving a sacrifice is like saying to Allāh, "You created me and I will use all of Your provision to obey You and to obtain Your love so that You will accept me and be satisfied with me." If a person goes to Mecca and comes back to act like a devil, this is not Ḥajj. If a person starts to steal and kill, then this person is worse than the devil.

Promise Allāh (ﷻ) that you are His servant and obey Allāh (ﷻ) and give everything as a sacrifice to Allāh (ﷻ). Come here, my beloveds. The coming days are the time of the pilgrimage and the ones who can do it can pay a sacrifice to protect your families. When Sayyidinā Ibrāhīm (ؑ), intended to slaughter his son and Allāh (ﷻ) prevented it, the Angel Jībrīl (ؑ) came down with a sheep as a sacrifice and told Ibrāhīm (ؑ) to give the meat to all of the poor people. This is the meaning of the sacrifice, to protect and guard you and your families and your fathers.

This sacrifice exists in Islām, Judaism and Christianity. Ibrāhīm (ؑ) is the prophet of all those religions and all of us believe in him. You will be holy and noble if you follow these holy and noble prophets (ؑ). This is the reality of unity. Allāh (ﷻ) says:

> Truly! This, your religion (or nation) is one religion (or nation), and I am your Lord; therefore, worship Me. (21:92)

We are the son of Sufism. This is the faith of all the prophets (ؑ). If anyone wants to pay a sacrifice at the special time of Sayyidinā Ibrāhīm (ؑ), it is a great thing. Anyone who wants to slaughter a sheep and pay a sacrifice, we can do this in the Holy Land and feed the poor and needy people. This is sunna until the Last Day, and no one can remove this sunna. It is in Islām, Judaism and Christianity. It is for poor people and you can feed your family from your sacrifice, also.

The reading continues, "Do as you were commanded by Allāh. Ismā'īl (ؑ) surrendered to all the commands of Allāh (ﷻ), but he did not surrender to Ibrāhīm (ؑ) as a human being, no. He surrendered to the divine essence, to Allāh (ﷻ) as reflected in Ibrāhīm. He surrendered to the divine image, to the divine reflection that was coming through Ibrāhīm (ؑ).

Ismā'īl (ؑ) said, 'Father, do as you were commanded.' Ibrāhīm (ؑ) tried seven times, but the knife would not slaughter Ismā'īl (ؑ). Then Allāh (ﷻ) sent something to ransom him and to purify him. He sent blood that would purify him. Allāh (ﷻ) sent down Archangel Jībrīl (ؑ) and Jībrīl said: 'Oh Ibrāhīm, you were truthful and you believed in the vision. You were doing what we asked, and We will ransom your son with a great sacrifice.' Allāh (ﷻ) made this sacrifice as a way of purifying him.

> Then, when they had both submitted themselves,
> and he had laid him prostrate on his forehead,
> And We called out to him: 'Oh Ibrāhīm!
> You have fulfilled the dream (vision)!'
> Truly! In this way We reward the good-doers.
> Truly, that was a manifest trial
> And We ransomed him with a great sacrifice;
> And We left for him (a good teaching)
> among generations in later times. (37:103 – 37:108)

So this great lamb came from the heavenly Garden as a sacrifice to purify the human being. This great sacrifice is equivalent to all of the animals, all of the birds and all of the human beings. This way of purifying oneself became the accepted way, from that time until today, until eternity. It became the way of purification that we must follow. But it is not as people understand; it is not to just slaughter an animal and eat it. It is a way of granting sacrifice and purification.

The Angel Jībrīl (عليه السلام) said to Ibrāhīm, 'You believed in the divine vision and so We will ransom you. We will save you and your son; we will purify you.' That is why anyone who wants to walk this path must also offer a sacrifice on behalf of his physical being, his heart, his soul and his spirit. This is the first step to walking the path of purification, the path toward Allāh, in the way of the people of Allāh, the people who walk in the way of purity. We have to offer a sacrifice to purify ourselves."

We have to offer a sacrifice to purify ourselves. The door is open if you want to pay a sacrifice. This is the sunna of Sayyidinā Ibrāhīm (عليه السلام), Sayyidinā Mūsā (عليه السلام) and Sayyidinā Muḥammad (ﷺ). You can write your name on a piece of paper. When we slaughter the sheep, we will ask Allāh (ﷻ) to accept the name of the person and family making the sacrifice. I will sacrifice it with my own hands, inshā'a-llāh. Give what you can. The cheapest sheep in Jerusalem is $130.

The Healing for Many Diseases

Cupping, Lyme Disease, Cancer, Citron

Wednesday, October 20, 2010 AM, USHS Year 2

لا إله إلا الله - لا إله إلا الله - لا إله إلا الله - محمد رسول الله عليه صلاة الله
لا إله إلا الله - لا إله إلا الله - لا إله إلا الله - ابراهيم رسول الله عليه صلاة الله
لا إله إلا الله - لا إله إلا الله - لا إله إلا الله - موسى رسول الله عليه صلاة الله
لا إله إلا الله - لا إله إلا الله - لا إله إلا الله - عيسى رسول الله عليه صلاة الله
اللهم انت السلام ومنك السلام و إليك يعود السلام
تباركت ربنا وتعاليت يا ذوالجلال والإكرام

Peace upon all the messengers,
Peace upon all the Beloved of Allāh (ﷻ),
Peace upon the followers, the gnostics, the Knowers who know Allāh (ﷻ),
Peace on all those who carry the message of unity,
Peace on all those who heal the bodies and the selves.

It is my great honor to be among all of you, my beloveds, and the poor slaves. Allāh (ﷻ) uses me to serve you and to serve all honest people; all people who will carry the message of unity, the message of mercy and love and justice. I wish you all the best in your path and to be among the honest worshippers.

I will start my lecture this morning and I'll give you the ways to heal certain diseases and sicknesses. You can make notes and I have also prepared details about certain diseases for you. Halima, can you distribute the notes?

I would discuss a disease that has been spread in America—Lyme disease. We have been working on a treatment for Lyme disease through many experiments, and the last one we did in Florida 3 days ago.

Two days ago Dr. Wadude healed one of our beloveds who was suffering and couldn't walk. He had a lot of pain and he came to me. I referred to my beloved son, Wadude, and I love him so much because he is honest and he serves humanity. Wadude did the healing for him under my supervision.

Doctors don't know the exact treatment for this disease. This is a dangerous situation. It is not an easy disease. The healing is not from me. It is from a ḥadīth. When Sayyidinā (our Master) Muḥammad was on his Night Journey, Sayyidinā Jībrīl (Gabriel) (ﷺ) told him:

> Tell your people. And advise them to do cupping.

In Arabic, cupping is known as ḥijāma. Sayyidinā Jībrīl (ﷺ) told Sayyidinā Muḥammad (ﷺ) that cupping will heal most diseases. The Prophet (ﷺ) used to do it twice a year and he was healed through it. He gives details about the dates and the months.

The body has arteries and veins that carry blood. If blood becomes black it means that the body carries a certain disease. Lyme disease is caused by deer ticks that carry 2 or more kinds of bacteria. If a tick with these bad bacteria attaches itself to a person, the bacteria start to reproduce in the blood and cause a lot of pain.

Dr. Abdullah is a physician, a specialist, in Portland, Praise Allāh (ﷻ), many years ago I healed him of a certain sickness. Dr. Abdullah diagnosed the disease in this beloved and Dr. Wadude did the cupping. How should we do cupping if someone contracts Lyme disease?

Cupping Technique for Lyme Disease

Cup spots in the back and both legs. After the cupping, you have to use an Arabic plaster. The ingredients of this plaster are the following:

4 big spoons of olive soap
4 big tablespoons of flour
5 eggs whites

1. Mix these ingredients together.
2. Get a thin cloth and place the mixture on it.
3. Cover it and put his thin cloth on the upper back up to the bottom of your neck.

Dr. Wadude knows the locations to cup. There are certain places and you are students who came here to obtain divine knowledge, help others, and heal others. I am preparing you to be specialists in this field. This is a divine healing. Congratulations to all of you. You are lovers. You love Allāh (ﷻ) and Rasūlu-llāh (ﷺ), and you love all of humanity.

I am so sorry, because I encouraged many of our beloveds to join this university. I don't know the unseen, but I can confirm by Allāh's knowledge that this university will be the best one in the U.S. I'm here to spread the message of love and freedom to all people and to teach you healing, and this university carries the same message. The University carries the same aim, the same goal, of teaching you divine healing.

This healing is perfect for Lyme disease and I want to tell you that it's also a perfect healing for other diseases, like the dangerous disease of cancer. For this illness Wadude did cupping on one of our beloveds.

She is feeling much better now, ma shā'a-llāh. She carried cancer in her back. You know about that? I remember everything.

Some people say I am getting old, but I am not. My grandfather lived to be 113 years old and our family lives for a long time. What is the secret? I will tell you the secret after a while. I will not hide anything from you. I love you. But I will tell you what Allāh (ﷻ) taught me. I don't know the unseen, but I believe in Allāh (ﷻ) and the knowledge we received through the prophets (ﷺ). I will never live in illusion.

Back to cancer. So you know about cancer, and the details of how cancer happens. It is from eating processed foods filled with chemicals, non-organic foods, and drinking water that is not clean, that is full of pollution. Try to obtain clean water like the original, pure rainwater from Allāh, the way it was before the human being destroyed the environment, used chemicals and caused pollution.

People will get diseases because of these substances. The human being started to purify water with filters and other treatments. I'm telling you: don't drink water if you are not sure if it is pure and clean. In the time of our grandfathers, our families used to drink clean water; they used wells and saved rainwater. There were no chemicals polluting the water at that time, so they would drink the water in their wells and save rainwater. It was safe because the earth was clean.

Cancer came because of these chemicals, and blood can become polluted by them. If blood becomes polluted, the body will not be able to defend itself and the person's flesh will be not healthy. If you have a piece of meat and leave it outside, what will happen to it? You will smell a bad fragrance, a bad smell. If someone has a piece of a body with cancer and puts it next to a piece of meat that was brought outside, you can't perceive a difference between them. Both of them are polluted.

I'm not telling you illusion. The flesh you put outside that becomes polluted and the flesh of a human being with cancer have the same fragrance. How can we treat this dangerous disease?

My beloved, I'm telling you, our Prophet (ﷺ) is healing us. How? Sayyidinā Muḥammad (ﷺ) says:

> The worst vessel to fill is one's stomach.

Why? The stomach is the house, the place of disease. Guard yourselves from certain foods to avoid this problem. Don't put those things in your stomach. If you follow this wisdom, you will guard and protect yourself from many diseases.

The stomach is a divine tool. The stomach will digest non-organic food, bread or meat, which will put it into your blood. Then your blood will be polluted by the polluted food.

When a baby comes to this life he is pure, but if his mother eats unhealthy food, she will send these diseases to her baby. My grandfather taught me not to eat anything except healthy, clean foods from the earth; vegetables, fruits and meats. Healthy ones, not ones injected with hormones or raised with other unhealthy practices as they do now. Because they use hormones and chemicals to raise chickens and sheep. don't eat eggs from chickens that feed on non-organic food. That will cause disease. We should eat the way all the prophets and messengers (عليهم السلام) taught us. They would not eat anything unhealthy.

We are discussing how cancer appears and starts to attack people. Poor food is, as I told you, one of the reasons of cancer. It is a very important reason. The most difficult situation is that people cannot diagnose it after a certain period of time. You eat the food with your mouth, your mouth starts to touch the food, your stomach processes it and puts what was in the food into your blood, which will then move all over your body.

Some people don't have the ability to resist those symptoms, so the disease will move through his hands, through his back and different parts of this body. The Prophet (ﷺ) told us this through knowledge he received through Sayyidinā Jībrīl (عليه السلام).

So to get rid of this polluted, bad, blood you can use cupping. The cupping will take only the bad blood, the polluted blood, from your body. From the time I was a child up until this moment I receive cupping twice a year.

I did not hear about this disease during the lives of my father and grandfather, and they lived for long periods of time, for more than one hundred years, because they were following the orders of Allāh (ﷻ). They were following the divine knowledge through all the prophets (عليهم السلام).

So as I mentioned, al-ḥijāma, cupping, will keep your body clean and healthy. If black blood and clots of blood stay in the body, they will cause many different kinds of disease. Cupping is the healing for many different diseases because it will remove the bad, unhealthy blood from your body.

We are not talking without the knowledge gained by experimentation. This is from the knowledge gained by many experiments. My wife couldn't walk. I did ḥijāma on her and it helped her, and so this is healing. This method of healing will help you to fully recover, with the permission of Allāh (ﷻ).

Sayyidinā Muḥammad (ﷺ) also told us:

> We are people who will not eat until we are hungry.
> When we eat, we do not fill ourselves to the brim.
> We fill one-third of our stomach with food,
> we fill the second third with water
> and we leave the third part for air.

Allāh (ﷻ) gave us the intellect and Allāh (ﷻ) ordered us to use our intellects. Only those who use their intellects know what I mean by using the intellect.

Where is water, what is water? Water helps you to digest food and air helps you to get the life, the breath. You should understand these principle things about this natural, divine knowledge, and you should teach others about them. Teach your students in the future about them. Allāh (ﷻ) created you from clay and He created your provision from clay, including trees, fruits and vegetables. Chose your food wisely.

Sayyidinā Muḥammad (ﷺ), as Sidi mentioned before, said the stomach is the place of disease. You will put the disease in your stomach because if you eat unhealthy food, unhealthy fruit and unhealthy water. If you put all of those unhealthy things in your stomach, it will become the place, the home of the disease.

So many difficulties will happen to the stomach if you use different kinds of spices, hot spices in your food. People use spices like crazy. You can sprinkle a small amount of spice but don't use too much, because that will cause many difficulties to the stomach wall, which will affect all of the other parts of your body. Even too much salt and pepper and other kinds of spices can hurt you if eaten in excess. See what happens if you put hot pepper on your hand. Can you imagine what will happen to your stomach? The walls of the stomach are thin and sensitive.

If you use too much salt it can hurt you. Be sure to use the salt you get from sea, the right one, the raw one, the natural one. It is natural and Allāh (ﷻ) put every mineral in salt in exact, precise amounts. That is enough for you. Don't use other kinds of salt. If you want to use spices, sprinkle only very little on your food. Maybe it will be more delicious with excess spices, but the side effects are horrible.

Use everything with wisdom, because everything will affect your stomach and the other parts of your body. Many people are suffering from their stomachs and Sayyidinā Muḥammad (ﷺ) said:

> Avoid 2 white things: salt and sugar.

You should use them in very limited amounts. If you have an alternative thing, you can use it; for example, you can use rocky salt.

We will talk about other diseases. There have been many experiments and it is wonderful. Maybe among you there are people who have received healing from AIDS or syphilis.

Treatment for AIDS and Syphilis

1. First of all, obtain some orange, lemon, grapefruit and citron.

2. Put them in blender with their rinds and don't peal them. Put every part of the fruit in there, even their seeds.

3. Blend them all together and then take two big tablespoons three times per day before meals.

You can check yourself, and you can go to the lab and you will find the results. If you continue this healing, everything will be fine. There will be no cancer, no syphilis anymore, inshā'a-llāh.

Why does this sickness come? Because most of us do not face Allāh (ﷻ).

Excuse me, I say this because I care about my beloveds everywhere. I care for the human being. When a woman marries a woman and a man marries a man, what happens? From these things, sickness comes. Allāh (ﷻ) forbids it in every religion: Christianity, Islam, Buddhism. Forbidden.

I am sure if anyone follows the order of Allāh (ﷻ) they will be real beloveds in the way of Allāh (ﷻ). They will be a real husband and a real wife for each other. Not like some men and women. This is not love. It is sickness. This is not right. Allāh (ﷻ) does not say yes.

Why did He create the man and the woman? From where do you come? Do you not come from your mother and your father? This is Allāh (ﷻ). He shows us everything. He cares about the human being, in the right way. This is my beloved Allāh (ﷻ).

Also, I like to say something about citron. There is special fruit called citron. It is the real, real medicine for influenza. It is the medicine for anyone who has influenza of any kind. This is only one. This is the medicine. This is for all influenza from the pots, from the chickens.

- You can eat citron with its skin. After 48 hours you will not see any influenza. You will be healed, inshā'a-llāh, completely.

This is the perfect, perfect, perfect medicine for children, for women, for men, for anyone. I have brought the seed and, of course, Ṣalīḥ will plant it.

Also, the fragrance of the flowers is very, very delicious. The fragrance of this tree will repel insects and bugs and will not let them be close to you. It is a holy tree, citron.

The Prophet (ﷺ) wrote:

> Citron is the medicine for many, many sicknesses.

This is what he (ﷺ) says in the Ḥadīth. These are some of our practices.

I'd also like to tell you how to heal kidney diseases. For kidney stones, people go to hospital and have surgery, but there are two kinds of natural healing for this condition.

Treatment for Kidney Stones

- Before each meal, take one medium spoonful of radish seeds. Continue this for 3 weeks. This will take the stones away from your kidneys. It will smash them, crush them.

- Another medicine is cranberry. Try to drink cranberry juice every day.

This is enough for today. I will not be able to give you all and everything in a few hours. But I have tried today to explain the cause of all diseases, why we have pain and diseases. Why? Because we are not following the advice of all the prophets (عليهم السلام).

We are not following the orders of Allāh (ﷻ).Keep this wisdom with you.

- Watch your stomach. Watch your food.
- The stomach is a third for your water, a third for your food and a third for your breath. Then the stomach will be healthy.
- Don't sleep on your back or on your left side. Sleep on your right side to help the stomach work correctly.
- Don't eat before your bedtime. Eat at least one hour before going to bed to keep your stomach healthy and to let her have time to digest the food you've eaten at night.

These are important things.

Inshā'a-llāh, I will pray for you and I will give you this protection du'ā'. This is a supplication and healing by using āyah from the Qur'ān and Ḥadīth. I'm a poor slave. I don't know the unseen. This is not my knowledge. This is the knowledge of all the prophets (عليهم السلام), the knowledge of Sayyidinā Muḥammad (ﷺ) and Ibrāhīm (Abraham) (عليه السلام). This is not from us.

If you don't understand what I'm saying, this is your problem. And I'm telling you if you understand something other than what I'm saying, it is a problem. All the time I mention this is from Allāh (ﷻ) and this is from the Prophet (ﷺ). Many people say, "Our shaykh is starting to forget." All people forget. I'm a human being.

Allāh (ﷻ) says in Qur'ān:

> And indeed We made a covenant with Ādam before, but he forgot, and We found on his part no firm will-power. (20:115)

Allāh (ﷻ) told Ādam (عليه السلام) something and Ādam (عليه السلام) forget, so the human being will forget. I speak what I know completely, I do not keep anything hidden. I speak, I am a human being. But Allāh (ﷻ) is perfect silence and He teaches us how to give in the right way.

Ibrahim's Sacrifice (عليه السلام) for the Face of Allāh (ﷻ) for All of Humanity

"The True Meaning of Ḥajj" on page 363 and "The True Beginning of Healing" from *Secret of the Spirit*
Thursday, October 21, 2010, USHS Year 2

لا إله إلا الله - لا إله إلا الله - لا إله إلا الله - محمد رسول الله عليه صلاة الله
لا إله إلا الله - لا إله إلا الله - لا إله إلا الله - ابراهيم رسول الله عليه صلاة الله
لا إله إلا الله - لا إله إلا الله - لا إله إلا الله - موسى رسول الله عليه صلاة الله
لا إله إلا الله - لا إله إلا الله - لا إله إلا الله - عيسى رسول الله عليه صلاة الله
اللهم انت السلام ومنك السلام و إليك يعود السلام
تباركت ربنا وتعاليت يا ذوالجلال والإكرام

As-salāmu ʿalaykum wa raḥmatu-llāhi wa bārakatuhu. Peace be upon you, beloveds. This is a holy day, a noble day. This is one of the blessed days. It is very close to Ibrāhīm's (Abraham's) journey (عليه السلام) to the Kaʿba, the holy Kaʿba in Mecca. This first house of Allāh (ﷻ) was been built for all of the people in Mecca. In 15 or 20 days, Ibrāhīm's journey (عليه السلام) will start and the people will start to make Ḥajj, pilgrimage, as Sayyidinā Ibrāhīm (عليه السلام) and all the prophets (عليهم السلام) did.

The Kaʿba is the first place. It was built for all people and they give a sacrifice for their selves, their hearts and their souls in order to receive Allāh's acceptance (ﷻ). These sacrifices all go to the needy and poor people.

I am asking Allāh (ﷻ) to guide you and help you to walk to Allāh (ﷻ). I am asking Allāh (ﷻ) to help you in your healing work, and I am asking Him to let you be among those who are honest and the lovers carrying the flag of love and mercy and justice to all the people. Inshāʾa-llāh

My son Ṣalīḥ will read for you. Open your hearts and take your chance. The angels (عليهم السلام) directed their faces toward Allāh (ﷻ), toward Mecca and Allāh (ﷻ) says:

> It is He who sends prayers upon you, and His angels, too. (33:43)

During Ḥajj thousands and thousands of the angels (عليهم السلام) will go to Mecca to pray upon you and ask Him to send His mercy to all of you. They will ask Him to stop the corrupters who start wars and fights and trials and difficulties. They will ask Allāh (ﷻ) to let all the people be one nation and Allāh (ﷻ) says:

> Truly! This, your religion (or nation) is one religion (or nation),
> and I am your Lord; therefore, worship Me. (21:92)

This is the order. This is from Allāh (ﷻ). Allāh (ﷻ) says:

> Oh people, We have created you from a male and a female,
> and made you into nations and tribes
> so that you may know (and love) one another.
> Truly, the most honorable of you with Allāh (ﷻ)
> is that who has taqwā (piety).
> Truly, Allāh is all-knowing, all-aware. (49:13)

A teaching given in Florida on October 17, 2010, called, "The True Meaning of Ḥajj" on page 363 of this book is read from the beginning.

"Peace be upon all the messengers of the prophets (عليهم السلام). Peace upon all the beloveds and all the followers of Allāh (ﷻ). I am asking Allāh (ﷻ) for all of you to be stable and firm on this path and to love all the prophets (عليهم السلام). I am asking Him to provide you with love and mercy for the whole world, your families, your sons and your daughters. It is my great pleasure to be among you.

This is the last day with you. I will not leave you. My spirit is with you. My supplications are always for you. I can feel all of the people who are suffering and who need prayers. I am asking Allāh (ﷻ) to send happiness to everyone. I direct my face to Allāh (ﷻ), asking Him to protect our world from the hurricanes, volcanoes and disasters. This is a great year with many events in the world. We are asking Allāh (ﷻ) to protect all people, all children and to heal the sick. He is the Healer, the Knower.

We talked yesterday about the journey of Sayyidinā (our Master) ʿĪsā (Jesus) (عليه السلام). Today we will talk about the father of all the prophets (عليهم السلام),

Sayyidinā Ibrāhīm (عليه السلام). He was also a father to his sons, Isḥāq (Isaac) and Ismāʿīl (Ishmael). He is the friend of Allāh (ﷻ), the khalīlu-llāh, the friend of Allāh (ﷻ) who carried the message of unity. He suffered a lot.

Sayyidinā Ibrāhīm (عليه السلام) was born in Ur, Iraq close to (Badin) Babel. When this noble prophet was twelve years old, his father would take him to his workshop. His father was a carpenter. The king at that time was named Nimrūd. He was a bad king who treated people like slaves without any mercy. Sayyidinā Ibrāhīm (عليه السلام) was thinking a lot about who provided for him and who gave him life. Could those idols do this? In the Qurʾān Allāh (ﷻ) tells us:

> When he (Ibrāhīm) saw the moon rising up, he said,
> 'This is my Lord.'
> But when it set, he said, 'Unless my Lord guides me,
> I will surely be among the people who went astray.'
>
> When he saw the sun rising up, he said,
> 'This is my Lord. This is greater.'
> But when it set, he said, 'Oh my people!
> I am indeed free from all that you join as partners.' (6:76-78)

Allāh (ﷻ), my Lord, is alive forever and never disappears. He is greater than any other thing you can imagine. After that he started to think that Allāh (ﷻ) was not like the human being because He created everything— the heavens, the skies, the animals and humankind—so how could He disappear? He said, 'My Lord, guide me to the right way.' Sayyidinā Jībrīl (Gabriel) (عليه السلام) came down to him and told him, 'Allāh (ﷻ) keeps within you the true words of Allāh (ﷻ) who created the skies and the heavens.'

Ibrāhīm's father told him (عليه السلام) to take the idols he made and to try to sell them. He took the stones and idols and started to call to the people, 'Who can buy something that will not do anything to them? They will not give you any benefit and they will not even harm you.' So no one bought anything from him.

He told his father that the people would not buy a god that would never help them or even cause harm to them. His father was angry with him and told him, 'You stopped our provision, how can I offer you food? You are not a good son.' He talked badly about him and told him he was a disobedient son. Ibrāhīm (عليه السلام) told his father, 'No I cannot do that.' He was very polite. He asked his father, 'How can you worship something that cannot give you anything or cannot help you? This is an error, a mistake, an illusion. No one with an intellect can accept this.'

His father was angry with him and told him to get out of his place. Ibrāhīm (عليه السلام) told him that our creator is Allāh (ﷻ). The people heard about this story. Ibrāhīm (عليه السلام) was thinking about how he could help those people. He was brave and bold. He wanted to make a change. He was a strong young man.

One day his king, Nimrūd, entered the place and worshipped the idols. Ibrāhīm (عليه السلام) was very intelligent and after they left, he took the axe and began ruining the idols. He left the big idol and hung the axe on its neck. In the early morning they went to pray and saw that their Gods were ruined. Who did that? They heard that it was Ibrāhīm (عليه السلام) who did it.

Nimrūd sent his soldiers to get Ibrāhīm (عليه السلام). They asked Ibrāhīm (عليه السلام) who did it. He pointed to the biggest idol with the axe and said, 'This one, the great one. The god with the axe around his neck did it. Look at him.' Nimrūd and the soldiers said to Ibrāhīm (عليه السلام), 'How can we talk to the idol? He cannot talk.' Ibrāhīm (عليه السلام) asked, 'Then how can you worship him? This god cannot defend himself. What kind of god is this?'

God (ﷻ) is strong, God (ﷻ) is great, God (ﷻ) is the Creator. This is the issue of Sayyidinā Ibrāhīm (عليه السلام) and all of the prophets (عليهم السلام). In spite of Nimrūd, Ibrāhīm (عليه السلام) was strong. He knew that Nimrūd could kill him but Ibrāhīm (عليه السلام) did everything for the face of Allāh (ﷻ). Sayyidinā Ibrāhīm (عليه السلام) lived to be 175 years old.

We return back to our story. They asked him, 'What should we do to Ibrāhīm (عليه السلام) who destroyed our Gods?' The devil, Iblīs, came looking like a man to the horrible king Nimrūd and said, 'I will tell you what to do with Ibrāhīm (عليه السلام). Gather a lot of wood, light the wood and put him in the fire.' This was the judgment of Iblīs.

Here was the miracle and the greatness of Allāh (ﷻ). Here you can see the nobility and how Sayyidinā Ibrāhīm (عليه السلام) was great. This is faith. The son of the truth will never be frightened. They do not fear anyone except Allāh (ﷻ). They believe Allāh (ﷻ) will defend them. The corruptors are weak. An insect, an ant is stronger than the corruptors, the criminals and the oppressors.

All the prophets (عليهم السلام) pay their selves, their souls and their hearts as a sacrifice for Allāh (ﷻ). This is the mercy of Allāh (ﷻ). They are strong and brave. This station, the son of the truth, does not fear anyone except Allāh (ﷻ). They are sure that Allāh (ﷻ) will send His victory to them. They are the winners and the corruptors are the losers.

All the prophets (عليهم السلام) pay their selves, their souls and their hearts as a sacrifice for Allāh (ﷻ). This is the mercy of Allāh (ﷻ). They are strong and brave. This station, the son of the truth, does not fear anyone except Allāh (ﷻ). They are sure that Allāh (ﷻ) will send His victory to them. They are the winners and the corruptors are the losers.

The prophets are the link to Allāh (ﷻ). Allāh (ﷻ) has everything. He has soldiers of this earth and of the heavens. The soldiers of the heavens are the angels (عليهم السلام) and the soldiers from the earth are the good doers. Sayyidinā Ibrāhīm (عليه السلام) is the perfect pattern, the example for all of us in order to teach us."

Ibrāhīm (عليه السلام) is the father of all the prophets (عليهم السلام). He is the Friend of Allāh (ﷻ). He is the carrier of the message of unity completely, in all of its qualities. He carries the qualities of Allāh (ﷻ), His are the 99 names and he knows the secrets and meanings of those names. He tried to fix the problems in this earth by using the message of unity. So Allāh (ﷻ) selected him to let him be His khalil, His close friend, a lover for Allāh (ﷻ). He took a divine shahāda promising that he was the lover of Allāh (ﷻ), khalīlu-llāh.

Ibrāhīm deserves this honored title because he carried the message from the beginning, completely. He paid himself as a sacrifice for all people. He sacrificed his heart, his soul, his body, and he let the spirit of love and justice and freedom spread all over the world. He was humble. He was asking Allāh (ﷻ) all the time to save and guard people and to keep people happy. His was always praying and supplicating for all people. He was a lover. He used to take care of all people because he knew that Allāh (ﷻ) is the Lord of all the worlds (including all the people) and that He is the Merciful, the Compassionate. The first one who told us about making a sacrifice was Sayyidinā Ibrāhīm (ؑ) and he explained it to all people.

The reading continues, "Allāh (ﷻ) does not accept the weak. You should keep your religion and protect the poor and needy people; then they will never fear kings, criminals and corruptors. What did Allāh (ﷻ) do to Hitler? He was great but Allāh (ﷻ) took him. Allāh (ﷻ) will send His angels (ؑ) for all those corruptors who do not follow the order of Allāh (ﷻ). Allāh (ﷻ) will destroy all of them sooner or later. Everything will have its time.

They gathered a mountain of wood and they brought Sayyidinā Ibrāhīm (ؑ) there. This is an example and a lesson for all people. He never feels frightened. They put him in a catapult and threw him into the fire. Look at how great Sayyidinā Ibrāhīm (ؑ) was. When they put him in the catapult, Ibrāhīm (ؑ) began to smile and ask them why they put him here. He said, 'Do you think Allāh (ﷻ) will leave me by myself?' They asked him, 'Who is your Lord, your Allāh (ﷻ)?' He told them, 'He is my creator. He will defend me and you will see by your eyes what Allāh (ﷻ) will do for me.'

Then they threw him and he was between the sky and the earth. Look at the son of the truth—Sayyidinā Jībrīl talked to him and asked him, 'Ibrāhīm (ؑ), do you need anything? Do you need any help?' Ibrāhīm answered, 'I do not need anything from you because Allāh (ﷻ) knows my situation. Allāh (ﷻ) does not need me to ask anyone except Him.'"

Look at this great prophet. He contains the depths and depends upon Allāh (ﷻ) completely. He never asked anyone but Allāh (ﷻ) for help. Look at him. He was polite with Allāh (ﷻ). And this situation was a great, great event. These people put him in the fire.

Ibrāhīm's name contains two phrases: "Ibrā" and "hīm." "Hīm" means that he fell in love with Allāh (ﷻ) and he was absent from this existence. He was in the world of al-baqāʾ, world of subsisting in Allāh. The Angel Jībrīl (عليه السلام) asked him, "Do you need anything, Ibrāhīm (عليه السلام)?" He told him, "From you, no, I do not need anything. Allāh (ﷻ) knows what I need." In this he is teaching us how to depend upon Allāh (ﷻ), how to trust Allāh (ﷻ) with our hearts, our bodies, our souls.

When Ibrāhīm (عليه السلام) paid the sacrifice, Allāh (ﷻ) accepted it from him. Ibrāhīm (عليه السلام) was sacrificing himself for all people when they put him into the fire. He was carrying the message of unity. This was the first sacrifice. This was first Ibrāhīmic sacrifice for all of you and the whole world. This is Ibrāhīm (عليه السلام), our first prophet to sacrifice himself in this world in order to let all people live happily, with lives full of mercy and peace. He is the father of all people. He gave everything. His word was a divine word.

In our ṣalāh we say, "Āllahumma ṣalli ʿalā Sayyidinā Muḥammad, wa ʿalā ʿāli Sayyidinā Muḥammad kamā ṣallayta ʿalā Sayyidinā Ibrāhīm, wa ʿalā ʿāli Sayyidinā Ibrāhīm, innaka ḥamīdun majīd. Āllahumma bārik ʿalā Muḥammad wa ʿalā ʿāli Sayyidinā Muḥammad kamā bārakta ʿalā Sayyidinā Ibrāhīm, wa ʿalā ʿāli Sayyidinā Ibrāhīm, innaka ḥamīdun majīd."

"Oh Allāh, send peace to our Master Muḥammad and to the family of our Master Muḥammad as You sent peace to our Master Ibrāhīm and the family of our Master Ibrāhīm. You are truly Praiseworthy, Glorious. Oh Allāh, send blessings to our Master Muḥammad and to the family of our Master Muḥammad as You sent blessings to our Master Ibrāhīm and the family of Ibrāhīm. You are truly Praiseworthy, Glorious."

We are carrying the message of Ibrāhīm (عليه السلام), the sharīʿa (divine law) and the ḥaqīqa (divine reality). We are trying to clearly tell the people on this earth about the sharīʿa and the ḥaqīqa. We never say anything except what is from Allāh (ﷻ) and from what Allāh (ﷻ) revealed to all the prophets (عليهم السلام) including: Sayyidinā Muḥammad (ﷺ), Sayyidinā ʿĪsā (عليه السلام) and Sayyidinā Mūsā (Moses) (عليه السلام). We would not speak from illusions and the black mind. We are speaking from Allāh (ﷻ). We are taking from the message He gave to all the prophets (ؑ), including Ibrāhīm (ؑ) and ʿĪsā (ؑ). We are the sons of the ḥaqīqa, the divine reality.

We are not for this dunyā. We are not to live in this dunyā. We are with Allāh (ﷻ). We are absent from other people. We are traveling to His presence, His divine presence. We are the sons of the truth. We are the sons of al-Ḥaqq. We have to worship Him. Allāh (ﷻ) says:

> And I did not create the jinn and human beings
> except they should worship Me. (51:56-57)

This is the journey of Sayyidinā Ibrāhīm (ؑ). He started his journey while he was young. He destroyed all of the idols. He knew that Allāh (ﷻ) would be with him. Allāh (ﷻ) would never leave His lover by himself, so he traveled to make Ḥajj.

The reading continues, "Ibrāhīm (ؑ) was brave and bold. He is the father of all the prophets (ؑ). He is khalīlu-llāh (ؑ), the close friend of Allāh (ﷻ).

Ibrāhīm (ؑ) went into the fire but Allāh (ﷻ) ordered the fire to be cool and peaceful for Ibrāhīm (ؑ). Before his body touched the fire, the wood changed into trees and green plants. There were different and beautiful trees, some fruitless and others with fruit like apples. Ibrāhīm (ؑ) was in a paradise full of flowers, watching the birds singing with happiness that Allāh (ﷻ) saved Sayyidinā Ibrāhīm (ؑ). This is Sayyidinā Ibrāhīm (ؑ), al-khalil. Many people believed in Ibrāhīm (ؑ) and his message and in the message of Sāra and Lūṭ (Lot) in Iraq and Palestine.

Then Nimrūd was sent a trial. It was his first punishment and it was a hard punishment. Allāh (ﷻ) wanted to prove to all people that Ibrāhīm (ؑ) was not coming from himself, that he was carrying the message of Allāh (ﷻ). Nimrūd started to have a lot of pain and he started crying out and screaming, 'Where is the physician?' The physicians told Nimrūd, 'No one can heal you except Ibrāhīm (ؑ).'

One of Nimrūd's guards came to Ibrāhīm (ؑ) and explained that Nimrūd was suffering and could not sleep. Ibrāhīm (ؑ) said that he would help him. He called one of his followers, a poor man, full of faith, whose

name was Rafed. Ibrāhīm (ﷺ) told him to take his shoes and hit Nimrūd on the head. The poor man said, 'How can I do that?' Ibrāhīm (ﷺ) said, 'Allāh (ﷻ) will be with you. Go.'"

So because he took his shoes to hit Nimrūd, they called him Rafed because he took the shoes.

The reading continues, "Through this Allāh (ﷻ) will let you see a picture of how He can belittle the corruptors."

Though this poor man did not have anything, he believed in Ibrāhīm (ﷺ) and the message of Allāh (ﷻ), so Allāh (ﷻ) made him powerful, more powerful than the king. The king was in need because of his health. The insect entered his brain and when it would move it caused Nimrūd pain. When Rafed hit him on the head, the insect would be calm. When he stopped hitting him, the insect would start to be active again and then Nimrūd would feel pain, and so he needed to be hit on the head again.

This is for all the corruptors who are trying to destroy this earth and steal money and steal houses. Allāh (ﷻ) is promising them. Allāh (ﷻ) will send them someone who will belittle them and it will be like what He did with Ibrāhīm (ﷺ) to Nimrūd with the insect and the shoes. This is Allāh's cure for all corruptors all criminals who destroy the peace and love and mercy and justice between people. Allāh (ﷻ) says, "I am the Powerful, I am the Dear, I am the Merciful, Compassionate."

The reading continues, "Sayyidinā Ibrāhīm (ﷺ) was the messenger of Allāh (ﷻ) and he spoke the truth. Therefore, the poor man took his shoes and said to Nimrūd, 'Your medicine is here.' This is the wisdom of Allāh (ﷻ). Allāh (ﷻ) will make the poor and weak people strong, brave and bold by His permission. He told Nimrūd, 'This is the physician.' He was very poor.

All of the people gathered to see the healing. They came to see how he would heal Nimrūd."

Judge yourself before Allāh (ﷻ) judges you. Sometimes we ask why we have a disease. Why we have lost a home. Ask yourself: do you eat the money of others? Do you break the hearts of others? Did you give help to poor and needy people? Did you help the poor and sick people? Do you have a lot of wealth?

Allāh (ﷻ) is the Just. Justice is one of His qualities. We should be straight. Allāh will protect anyone who is straight and gives mercy to all people. He will protect those who are polite, full of mercy. He protects those who cry and feel the suffering of those who suffer. This is the real medicine.

The reading continues, "He said to take away Nimrūd's throne full of gold, jewels and diamonds and throw it to the earth. Nimrūd took it all and threw it to the ground. Then the poor man took his shoes out and put them next to the throne of the king. Look at this picture. This is a poor, honest believer. He began to hit Nimrūd. After the second time, Nimrūd began to feel pain in his head. Sayyidinā Ibrāhīm (ﷺ) told the poor man to sit down when he was finished hitting him.

After one half hour Nimrūd started to scream out that he had severe pain. What was the matter? It was an insect that had entered through his nose, crawled into his brain, and started to eat it. Nimrūd started to scream. This is the miracle. It is a very small insect. Allāh (ﷻ) judged Nimrūd. There are many killing insects that you can see with your eyes.

Welcome to all the corruptors and others who do not follow Allāh's orders. I am asking Allāh (ﷻ) to keep you and to guard you and to let you to be honest with Allāh (ﷻ), the God (ﷻ) of all the prophets and messengers (ﷺ). This insect killed him. He was dead now and their custom was to put him into the earth, into dust.

After this, Sayyidinā Ibrāhīm (ﷺ) went to Palestine, the Holy Land. It is the throne of Allāh (ﷻ). It is the first Qibla, the direction toward which the Prophet Muḥammad (ﷺ) and all of us were told to pray. Ibrāhīm (ﷺ) traveled from Ur, the land of Padanine in Iraq to Canaan, the Holy Land, to Ur-Salām (Jerusalem), the land of peace.

No one can change Jerusalem. It will be the land of peace, despite everything. It is peaceful for everyone without discrimination. In a ḥadīth qudsī Allāh () said:

> Yā Quds (Oh Jerusalem).
> You are honored by My light and you are My heaven.
> You are the land of gathering and suffering.
> In the Hereafter it will be as if you were a bride to your groom.
> Whoever caused you pain will receive My anger and punishment.

Sayyidinā Ibrāhīm () had two sons. He had his first son, Ismāʿīl (), when he was 86 years old and he had his second son, Isḥāq (), when he was 100 years old. Sayyidinā Ismāʿīl () was a prophet and his mother, Hajjar (), was the daughter of the king from Habasha.

When Sayyidinā Ibrāhīm () and Sāra (), his first wife, traveled to Egypt, Pharaoh gave Hajjar () as a gift to serve Sāra (). Sayyidinā Ibrāhīm () and Sāra () did not have a son at the time. He asked Allāh () for a son, and so he married Hajjar () and they had a son, Ismāʿīl (). However, Sāra () felt jealous and she asked Allāh () for a son. This is human nature. She loved her husband. How can another women come and share her husband? It was a normal thing to feel this way."

This is normal. The woman does not want anyone to share her husband. I agree with her.

The reading continues, "Could you bear to see your husband with other women?

Sayyidinā Ibrāhīm () sent supplications to Allāh () to send Sāra () a son. She had her son when Sayyidinā Ibrāhīm () was 100 years old. It is a miracle of Allāh (). She had Sayyidinā Isḥāq () and after Sayyidinā Isḥāq () came Yaʿqūb (Jacob) (). Yaʿqūb () had eleven sons and one of them was Sayyidinā Yūsuf (Joseph) (). All of them were holy and noble.

There was a problem with jealousy between Sāra () and Hajjar (). By the order of Allāh (), Sayyidinā Ibrāhīm () took Hajjar () and his son Ismāʿīl () on al-Ḥijra (emigration). Why? The first house of Allāh ()

had been built in Mecca: the Kaʿba. Who built the Kaʿba? The first person to build it was Ādam (ﷺ) with the help of the angels (ﷺ). Allāh (ﷻ) says in the Qur'ān:

> And (remember) when Ibrahim and Ismāʿīl
> were raising the foundations of the House (the Kaʿba), saying,
> 'Our Lord! Accept (this) from us.
> Truly! You are the All-Hearer, the All-Knower.' (2:127)

Hajjar (ﷺ) and Ismāʿīl (ﷺ), who was an infant, were in this place with no food or water, but Ibrāhīm (ﷺ) knew that Allāh (ﷻ) would be with them. Hajjar (ﷺ) began to walk back and forth looking for water. The baby began hitting the earth and the water came out from under his feet. This was another miracle. Hajjar (ﷺ) saw the water and she started to drink it. The Bedouin people asked her if they could have some water. She (ﷺ) said, 'This is the water of Allāh (ﷻ).'

Later Sayyidinā Ibrāhīm (ﷺ) returned to them. He knew that they would be fine and that Allāh (ﷻ) would take care of them. This was the order of Allāh (ﷻ). Allāh (ﷻ) had prepared something. There is an āyah in the Qur'ān describing the beautiful picture of how Sayyidinā Ibrāhīm (ﷺ) had strong faith and that he told Allāh (ﷻ) about leaving his wife and his son in this desert where there was no water or plants. There was nothing. He prayed, 'Please Allāh (ﷻ), let the people love them and let the House be close to them.' The Ḥajj (pilgrimage) started here.

At this moment you can still find the water that appeared for Hajjar (ﷺ) and Ismāʿīl (ﷺ), this miracle, and drink from it. The name of this water is Zamzam. If you drink this water with the intention for Allāh (ﷻ) to heal you, Allāh (ﷻ) will heal you. This water of Zamzam is different than any other water on this earth. Geologists and scientists have tested it and taken samples of it and they found out that it contains more than twenty elements and that it is different than any other water on earth. The scientists made their reports and now you can find the water of Zamzam everywhere. This is a divine issue. Now I will ask my son to read to you."

The reading, 'The True Beginning of Healing' from *Secret of the Spirit*[29] is read from the beginning.

"Who is Ibrāhīm (⁕)? Ibrāhīm (⁕) is the father of all the prophets. He is the father of all the prophets and Allāh (⁕) once inspired him in his sleep. Ibrāhīm (⁕) explained to his son that he saw a vision in which he was slaughtering him. He did not see him in a dream or vision, but it was a true state of seeing. He said, 'I see that I am slaughtering you,' but it did not mean slaughtering in the way that people think. It had a deep meaning. It had a very deep meaning, which meant, 'I am slaughtering all of the animal qualities within myself. I am slaughtering the physical diseases; I am slaughtering the psychological diseases and all the selfish and non-godly qualities.'

> And, when he (Ismā'īl ⁕) was old enough to walk with him,
> he (Ibrāhīm ⁕) said, 'Oh my son! I have seen in a dream
> that I am slaughtering you (offering you in sacrifice to Allāh),
> so what do you think!' (37:102)"

When Allāh (⁕) revealed for Ibrāhīm (⁕) to kill his son, Allāh (⁕) wanted to teach people how to obey Allāh (⁕). We see how to obey Allāh (⁕) through how Ismā'īl (⁕) gave himself to his father and told him to follow the order of Allāh (⁕). This is how to obey Allāh (⁕). This is how sons should obey their parents. This is a very important point. Allāh (⁕) wanted to purify the heart of His Ismā'īl (⁕). He was preparing him to carry the eternal message, the message of unity, and to be a divine slave and a complete messenger for Allāh (⁕).

Are you ready to give your self, your soul, your heart and your intellect as a sacrifice for the face of Allāh (⁕)? Sayyidinā Ibrāhīm (⁕) did. If you want this, give your sacrifice to Allāh (⁕) and Allāh (⁕) will purify you. Allāh (⁕) wants to purify the family of Sayyidinā Ibrāhīm (⁕), and from Sayyidinā Ibrāhīm (⁕) all of the other prophets, including 'Īsā (⁕) and Muḥammad (⁕). Are you are ready to carry the real message that is from the divine presence, from al Ḥaqq? Allāh (⁕) wants to purify all of you by using His divine water. This is very deep issue. This is the walking to Allāh (⁕) and this is the emigration of Sayyidinā Ibrāhīm (⁕) when he went to the Ka'ba. When he went to Mount Arafat and he

---

[29] Sidi Muhammad, *Secret of the Spirit*. Pope Valley: Shadhiliyya Sufi Center, 2010, pp. 419-435.

ordered the people all people come pay their sacrifices for the face of Allāh (ﷻ) to all the needy and sick people.

This is not from me. It is from Allāh (ﷻ) to Sayyidinā Ibrāhīm (ﷺ), to Sayyidinā Mūsā (ﷺ), to Sayyidinā ʿĪsā (ﷺ), to Sayyidinā Muḥammad (ﷺ). These are the tools you can use to purify yourself. These are holy, holy tools, they provide a holy means for you to purify your body and your soul. This is not from us, we are a poor slave. We never talk except what Allāh (ﷻ) ordered us to say and except what the prophets and the messengers (ﷺ) revealed to us. This sacrifice will protect you and your families and everything.

The reading continues, "When Sayyidinā Ibrāhīm (ﷺ) said, 'I saw in my dream,' it was not a dream. For a prophet (ﷺ) it was real, not an illusion, because he was seeing by the light of Allāh (ﷻ). Allāh (ﷻ) let him see beyond what normal people see, for he was a prophet and messenger."

Dreaming is not one of the qualities of the prophets (ﷺ). It was a vision from Allāh (ﷻ) for him. It was real.

The reading continues, "He was a noble one. He saw by His eyes and he heard by His ears this divine order. He said, 'I have seen.' He did not say, 'I had a dream' but he said, 'I see with my eyes that I am slaughtering you.' His son Ismāʿīl (ﷺ) told him, 'Please, my father, do what Allāh (ﷻ) has commanded you to do. This is a divine order.'"

Nowadays, sons and daughters disobey their parents. This is not from Allāh (ﷻ). Many people, many sons and daughters remember their parents only at Christmas. This not right. This is disobedience. They should pay their respect and they should obey them and be close to them and feel them because they raised them. They were suffering with worry for them and asking to Allāh (ﷻ) to let them be happy. This is the sharīʿa of Allāh (ﷻ).

The reading continues:

> **"He (Ismāʿīl ﷺ) said, 'Oh my father! Do that which you are commanded, inshāʾa-llāh (if Allāh wills),**
> **you will find me to be one of the patient ones.'**

The child of Ibrāhīm (ؑ) was also a prophet. He was around nine years old and he said to his father Ibrāhīm (ؑ), 'Oh my father, do as you were commanded,' because he understood that what Ibrāhīm (ؑ) was telling him was, 'I want to purify you.' So he said, 'Purify me; do as you were commanded,' because he believed that the one who commanded his father was Allāh (ﷻ). Because the prophet's vision is a godly vision, it is direct knowledge from Allāh (ﷻ). He knows that Ibrāhīm (ؑ) was his father, biologically speaking, but he was Ibrāhīm's very soul when we talk from the spiritual perspective.

When Ibrāhīm (ؑ) took his son to the mountain of Arafat...this mountain is where Muslims go for pilgrimage and there is a belief that all of the prophets (ؑ) went to this mountain. Mūsā (ؑ) went to this mountain and all other prophets (ؑ) went there, as well. It is not as some ignorant Muslims and other ignorant people understand it. I also visited that mountain for seven years and I saw divine visions in it, scenes in it, in a true way of seeing.

Going back to our story, Ibrāhīm (ؑ) took his son and put him on the altar and took the knife in his hand. People thought that he was truly going to kill his son, but who could ever kill his son? What happened to the sharp knife at this point? It became water. It was moving as water moves. It was a purification operation, it was not a true killing. He kept trying to use the knife, but it turned to water. When the knife turned to water, it could not really slaughter his son.

Ibrāhīm's name (ؑ) has two syllables. Ib-rāhīm. It means to become the merciful father, which means to become absent from everything except Allāh. It means to be absent from your animal self and to get in touch with your divine essence. The divine essence is far from the animal essence; it is the godly essence. In this instance Ibrāhīm's hand (ؑ) was a divine hand. His hearing, his seeing, all of his senses were luminous. He was full of light. All of his senses were full of light and he was a luminous being. Ismāʿīl (ؑ), his son, was also full of luminous light. Can a knife really slaughter light? It cannot go through light and hurt it. So they became light, and that is why the knife couldn't slaughter him.

Do you truly want to be like that, to be an Ibrāhīmic being or an Isḥāq-like being or an Ismāʿīl-like being? Do you want to be like those beings, to be one with them? So, do what Ismāʿīl (ؑ) did. He said, 'My father, I surrender fully to you. Do as you are commanded by Allāh (ﷻ).' Therefore he surrendered to all of the commands of Allāh (ﷻ).

The meaning of this sacrifice was as one of the gnostics says: there are special people, special places and special times for Allāh (ﷻ). Allāh (ﷻ) guided Ibrāhīm (عليه السلام) who was a special person. A special place was Mecca because it was the first place to worship Allāh (ﷻ). The angels (عليهم السلام) felt this place. The special time was the time Allāh (ﷻ) stated to do your pilgrimage, and Sayyidinā Ibrāhīm (عليه السلام) was the first one to establish the pilgrimage. All the prophets (عليهم السلام) made pilgrimage. Allāh (ﷻ) ordered the people to make Ḥajj (pilgrimage) at a special time. This is an exact time which is 10 Ḥijja. No one can change it. Allāh (ﷻ) fixed this date. Therefore, for Allāh (ﷻ) there are special people, special places and special times.

When you go on Ḥajj, Allāh (ﷻ) will remove all of your sins. This is a new birth for you. You will feel the jalāl (majesty) of Allāh (ﷻ). Everyone puts on white clothes, the clothes of death, to gain admittance and announce that, 'We are Your servants.' All people are the same. No one is better than any other. No one can say, 'I am king.' Men and women are all together and are the same. There is no difference between them. You will see all people in the same clothes, the clothes of death, the white clothes.

Who will gather the people? The voice of Sayyidinā Ibrāhīm (عليه السلام). If you could see the Ibrāhīmic view over there...it is unbelievable. Your heart will be absent when you see the view of Sayyidinā Ibrāhīm (عليه السلام) calling the people to come. The gnostic does not think of anything except Allāh (ﷻ) and they call, 'Yā Allāh (ﷻ).' There are no other words except Yā Allāh (ﷻ) and fear and jalāl. Hearts will be humble and with Allāh (ﷻ), never looking right or left, so that Allāh (ﷻ) will send His mercy.

As I mentioned, there are special places and special times. This is the will of Allāh (ﷻ). When the divine order was sent down to Sayyidinā Ibrāhīm (عليه السلام), he told Ismāʿīl (عليه السلام), 'I am seeing in my dream that I am slaughtering you.' Yawm al-Arafat is the slaughtering day, the pilgrimage day. What is the wisdom in this?"

Do you want to be with them? Do you want to pay the sacrifice for your heart and your soul? Those are very holy days you will share with the people who go to Mecca on Ḥajj, so if you want to pay the sacrifice for the face of Allāh (ﷻ) to purify your heart and your soul, you can. Inshā'a-llāh. I will take it to the Holy Land to slaughter a sheep. It costs between $130-$300. Anyone who wants to pay, I am ready to slaughter the sacrifice for the face of Allāh (ﷻ) and to give it to the poor people. If you want, if you can, you can give a big sacrifice or a small one. If you want to do that, bismi-llāh. If you do not want to do that, bismi-llāh.

The reading continues, "They will not arrive to Allāh (ﷻ) unless they are absent from this existence, not of this place or of this time. Allāh says, 'If you really want Me and you are honest, then come to Me as I wish and you can fulfill this wish by obeying My orders. Do not disobey Me.'

The son is very appreciative to his parents. He told Ibrāhīm (عليه السلام) to kill his son. It meant: give the dearest thing to you for the face of Allāh (ﷻ). In giving a sacrifice Allāh (ﷻ) does not want you to kill your son. He wants you to give Him the dearest things to your heart.

Allāh (ﷻ) is the Rich. Allāh (ﷻ) wants you to walk from the world of al-fanā', annihilation into God, to the world of al-baqā', subsistence in God, and to be with Allāh (ﷻ) and nothing else. Behave yourself and carry the qualities of Allāh (ﷻ). Do not be attached to this dunyā. Be straight and be honest and do not lie. Do not kill. You should walk and obey Allāh (ﷻ) in your eyes, in your intellect, in your heart and in your spirit. This is the meaning of the pilgrimage, the Ḥajj. Leave everything behind and remember Allāh (ﷻ).

You must give a sacrifice. What is a sacrifice? It is to slaughter a sheep, which means to behave well in your self, your heart and your soul. Come humbly toward Allāh (ﷻ) and carry the message of Sayyidinā Ibrāhīm (عليه السلام) and the message of peace and mercy. Do not cause any pain to anyone. Then you will establish your pilgrimage.

If you go on Ḥajj 100 times, Allāh (ﷻ) will not accept any of them if you cause pain to others upon your return. Allāh (ﷻ) will not accept your offering. Allāh (ﷻ) will not accept it. Purify yourself from all your sins and give your heart a sacrifice, your soul a sacrifice and your body a

sacrifice. Giving a sacrifice is like saying to Allāh, 'You created me and I will use all of Your provision to obey You and to obtain Your love so that You will accept me and be satisfied with me.' If a person goes to Mecca and comes back to act like a devil, this is not Ḥajj. If a person starts to steal and kill, then this person is worse than the devil.

Promise Allāh (ﷻ) that you are His servant and obey Allāh (ﷻ) and give everything as a sacrifice to Allāh (ﷻ). Come here, my beloveds. The coming days are the time of the pilgrimage and the ones who can do it can pay a sacrifice to protect your families. When Sayyidinā Ibrāhīm (ﷺ), intended to slaughter his son and Allāh (ﷻ) prevented it, the Angel Jībrīl (ﷺ) came down with a sheep as a sacrifice and told Ibrāhīm (ﷺ) to give the meat to all of the poor people. This is the meaning of the sacrifice, to protect and guard you and your families and your fathers.

This sacrifice exists in Islām, Judaism and Christianity. Ibrāhīm (ﷺ) is the prophet of all those religions and all of us believe in him. You will be holy and noble if you follow these holy and noble prophets (ﷺ). This is the reality of unity. Allāh (ﷻ) says:

> Truly! This, your religion (or nation) is one religion (or nation), and I am your Lord; therefore, worship Me. (21:92)

We are the son of Sufism. This is the faith of all the prophets (ﷺ). If anyone wants to pay a sacrifice at the special time of Sayyidinā Ibrāhīm (ﷺ), it is a great thing. Anyone who wants to slaughter a sheep and pay a sacrifice, we can do this in the Holy Land and feed the poor and needy people. This is sunna until the Last Day, and no one can remove this sunna. It is in Islām, Judaism and Christianity. It is for poor people and you can feed your family from your sacrifice, also.

Do as you were commanded by Allāh. Ismā'īl (ﷺ) surrendered to all the commands of Allāh (ﷻ), but he did not surrender to Ibrāhīm (ﷺ) as a human being, no. He surrendered to the divine essence, to Allāh (ﷻ) as reflected in Ibrāhīm. He surrendered to the divine image, to the divine reflection that was coming through Ibrāhīm (ﷺ).

Ismā'īl (ﷺ) said, 'Father, do as you were commanded.' Ibrāhīm (ﷺ) tried seven times, but the knife would not slaughter Ismā'īl (ﷺ). Then Allāh

(ﷻ) sent something to ransom him and to purify him. He sent blood that would purify him. Allāh (ﷻ) sent down Archangel Jībrīl (ؑ) and Jībrīl said: 'Oh Ibrāhīm, you were truthful and you believed in the vision. You were doing what we asked, and We will ransom your son with a great sacrifice.' Allāh (ﷻ) made this sacrifice as a way of purifying him.

> Then, when they had both submitted themselves,
> and he had laid him prostrate on his forehead,
> And We called out to him: 'Oh Ibrāhīm!
> You have fulfilled the dream (vision)!'
> Truly! In this way We reward the good-doers.
> Truly, that was a manifest trial
> And We ransomed him with a great sacrifice;
> And We left for him (a good teaching)
> among generations in later times. (37:103 – 37:108)

So this great lamb came from the heavenly Garden as a sacrifice to purify the human being. This great sacrifice is equivalent to all of the animals, all of the birds and all of the human beings. This way of purifying oneself became the accepted way, from that time until today until eternity. It became the way of purification that we must follow.

But the sacrifice is not as people understand; it is not to just slaughter an animal and eat it. It is a way of granting sacrifice and purification. The Angel Jībrīl (ؑ) said to Ibrāhīm, 'You believed in the divine vision and so We will ransom you. We will save you and your son; we will purify you.'

That is why anyone who wants to walk this path must also offer a sacrifice on behalf of his physical being, his heart, his soul and his spirit. This is the first step to walking the path of purification, the path toward Allāh, in the way of the people of Allāh, the people who walk in the way of purity. We have to offer a sacrifice to purify ourselves."

The door is open, my beloveds, if you want to pay a sacrifice. This is the sunna the Sayyidinā Ibrāhīm (ؑ), Sayyidinā Mūsā (ؑ) and Sayyidinā Muḥammad (ﷺ). You can write your name on a piece of paper and then put it with what you wish to give to slaughter a sheep. We will ask Allāh (ﷻ) to accept the name of the person or people and families making this sacrifice. I will sacrifice it with my own hands. Inshā'a-llāh, give what you can. So, my beloveds, if you are ready in this holy time, come to me now. Come with your hearts ready for purification and ask Allāh (ﷻ) to create a new you and make the real tawba at this time. I bring a special gift for you, a special paper, so if you are ready come now.

Sidi gives the promise.

Remedies for Healing in the Way of Allāh (ﷻ)

Remedies and the Protection Healing
October 26, 2010 AM, USHS Year 3

لا إله إلا الله - لا إله إلا الله - لا إله إلا الله - محمد رسول الله عليه صلاة الله
لا إله إلا الله - لا إله إلا الله - لا إله إلا الله - ابراهيم رسول الله عليه صلاة الله
لا إله إلا الله - لا إله إلا الله - لا إله إلا الله - موسى رسول الله عليه صلاة الله
لا إله إلا الله - لا إله إلا الله - لا إله إلا الله - عيسى رسول الله عليه صلاة الله
اللهم انت السلام ومنك السلام و إليك يعود السلام
تباركت ربنا وتعاليت يا ذوالجلال والإكرام

As-salāmu ʿalaykum wa raḥmatu-llāhi wa bārakatuhu. I am asking Allāh (ﷻ) and His prophets (عليهم السلام) and all the angels (عليهم السلام) to let you be among the loyal and sincere people and to let you be healthy. I am asking Him to help you carry the message of al-Ḥaqq, the message of unity, the message of all the prophets (عليهم السلام). I direct my face by the secret of Sayyidinā (our Master) Muḥammad (ﷺ) to hear the patient and to guard them from all evils. He is able to do everything. We depend upon You and Sayyidinā Muḥammad (ﷺ) and all of Allāh's beloveds depend upon You.

My beloveds, I think this is the last meeting for us and I hope to come back again and again. I leave among you my dearest wife. I know she is a proper lady, a very polite lady and she carries the Qurʾān. She knows Arabic and she contains the knowledge of reality. I am asking Allāh (ﷻ) to guard her and give her the strength to carry the message, my message. She will carry my message, inshāʾa-llāh.

When you become sick it acts as a sacrifice for your mistakes. All the prophets and Sayyidinā Muḥammad (ﷺ) say:

> Of anyone of you is haunted by a small darkness,
> I will feel your pain.

It is a test in this world and also it will lead you to a station closer to Allāh (ﷻ). Sayyidinā Ibrāhīm (Abraham) (عليه السلام) experienced sickness and all the prophets, including Sayyidinā Muḥammad, experienced sickness. (ﷺ) have been sick.

Allāh (ﷻ) says:

> Allāh is with the patient ones. (2:153, 2:249, 8:66)

Part of healing is patience. I am saying, and Allāh (ﷻ) is my supporter, this class will, inshā᾽a-llāh, be guided by Allāh (ﷻ).

There are many healings you never hear about and many sicknesses for which you do not know the medicine. I put many methods of healing in my books. I am very sorry not all of you have read the books and understood what I explained in detail.

These healings are not from me, but from others. They are from the gnostics, and they received the healings from the prophets, from Sayyidinā Ibrāhīm (ﷺ) and Sayyidinā ʿĪsā (Jesus) (ﷺ). The prophets (ﷺ) received this knowledge from Allāh (ﷻ) and from Sayyidinā Jībrīl (Gabriel) (ﷺ).

Lyme Disease

I will start with a dangerous disease that no one knows how to heal, even in this country and in other countries. Sayyidinā Muḥammad (ﷺ) learned about when he was on his night journey. Sayyidinā Jībrīl (ﷺ) told Sayyidinā Muḥammad (ﷺ) to tell his nation to begin using cupping.

Cupping is the healing for every disease. Sayyidinā Jībrīl (ﷺ) taught him how to do cupping and the Prophet (ﷺ) taught one of his followers how to do cupping on him. He was the first one to do cupping and he used to do cupping on an individual twice, period.

Lyme disease is an unknown disease and a very dangerous disease with many side effects. I taught my son, Dr. Wadude, how to do cupping. I taught him the spots on the back and he has healed many people, including my wife and others.

Lyme disease is dangerous and causes pain in your legs, knees, back and your head because of the black blood. Black blood is not healthy blood. When a person does cupping it takes away this black blood.

How to Prepare Arabic Plaster

After cupping I recommend you make the Arabic plaster.

3 Tbsp of olive soap
3 Tbsp of flour
5 egg whites

1. Mix all ingredients together. Put the plaster on a thin cloth.

2. Start at the upper back and work down, covering the entire back with the plaster.

3. Let the plaster sit for 24 hours, at which time it should begin to fall off.

4. Do not let it get wet. Have the person sleep on their stomach. The plaster will take away all of the pain.

Treatment for Tapeworm: Pumpkin Seeds

A tapeworm enters the stomach and eats all of the food you consume. It is about 1 meter long. Its mouth is located at the beginning of the stomach. When a person has a tapeworm he will lose all his food which will make him very weak and unable to walk. He will not be able to eat. How will he survive?

I used this myself 17 years back and have repeated this healing many times. What is the healing for tapeworm? Pumpkin seeds.

1. Take ½ pounds of raw pumpkin seeds and eat it in 1 day. Do not cook them. You can put them under the sun and then eat them.

2. After ½ hour eat 15 cloves of garlic. Why? The garlic will act like a knife. It will burn the skin of the tapeworm and kill it.

3. Once it is dead how will you expel it? Drink 3 Tbsp of castor oil with mint tea. After ½ hour you will have diarrhea and everything will clear out.

After doing all of this you will be very hungry. This remedy kills all the babies and eggs of the tapeworm. I healed a girl named Maḥbuba with this treatment. She was doing her exercises and fell down and no one knew what was wrong. She had this worm. To this day this healing is used in Palestine and al-Aqṣā and I have used it many times with many patients. You should write it down and understand it. This is made with all natural ingredients.

Treatment for Kidney Stones

Many people suffer from kidney stones. They go to hospitals and try to get rid of these stones with surgery and other methods. Healing kidney stones is very easy and there are 2 ways.

Remedy #1: Radish Seeds

1. Use the radish seeds of the long radish variety. Eat the seeds every morning after crushing them. Take a spoonful before breakfast and continue doing this for 1 week.

2. When you go to the restroom try to watch your urine. You should see something like ash.

Remedy #2: Cranberry Juice

- If the stone is like copper this will melt it. Take fresh cranberries and crush them. Drink a small cup of this juice 2 times a day. I do not think you will find this medicine in books or from physicians.

Hypertension (High Blood Pressure)

First, you should understand that different kinds of foods affect your blood pressure. You should avoid all non-organic foods. Eat only organic foods, 100% natural. This is the first reason for high blood pressure. Do not be angry, do not think a lot. That will affect you, of course. Do not let your mind be busy with thoughts, because it will affect your heart. If you are angry and start to think your blood pressure will not be stable. Do not think about what happened in the past, because that will keep your mind busy with the past. The brain will be busy and the heart will be busy and that will affect the blood. High blood pressure happens because of anger, grief and sadness. Protect yourself and your body. This is the truth.

Anger, grief and sadness also cause other diseases. What do you do if you are angry or sad? Direct your face to Allāh (ﷻ) and ask Allāh (ﷻ) for healing and read from the Qur'ān. When you read or listen to the Qur'ān you are talking to Allāh (ﷻ). When you pray to Allāh (ﷻ) you are talking to Allāh (ﷻ). Allāh (ﷻ) says:

> Remember Me, I will remember you,
> and be grateful to Me and never be ungrateful to Me. (2:152)

Ask Allāh (ﷻ) for forgiveness, praise Allāh (ﷻ), direct your face to Allāh (ﷻ). You are asking Allāh (ﷻ) and He is the Only One who can give to you. No one can give to you except Allāh (ﷻ). Allāh (ﷻ) says:

> And when My slaves ask you concerning Me,
> then (answer them), I am indeed near.
> I respond to prayers when they call upon Me. (2:186)

Ask Allāh (ﷻ). Ask Allāh (ﷻ) and do not ask anyone else. I will pray for you. The brother will pray for his brother. I will pray that Allāh (ﷻ) heal you. Allāh (ﷻ) ordered us to send our supplications. Allāh (ﷻ) says on the tongue of His Prophet (ﷺ):

> Oh My worshipper, be to Me as I want you to be
> and I will be to you as you want Me to be.

There are natural plants that heal high blood pressure.

Remedy for High Blood Pressure: Olive Leaf

1. Take 2 big Tbsp. of olive leaf and boil it for 25 minutes.

2. Drink the water and it will heal you.

It will reduce high blood pressure. I am very sure about this healing.

Treatment for Fever: Vinegar and Water

Many people go to the pharmacy and get medicine to treat a fever. I will tell you that you can get rid of a fever or high temperature by using plants.

1. Take 2 Tbsp. vinegar and mix with it with 2 Tbsp. water.

2. Take a thin cloth and put it in the mixture and wring it out.

3. Put the cloth on your body for 5 minutes.

After 5 minutes the temperature will be reduced. If you touch the cloth you can feel that it is hot because it has absorbed the heat. You can do this for yourself, men, women, or children. Put this cloth around the neck and between the legs. You can do this for a baby. Many people have tried this healing and I have confirmed the results.

Weight Loss/Hemorrhoids

Let me tell you about another important case. Many people want to lose weight, especially ladies. She looks at herself and thinks she is fat and wants to lose some weight. First of all, do not eat a lot. Sayyidinā Muḥammad (ﷺ) said:

> We are people who will not eat until we are hungry.
> When we eat, we do not fill ourselves to the brim.
> We fill one-third of our stomach with food,
> we fill the second third with water
> and we leave the third part for air.

The stomach is a machine. Why do you bother this machine and destroy it? When you put many spices and foods and peppers in it, it will affect the stomach and cause many diseases. All that food, pepper and salt destroys the stomach. The stomach has a thin wall.

Spices and peppers will cause hemorrhoids. How can you heal this disease? First, do not eat a lot. Keep one-third of the stomach for food, one-third for breath and one-third for water. If you have hemorrhoids use honey.

Treatment for Hemorrhoids: Honey

1. Take a small piece of cloth and dip it into honey and shape it into a capsule form.

2. Insert it into your rectum at bedtime and leave it in all night.

3. In the morning you will pass it when you go to the restroom.

Everything will be fine in 7-8 days. This is a very good cure and you will be better after 7 or 8 days.

Treatment for Weight Loss: Apple Cider Vinegar

Apple cider vinegar is the healing for weight loss. How can you keep our weight at a normal level?

1. Take 2 Tbsp. apple cider vinegar and add 3 Tbsp. of water.

2. Mix it together and drink every morning and before each meal.

Weigh your yourself when you start. For example, if you weigh 100 pounds to start and you take the vinegar for 1 month, then when you weigh yourself again you will weigh 70 pounds or 50 pounds. You will weigh ½ your weight. This is your natural weight. Do not take chemicals. Your meals should be an exact amount as I have told you. One-third of your stomach is for food, one-third is for breath and one-third is for water.

I mention this in all of my books. I feel sad because you don't read the books and you do not focus on those things. You do not understand and you go to doctors and give them your money. I am telling you, this is a treatment and you can do it. Yes, of course we need to go to hospitals in certain cases, but there are many diseases you can heal yourself. If you need X-Rays or an MRI or something you need to go to the doctor. I am not telling you to stop going to the doctor. There are certain cases.

Sayyidinā Muḥammad (ﷺ) ordered us to heal ourselves, to go to hospitals or doctors if needed.

Sayyidinā Muḥammad says:

> Heal yourself.

How can you heal yourself? If you have something wrong with your eyes go to a physician or an eye specialist. I am not telling you to not go to the doctor. Go to doctor, to a specialist; try more than one doctor. Go to the doctor who carries mercy in his heart.

Treatment for Skin Tags / Warts

Sometimes there is a part of the body, in Arabic we call it tallul. It is horrible and people feel uncomfortable when they see it. Tallul is like a wart or a skin tag. How do you heal tallul? Very simply but carefully. You should do it. To get rid of it you burn it.

1. Once daily, in the morning or night, dip a cloth into straight apple cider vinegar and then rub the area around the skin tag or wart with it. It will hurt but it is not too strong.

2. Do this for 1 week and it will disappear completely.

Treatment for Premenstrual Pain: Ginger and Cinnamon

Young girls who are not yet married sometimes have pain before their menses. She will sometimes feel bad pain that she can put up with for a day or two before she gets her period. There is a cure for this with ginger and cinnamon.

1. Take ½ tsp. raw ginger and ½ tsp. cinnamon stick and boil them in 2 cups of water.

2. Drink one glass in the morning and 2 or 3 hours later drink the second glass.

The young girl or woman who does this will clean out everything dirty from her stomach. This is very effective medicine. She will feel okay and have no more problems.

Protection Healing

I would like to give you something to heal people, because you will be healers, inshāʾa-llāh. There is a protection and I will teach you how to use it.

1. Make wuḍuʾ.

2. Pray 2 rakʿāh.

3. Ask Allāh (ﷻ) to give healing through your hands to heal this patient.

4. Say "astaghfiru-llāhu-l-aḍhīm" 100 times to make tawba for the client and yourself.

5. Follow the orders of Allāh (ﷻ).

6. Read the Arabic on the healing paper.

Our healings are not from the mind and not from us—they are from Allāh (ﷻ). So pray 2 rakʿāh to Allāh (ﷻ) asking Allāh (ﷻ) to help you to heal this patient. I will let you know how to use this protection paper. There are 2 papers, one in Arabic and one in English. You read the English one.

Wadude: Do people need to take a promise from you to do this healing? There are students in other communities who want to learn this healing, do they need to take a promise from you before they can do it? Can other muqqadams teach this healing?

Sidi: Yes, sure, they can teach this healing. You have permission to use this protection, but no one else can use it without permission. Muqqadams have permission to teach this healing. Muqaddams can give permission to students to use this healing.

This is the complete healing. I am sure Allāh (ﷻ) will protect you and your patient. You will also be guarded with this protection while you are giving it to others. It will keep you safe. Allāh (ﷻ) will heal the person even if he has a jinn or a devil. If it will not leave him through these āyah then the jinn or devil will be burned. Advise the patient who has a jinn to put the protection paper under his pillow.

Ibrāhīm and Wadude and all of my beloveds have permission to do this protection. Keep your promise and renew your promise. Come and take the promise again.

Sidi gives a promise.

Wadude: You have permission to make copies of the Arabic paper to give to clients when you give them a healing. After you give the healing, fold it and roll it and tape it up and have them put it under his or her pillow. Tell the client this is only for them. They are not to give it to other people or to make copies of it or to give it out. You can prepare the protections ahead of time to give out during the healing sessions.

Sidi: It will have no benefit to anyone other than the person who received the healing. The opposite will happen, he will get bad things. Without permission no one can use this healing.

Allah's Orders Are a Gift (ﷻ)
"A Drop of the Love" and Music
Friday, October 20, 2010 PM, San Diego

لا إله إلا الله - لا إله إلا الله - لا إله إلا الله - محمد رسول الله عليه صلاة الله
لا إله إلا الله - لا إله إلا الله - لا إله إلا الله - ابراهيم رسول الله عليه صلاة الله
لا إله إلا الله - لا إله إلا الله - لا إله إلا الله - موسى رسول الله عليه صلاة الله
لا إله إلا الله - لا إله إلا الله - لا إله إلا الله - عيسى رسول الله عليه صلاة الله
اللهم انت السلام ومنك السلام و إليك يعود السلام
تباركت ربنا وتعاليت يا ذوالجلال والإكرام

As-salāmu ʿalaykum wa raḥmatu-llāhi wa bārakatuhu. Peace be upon you, my beloveds. I thank Allāh (ﷻ) for letting me be here among all of you in this country, and I thank all of you. I ask Allāh (ﷻ) to protect all of you and to protect your hearts, your souls, your selves and your bodies from everything. I ask Allāh (ﷻ) to give you and your beloveds love, peace, mercy, freedom and justice, because you are honest, seeking the truth and raising the flag, the message of Allāh (ﷻ).

I can see myself flying in this earth, seeing all people live happily in this life, full of love and mercy, without any discrimination. The prophets (ﷺ) are confirmed and as Allāh (ﷻ) said to all the prophets (ﷺ):

> All people who carry the message of unity and who have faith
> are the beloveds of Allāh (ﷻ).

I am asking Allāh (ﷻ) to let you be happy and blessed and to let us see the whole world as one nation. As Allāh (ﷻ) says:

> Truly! This, your religion (or nation) is one religion (or nation),
> and I am your Lord; therefore, worship Me. (21:92)

Carry the sharīʿa, the divine law, and the ḥaqīqa, the divine reality. All the prophets (ﷺ) carried the sharīʿa and the ḥaqīqa. You received the message through them, the message of Sufism. We can define Sufism as iḥsān, excellence. What is the meaning of excellence? Excellence is to worship Allāh (ﷻ) as if you see Him (ḥadīth).

Islām means to be surrendered, to obey Allāh (ﷻ). The root of the word Islām is from the word peace, as-salām. In the Syriac language, Islām means peace, as-salām. In the Hebrew language, it also means peace. This is also old Hebrew from our Master Ibrāhīm's (Abraham's) time (ﷺ). What is the meaning of Isrāʾīl (Israel)? In the old Ibrāhīmic language it means the slave of Allāh (ﷻ), ʿAbd Allāh. It means peace.

Sayyidinā (Our master) Ibrāhīm (ﷺ) is the prophet who emigrated to Allāh (ﷻ). He is the father of all the prophets (ﷺ). The meaning of the name Ibrāhīm is to let go of everything and to fall in love. It means peace. In Sayyidinā Muḥammad's name (ﷺ), the first "mim" means "We send you as a mercy to all the worlds." This is the raḥma, the mercy. These are some of the secrets within these names.

I encourage you to understand the meaning of these words and to work for peace through spreading the message of unity, lā ʾilāha ʾilla-llāh. Follow all of the prophets and messengers (ﷺ). They are the leaders of all worlds for all eternity. They are the real leaders.

I am asking Allāh (ﷻ) to gather all people, all castes, all different religions, under the same flag: the flag of unity, real mercy, real justice, real freedom and real peace. Āmīn.

Now, you will listen to a beautiful song. It is food for your soul. My son will tell you something of love's real meaning. You can feel the fragrance of love and you can feel the fragrance of the Holy Land. After this song, you will listen to a beautiful song about the Holy Land.

"A Drop of the Love," and an introduction Sidi gave in Portland are read and accompanied by Shaykh Yasīn at-Tuhamī's music. This was Sidi's commentary on the song before he actually heard it. It is available on YouTube under "Sidi, A Drop of the Love."

The lyrics of the music
are bold, italicized and indented.
The reading is in bold text.
Sidi's live commentary is in plain text.

The reading begins, "Peace be upon you and peace be upon all of the prophets and all the beloved gnostics, all of them (عليهم السلام). Āmīn.

On this holy day, I am among you. I am here in my form, in my body. But when I leave and return to the Holy City, al-Quds, Jerusalem, I want you to know that I will keep my heart and my spirit praying for you and for everyone who is crying from the deep suffering in this world. I cry from my deepest spirit. I ask Allāh (ﷻ) to send His peace and His mercy and His love and His freedom and His justice to all people everywhere. Āmīn.

I ask that He help those who are crying from deep sickness everywhere. I ask that He send angel healers (عليهم السلام) for everyone who is crying from deep sickness, that He clean this heart, clean this land, clean all the earth everywhere from the bad sicknesses, from the bad diseases and from cancer. Āmīn.

I pray for Allāh (ﷻ) to stop wars everywhere, to send the wind of peace and to see the flag of unity from Allāh (ﷻ) go directly to every heart. Please, Allāh (ﷻ), answer our supplications, for we are between Your hands and we are Your poor servants. The poor people here are praying for You and for Your essence, for You created us and You provide for us. We direct our faces to You, asking for You to heal us, to heal our daughters and our sons and our beloveds all around the world. We complain to You of our weakness and our poverty and we take refuge in You, for You are the Only One. So please, Allāh (ﷻ), answer our questions and our supplications. Āmīn.

My beloveds, my heart is crying for those who are crying, for those who are crying from the deep suffering in all the world. Āmīn, Āmīn, Āmīn.

If you live a true life full of love, and you love humanity, love Allāh (ﷻ) and give everything to help others if they need help....if you give everything for the poor and sick people, this is your provision from Allāh (ﷻ). Allāh (ﷻ) lets you do this and lets you help others, so that in reality, you may help yourself. It is a gift from Allāh (ﷻ) to you and to others to be able to help those who are less fortunate. This is a holy thing.

My beloveds, do you want to live in the ocean? Do you want to swim in the ocean of love? Then come to the mercy of Allāh (ﷻ), for the door is open. Yes, the door is open and there is no separation in the world of Allāh (ﷻ). There are no words of separation or discrimination.

How can we come to the mercy of Allāh (ﷻ)? By praying and worshipping and following the orders of Allāh (ﷻ). We are the sons and daughters of Sufism. Allāh (ﷻ) selected us to be His beloveds because we follow His orders.

Me, I am poor and I do not have anything in my hands. There is no separation between me and you. We are one body, one heart and one spirit. We are manifestations of Allāh (ﷻ); we are divine manifestations. Even though we are different in color and language, there is really just one language—the language of Allāh (ﷻ)—which is in your heart."

Yes, this is the reality of humankind. Allāh (ﷻ) created us with His Hands. He told the angels (ﷺ):

> I will be creating a human being out of mud.
> When I finish forming him and fashioning him
> and breathe into him out of My spirit
> prostrate yourselves to him. (38:71)

This is an order. He ordered the angels to prostrate in front of this manifestation of Allāh (ﷻ). Humankind carries within it the whole world. Allāh (ﷻ) created him with His Hands. Many people confirmed that the clay Allāh (ﷻ) used to create Ādam (ﷺ) is from holy places: al-Quds (the Holy Land) and Mecca at the Kaʿba, which was the first place built for humanity.

Sayyidinā Muḥammad (ﷺ) says:

> You can travel to the three places from Mecca
> because it was the first place.

This was said because Mecca is the place to which we make Ḥajj, pilgrimage. The three places described in the Ḥadīth are: the Kaʿba, the Holy Land (Jerusalem), and the Prophet's mosque in Medina. These three places are holy places. You make pilgrimage to these places and worship Allāh (ﷻ) there.

Allāh (ﷻ) created you, oh human being. Your father Ādam (ﷺ) has been created from clay from these three places, and for this reason these places are holy. One prayer in Mecca equals 1,000-2,000 prayers anywhere else. In Jerusalem, the Holy Land, al-Quds, one prayer equals 1,000 prayers anywhere else. In the al-Aqṣā Mosque it is the same. You are holy. Allāh (ﷻ) says:

> I will be creating a human being out of mud.
> When I finish forming him and fashioning him
> and breathe into him out of My spirit
> prostrate yourselves to him. (38:71)

You carry His spirit. You are holy, so keep your nobility. Carry the message of unity and follow His orders: peace, justice, freedom, love and mercy. Guard yourselves and you will stay holy. Allāh (ﷻ) will love you while you are obeying Him, but if you disobey Him Allāh (ﷻ) tells us:

> When Allāh said to the angels, "Prostrate to Ādam"
> and all the angels prostrated except Iblīs
> Allāh asked him, "Oh Iblīs, why did you not prostrate?"
> He said, "I am better than him.
> You created me from fire
> and you created him from clay." (38:72-38:76)

So Allāh (ﷻ) told him:

> Then get out of here, for truly you are outcast. (38:77)

So do not follow Iblīs or you will be far from the mercy of Allāh (ﷻ). Iblīs said to Allāh (ﷻ):

> My Lord! Give me respite until the Day all are resurrected.
> (38:79)

Iblīs did not ignore Allāh (ﷻ). He told Him:

> I will sit in wait for them, I will try to mislead them.

Iblīs affirmed that the path of Allāh (ﷻ) is the straight path and Iblīs told Him:

> By Your might, then I will surely mislead them all,
> except Your chosen slaves among them. (38:82-83)

Why? Because Allāh (ﷻ) guards and protects them. Even if they sin, Allāh (ﷻ) opens the door of tawba. Those who worship Allāh (ﷻ) and do good deeds will have their tawba accepted by Allāh (ﷻ) and He will open the door for them. Disobedience cannot be in Allāh's heaven. We are asking Allāh (ﷻ) to let those of you who obey Allāh (ﷻ) carry His message and His love.

The reading continues, "You can recognize, know and understand this message, this language of the heart, by what is in your heart. This is why it's important to purify your heart. This is one language we can all understand. We can understand each other through the language of the spirit and the heart. This is the highest station.

Excuse me for this introduction. This is just some of the deep meaning of the love. This is like a drop from the ocean, so excuse me. I keep many things inside and everything comes in its time. Now we will begin the song and you can hear some of what I have explained in this song.

Music plays.

> *When He talks with me,*
> *He allows me to be with Him completely.*
> *I understand what He says.*
> *I am always ready to drink.*
> *I do not speak another word after that.*
> *His word is enough for me,*
> *because it comes from the One who loves me,*
> *the One who has cared about me all my life.*
>
> *Yes, I am in that situation,*
> *I am absent from everything that people see,*
> *because I am with Him,*

through my body, my self and my spirit.
In reality, there is not even a choice for me.
It is not easy to be in this situation
if you do not surrender completely to your Beloved.
He wants a special sacrifice from you through His beloveds,
through the Beloved who created you.
Listen to what He means.

The reading, "A Drop of the Love" begins in the middle, "Oh, Allāhu Akbar. I just want to be alone with my beloved God (ﷻ) in this life. This is the life I am waiting for—to not look left or right but to be only between His arms. Yā Allāh (ﷻ). Yā Allāh (ﷻ).

That is what I wait for. I wait to drink from His source and to swim in His ocean. Because of this I follow his commandments. Yes, yes, I follow what He says. When I mention the one I fall in love with..."

I would like to tell you that you are not the only one who asks Allāh (ﷻ) for love. Many within His creation ask Him for the same thing. You can see Him day and night. Can you hear the voices of the seas and rivers? Can you hear the voices of the birds? Can you listen to their music? Their music praises Allāh. Everything is praising Allāh (ﷻ). Every creature has its own praise, even the mountains. Allāh (ﷻ) talked to the mountains. He ordered them:

> And indeed We bestowed grace upon Dāwūd (David) from Us:
> "Oh you mountains, glorify (Allāh) with him! And you birds!
> And We made the iron soft for him." (34:10)

With who? With Sayyidinā Dāwūd (ﷺ). He is the prophet of Allāh (ﷻ). He used musical instruments to praise Allāh (ﷻ) and Allāh (ﷻ) ordered the mountains to sing with him. He said, "Praise Me with Dāwūd." Allāh (ﷻ) even ordered the birds to praise Him with Dāwūd. Allāh (ﷻ) says:

> Had We sent down this Qur'ān upon a mountain,
> you surely would have seen it humbling itself
> and rent asunder in awe of Allāh. (59:21 and tafsir)

The trees move left and right, praising Allāh (ﷻ). Everything in this world is praising Allāh (ﷻ) and many creations before you have praised Allāh (ﷻ).

Allāh (ﷻ) has told you:

> If you give thanks, I will give you more. (14:7)

Let the trees praise Allāh (ﷻ). They give their fruits to you. They give food and beautiful fruits to you. They are obeying Allāh (ﷻ).

Allāh (ﷻ) wants you to live happily in this life. Don't cause any corruption on this earth or to the trees. If you guard the earth, if you listen to the trees, then Allāh (ﷻ) will give you more. It is provision from Allāh (ﷻ). Everything in this world is provision from Allāh (ﷻ). If you cut down trees or poison the water...even the rocks are a mercy from Allāh (ﷻ). What are the corruptors doing now?

We thank Allāh (ﷻ) for all of His provision: the trees, the mountains, the rocks, the seas, the birds, everything. The corrupters cause many bad things and they poison this existence. Everything in this existence worships and praises Allāh (ﷻ).

This music is food for your spirit. It is the music of the rivers, of the trees and of the mountains. Don't cause any harm or pain to them. The wind is a mercy from Allāh (ﷻ) that lets you breathe cool air. Allāh (ﷻ) lets the wind sing its songs, beautiful melodies. All of these things know the love and give the love. Why do you cause pain to others? When you cause pain to others, you cause pain to yourself. This is a great provision.

Many people cannot understand the divine language. They say "What is the meaning of music?" Music carries divine melodies. You should understand it with your spirit and in this way it can be food for your spirit. Listen, Allāh (ﷻ) does not forbid us from listening to music. Music is within His divine existence. This is one of the meanings of music, one of the meanings of love. It is a correct one. Allāh (ﷻ) ordered all the prophets (ﷺ) to read all the holy books with a divine melody.

Music plays.

> ***"When I mention the one I fell in love with, my Beloved One,***
> ***I am happy, even if I see Him only in my dreams.***

The reading continues, "My hearing witnesses that I love You. The dream that comes to my eyes, to my ears, to my heart, all of them witness that I love You. My ears, my eyes, everything that God (ﷻ) gave me witness that I love You. They witness that I do not return back. Always, I keep my deep spirit with my Beloved who loves me, Allāh (ﷻ). Even if I am far away and do not see Him, He does not go far away. He never leaves me, not for one moment.

This is my chance. This is my chance to be with Him. This, my beloveds, is the real wedding. It is my pleasure to hear my remembrance within my witnessing, to hear and feel my remembrance within my love. Oh, I am so lucky that He took me in His arms, that Allāh (ﷻ) took me into His arms and that He supports me in obeying His orders and that He helps me to always be in His eternal world. This is my pleasure and this is my hope. This is my end and this is my goal, that He puts me in front of His eyes and takes care of me. Āmīn. It is my deep wish to see all of you who love Allāh (ﷻ), everyone, in this holy station. Āmīn.

I want to see the whole world dance with each other, to be real beloveds, to have a real wedding with Allāh (ﷻ). I want to see all of the beloveds who love Allāh (ﷻ) live in the ocean of His love. Āmīn. Āmīn. I want them all to reach and to hear the divine station, for Allāh (ﷻ) wants to position all of His creatures in this station. If they obey His orders (ﷻ) and the orders carried out by all the prophets (ﷺ), and if they carry the message of unity through the love that Allāh (ﷻ) gifted us, they will be clean. To be clean gives life to you and to everyone who is in this state, in this place and everywhere.

He loved us, so He gave us the gift of His sharīʿa, His rules, His orders. He taught us His prohibitions and what we should not do. It is Allāh's gift to us to clean us, to clean our hearts to know His love, because He loves you. He loves you and you love Him. If you follow His orders, you will be in His loving presence all the time. There is no life except within Him, and this is why it is important to follow Him, to obey Him, and to be between His hands as He wishes. Because He said:

> I will be with you everywhere and anywhere. (20:46 and Tafsir)

My beloveds, this is the truth. How do you want to walk to Allāh (ﷻ)? This is the walking. I have explained it in all my books. This is what you need to know. If you speak from an ugly mind, you will not be able to reach Allāh (ﷻ). You will forget Him and you will turn away from Him. You will leave His Garden and you will go into the material world, the rubbish world, the recycle bin.

Allāh (ﷻ) wants to give you sweets, but you do not want them. What are you trying to say? You claim that you are a slave, but you do not follow His orders. You do not follow the commands that He sent down to His prophets and messengers (ﷺ). So how, then, are you a slave?

Some people say they are lovers but they kill others. They are killers. They break hearts. Some people say they are lovers but they are thieves. What is that? Return back to Allāh (ﷻ)! The cure, the healing, is in Allāh (ﷻ). He provides us with everything. After that, how can anyone disobey Allāh (ﷻ) and follow the shayṭān, Iblīs? Allāh (ﷻ) says:

> (Escape to) Allāh, the true Guardian-Protector. (Tafsir of 2:257)

Allāh (ﷻ) is the supporter of those who are honest. Allāh (ﷻ) will forbid those who disobey Him from tasting the love. They will not be able to taste the love. Those who love Allāh (ﷻ), those who follow His divine law, will be under the tent of Allāh (ﷻ). They will be in the Garden with spreading branches where you can always find His provision.

> Say, 'If you love Allāh (ﷻ) then follow me.' (3:31)"

Oh, Allāh (ﷻ)!

The reading continues, "Allāh (ﷻ) gives me this special gift, Allāh (ﷻ), the only truth, al-Ḥaqq, He gave me a message for those who have already heard the divine call, but disobeyed. I hope and I ask Allāh (ﷻ) to open their hearts, their spirits and their minds to be among those who receive His mercy and purification. His message is the message of the Most Compassionate, the Most Merciful.

Music plays.

I remember His name.
I enjoy remembering Him, even if all of you blame me.
It doesn't matter, I love Him.
Yes, I love Him.
Ḥabībi, my love, my spirit.
Mention my Lover, mention His name,
Even in my dreams, mention His name.

My love, my spirit, when you mention the name of Allāh (ﷻ) with sincerity in your heart, it is not just your tongue that says the name. Every part of you is saying the name. Your trillions of cells are saying the name of Allāh (ﷻ) when you say it with sincerity. My love, my spirit, by mentioning the One I love, I will have eternal life.

My beloveds, keep repeating, keep mentioning and keep remembering. Keep giving the water of life to your hearts and your spirits so that you can continue to be in Allāh's order, the divine order in which He commanded us to reside.

It is the holy order to carry Your message and to save all people from suffering around the world, and not only this world, but in all of Your worlds that You created and gave the real life. You asked and ordered them to carry the flag of happiness, pleasure and spirit, which will send love to their hearts, for You are our love. You are our Lord (ﷻ). Oh, my Lord (ﷻ).

I will not listen to people who say many different things, who try to distort the orders of Allāh (ﷻ) or make the orders of Allāh (ﷻ) confusing. They live in illusion, in pictures that they talk about with false tongues. This is not what Allāh (ﷻ) wants. He wants you to throw your self, your heart and your spirit between the arms of Allāh (ﷻ) under His religion of unity. He wants you to follow everything that He says and then you will be a pure one.

Do not choose another way, my children. Do not choose dark and false ways. Be in the ocean of your Beloved, under His command, under what He says for you to do because He cares about you. He wants you to be and to live in the way that He wants for you. You will be in His ocean, full of love.

This is the life for you, my daughters, my sons, my children. I will open my life and my spirit to every one of you who wants life. This life has already been given by Allāh (ﷻ). The provision comes from Allāh (ﷻ).

Many, many thanks Allāh (ﷻ), for You gave me the water of mercy. I ask You to accept my supplication and to give this holy water of mercy to others, to all my children, and to allow them to live a good life."

This is the right thing, this is the life you want to have. If you would like to live a life full of mercy and love and to know the essence of what you carry, I will explain how to reach and how to be in the real place without murder like the murder between the governments. No. Allāh (ﷻ) gives you complete freedom to swim in the ocean of love and mercy and to sing the song of Allāh (ﷻ) through your being. This is what I mean.

The reading continues, "When you love Allāh (ﷻ), when you trust Allāh (ﷻ), when you remember Allāh (ﷻ), then in one moment you can be in His Garden. If you taste, you know what I mean. I am going to open the door for you."

Now! Now! It is important to be in the garden of Allāh (ﷻ). When you know how to understand, as I explain to you now.

The reading continues, "This is what Allāh (ﷻ) says:

> **Come, come to My paradise!**

He opens the door to be in the Garden now."

Not tomorrow!

The reading continues, "So do not wait, my beloveds."

Be the son of your moment. Be the daughter of your moment. This is what Allāh (ﷻ) opens. Why do you want to close the door in front of your face?

The reading continues, "Your Beloved is waiting for you. He wants to make a real wedding for you. This is the real life and there is no doubt."

There is no wedding like this wedding. It means the love of Allāh (ﷻ). There is no murder, there is no end, there is no beginning when He says, "I am Allāh (ﷻ)." Come. Bismi-llāh. The door is open.

Allāhu Akbar!

The reading continues, "This is the real life. There is no death, only life. This means to follow what He says. If you listen and follow what comes from the dirty water, how can you be in the real life? No one can do this. This is the real death. Drink the water of Allāh (ﷻ), my beloveds, the tawḥīd, the unity."

This is the real life, without anything, only Allāh (ﷻ).

The reading continues, "I want you all to say, 'Lā ʾilāha ʾilla-llāh.'"

Audience: Lā ʾilāha ʾilla-llāh!

The reading continues, "Don't just say this with your tongue. Say it with your heart and your spirit. Use what He gave you in the way He wants. I want you to use your hands, your legs, your mind and your hearts only for what Allāh (ﷻ) has ordered. I want you to follow what He sent through His beloved prophets (عليهم السلام). Then, my children, you will be happy. Do not think you will die, because you will have eternal life.

So, my children, if you are ready, I want you to come to me now. If you are ready to open your heart, to know and feel a drop of this love, if you are ready to know how to give the real love to your beloved, how to give the real life to your children and your parents and your brothers and sisters, do not be shy. Come to me now and let me pray to open your heart with the water of this mercy. Let me help you pray to know this love, to swim in this ocean now. Come, my beloveds. Come to me now."

This is a holy hour. It is a very special chance for you to be with Allāh (ﷻ). Come to Allāh (ﷻ). Come to me. I am a poor slave, I am a servant. I will serve you. I will die for you. I will die for you through all the prophets' instructions, through all of Allāh's orders, to take you to Allāh (ﷻ).

I am following Sayyidinā Ibrāhīm (عليه السلام), Sayyidinā Mūsā (Moses) (عليه السلام), Sayyidinā ʿĪsā (Jesus) (عليه السلام), Sayyidinā Muḥammad (ﷺ) and all the prophets (عليهم السلام). I am following their laws. There is nothing in this from my self. There is nothing in this from my head. I received this information from the presence of Allāh (ﷻ).

I will serve you. I am a servant of the dust you walk on. You should be like this. All people should be like this. Be lovers. Keep the love in your hearts, the complete peace, the complete mercy and the complete freedom, to be one body, one heart, one spirit.

Sidi gives the promise.

The Family's Beautiful Fragrance

"The Beloveds of God" from *Conversations in the Zawiyah*

November 8, 2010

لا إله إلا الله – لا إله إلا الله – لا إله إلا الله – محمد رسول الله عليه صلاة الله

لا إله إلا الله – لا إله إلا الله – لا إله إلا الله – ابراهيم رسول الله عليه صلاة الله

لا إله إلا الله – لا إله إلا الله – لا إله إلا الله – موسى رسول الله عليه صلاة الله

لا إله إلا الله – لا إله إلا الله – لا إله إلا الله – عيسى رسول الله عليه صلاة الله

اللهم انت السلام ومنك السلام و إليك يعود السلام

تباركت ربنا وتعاليت يا ذوالجلال والإكرام

My beloveds, as-salāmu ʿalaykum wa raḥmatu-llāhi wa bārakatuhu. I am asking Allāh (ﷻ) to let you be among His beloveds and among the beloveds of Sayyidinā (our Master) Muḥammad (ﷺ). I am asking Him to let you be firm on his path, to let you be sincere. I am asking Allāh (ﷻ) to purify your hearts, your intellects, your souls, your selves, your bodies, and that of your families and all of your beloveds.

These are holy days. This is the second day of Dhul Ḥijja, the month of pilgrimage. This is the month of pilgrimage for Sayyidinā Ibrāhīm (Abraham) (عليه السلام) and all the worshippers, the believers, the prophets (عليهم السلام) that Allāh (ﷻ) sent down to this lower world to carry the message of peace, love, mercy and justice to all the people without any discrimination, following the orders of Allāh (ﷻ). Allāh (ﷻ) says:

> And truly, this is My straight path, so follow it. (6:153)

Allāh (ﷻ) says:

> Truly! This, your religion (or nation) is one religion (or nation). (21:92)

We do not discriminate between any nation and we believe in all the prophets (عليهم السلام): Sayyidinā ʿĪsā (Jesus) (عليه السلام), Sayyidinā Mūsā (Moses) (عليه السلام), Sayyidinā Ibrāhīm (عليه السلام) and Sayyidinā Muḥammad (ﷺ).

It is a great honor to be among you during these holy days in this holy month. These are pleasant days.

> The Ḥajj is (in) the well-known months (the 10th month, the 11th month and the first ten days of the 12th month). (2:197)

On those 10 days, as mentioned in the Qur'ān, one prayer equals thousands of prayers. Also, praising Allāh (ﷻ), worshipping Allāh (ﷻ) and fasting on those days equals a thousand months of worship (97:3). We should follow Allāh (ﷻ) and be humble, purifying our hearts and souls as Allāh (ﷻ) wants for us.

We're asking Allāh (ﷻ) to gather every good deed for us. He is able to do this. This day, as I mentioned, is a blessed day, a great day. Purify yourself from this dunyā, from this lower world, and then you will be real children between Allāh's hands.

Allāh (ﷻ) created you to worship Him. Be humble with Allāh (ﷻ) and with all people. Sayyidinā Muḥammad (ﷺ) said:

> All creatures are the children of Allāh (ﷻ),
> and the most beloved to Him
> are the ones who are most beneficial to His children.

Direct your purified face, purified vision and purified hearing toward Allāh (ﷻ) and Allāh (ﷻ) will accept you. You have to purify your heart from everything in this dunyā, and Allāh (ﷻ) is able to do everything.

At this time, you are in the healing school. There is no discrimination in this university because this is the religion of divine unity. Lā ʾilāha ʾilla-llāhu. There is only one God (ﷻ).

This university opens its heart to all people without discrimination who follow all the prophets (ﷺ). We have to study and obtain knowledge from this university because this university teaches and follows the message of God (ﷻ).

I direct my speech to all of you: open your hearts, open your eyes and open your ears to this divine knowledge. This divine knowledge has come down to all the prophets (ﷺ), and I'm not saying that this knowledge is from me. It's not from me. It is from Allāh (ﷻ) to all the prophets. When you have this divine knowledge you'll be able to heal yourself and others. This is from Allāh (ﷻ) to Allāh (ﷻ), to all the prophets (ﷺ) and to all of you.

The first thing to do in your hearts and intellects if you wish to obtain this divine knowledge is: don't backbite others. Don't use your eyes for forbidden things.

I am a slave, a poor servant, trying to give you the divine instructions. They are not from my head. They are from Allāh (ﷻ) through all the prophets (ﷺ). We are the children of Ādam (ﷺ) and we take care of our family.

This life is like a ship and our family is a ship. This ship, this family, carries men and women who should carry the love. They should be similar to each other and love each other as Allāh (ﷻ) ordered us through Sayyidinā Muḥammad (ﷺ) and all the prophets (ﷺ), including: ʿĪsā (ﷺ), Mūsā (ﷺ) and Ibrāhīm (ﷺ). Sayyidinā Muḥammad (ﷺ) said:

> The best one is the one who takes care of his family.

And he (ﷺ) says:

> Take care of your women, your wives and daughters.
> Keep their hearts and their bodies safe.

The husband should give his wife pure love and he should give his entire self, his entire heart to her because she is his mirror, his pure mirror, and he has to take care of this mirror. The wife is the mirror of her husband and the husband is the mirror of his wife. Love and peace need to exist between them, reflecting in this mirror, in order for this ship to sail safely.

Listen to this reading to learn how the husband should be with his wife and how they should follow the orders of Allāh (ﷻ), serving each other and being honest, because Allāh (ﷻ) says that we are from each other. Allāh (ﷻ) created us out of clay. Be humble. Be humble. Āmīn.

The reading, "The Beloveds of God" from *Conversations in the Zawiyah*[30] is read, "Bismi-llāhi-r-raḥmāni-r-raḥīm. The Beloveds of God. I want to speak about the prophets (ﷺ) and the father of the light (Muḥammad ﷺ) and how all the prophets lived with their wives. Listen. Listen with the ear of your heart, my sons and my daughters, to hear what I say because this is a very important subject and it is from the order of God (ﷻ) to speak to you about how to live as husband and wife and be beloveds of God (ﷻ).

Now, I have given you many subjects before to help you to know yourself, to find the key to open the hidden treasure that is inside of you. After you have walked in the way and lifted the veils of darkness to see the light of God (ﷻ), He will bring you a step higher to see Him in the face of your beloved.

The understanding of God (ﷻ) and all that His love means to you is completed by the sharing of the deep secret love with another, because it is putting the essence of all the teachings and all the books and all the sciences and all that God (ﷻ) has given to you into manifestation through the love that you share with your beloved.

Everything before has been a preparation for seeing the light of God (ﷻ) in the eye of your beloved. You have cut through many stones in your way, for the world is full of darkness and trouble and many things have come before you. But it is necessary to erase everything, to erase everything, and to leave your past behind. Come to your beloved with a clean heart in order to live in the heart of God (ﷻ), for He wants to show you the true picture of Himself in the face of your beloved.

It is necessary to be careful with those whom God (ﷻ) gives us to care about, because they really are jewels. Their hearts are pure and clean and through them you can see the true image of God (ﷻ). With your beloved you share a love whose depths cannot be fathomed, because it is the love of God (ﷻ). His secret is in the love. It is important for you to care for your beloved as if you were caring for God (ﷻ) and to speak to your beloved as if you were speaking to God (ﷻ). At every moment you

---

[30] Sidi Muhammad, *Conversations in the Zawiyah*. Petaluma: Sidi Muhammad Press, 1999, pp. 24-28.

stand facing God (ﷻ). God (ﷻ) is your beloved. You must be polite with your beloved and give your whole self to this love.

Now, sometimes God (ﷻ) manifests through your beloved as the jamāl (His beauty) and sometimes as the jalāl (His severity). He who cannot accept both is not the unity, because he is manifesting what he wants to see of himself. Give love to your beloved. It will change the darkness to the light and the jalāl into a garden of love. Care for your beloved. Make sure each word and action contains only the love of God (ﷻ) and His politeness."

You have to keep the family sacred. You can see there is no family now. The family has been destroyed all over the world—in Africa, America and the Middle East. We used to live in a beautiful way with our families. Our families were happy and we helped each other.

Now people say, "We want freedom." But what kind of freedom do they want? A wrong type of freedom. When a child is 18 years old his parents will tell him, "Get out of my home." Where is the family in this? There is no family. One hundred years ago the family gathered together, all of the children and grandchildren, and they lived in peace. If a man looked at his home and asked, "Where is my daughter?" or, "Where is my son?" his children were there and they would take care of him.

This issue has really caused a big mess in the world. Mothers used to take care of their children. Now you can't find them doing so—they're only taking care of their husbands. Where are her children? Where are her sons and daughters? This is not the law of Allāh (ﷻ). The law of Allāh (ﷻ) says that children should be loved. Parents should give them love to let them be happy. Now, if a mother has five kids, there is no one around to support her if she gets sick. This is the situation now.

I want to tell you: sickness does not just occur in the body. Sickness also occurs in the emotions, the heart and the intellect. We need to correct this and teach people how to establish the real family. This is the principle healing for the whole world. Today, if a parent enters his home he will not find his children there; this causes the intellect to constantly question, "Where are my children? Where are my sons? Where are my beloveds? I want to smell their fragrances."

Life is not just about eating and drinking. If a family lives in a castle or a palace, it doesn't mean anything without children, without grandsons and granddaughters. This is a real sickness. This issue causes pain. We should re-connect the family to eliminate this sickness in this dark world. This is a dark world, and unhealthy families darken it. A prison is better than some homes because in prison you can at least find people to talk to, but at home you can only find old men and women with no one around them.

These are not the teachings of Allāh (ﷻ). The real healing is to stop what we are doing and follow the sharīʿa (divine law) of the family as our great-grandparents did. This is the most important issue and I want to focus on it. Sayyidinā Muḥammad (ﷺ) was asked:

> "To whom should we give our attention and caring?"
> He (ﷺ) answered, "Your mother."
> He asked him (ﷺ) again, "Who?"
> He (ﷺ) told him, "Your mother."
> After he (ﷺ) repeated, "your mother" three times
> the Prophet (ﷺ) said, "Your father."

So, the Prophet (ﷺ) said for you to give to your mother 3 times, because she gave you life and love.

Today, you can find the father and mother alone with no grandchildren, daughters or sons. They barely talk to each other. There is no happiness. This is a symptom of sickness within the intellect. This is the real sickness. This is the real sickness. Most families are suffering from this sickness. There is no purity inside their homes. We can't deny this. Destruction has reached the family. The mother is suffering, the father is suffering. Their intellects are asking, "Where are my kids? Where is my family?" This is the real disease.

Establish the family. Give it the love. Give love to your children like our fathers and mothers gave it to us. This is a fruitful tree. You need this tree. If this tree doesn't produce a shadow you won't want to sit under it, and you need to sit under it. The child is a fruit and you are the tree. Parents want to see their fruits.

Now, look at the daughter. She remembers her parents when she wants to say happy birthday. She just calls them to say happy birthday and that's it. They gave her everything, they love her, and they want to see their fruits around them. Your parents want to hear your voice and see your face. The voices of our beloveds are a melody that feeds our bodies, our intellects, our spirits. This is a fact. All these diseases are a result of the family's destruction. I'm trying to let you know how to heal this disease.

The reading continues, "So, my beloveds, I want you to understand what God (ﷻ) wants from you in every moment. What He wants for you is to be the father and the mother, the sister and the brother, the wife and the husband to your beloved. To be everything at any time. And do not search for your beloved in any other place, because he holds all the qualities of God (ﷻ). And you, also, are the beloved of God (ﷻ). There is no separation between you because you both carry the soul of God (ﷻ). The husband does not make a difference between his wife and himself, and the wife does not make a difference between her husband and herself. They are one. There are no numbers in the truth.

From the picture I have given you, from the religion of your soul, the soul of God (ﷻ) and of the guide, send mercy to your beloved; in this giving you are sending mercy to yourself. Life in the marriage of beloveds is for each to be holy and to care about one another. This marriage is like a holy tree, a holy tree whose roots grow deep into the earth and the earth is the heart of God (ﷻ).

How do you nourish this tree? You nourish it by giving it love, by giving it love and clean water, water that has been cleansed of all the troubles of this world. Now it is necessary for the tree to grow strong in order to give shade to all the lovers of God (ﷻ) who are beneath it. And when nourished, her roots will grow deep into the earth, becoming all the qualities of God (ﷻ) and covering the universe with its essence. This is the Tree of Life, and it is necessary for it to be nourished with the love of God (ﷻ). Then it will give the holiest of fruits and, with His permission, have the sweetest of flowers, because it comes from one source. Surround her with love and clean water.

So, how do you do this? By helping each other. Help each other while walking in the way to remove all obstacles that come before you. Let nothing stand in the way of this love, for the heart of your beloved is like a glass and it is necessary to take care of it so that it will not break, for if it breaks you will have broken yourself. You will have misused its care and then God (ﷻ) will take you from His garden. The heart of your beloved is like a jewel and there are responsibilities for caring for this heart.

Your time together as beloved has three parts. The first is for yourself; the second is for your wife or husband; the third is for your children. And from all of this, you can give. You can give to your mother or your father, your sisters and your brothers."

Keep building the family. Build the family. Don't reject your sons and daughters, your relatives, you cousins, your kin. Give them mercy, love and justice. Help them. You should even give your neighbors the love. Let the area you live in be full of love and happiness, full of peace. Heal them. The one Allāh (ﷻ) loves the most is the one who loves others and who says a kind word to them (ḥadīth). Don't reject your family and your relatives, your neighbors. Give them love in order to establish the heaven of love. This is real healing.

If your neighbor is sick, how can you help him and heal him? You can heal him with love, with support. They will be your beloveds. If you give love you will receive love. Be wise and teach them how we should be brothers to each other without discrimination. Whether he's black or white, he's your brother. You are both from the same mother and the same father (Adam and Hawwā' ؉).

This is the real healing for all people. Sometimes you hear about a person who has a mental or psychic disease. Why? Because he lives by himself. He has no family, no sons, no relatives. What kind of life is he living?

The human being is the brother of other human beings. Heal him with good, kind words, full of love and mercy. This is the way. Then, you will find all people happy and cured from their illnesses. Many people lose their intellects and their minds and they have a lot of money, but the money doesn't help them to be happy. They feel depressed and frustrated and they get sick. They will leave this dunyā, they will die, leaving everything behind them because of what their hands have earned.

Allāh (ﷻ) guided us in how to live, how to love each other. Don't fight each other. Don't be aggressive. Don't be an oppressor. Why do people fight each other? Because they are sick. You can even find the cause of war in this disease. You will leave this dunyā and you will leave everything behind you.

The reading continues, "All of these parts are for God (ﷻ) and if you walk straight and you give your whole self for the love of God (ﷻ), He will give you a life of happiness and peace. What more could you want?

Now, the husband is like the father of the universe. First, he begins in the home where his example is like the earth, which anyone can walk upon and take what they want. The husband's soil is the ground of love and he stands strong as the source of love and understanding in the family. Behind his strength is the mercy of Allāh (ﷻ). God (ﷻ) has made him a captain of the ship in order to provide for his family. His wife can come to him at any time and he gives her the love and the caring of God (ﷻ). He is the support and strength of the family, maintaining the home in balance. The way of every prophet (ﷺ) has been to help his wife, not making a difference between her and himself. She is his equal.

The father of the light, our Prophet Muḥammad (ﷺ), may Allāh (ﷻ) bless him and send him peace, helped his wife with everything. He cleaned, he cooked, he sewed, he brought water from the well, he brought coal for the fire and he played with the children at home. This is the way of every prophet. God (ﷻ) says, "Know that your wife is your mirror. Through her reflection you can see yourself, and if she remains in your heart, then you can see Me through the eye of your heart. This is only true if you care for this heart and send her love."

Yes, my son, when your work is finished, if she has not finished her work it's necessary to help with what's needed. The responsibility of the husband is great. He must provide love where love is needed and help without being asked, keeping peace within the family and knowing that there is no kingship in being a captain.

The wife is not a servant for her husband, nor is the husband a servant for his wife. They are both slaves for God (ﷻ). If God (ﷻ) is your Beloved, then you are slaves for each other. And if you treat her as a jewel and appreciate everything that is done as if it were coming from the hand of God (ﷻ), then she will be happy and not turn outside. She will keep the home as if it were a loving garden.

The wife is the mother. Not only are her family her children, all the world are her children. She is a fountain of love, showering the world with her water. Its source is a deep spring flowing directly from God (ﷻ). She has the love to give without asking anything in return, without holding anything back, because her giving has no end. She knows that caring for her family is the expression of her love for God (ﷻ) and anyone can come to her for anything at any time. She gives patience and understanding without end. Her home is kept as a place of beauty. She prepares food as if her Lord were a guest for dinner.

She is the most precious of jewels and she must open the jewel inside of herself. This jewel is hidden within the deepest valley, holding all of the wisdom of the love of God (ﷻ). If she reaches this valley, she will know the meaning of the love she gives. When she speaks with her husband she must know that she is speaking with God (ﷻ). Every word she speaks is a prayer, and it is the same for her husband because everyone is the face of God (ﷻ). If anyone is impolite with this reflection, then he is impolite with God (ﷻ). If a husband feels that his home is a garden which contains a loving wife, then he will not turn outside. He will feel peace and happiness in his heart."

This is the truth and these are the elements of how to heal the heart, the intellect, the body and the soul. You have to follow this guidance. These are instructions from Allāh (ﷻ), not from any human being. Allāh (ﷻ) teaches us how to keep the body holy and how to keep the family strong, meaning the mother and father. If you are polite to each other, love each other, help each other, then you will serve each other. There is no boss here; there is no president here. No. She is he and he is she.

Help each other to keep this holy structure. Don't leave space for devils to enter. Don't listen to those who are estranged from Allāh (ﷻ). This is the only healing. This way your children will grow up as strong men and women carrying the divine love, carrying the divine message.

This is the tree. You are the tree. You are the mother and the father. You are the tree. You will give good fruits: beautiful hearts, beautiful souls, beautiful intellects. Your children are your fruits. Everything will be healthy if the mother and the father are healthy.

The reading continues, "It is necessary for every child born from this holy marriage to see only light from the beginning."

Your marriage will be holy and blessed if the food between you is love, peace and justice. Then your earth will produce good, wholesome fruits. If you follow these instructions when you get married, you can be like the tree that gives fruits and the leaves that give shade to others. You will hear the melodies of the trees and you will hear the melodies of the rivers.

In order to achieve this, you have to drink pure water and you have to behave yourself. Be well-behaved. Don't carry hatred—carry the qualities of God (ﷻ). His names are al-Laṭīf, the Gentle, and ar-Raḥīm, the Merciful. Be like Him. Why does Allāh (ﷻ) give you all of the divine names? He gives them to you so that you can obtain knowledge from them. You are here to obtain knowledge about healing, so my advice to you is: heal yourself.

Heal yourself. Follow the prophets (عليهم السلام). Be gentle. Be gentle. Be beautiful. Be a world full of beauty; don't be a world full of darkness. In this way, we can know how to heal ourselves. If you recover and heal yourself, you will see yourself in a different way. You will find the beauty and feel how beautiful you are. Then, you can heal others.

If someone comes to you asking for help, asking for you to heal him, you should ask him, "How are you doing?" He will tell you, "I am suffering. I am in pain. I have many nightmares or illusions." Then, you should ask him, "Why do you think you are like this?" He will answer, "I am alone. I feel lonely." Why? This is from what your hands have earned. You are the heavens. You are the tree. This is why you put your fruits out on the streets (out in the world).

Teach the love. Teach your sons and daughters love and mercy. Allāh (ﷻ) will ask the father and the mother, "How did you deal with your children?" He will ask if you gave them the love or not. So Allāh (ﷻ) says, "My servant, know me and obey Me. I will give to you and I will answer you. I am very close to you and I will answer your supplications." This is the principle issue.

You are here to learn healing. The knowledge and instruction this university contains is from Allāh (ﷻ) and all the prophets (ﷺ). Open your hearts. The University opens her doors to all people, regardless of religion and who they are. It is open to all people who believe there is one God (ﷻ) and to all those who seek to obtain love, truth, justice and freedom by following the Merciful, the Compassionate, ar-raḥmāni-r-raḥīm. We are different from other universities because we are trying to teach our students how to be happy.

This knowledge, these references, are from Allāh (ﷻ). The name of this university is "The Spiritual University for All People Seeking the Truth," and its students will receive the truth through God's knowledge. No one can heal himself or others without following Allāh's divine knowledge. As I mentioned, start with yourself. Heal yourself, heal your spirit and heal your intellect. Allāh (ﷻ) says:

> It is He who has created for you hearing, eyes and hearts.
> (23:78. See also 32:9, 46:26, 67:23)

He gave you two eyes, lips and a heart. Allāh (ﷻ) says in a ḥadīth qudsī:

> My heavens and My earth cannot contain Me.
> Only the heart of My faithful, honest servant contains Me.

You can contain Allāh (ﷻ). Your heart should contain all of the divine qualities. You should carry all the divine qualities, and then you will be a successful healer. Without doing this, there is nothing. The reason for all diseases, like cancer, high blood pressure, etc., is lack of love: selfishness, anger and sadness. These things cause disease because the human being starts to think and think without guidance. So, we are telling you about the qualities of Allāh (ﷻ), the qualities of God (ﷻ). Carry these divine names. Allāh (ﷻ) says on the tongue of His Messenger (ﷺ):

> Oh My worshipper, be to Me as I want you to be
> and I will be to you as you want Me to be.
> Love Me and I will love You. (tafsir)

He loves you and then you love Him. The love of Allāh (ﷻ) will purify you if you search for the reasons behind a certain sickness or situation. If you are not feeling well, if you are not happy, ask yourself why you are sad. You are sad because you've lost your daughters or your sons; you're sad because you've lost your family. Your eyes can't see the beauty. There is no love. You have lost the love. If we make mistakes Allāh (ﷻ) has ordered us to do what the Qur'ān says:

> Say: "Oh My slaves who have transgressed against themselves!
> Do not despair of the mercy of Allāh.
> Truly, Allāh forgives all sins.
> Truly He is Often-Forgiving, Most Merciful." (39:53)

Make your tawba (repentance). Make your tawba. Tawba is quite enough; it is enough to wash your lips, your eyes and your ears. Do tawba if you use your ears to spy on others and your heart is full of diseases. How can you heal all of these things? Tawba. Tawba will teach you how to heal yourself and how to heal others. All of us make mistakes except for the prophets (ﷺ).

Allāh (ﷻ) explained to us how to make tawba, the tawba for your intellect, for your hands, for your soul and for your heart. If you are honest and make a true tawba, be sure that you will not feel sad anymore or have disease. This is the beginning of healing.

I gave this lecture and I will repeat it again and again and again. And I want to repeat again and again so that you understand the reasons for these diseases and you know how to heal them. If you follow Allāh's orders He will heal you. Allāh (ﷻ) is the Provider. Many our beloveds have come to me saying, "Oh, Sidi! I lost my job. I sold my home. I don't have anything." So, judge yourself before the Day of Judgment. Why didn't you act wisely? Allāh (ﷻ) says He will not ask you for what is beyond your ability.

Don't transgress against yourself and others. Do the things you can do. If you cannot carry 200 pounds on your shoulders why did you take on this weight? Carry what you can, because you will cause pain for your body and you will fall down, otherwise. Then you will say, "Allāh (ﷻ) did this to me." You did this to yourself! This is because of what your hands have earned. This is the truth.

The human being should be wise and he should not let his intellect be busy with Illusions and pictures. Allāh (ﷻ) created you free, He gave you a heart and He gave you eyes to use in the right way. Don't think like the foolish or crazy people. They will not be able to help you or heal you. Their thoughts or ideas will make you sad because you are following crazy people. They are corrupters. This is the truth. They hate humanity and they are losers.

Follow the divine orders. Follow all of the holy books. All of the holy books have been sent to all the prophets (ﷺ). Follow the Qur'ān and follow the divine law. You will be a healer and you can heal others. This is my advice. You are my beloveds. You are students in this Sufi University. You can be successful healers by following those instructions. Āmīn.

The reading continues, "It is necessary for every child born from this holy marriage to see only light from the beginning and to grow up in a happy home full of love. Teach him the meaning of courtesy. Teach him politeness toward his mother and father and do not leave him to follow his own impulse, but guide him in everything. For if he is left to follow his own impulses, he will feel the troubles of the darkness and God (ﷻ) will ask both the parents why the child was left on his own. It is also from this message to not give the child after he or she has grown up to anyone who is not from the family of God (ﷻ). Others do not know the meaning of politeness in the same way.

In the religion of God (ﷻ) the woman is like a jewel and it is necessary for the man to drink from the cup of her wine because its essence is the deep, secret love of God (ﷻ). My sons and daughters, if you knew what God (ﷻ) has given to you, you would not do or say anything to break the heart of your beloved. The key to living a life with a beloved is to give each other what each person needs. I'm sure that if everyone does all

that I have said you will live this day in the Garden and feel peace in any place and in any religion, for this message knows no difference between people or religion.

There is no life like this life because you live all the time with God (ﷻ). You pray all your time with God (ﷻ). So I send my voice to all the world and carry everyone in my heart. Lā 'ilāha 'illa-llāh. Āmīn."

I hope you have understood this teaching and what I have said to my beloveds. I hope everyone accepts what he has and knows how to walk in order to heal himself and others, from beginning to the end. This is a deep subject that I have given in many, many countries, in Europe and here, also. I hope everyone understands what I mean. Āmīn. Āmīn.

Sidi gives the promise.

Appendix I: Prophets (﵇), Angels (﵇), Awliya (﵁)

Prophets (﵇)

English	Arabic	Description
Aaron	Hārūn (﵇)	The cousin of Mūsā (﵇) who helped him in his mission.
Abraham	Ibrāhīm (﵇)	Father of the prophets (﵇) Friend of Allāh (ﷻ) Father of Ismāʿīl (﵇) and Isḥāq (﵇) Second human builder of the Kaʿba
Ādam	Ādam (﵇)	Father of humanity The first prophet in the body The first human builder of the Kaʿba
David	Dāwūd (﵇)	Bringer of the Zabūr (Psalms) Slayer of Jalūt (Goliath)
Enoch	Idrīs (﵇)	Predecessor to Nūḥ (﵇) Raised to Heaven by Allāh (ﷻ)
Isaac	Isḥāq (﵇)	Father of the Jewish line Second son to Ibrāhīm (﵇) via Sāra (﵁)
Ishmael	Ismāʿīl (﵇)	Father of the Islamic line First son to Ibrāhīm (﵇) via Ḥajjar (﵁)
Jacob	Yaʿqūb (﵇)	Father of Yūsuf (﵇) and the 12 tribes of Israel Son of Isḥāq (﵇)
Jesus Christ	ʿĪsā (﵇)	Son of Maryam (Mary) (﵇) The Spirit of Allāh (ﷻ) The Messiah (al-masīḥ) Bringer of the Injīl (Gospel)
Jethro	Shuʿayb (﵇)	Mūsā's father-in-law (﵇) and teacher.
John the Baptist	Yaḥyā (﵇)	Son of Zakariyā (﵇) Forerunner of ʿĪsā (﵇)
Jonah	Yūnus (﵇)	Swallowed by a large fish (whale) prophet in Ninevah

Prophets (عليهم السلام)

English	Arabic	Description
Joseph	Yūsuf (عليه السلام)	Son of Yaʿqūb (عليه السلام) prophetic dreamer
Khidr	Khidr (عليه السلام)	Mūsā's teacher (عليه السلام)
Lot	Lūṭ (عليه السلام)	Ibrāhīm's nephew (عليه السلام). Prophet of Sodom and Gomorrah
Moses	Mūsā (عليه السلام)	The Converser with Allāh (ﷻ) Bringer of the ten Commandments, the forty Scrolls of Ibrāhīm (عليه السلام) and Mūsā (عليه السلام) and the five books of the Old Testament Freed the Jews from Pharaoh
Muhammad	Muḥammad (ﷺ)	The Seal of the prophets (عليهم السلام) The Beloved of Allāh (ﷺ) The Light of Allāh's Face (ﷺ) First prophet in spirit Receiver of the Qurʾān
Noah	Nūḥ (عليه السلام)	Built the ark and the ship of safety
Solomon	Sulayman (عليه السلام)	Son of Dāwūd (عليه السلام) Has command over all creatures, including the jinn (spirits)
Zachariah	Zakariyā (عليه السلام)	Father of Yaḥyā (عليه السلام) Guardian of Maryam (عليها السلام)

Angels (عليهم السلام)

English	Arabic	Description
Raphael	Isrāfīl (عليه السلام)	He will blow the horn at the end of time, announcing the Day of Resurrection
Azrael	Izrā'īl (عليه السلام)	The angel of death
Gabriel	Jībrīl (عليه السلام)	The angel of revelation to the Prophet Muḥammad (ﷺ). The Holy Spirit
Michael	Mīkā'il (عليه السلام)	The angel of health. He provides rain and rewards earned to all creatures.
Munkar and Nakīr	Munkar and Nakīr (عليهما السلام)	These two angels question you after death.
Recording angels	Kirāmān Kātibīn (عليهم السلام)	There are 2 of them, one on your right side recording your good deeds and one sits on your left side recording your bad deeds.

Awliya (رضي الله عنهم)

Name	Description
ʿAbd as-Salām ibn Mashīsh (رضي الله عنه)	The guide of Abu-l-Ḥasan ash-Shādhulī (رضي الله عنه)
ʿAbd al-Qādir al-Jilani (رضي الله عنه)	Was a Persian Imām, Sufi shaykh and the originator of the Qadiri Sufi order.
Abu Bakr aṣ-Ṣādiq (رضي الله عنه)	Was one of the Prophet's closest companions. The Prophet (ﷺ) married his daughter, ʿĀ'isha (رضي الله عنها), and he was the first righteous caliph.
Abu-l-Ḥasan ash-Shādhulī (رضي الله عنه)	The originator of our ṭarīqa.
ʿĀ'isha bint Abu Bakr (رضي الله عنها)	The Prophet's favorite wife after the death of Khadīja (رضي الله عنها); daughter of Abu Bakr aṣ-Ṣādiq (رضي الله عنه)
ʿAlī ibn Abu Ṭālib (رضي الله عنه)	The Prophet's cousin (ﷺ) and one of his closest companions. Husband of Fāṭima (رضي الله عنها). ʿAlī (رضي الله عنه) was the fourth righteous caliph.
Asiya (عليها السلام)	The Mother of the Prophet Mūsā (عليه السلام). One of the 4 greatest women of all-time (with Maryam عليها السلام, Fāṭima عليها السلام and Khadīja عليها السلام)

Awliya (ؓ)

Name	Description
Bilāl ibn Rabāḥ (ؓ)	A companion of the Prophet Muḥammad (ﷺ), best known for the Call to Prayer.
Bilqīs (ؓ)	Queen of Sheba, wife of the Prophet Sulayman (ؑ).
Fāṭima (ؓ)	Daughter of the Prophet Muḥammad (ﷺ) One of the 4 greatest women of all-time (with Maryam ؑ, Asiya ؓ and Khadīja ؓ), Wife of ʿĀli ibn Abī Ṭālib (ؓ), Mother of Ḥasan and Ḥusayn (ؓ)
Ḥajjar (ؓ)	Second wife of the Prophet Ibrāhīm (ؑ) Mother of the Prophet Ismāʿīl (ؑ)
Hawwāʾ (ؓ)	Eve, the wife of Ādam (ؑ)
Khadīja (ؓ)	The first wife of the Prophet Muḥammad (ﷺ) and the only one who bore him children. One of the 4 greatest women of all-time (with Maryam ؑ, Fāṭima ؓ and Asiya ؓ)
Sidi Ibrāhīm ibn Adham (ؓ)	An ascetic who, in later legend, was portrayed as a prince who gave up his court to be a wandering lover of Allāh. He lived in the 8th century A.D.
Maryam (Mary) (ؑ)	Mother of ʿĪsā (ؑ), One of the 4 greatest women of all-time (with Asiya ؓ, Fāṭima ؓ and Khadīja ؓ)
Muḥyi-d-dīn ibn al-ʿArabī (ؓ)	One of the most famous and influential Ṣūfī saints, scholars and writers in the history of Islām. He is known as the "Shaykh al-Akbar."
Rābiʿa al-ʿAdawiyya (ؓ)	Was a passionate lover of God (ﷻ) and the first Ṣūfī saint. She extolled the way of divine love and intimacy with Allāh (ﷻ).
Salmān al-Fārisī (ؓ)	One of the Prophet's companions (ﷺ) who helped significantly during the Battle of the Ditch.
Sāra (ؓ)	Wife of Ibrāhīm (ؑ), Mother of Isḥāq (ؑ)
Suhayb ar-Rūmī (ؓ)	A companion of the Prophet (ﷺ). Considered as a possible successor for ʾUmar ibn al-Khaṭṭāb (ؓ).
ʿUmar ibn al-Khaṭṭāb (ؓ)	Was one of the Prophet's closest companions. Known for his strength of character, he was the second righteous caliph.
Zulaikha (ؓ)	The wife of the Prophet Yūsuf (ؑ)

Appendix II: Glossary of Arabic Terms

Adab: politeness, manners.
Ādhān: the call to prayer. The call to prayer is given to indicate that the time of a specific prayer has arrived.
Ākhira: the hereafter, the next life.
ʿAlaq: literally means a clot of blood. In the Qurʾān its outward meaning is the second stage of embryonic development, where the fetus appears as a clot of blood.
ʿAlayhi-s-salām (عليه السلام)**:** literally translated as "peace be upon him." It is polite and customary to say this after mentioning any of the prophets (عليهم السلام). Variations include: ʿalayhim as-salām (عليهم السلام) (masc. or mixed plural), ʿalayha-s-salām (عليها السلام) (feminine singular), ʿalayhuma-s-salām (عليهما السلام) (for 2 people or angels (عليهم السلام), masc. or mixed).
Al-ḥamdu li-llāh: literally translated as "all praises to God (ﷻ)." It is polite and customary to say this in response to a query about your state or your health (i.e. how are you?). In doing so you recognize that no matter what is happening in your life, Allāh (ﷻ) is to be praised because everything in your life is from His Raḥmān (never-ending mercy).
Āmīn: Amen. Assent. "So be it."
ʿArafa: Mount Arafat, the mountain where Ibrāhīm (عليه السلام) was going to sacrifice his son, but instead Allāh (ﷻ) allowed him to sacrifice a sheep.
As-salāmu ʿalaykum: This is the greeting Allāh (ﷻ) told the Prophet Muḥammad (ﷺ) to use when greeting believers. It means "peace be upon you."
As-salāmu ʿalaykum wa raḥmatu-llāhi wa bārakatuhu: An extended version of "as-salāmu ʿalaykum," this translates as "May the peace of God (ﷻ) be upon you, and His mercy and blessings."
Ash-Shāfī: "The Healer," which is one of the attributes of Allāh (ﷻ).
Astaghfiru-llāh al-ʿaḍhīm: This phrase is used during tawba to ask for Allāh's forgiveness. When using it you are asking Allāh (ﷻ) to veil your faults and forgive you while acknowledging His enormity, greatness and power to do so.
Ākhira: the hereafter, the next life.
Awrād: plural for *wird*. See *wird*.
'Āyah: a verse in the Holy Qurʾān.
Azal, al-: pre-eternity, eternity without beginning.
Baqā': subsistence; the state of subsistence which occurs after the fanāʾ where you are established in and by the qualities of Allāh (ﷻ).
Barzakh: the intermediary state in which the soul waits after passing away. While in the barzakh the soul considers its actions during its life and awaits the Day of Judgment.
Baṣīr, al-: The name of God (ﷻ) that means, "the All-Seeing." Allāh (ﷻ) lends us His quality of seeing, and that is why we can see.

Bay'a: the promise made by a novice with God (ﷻ) through the spiritual master; originally the covenant between Allāh (ﷻ) and the believers in the soul world when He asked them, "Am I not your Lord?" They answered, "Yes (bala), You are our Lord in truth."

Bismi-llāh: literally means, "In the name of Allāh (ﷻ)." It is traditional to say, "Bismi-llāh" before undertaking any action in order to sanctify it.

Bismi-llāhi-r-Raḥmāni-r-Raḥīm: "In the name of Allāh (ﷻ), Most Merciful, Most Compassionate."

Dhikr: the remembrance of God (ﷻ) through the remembrance of the tongue, the remembrance of the heart or the remembrance of the spirit.

Du'ā': a personal prayer as distinguished from the ritual prayer (aṣ-ṣalāh)

Dunyā: the material world.

Fanā': the death of the nafs/self/ego; to die before one dies; to die to the world; to annihilate into God's reality (ﷻ).

Faqīr: the poor; the initiate with the quality of material and spiritual poverty. This is considered a central virtue. Variations: fuqarā' (pl.).

Farḍ: The acts obligatory for the Muslim (the five pillars).

Fātiḥa, al-: Al-Fātiḥa is the opening chapter, or sūra, of the Holy Qur'ān. It is said to contain the essence of the entire Qur'ān within it. Al-Fātiḥa is recited at least seventeen times daily by Sufis and Muslims during the obligatory, five times a day prayer (ṣalāh). This sūra is fundamental to the Sufi's understanding of his religion.

Fiqh: Fiqh is the development of the sharī'a, Islamic law, based on the Qur'ān, the Sunna, and rulings and interpretations made by Islamic jurists. In Sunni Islām there are four schools of jurisprudence: Hanbali, Shafi'i, Maliki and Hanafi.

Five Pillars of Islām: 1. Testifying that there is no God (ﷻ) but God (ﷻ) and that Muḥammad (ﷺ) is His messenger, 2. Praying ṣalāh five times daily, 3. Paying a percentage of your assets in zakāh (charity) yearly, 4. Fasting during the month of Ramaḍān, 5. Making Ḥajj (pilgrimage) to Mecca once in your lifetime if you can afford to do so.

Ghusl: the complete ablution which returns you from a state of janāba (ritual impurity).

Ḥadīth: traditions relating to the actions and sayings of the Prophet (ﷺ) recounted by his companions (رضي الله عنهم). For instance, a famous ḥadīth states, "In order to know, you need to taste." Sayings from Ḥadīth Qudsī are sayings where Allāh (ﷻ) speaks with the tongue of the Prophet (ﷺ) (where the "I" refers to Allāh (ﷻ) speaking in the first person). For example, a famous ḥadīth qudsī is, "My heavens and My earth cannot contain Me. Only the heart of My faithful worshipper contains Me."

Ḥaḍra: The technical term for the dhikr our ṭarīqa and other ṭarīqāt do as a group standing in a circle.

Ḥaḍrat: divine presence.

Ḥajj: the pilgrimage to Mecca that is mandatory for a Muslim to make once in his or her lifetime if there is the means to do so. Ḥajj occurs days 7-13 of the month of Dhul Ḥijjah. A number of special rites comprise the Ḥajj, some of which include: circumambulating the Ka'ba seven times counter-clockwise, running seven times between the hills of Ṣafā and Marwā, praying and reciting Qur'ān on Mount 'Arafa

(Arafat) and throwing stones while in Mina. After Ḥajj there is a three-day holiday, ʿEid al-Adha, during which there is feasting and celebration.

Ḥāl: mystical state, grace from Allāh (ﷻ); something coming down into the heart. Sidi Junayd (ؓ) says, "Al-aḥwal are like flashes of lightning."

Ḥalāl: lawful or legal. Anything that is ḥalāl is permissible to do, eat or have. Ḥalāl is the opposite of ḥarām.

Ḥaqīqa: the divine truth, the divine reality or the essential reality of Allāh (ﷻ).

Ḥarām: forbidden or unlawful. Muslims should not engage with anything that is ḥarām. Certain behaviors, foods and objects are ḥarām. Ḥarām is the opposite of ḥalāl.

Ḥubb: love.

Iblīs: Satan. Iblīs is the personal name for the devil (ash-shayṭān); the jinn who refused to bow to Ādam (ؑ).

Iḥsān: excellence in action. Worshipping God (ﷻ) as if you see Him. The highest of three levels of worship.

Imān: faith, trust, belief; The second of three levels of worship.

Injīl: the Gospel. This term is not precisely defined in the Qurʾān but it is safe to say that the Gospel includes the authentic teachings of ʿĪsā (ؑ).

Insān al-kāmil: literally means "the perfect man." It is a term that is used honorifically for the Prophet Muḥammad (ﷺ) and ibn al-Arabī (ؓ) discusses at length in relation to the quṭb.

Inshāʾa-llāh: literally means "if God (ﷻ) wills." It is used to express the dependence of man's will on God's will (ﷻ). We are told not to say regarding anything, "I am going to do that tomorrow," without also saying, "if God (ﷻ) wills." (ḥadīth).

Islām: surrender; the word Islām is derived from the word as-Salām (peace); The first of the three levels of worship (Islām, Imān, Iḥsān). Islām is the religion brought by the Prophet Muḥammad (ﷺ).

Istikhāra: a practice where in order to receive guidance from Allāh (ﷻ) the petitioner does 2 voluntary rakʿāh (in addition to the obligatory ṣalāh) and recites a special prayer in addition to some other steps. For the exact procedure contact the Shadhiliyya Sufi Center.

Jabarūt: formless world; world of infinite eternal power and possibility.

Jahannam: the pit of the hellfire.

Jalāl: quality of severity, difficulty, majesty, glory and exaltation.

Jamāl: quality of beauty, easiness.

Jedda: the city Hawwāʾ (Eve) (ؑ) was born.

Jihād: holy war; inner struggle. This term primarily refers to the inner struggle that occurs when the nafs are not in surrender and obedience to Allāh (ﷻ). Inaccurately, it commonly refers to the outer struggle which can manifest as a holy war between people or cultures.

Jinn: inhabitants of the world of the Malakūt, the subtle world created of "smokeless fire." There are believing jinn and unbelieving jinn.

Jumʿa: the Friday congregational prayer.

Kaʿba: the holy house in Mecca first built by Ādam (ؑ) and re-built by Ibrāhīm (ؑ) (Abraham) (ؑ), Ismāʿīl (Ishmael) (ؑ) and Isḥāq (Isaac) (ؑ). The place of pilgrimage. The house contains the black stone which came from Heaven. It was white but now is black from the sins of those who have touched it.
Khalwa: spiritual retreat where chants are recited all night until dawn.
Khuṭba: the sermons given during Jumʿa, the Friday congregational prayer.
Lā 'ilāha 'illa-llāh: translated as: "there is nothing worthy of worship except God (ﷻ)." Attesting to the truth of this statement is one-half of ṭawḥīd, the declaration of God's oneness and unity (ﷻ).
Lāhūt: the world of the divine essence.
Laylā: the essence of the deep, secret love of Allāh (ﷻ). Also, the beloved of Qays (ؓ).
Lawāmma: the station of blaming, still questioning.
Leader of Guidance: The inheritor of the divine knowledge of the prophets (ؑ). This person can be of any race, religion, ethnicity or gender. Some of these people are out in the world spreading the divine message and others are told to live in seclusion and pray for others.
Mā shā'a-llāh: literally, "Allāh (ﷻ) willed it." It is said when you see something good to protect yourself and the other person from envy.
Mahdī, al-: The Prophet Muḥammad (ﷺ) spoke about Al-Mahdī, foreseeing that he would be a khalīfa of Allāh who would, "return the religion to its former position." The Prophet (ﷺ) said that al-Mahdī would, "fill the earth with justice as it is filled with in justice and tyranny. He will rule for 7 years. (Abu Saʿīd al-Khudri)" He will come from the Prophet's family and lineage and come from Mecca. Most Sunni Muslims (like Sidi) believe he hasn't been born yet and that ʿĪsā (Jesus) (ؑ) will return at the same time. Inshā'a-llāh.
Malakūt: the world of the heart and soul which contains the spiritual presence of the Prophet (ﷺ). It is the world of the unseen, the angels (ؑ), the jinn, heaven and Hell. It is where we go after we die, also known as the second world, until we travel through all of the worlds to reach Allāh (ﷻ).
Maqām: spiritual station.
Marwā: The name of one of the hills Ḥajjar (ؓ) ran between when Ibrāhīm (ؑ) left her in the desert with only her son, Ismā'īl (ؑ).
Masīḥ, al-: literally, "Messiah." The title given to ʿĪsā (ؑ) (Jesus) (ؑ).
Masjid: a mosque; where Muslims gather to pray.
Masjid al-Aqṣā: the mosque in Jerusalem at the Dome of the Rock. This is where Sidi works.
Mawjūd: omnipresent being, ever-present being; all-pervading being, or immanent.
Misbaḥa: prayer beads hung on a string for easy counting.
Monotheism: the belief that there is only one God (ﷻ).
Muḥammadan light (ﷺ): The light that Allāh (ﷻ) originally took from His face (His essence) when He gave the first command, "Be." This is the essential light upon which everything else rests, and it is the highest light in existence. It is most strongly embodied in the Prophet Muḥammad (ﷺ).

Muḥyī, al-: the name of Allāh (ﷻ) that means, "the Giver of Life."
Mulk: the physical state or material world. All that you can see and everything you can experience with the five outer senses.
Muqaddam: the word is derived from the quality of Allāh (ﷻ), "the Initiator." A muqaddam is typically the representative of a shaykẖ or spiritual master. One who is authorized to give instruction and initiate disciples in certain Ṣūfī orders. In Sidi Muḥammad's order, a muqaddam is given the responsibility of opening the doors of the local community, inviting new people to the path, and giving the message of God's peace, love, mercy, justice and freedom without discrimination.
Murabbi: a rank in Sidi Muḥammad's ṭarīqa given to those who deeply support the spiritual walking of all people in the ṭarīqa. These beloveds provide organizational development and administrative support for the University of Spiritual Healing and Sufism, and the ṭarīqa as a whole.
Murīd: the seeker on the path to Allāh (ﷻ).
Nafs: the self, the soul which resides alongside the spirit. Sidi Muḥammad defines the nafs as, "your perceptions, hearing, feeling, the voices in your mind, and the desires of your heart that say this and that or ask why or what." (page 47 of *Music of the Soul*)
Naqīb: literally means, "One who cares for the people." It is a rank and a responsibility Sidi gives some of his students in different communities around the country.
Pharaoh: used specifically to reference the Pharaoh who oppressed the Jews, Tutankhamen. Used generally to refer to an oppressor.
Qibla: the direction the seeker faces when praying ṣalāh. Initially, the qibla was Jerusalem, but during the Prophet's lifetime Allāh (ﷻ) revealed that it should be changed to the Kaʿba in Mecca.
Raḍiya-llāhu ʿanhā (ﷺ): The feminine singular form of the honorific you add after the name of a companion of the Prophet (ﷺ) or a saint. Variations include: raḍiya-llāhu ʿanhu (ﷺ) (sing. masc.), raḍiya-llāhu ʿanhum (ﷺ) (pl. masc.), raḍiya-llāhu ʿanhumā (ﷺ) (any 2 people), and raḍiya-llāhu ʿanhunna (ﷺ) (2 women).
Rakʿāh: one cycle of standing, reciting the Fātiḥa, bowing, kneeling, testifying to Allāh (ﷻ) as Lord and Muḥammad (ﷺ) as His messenger, and prostrating during the ṣalāh.
Ramaḍān: the 9th month of the Islamic calendar, Ramaḍān is considered the holiest month of the year. Muslims spend the month fasting from dawn until dusk, offering extra worship, giving charity to the poor, and deeply drinking from the overflowing blessings of Allāh (ﷻ).
Ṣabūr, aṣ-: The name of Allāh (ﷻ) that means, "the Patient."
Sacrifice: an important and deeply holy act of self-purification. A "sacrifice" is given when you need to repent for something you have done and cannot complete it (because you cannot right the wrong). A sacrifice is a donation of $500 which is used to buy and painlessly kill a sheep in a sacred way. The meat is given to the poor and hungry as food.

Ṣaddaqa: voluntary charity as opposed to zakāh, which is the obligatory almsgiving ordered by Allāh (ﷻ) (one of the five pillars of Islām).
Ṣafā: purity. A word from which "Sufism" is etymologically derived.
Ṣalāh: Ṣalāh is a physical act of worship, done in groups or by oneself, that engages the body, mind, heart, soul and spirit. The form, which includes standing, reciting, bowing, kneeling, testifying, and prostrating, is specific and is done in the same way all around the world. It is one of the five pillars of Islām.
Ṣalla-llāhu ʿalayhi wa sallam (ﷺ) : literally: may the blessings and peace of Allāh (ﷻ) be upon him. It is polite and customary to always say this after mentioning the name of the Prophet Muḥammad (ﷺ).
Ṣawm: fasting.
Sayyid: master, lord (this word usually refers to people, not Allāh (ﷻ)). It's a term of address for a person of high class. Variations: Sayyidinā (our Master), Sayyida (Lady), Sayyidī (my Lord), Sayyidatī (my Lady, feminine), Sayyidatunā (our Lady).
Shahāda: to observe, witness or testify; the first of the five pillars of Islām is to bear witness that there is no God (ﷻ) but Allāh (ﷻ) (Lā ʾilāha ʾilla-llāh) and that Muḥammad (ﷺ) is the messenger of Allāh (ﷻ) (Muḥammadan rasūlu-llāh).
Sharīʿa: the law of Islām as revealed in al-Qurʾān and the Sunna—the traditions of the Prophet Muḥammad (ﷺ).
Shayṭān: Satan, the devil, Iblīs.
Shaykh̲: literally: old man or elder. The master who can give effective instruction for students on the spiritual path. He possesses a degree of spiritual realization and can bring others to his degree.
Shirk: considered the greatest transgression in Islām. It is the worship of something other than Allāh (ﷻ). This can range from the obvious, such as worshipping a statue of a cow, to the subtle, such as worshipping power, money, beauty, etc.
Shukran: thank you.
Sirr: your innermost secret; the spiritual center of your being which is said to be located (metaphorically) in the heart; the place of union with Allāh (ﷻ).
Soul: the soul was formed when Allāh (ﷻ) breathed His spirit into the dust which became Ādam ﷺ (humankind). It rose as a vapor.
Subḥānahū wa taʿālā (ﷻ): literally means, "glorious and exalted is He," and is used honorifically when mentioning Allāh (ﷻ).
Subḥāna-llāh: literally: all exaltation to Allāh (ﷻ).
Ṣūfī: see faqīr. The name is thought to have come from the rough woolen garments worn by the early Sufis.
Sufism: the science of direct knowing of Allāh (ﷻ).
Sunna: the spoken words and actions of the Prophet Muḥammad (ﷺ) that have become the example to follow.
Sūra: a chapter from the Holy Qurʾān.
Tajallī: revelation; coming forth into the light; the unveiling of divine secrets; illumination.
Taqwā: reverence, piety, awe of God (ﷻ).

Tarāwīḥ prayers: additional prayers (cycles of ṣalāh) offered each night during the month of Ramaḍān. The blessings given during tarāwīḥ prayers are extraordinary. The tradition of the Prophet (ﷺ) was to do at least eight rak'āh per night during Ramaḍān.

Ṭarīqa: the path, the way, school or brotherhood of mystics. It is the bridge between the sharī'a and the ḥaqīqa.

Ṭawāf: circumambulation around the Ka'ba

Tawba: literally: to return. It indicates the process of tawba that the Prophet Muḥammad (ﷺ) did seventy times each day (ḥadīth).

Tawḥīd: the oneness and unity of Allāh (ﷻ).

Tawrā: The Torah, which is the holy book brought to the Jewish people by the Prophet Mūsā (ﷺ) (Moses) (ﷺ).

'Umrah: is a pilgrimage to Mecca that can be done any time of the year. The aspirant walks around the Ka'ba in a counter-clockwise direction seven times, walks between the two hills of Ṣafā and Marwā (the two hills Ḥajjar ran between when Ismā'īl (ﷺ) was crying for water) and cuts his or her hair (women usually just cut a little while men shave their heads). 'Umrah can be done right before doing Ḥajj or it can be done separately at another time of year.

Valley of Ṭuwā: The valley in which Mūsā (ﷺ) annihilated his nafs and attained gnosis.

Warīth: A leader of guidance. the heir or inheritor of the Muḥammadan presence (ﷺ) who is the representative and picture of the Muḥammadan presence (ﷺ) in his time. His orders are the orders of our beloved Prophet Muḥammad (ﷺ).

Wird: A "wird" is a specific set of recitations given to the seeker by his guide. The standard wird in Sidi Muḥammad's ṭarīqa is to recite the following twice a day: "astaghfiru-llāh al-'aḍhīm" 100 times, "Allāhumma ṣalli 'alā sayyidinā Muḥammad wa ālihi wa sallam," 100 times, "Lā 'ilāha 'illa-llāh," 100 times and, "Allāh (ﷻ)" 100 times.

Wuḍu': ablution, ritual purification. For information on how to do wuḍu' see *The Reliance of the Traveler* by Ahmad ibn Naqib al-Misri.

Zabūr: the Psalms brought by the Prophet Dāwūd (David) (ﷺ).

Zakāh: obligatory charity. One of the five pillars of Islām.

Zāwiya: a place people go to be in retreat from the world, so that they can spend all of their time, without distraction, with Allāh (ﷻ).

Index

A

Aaron. *See* Prophet Hārūn
abortion, 123
Abraham. See Prophet Ibrāhīm
Abu Bakr, 81
abuse, healing it, 156
adab, 58, 59, 61, 272, 278, 279, 449
  fitra, 41
  is from love, 99
  live life in, 258
  needed for fanāʾ and baqāʾ, 206
  of Ibrāhīm (ﷺ), 272
  of prophets, 81
  of the bee, 61
  of the winner, 257
  of USHS teachers, 355
  when you see something you admire, 245
  with parents, 443
  with beloved, 434, 439
  with children, 201
Adam. *See* Prophet Adam
AIDS, 382
ʿĀʾisha, 48, 447
al-Fātiḥa, 43
ʿĀli ibn Abu Ṭālib, 447
alif, 52, 174, 193, 265
Allāh's knowledge
  secret of is through love, 58
Allāh's orders
  are a gift of love, 186, 303, 424
  follow them to walk quickly, 175
  obey them, 53, 55-56, 61, 64, 81, 94, 193, 249, 325, 336, 443, 455
al-Mahdī, 311
Anak, 42
Angel Isrāfīl, 76, 447
Angel Izrāʾīl, 34, 35, 71, 447
Angel Jībrīl, 82, 192, 193, 232, 283, 375, 377, 380, 388, 391, 403, 404, 407, 447
  and Ibrāhīm, 366, 374, 392, 404
  appeared to Maryam, 318, 340, 347
  asking Ibrāhīm if he needed anything, 283
  gave Ibrāhīm sacrifice, 288, 374
  gave Ibrāhīm guidance, 364
  gave message to prophets, 166, 192
  ḥadīth about Ramaḍān, 232
  night journey, 115
  on Day of Judgment, 82-83
  telling Muḥammad about Day of Judgment, 231
  told Muḥammad: Read, 39
  told Muḥammad: do cupping, 377
Angel of Death. *See* Angel Israʿīl
angels
  asked to prostrate, 359
  come after death, 34
  recording, 21, 248
  thousands go to Ḥajj, 387
anger, 24, 368, 396, 410, 441
apple cider vinegar, 335, 412, 413
al-Aqṣā Mosque
  night journey, 115
Arabic
  learn it, 333
  letters contain secrets, 193, 257
Arabic plaster, 377, 408
Arafat, 371, 400
arteries in the brain, 328
Asiya, 111, 336, 447, 448
Azrael. *See* Izrāʾīl

B

Babel, 266, 363, 388
babies, 127
backbiting, 24, 245
  don't do it!, 432
  how to repent for it, 246
baqāʾ, 100, 104, 168, 194, 206, 220, 222, 225, 373, 392, 402, 449
  can't reach without adabʾ, 206
  baqāʾu-l-bi-llāh, 97, 219
barzakh̲, 32

be satisfied, 171
bee, be like one, 61
Bilqīs, 60, 293
birds, 59, 404
  Allah will provide for you, 171
  why they are happier than us, 99
birth
  choosing a caretaker, 126
black blood, 327, 380, 407
black mind, 43
black seed, 326, 327
  use for sexual strength, 326
blood
  black blood, 327, 380, 407
  circulation, 339
  clots, 327
  pressure, 409, 410
breast cancer, 198
breast milk
  is pure love, 198
breastfeeding, 336
breasts, 198
Burāq, 114

C

calcium absorption, 338
Canaan, 266, 287, 368, 395
cancer, 133, 178, 292, 329, 378, 379, 380, 382, 418
  breast, 198
castor oil, 408
cave, sleepers of the, 313
charity, 454
child rearing, 200, 201
cinnamon, 413
citron, 382, 383
cranberry juice, 384, 409
creation
  He created everything for you, 54
cremation, 33, 34
crush your nafs, 259
cupping, 327, 377, 378, 380
  Angel Jībrīl gave order to Muhammad (ﷺ), 377
  lyme disease, 377, 407
  sunna is twice yearly, 377

D

dates, 343
David. *See* Prophet Dāwūd
Day of Judgment, 19, 25, 36, 41, 43, 45, 47, 48, 71, 79, 81, 84, 157, 196, 358, 442, 447, 449
  all senses & body parts will be judged, 233
  blowing of trumpet, 76
  every nation will be on their knees, 45
  father will ask son for help, 48
  Ḥadīth about, 48
  how did you spend money, 49
  Jerusalem will be the bride, 342
  judge yourself before, 236
  maryrs, saints, gnostics, 77
  really beautiful passage, 82
  sweat will almost drown them, 81
  the Prophet intercedes, 83
  what happens if you have wronged others, 25
  your book, 78
death, 29, 32, 34, 35, 68, 71, 74, 92, 97, 103, 205, 219, 224, 307, 350, 359, 361, 372, 401, 428, 447, 450
  after, 34-35, 44
  afterwards a wedding for you, 35
  afterwards the angels come, 34
  by Viagra, 326
  die before you die, 96, 217, 273
  for the disobedient, 35
  fragrance of essence of person, 34
  is to be between His arms, 258
  prepare for it, 72
  questioning angels, 35
  real tawba makes it not smell bad, 242
  Sidi's grandfather's example, 34
dhikr, 175
  your trillions of cells, 144, 188, 305, 426
diarrhea, 408

Die before you die, 96, 217
disciples, 313, 316, 347
asked for a meal, 317, 322, 347, 352
carried the message, 316, 347
followed allprophets, 317
needed confirmation, 323, 355
divine knowledge, 40, 44, 153, 172, 192, 193, 194, 201, 208, 213, 217, 269, 333, 378, 380, 381, 431, 441, 452
direct yourself toward Allāh, 263
divine light, 234, 240, 243
divine love, 29, 62, 235, 238, 448
drop of, 261
divine meeting, 255
divine mirror, 359, 374, 403
divine music, 62
divine presence, 19, 20, 157, 196, 239, 243, 244
divine qualities, 241
divine wedding, 80, 81, 252, 255, 256
don't say "I", 39-40, 64, 97
don't say, "Allāh spoke to me", 301
don't say, "I see Allāh", 195, 301
don't say, "I see", 212

E

eating,
don't eat ḥarām foods, 154
don't overeat, 177
eat only organic, chemical-free, 155
egg whites, 327, 408
eggs, of woman, 122
emigration
He will take care of you, 92
envy, 23, 245, 452
how to prevent, 245

F

faith. *See* imān
family, 434
build it, 437
disintegration of, 434
extend to neighbors, 437
is a shi, 432
is sick, 435
fanā᾿, 104, 168, 176, 182, 194, 206, 225, 373, 402, 449
fasting. *See* ṣawm
Fātiḥa, 27, 174, 450
inner meaning of āyah, 174
fetal development, 122
fever, 338, 411
Firʿown, 110, 111
his body is still preserved, 45
fish, 155
five pillars of Islām, 454
flute of Dāwūd, 102, 223
food, 155
don't eat ḥarām foods, 154
eat only organic, chemical-free, 155

G

Gabriel. *See* Angel Jībrīl
gametes, 122
Garden, the 80, 185, 244, 252
garden of knowledge, 175, 263
garden of peace, 175
garlic, 329, 330, 331, 408
garlic oil, 329, 330, 331
ginger, 413
gnostics
are sometimes absent, 69
their trust and belief, 66
gratitude, 171
grave, 33, 35, 42, 72, 76
are you the only one, 34
Day of Judgment, 76
of the Prophet (ﷺ), 33
greatest name, 29, 198
grief, 410

H

Ḥajj, 6, 100, 101, 221, 369, 386, 387, 393, 397, 401, 402, 419, 431, 450, 452, 455
Allāh removes your sins, 372

meaning of, 373
special time, 372
subsist in Allāh, 373
the real, 260
thousands of angels, 387
you're on it when...260
Hajjar, 369, 396
daughter of a king, 368
looking for water, 369
ḥaqīqa, 1, 3, 63, 64, 229, 455
carry and Allāh's doors open, 257
carry it, 416
emigrate to, 261
of Ibrāhīm, 392
ṣalāh is full of, 336
Haṭim, 110, 114
Hawwā', 10, 448, 451
healer, message of unity, 194
healers, characteristics of, 156
healing
abuse, 156
intake interview, 155
knowledge in Sidi's books, 303
Letter of the Prophet Healing, 326, 362, 414
patience, 407
healing paper, 414
hearing in the wrong way, 245
heart, 211, 212
in utero, 125
Hell, 42, 78, 83
Anak, 42
hemorroids, 411
holy books, 36, 52, 90, 164, 192, 202, 301, 344, 423, 443
Allah speaks to you, 301
honey, 61, 84, 326, 327, 411, 412
Hoopoe, 293
Hudhud, 293
humble, be, 98
husband, 432, 436, 439
not a servant, 439

I

Iblīs, 451
Ibrāhīm ibn Adham, 69
iḥsān, 416, 451
imagination, 360
imān, 36
immaculate conception, 349
'Imrān, family of, 82
infancy, 127
influenza, 383
Injīl, 242, 451
intention, 247
intimacy with Allah, 95, 216
Isaac. *See* Prophet Isḥāq
Ishmael. *See* Prophet Ismā'īl
Islām, 6, 36, 279, 374, 403, 447, 448, 450, 451, 454, 455
fasting, 231
is divine peace, 193
meaning of, 417
istikhāra, 131-132, 165, 451

J

Jabarūt, 75, 78, 80, 103, 194, 213, 224, 451
is the world of fear, 77
the eternal world, 89
Jacob. *See* Prophet Ya'qūb
Jahaliyya time, 110
jealousy, 23, 24
Jerusalem, 87, 133, 177, 239, 287, 343, 360, 368, 375, 395, 396, 418, 419, 420, 452, 453
etymology, 266
help the people there, 342
is His heaven, 342
will be His heaven, 368
Jerusalem Kindergarten, 87
Jesus. *See* Prophet 'Īsā
jinn, 60
Joseph. *See* Prophet Yūsuf
Judge yourself first 36, 395
Junayd, Sidi al-, 66

K

Kaʿba, 100, 101, 221, 369, 386, 397, 398, 450, 452, 453, 455
  building of, 252
  night journey, 114
  Rābiʿa's journey to, 259
Khadīja, 113
kidney stones, 383, 409
kidneys, 339
Kun, 10, 37, 98, 220, 321, 352

L

Laḥūt, 75, 103, 213, 224
Laylā, 97, 101, 219, 223, 298, 452
let go of everything
  to swim in the divine ocean, 92
let go of the past, 156
Letter of the Prophet Healing, 326, 362, 414
liver, in utero, 125
Lot. *See* Prophet Lūṭ
love, 56, 58, 99, 220
  Allah guides us with it, 61
  door to divine knowledge, 210
  first condition of entering, 135, 180, 295
  first degree of, 58
  gives me life, 91, 211
  If you love someone..., 53
  needs to be tasted, 59
  secret of divine knowledge, 58
  signs of, 58
  with your heart and soul, 62
Lyme disease, 376, 377, 378, 407

M

Mā shāʾa-llāh
  is the adab, 245
Malakūt, 32, 49, 75, 77, 103, 194, 224, 239, 451, 452
  arrival after purified body, 195
  travel to during ṣalāh, 194
Maryam, 5, 82, 308–24, 340, 341-344, 347, 348, 446-448
  asked about pregnancy, 343, 349
  giving birth to ʿĪsā, 343
  immaculate conception, 349
  ʿĪsā son of Maryam, 322, 352
  was pure, 318, 347
milk, 117
mint tea, 408
mirror, you are, 53
money
  give it away as tawba, 87
  use only for good, 53
  you will be asked about it, 49
Moses. *See* Prophet Mūsā
mother, 126, 127, 319, 349
  fountain of love, 439
  ḥadīth about, 435
mountain
  metaphor for heart, 28, 301
  praised Allāh with Dāwūd, 52
Muḥyi-d-dīn ibn al-ʿArabī, 66, 274, 448
Munkar, 35
music isn't forbidden, 423

N

nafs
  crush them!, 259
Nakīr, 35
neighbors, treat like family, 437
nervous system, 339
Night Journey, 115
  cupping, 377
nightingale, 59, 60
Nimrūd, 285, 287, 363, 365, 388-389, 393, 394
  his death, 368
  his punishment, 367
Noah. *See* Prophet Nūḥ
nutrition, 177, 332, 379, 381, 411
  don't eat ḥarām foods, 154

O

olive leaf, 410

olive oil, 54, 328, 329
olives, 54
onion oil, 329, 330
orders of Allah
  are a gift of love, 186, 303, 424
  follow them to walk quickly, 175
  obey them, 53, 55-56, 61, 64, 81, 94, 193, 249, 325, 336, 443, 455
oxygen, 328

P

Palestine, 367, 368, 393, 395, 409
parenting, 200, 201, 434
parents
  honor them, 128
past, let go of it, 156
Pharaoh. *See* Firʿown
politeness. See adab
poor people, 12, 32, 86, 403, 453
  fast to feel like them, 177
  fed by sacrifices, 374, 386
  gave Nimrūd medicine, 367
  giving to helps us, 87
  help them, 31-32, 86, 175, 395
  help to be forgiven, 26
  helping is sunna, 403
  know how they feel, 231
  protect them, 366, 391
  Rābiʿa loved, 9
  Ramaḍān helps, 248
  received Ibrāhīm's sacrifice, 374
pray
  and follow practices, 165
  only to Him, 38
pregnancy, 122
premenstrual pain, 413
Prophet Ādam, 10, 82
  Muḥammad's ascension, 115
  will be asked for intercession, 81
Prophet Dāwūd, 46-47, 52, 60, 138, 149, 190, 289-290 295, 422, 446, 455
  flute, 102, 223
Prophet Hārūn, 64
  Muhammad's ascension, 116
Prophet Ibrāhīm, 100, 221, 248, 265, 268, 363, 370, 371, 398, 400, 452
  adab of, 272
  and Ismāʾīl, 374, 403
  birthplace, 266, 363
  emigration during Ramaḍān, 248
  father of Muslims, 266
  fire be cool, 367
  Ḥajj, 372
  Hajjar, 368
  Hajjar & Ismāʾīl, 369
  Hajjar & Sāra, 368
  his garden, 367
  his sons, 368
  his station, 264
  his table of knowledge, 279
  insight, 267
  investigated idols, 364
  khalīl, 264, 390
  meaning of his name, 265, 271, 392, 417
  miracles of, 113
  Muḥammad's ascension, 116
  needs nothing Jībrīl, 366, 392
  pray upon him in ṣalāh, 392
  refused to sell idols, 364
  sacrificed for entire world, 392
  sacrificing his son, 370, 398
  shaykh of all prophets, 297
  surrender of, 274
  the fire, 365, 366
  trick with idols, 365
  visions vs. dreams, 370
  went to Palestine, 368
  when the knife became water, 371, 400
  will be asked for intercession, 82
Prophet Idrīs, 115
Prophet ʿĪsā, 265, 308-324, 340, 341, 448
  asks for divine table, 355, 356
  carried Allāh's spirit, 349
  defended Maryam, 349
  disciples, 313, 317
    follow all prophets, 317
    pray as they did, 315, 345

first words, 319, 348
healed the sick, 341
his birth, 343
Muhammad's ascension, 115
on Day of Judgment, 341
spirit from God's order, 320, 351
spoke right after birth. *See*
table of, 316, 322, 323, 347, 352, 353, 354, 355, 356, 357, 358
Allāh responds to request, 359
full of everything, 357
was a sign from Allāh, 357
was like Adam, 318, 348
Prophet Isḥāq, 265, 277, 363, 368, 369, 388, 396, 448, 452
Prophet Ismāʾīl, 265, 288, 363, 368, 372, 373, 374, 388, 396, 399, 400, 401, 403, 452
being sacrificed, 370, 398
Mecca, 369
prepped for prophethood, 398
surrendered, 370
Prophet Lūṭ, 287, 367
his grave, 33
Prophet Muḥammad, 41, 265, 344, 449, 454
all prophets took bayah with, 118
always helped wife, 438
black spot removed, 114
Burāq, 114
cried for the poor, 110
meaning of name, 417
mercy to all, 297
miracle of, 113
night journey & ascension, 114
rain was a sign of his coming, 112
story of, 112
told to Read!, 113
was a prophet before Adam, 110
was an orphan, 112
was sent to all people, 110
will ask for intercession for us, 83
Prophet Mūsā, 27, 45, 64, 110, 111, 117, 237, 265, 301, 455
early life, 110
miracle of, 113
Muḥammad's ascension, 116
Oh my Lord, show me Yourself, 28
parted Red Sea, 113, 248
prophet of dignity, justice, 297
staff turned into snake, 113
went to Arafat, 371, 400
Prophet Nūḥ, 13, 14, 82, 246
will be asked for intercession, 82
Prophet Sulayman, 60, 293, 446, 448
story of nightingale, 59
Prophet Yaḥyā, 115
Prophet Yūsuf
Muhammad's ascension, 115
Prophet Zakariyā, 176
prophetic visions, 370
prophets
before their deaths, 33
follow all of them, 195
love so deep, 62
obeyed Allah's commands, 62
took bayah with Muḥammad, 119
we believe in all of them, 193
prostration, real, 100, 220
pumpkin seeds, 408

Q-R

qibla, 453
Rābiʿa al-ʿAdawiyya, 5-15, 57, 66, 448
journey to Kaʿba, 259
radish seeds, 383, 409
rain, 246
Rajab, 37, 66
Ramaḍān, 66, 230, 231, 232, 248
3 parts, 232
month of the poor, 247
Raphael. *See* Angel Israfīl
real Islām, 454
real life, the, 7, 32, 95-99, 101, 103-105, 145, 181-184, 188, 216-220, 222-227, 246, 253, 255, 258, 260, 261, 271, 273, 274, 279, 306, 307, 333, 426, 428
recording angels, 21, 248
returning people's rights, 25

S

sacrifice, 322, 370, 398, 402
  Allāh's way to purify yourself, 375
  how it helps tawba, 26
  in religions of the Book, 374
  is sunna, 374
  Ka'ba built for, 386
  of Ibrāhīm's son, 370, 398
  offering a, 26
  teaches meaning of love, 185
sadness, 410
ṣalāh, 18, 39, 59, 63, 100, 131, 162, 165, 173, 193, 221, 242, 336, 337, 343, 349, 392, 450, 451, 453, 455
  benefits everyone, 339
  blood circulation, 175
  detailed description of, 172
  do it, 172
  first station of, 174
  God speaks to you through it, 63
  is a physical exercise, 339
  is your connection to Allāh, 172
  meaning of, 64
  need it to travel to other worlds, 194
  Prophet's ascension, 117
  safeguard it, 337
  spiritual meaning of, 194
  when the Prophet received it, 117
Sāra, 367-369, 393, 396
ṣawm, 27, 28, 135, 176, 177, 180, 230, 295, 431, 453, 454
  angels, 230
  is not a prison, 231
  mercy for your body, 177
  of eyes, 176
  of mind, 176
  of the tongue, 20
  tawba is 1st step, 231
  true, 251
scientists
  how they will be judged, 44
seeking forgiveness, 24, 26
sex, 326
Sha'ban, 66
sharī'a, 53, 63, 64, 144, 186, 187, 193, 195, 229, 240, 257, 303, 305, 336, 392, 399, 416, 424, 425, 443, 455
  carry and Allāh's door is open, 257
  carry it, 416
  is a door to the ḥaqīqa, 64
  is healing, 435
  learn Arabic to understand it, 193
  obey it, 64
  of Ibrāhīm, 392
  received by the Prophet through Jībrīl, 193
  ṣalāh is full of, 336
Sidi Ibrāhīm ibn Adham, 69
signs of love, 58
sin, the fragrance of, 243
sixth sense, 173
skin, 338
skin tags, 413
sleep
  imagination, 360
sleepers in the cave, 313
Solomon. *See* Prophet Sulayman
special people, places, times 153, 195, 372, 401
  for tawba, 237
sperm, 44, 113, 122
spirit, 39
spiritual food, 172, 336, 358
spleen
  in utero, 125
spontaneous imagination, 360
stations of the way, 23, 24, 174, 175, 195, 262, 266, 333
  Ibrāhīm reached, 266
  in ṣalāh, 174-175
  travel beyond heart stations, 176
  travel by keeping ṣalāh, 175
stomach, 61, 154, 177, 327, 330, 332, 334, 335, 379, 380, 381, 382, 384, 408, 411, 412, 413
  filling it, 177, 332, 379
  is a divine tool, 379
Story of the Transgressor and the Real Gnostic, 237

Story of Sidi and the Birds, 46
Story of Sidi Ibrāhīm ibn Adham, 69
Story of Sulayman, Hudhud and Bilqīs, 293
Story of the Gnostic and Sinner, 67
Story of the Prophet's First Revelation, 112
Sufis, 316, 346
sunna
- and Qur'ān contains all knowledge, 217
- is part of sharī'a, 193

sweat, 338
syphilis, 382

T

table of 'Īsā, 316, 322, 323, 347, 352, 353, 354, 355, 356, 357, 358
- Allāh responds to request, 359
- full of everything you need, 357
- was a sign from Allāh, 357

table of Ibrāhīm, 279
tapeworm, 408, 409
tawba, 17, 192, 449
- don't be afraid, 67
- for family issues, 442
- greatest for Ramaḍān, 232
- If you don't make it, 25
- is always available, 67
- is like changing oil in your car, 19, 157, 196
- of the body, 245
- of the heart, 24
- of the hearts, 233
- of the mind, 232
- of the physical body, 20
- of the soul, 22
- return people's rights or else, 25

temperature regulation, 338
Torah, 242
Treatment for
- AIDS and Syphilis, 382
- Cancer Prevention and Erradication, 329
- Fever, 411
- Hair Loss, 330
- Hemorrhoids, 412
- Hypertension, 409
- Impotence and Infertility, 331
- Kidney Stones, 383, 409
- Mouth, Tongue, Lip Inflammation, 327
- Poor Memory, 328
- Premenstral Pain, 413
- Purify the Blood, 326
- Skin Disorders, 330
- Skin Tags / Warts, 413
- Tapeworm, 408
- Weight Loss, 332, 335, 412
- tree of life, 9, 92, 251, 316, 346, 436

trumpet, blowing of, 76
two paths, 68, 85, 94

U

'Umar ibn al-Khaṭṭāb, 185
unity, 19, 42, 64, 66, 80, 133, 143, 145, 166, 167, 178, 186, 188, 193, 204, 205, 229, 240, 251, 265, 277, 279, 285, 287, 292, 303, 306, 307, 315, 340, 342, 345, 354, 376, 388, 390, 403, 406, 416, 417, 420, 424, 426, 428, 434, 452, 455
- all prophets asked for it, 236
- beliefs of, 321, 351
- carried by all prophets, 314, 345, 350
- carried by Ibrāhīm, 266, 268, 392
- embody message of to heal, 194
- reality of, 374

USHS, 153, 325, 331, 332, 355, 378, 431
- Allah gives divine knowledge, 154, 441
- doesn't discriminate, 431, 441
- don't go to other universities, 304
- follows God's message, 354, 431
- is carrying the message, 325, 354
- is holy food for your spirit, soul, mind and body, 354
- is special, 191
- join and be blessed, 154, 333, 354, 378

should be at the Land, 153, 195
teachers follow Allāh, 154
teachers' adab, 355
teaches divine law, 194, 325
teaches from Allāh and all prophets, 441
teachings are divine, 303
tell your friends to come, 191
will be best in U.S., 378
you can be successful healer, 443

V

Viagra, 326, 331
vitamin D, 338

W

warts, 413
water of the love, 55, 58, 241, 272
we are all the same, 250
weight loss, 412
white mind, 39, 249
wife, 432, 436
not a servant, 439
wine of divine knowledge, 94, 215
wine of love, 58
witness, 454
your body is a, 79
woman, 294
woman who didn't feed her cat, 42
womb, 318, 347
wuḍu', 338
benefits of, 338

Y

Ya'qūb, 265, 277, 369, 396
Yawm al-Jabarūt, 43
your body
will be your witness, 79
Yūsuf, 265, 369

Z

Zachariah. *See* Prophet Zakarīya
zakāh, 311, 319, 343, 454
Zamzam, 110, 114, 370, 397

Quran Index

A

Allah chose Ādam, Nūḥ...(3:33), 82
Allāh is ever All-Hearer, All-Seer (4:58, 4:134, see 17:1, 19:65, 20:56, 22:61, 22:75, 31:28, 40:20, 40:56, 42:11, 58:1), 121
Allāh is the light of the heavens and the earth. (24:35), 242, 255, 315, 328, 346
Allāh is with the patient ones. (2:153, 2:249, 8:66), 407
Allāh will protect you. (5:67), 121
"Am I not your Lord?" And they said, "Yes." (7:172), 38, 119, 254
And (I have) shown him the two ways (good and evil). (20:10), 94, 198
And (remember) when Ibrahim and Ismāʿīl (Ishmael) were raising the foundations of the House (the Kaʿba) (2:127), 253, 369, 397
And (remember) when the angels said: "Oh Maryam! Truly, Allah has chosen you." (3:42), 309
And Allāh grants respite to none when his appointed time comes. (63:11), 71
And had you been severe and harsh-hearted... (3:159), 278
And He taught Ādam the names of all things (2:31), 40
And I did not create the jinn and human beings except... (51:56-57), 250, 393
And Ibrāhīm's invoking for his father's forgiveness... (9:114), 280
And indeed We bestowed grace on Dāwūd from Us... (34:10), 47, 52, 290, 422
And indeed We bestowed upon Ibrāhīm his (portion of) guidance. (21:51-53), 268
And mention in the Book Ibrāhīm. Truly, he was a man of truth... (19:41), 277
And she who guarded her chastity (Maryam): We breathed into her... 21:91), 309
And strive for Allāh with the endeavor which is His right. (22:78), 266
And Sulayman inherited (the knowledge of) Dāwūd... (27:16), 60
And take a provision (with you) for the journey, but the best provision is at-taqwā. (2:197), 249
And the earth will shine with the light of its Lord...(39:69-70), 76
And the trumpet will be blown, and all who are in the heavens... (39:68), 76
And they have not honored Allah with the honor that is due to Him... (39:67), 76
And those who disbelieved will be driven to Hell in groups (39:71), 78
And those who kept their duty to their Lord will be led to Paradise in groups (39:73), 80
And truly, this is My straight path, so follow it. (6:153), 354, 430
And wait patiently for the judgment of your Lord... (52:48), 256
And We have made from water every living thing. (21:30), 55, 58, 148, 289
And when Allāh will say (on the Day of Judgment), "Oh ʿĪsā, son of Maryam! (5:116), 341
And when My slaves ask you concerning Me, (2:186), 133, 178, 237, 292, 302, 410
And, when he (Ismāʿīl) was old enough to walk with him... (37:102), 370, 398
Ask forgiveness from your Lord; for He is Oft-Forgiving...(71:10-12), 246
As-salāmu ʿalaykum! You have done well...(39:73), 252

B

But those who obey Allah's orders and keep away... (2:212), 11
But We have made it (this Qur'ān) a light (42:52), 271
By Your Might, then I will surely mislead them all (38:82-83), 421

D

Do not be afraid: for I am with you... (20:46), 65, 135, 180, 293
Do they not reflect within themselves (so that you may understand)? (30:8), 360

E

Each one (of His creatures) every one knows his ṣalāh... (24:41), 59, 290
Escape to Allah, the true Guardian-Protector (Tafsir of 2:257), 143, 187, 305, 425
Except the one who brings Allāh a whole heart...(26:89-90), 136, 180

F

Fear Allah, (and guard yourselves against evil), if you have faith. (5:112), 311
From her (the earth) We create you and into her We will return you. (20:55), 35, 47

H

Had He so willed, He would, indeed, have guided you all. (6:149), 274
Had We sent down this on a mountain... (59:21), 422
He created you and fashioned you in the best mold. (95:4), 291, 320
He is a spirit from My command. (17:85), 320, 351
He is with you wherever you are. (57:4), 298
He loves them, so they love Him. (5:54), 11, 52, 185, 204, 230, 240, 252, 291

I

I am emigrating to my Lord. He will guide me! (37:99), 27, 245, 248, 249, 297
I am going to create a man from dried clay of altered mud. (15:28-29), 37, 38
I am going to send it (the table) down unto you... (9:33), 359
I am the Most Merciful, Most Compassionate. (see 1:1, 1:3, 2:163, 27:30, 41:2, 59:22), 121
I breathed into him out of My spirit (My own light) (so pray for them). (35:71 and Tafsir), 21, 309
I created you, fashioned you perfectly. (82:7), 125
I do not seek any provision from them nor do I ask them to feed Me. (51:56-57), 84
I will be creating a human being out of mud (38:71), 315, 318, 346, 348, 356, 419, 420
I will be with you everywhere and anywhere. (20:46 and Tafsir), 143, 186, 303, 424

I will teach you that which you did not know before. (2:151), 121
If anyone kills a person or spreads mischief in the land—it is as if he has killed all humankind. (5:32), 53, 63, 350
If you give thanks, I will give you more. (14:7), 147, 160, 423
Indeed, this is in the former scripture—the scripture of Ibrāhīm and Mūsā, (87:18-19), 299
Indeed, We have sent it (the Qur'ān) down in the night of al-Qadr (91:1, 4, 5), 12
It is He Who has created for you hearing, eyes, and hearts. (23:78. See also 32:9, 46:26, 67:23), 441
It is He who sends ṣalāh (prayers) upon you, and His angels, too. (33:43), 290, 387

N

Not a word does he (or she) utter but there is a watcher...(50:18), 137, 245

O

Oh Allāh, our Lord! Send us from Heaven a table spread (5:114), 355
Oh anta! Enter your dwellings, lest Sulayman and his hosts crush you... (2:18), 293
Oh assembly of jinns and men! If you have power to pass beyond the zones of the heavens and the earth... (55:33), 173
Oh my Lord, show me Yourself that I may look upon You. (7:143), 28, 168, 206, 301
Oh people, We have created you from a male and a female, and made you into nations and tribes...(49:13), 51
Oh people, We have created you from a male and a female, and made you into nations and tribes...(49\13), 42, 51, 290, 344, 354, 387
Oh you who believe, when you rise up to ṣalāh...(5:6), 337
Oh you who have come to believe, bow and prostrate yourselves... (22:77), 339
Oh, you human being. (49:13), 243
Or is he not informed with what is in the pages of Mūsā and of Ibrāhīm...(53:36-37), 299

R

Read, in the name of your Lord who has created (everything). (96:1), 39
Remember Me, I will remember you...(2:152), 146, 150, 251, 410
Remember when the disciples said: 'Oh 'Īsā, son of Maryam (Mary)!' (5:112), 316, 347

S

Safeguard the ṣalāh, and especially the middle ṣalāh, (2:238), 337
Say (oh Muḥammad to mankind): "If you love Allāh then follow me. (3:31), 300
Say, "Are those who know equal to those who don't know?" (39:9), 333
Say: "If you love Allāh then follow me." (3:31), 102, 144, 187, 223, 305, 425

Say: "Oh My slaves who have transgressed against themselves! (39:53), 30, 162, 234, 236, 442
Say: "Oh people of the book! Let us agree..." (3:64), 243
Say: He is Allah, the One and Only. (112:1, 112:3), 318, 347
So this day We shall deliver your (Pharaoh's) body...(10:92), 45
Such is the seizure of your Lord when He seizes...(11:102), 27

T

Take off your shoes for you are standing in the holy valley of Tuwa. (20:12), 28
That the recording angels record all of your actions...(50:17), 21
The example of the creation of Jesus is like the example of the creation of Ādam. (3:59), 318, 348
The one who comes with tawba and a full heart (5:39), 67
Then get out of here, for truly you are outcast. (38:77), 420
Then she (Maryam) pointed to him (ʿĪsā). (19:29-32), 311, 319, 343, 349
Then, when they had both submitted themselves (37:103-37:108), 375, 404
There has come to you a messenger from among yourselves. (9:128), 337
They (animals) are but nations like yours (6:38), 46
They [those who cover up the truth] want to extinguish Allāh's light...(9:32), 13, 357
This, your (human) nation, is one nation, and I am your Lord so worship Me (alone). (21:92), 94, 151, 191, 239, 307, 374
Truly, I am going to create humankind from clay. (38:71), 131, 240
Truly, We did offer the trust to the heavens and the earth...(33:72), 11, 40, 56
Truly, We have sent it (this Qur'ān) down in the night of al-Qadr. (97:1), 231

U-Z

Unless he repents, believes, and works righteous deeds...(25:70), 235
We have certainly created the human being in the best mold. (95:4), 351
We have not sent you but as a mercy for all the worlds. (21:107), 110, 229, 344
We make no distinction between any of His messengers. (2:285), 321, 352
We will soon show them Our signs in the universe...(41:53), 19
We wish to eat thereof (of that spiritual sustenance) and to satisfy our hearts (5:113), 317, 323, 353, 354
What! Did you then think that We had created you in vain...(23:115), 230
When Allāh said to the angels, "Prostrate to Ādam" (38:72-38:76), 309, 420
When he saw the moon rising up, he said, "This is my Lord." (6:76-78), 281
Who is he that will lend to Allāh a goodly loan so that He may multiply it to him many times? (2:245 and see 57:11, 5:2, 57:18, 64:17, 73:20), 86, 88, 322
Will You place upon the earth those who will make mischief and shed blood, (2:30), 236

Hadith Index

A

All creatures are the children of Allāh, 52, 62, 105, 147, 164, 203, 290, 314, 431
Allāh is beautiful and He loves beauty, 241
Allāh told the Prophet, "Read", 39
Allah gives respite to the oppressor, but when He takes him over, 27
Ask Allāh for forgiveness three times, 33
Avoid 2 white things: salt and sugar, 382

B

Be in thousand-fold peace. (alfu salām), 175

C

Citron is the medicine for many, many sicknesses, 383

D

Die before you die, 96, 217
Do not cause harm to yourself or others, 185

E

Give the poor their rights, take care of them, 31

H

Have mercy on the ones on earth and the One in heaven will have mercy upon you, 284
He said, "Be.", 321, 352
Heal yourself, 413

I

I ask for forgiveness seventy times a day, 234
I was a prophet before Adam was made from clay, 110
If anyone of you is haunted by a small darkness, I will feel your pain, 41, 406
If you are honest with Allāh and depend totally on Allāh, Allāh will provide for you like He provides for the birds, 171
If you pass close to the Garden, drink, 5

K

Know that any group of people who sit and mention Allāh, angels, 5

O

Oh Allāh, in the time before the Day of Judgment, You will find some people pretending they are religious, 84
Our deeds are judged by our intensions, 247

P

Prophet's night journey and ascension, 110

T

Take care of your women, your wives and daughters, 432
Tell your people. And advise them to do cupping, 377
The best one is the one who takes care of his family, 432
The closest we can be with God is when we pray and are on our knees, 18, 256
The first thing Allāh created was the light of your Prophet, oh Jabbār, 110
The grave could be the Garden or it could be Hell, 33
The worst vessel to fill is one's stomach, 177, 332, 379
There is a piece of flesh inside the body; it is the heart, 212
Those who ask Allāh for forgiveness and pray at midnight, 38
Those who believe in Him are in the Garden now, 32, 57, 139, 146
To whom should we give piety?, 435
Treat people with good manners. Be kind to them. Be sweet to them, 156
Two of the worshippers will not be in the Fire, 176

W

We are not people who will eat until we are hungry, 177, 332, 381, 411

Y

You are very close to Allāh when you are in prostration, 18, 256
You live, in this moment, in the Garden, 213
You will be very close to God when you pray to Allāh, 38

Hadith Qudsi Index

I have prepared for My righteous servants what no eye has ever seen, 241
I was a hidden treasure and I loved to be known, 53, 54, 63, 136, 181, 259, 289, 295
My heavens and My earth cannot contain Me, 18, 24, 28, 40, 212, 253, 301, 441
My servant continues to draw near to Me with voluntary works, 55, 103, 173, 224
Oh My worshipper, be to Me as I want you to be and I will be to you as you want Me to be, 185, 244, 299, 410, 442
Oh son of Ādam, were you to come to Me with sins nearly as great as the earth, 234
Oh, My worshipful slave, if you did not make mistakes I would create another creation that would make mistakes, 29, 68, 150, 167, 205, 189, 233
Yā Quds (Oh Jerusalem), 368, 396
You (Jerusalem) are My heaven, from My countries, 342

Yes! Please send me a FREE Supplemental Packet.

If you return this form to the SSC Gift Shop, they will send you, free of charge, a supplemental packet with even more of Sidi's 2010 teachings. Inshāʾa-llāh, this packet will be available in May 2011.

Order Form

First Name ______________________________________

Last Name ______________________________________

Mailing Address __________________________________

____

____

Phone Number ____________________________________

Email ____

Sufi Name (optional) ______________________________

SSC Gift Shop
(707) 865-0700, ext. 22

May Allāh (ﷻ) bless you!

Gently tear or cut here

20393600R00271

Made in the USA
San Bernardino, CA
09 April 2015